Year by Year & D[...]
the Los Angeles An[...]

❖❖❖

ANGELS
JOURNAL

❖❖❖

JOHN SNYDER

Copyright © 2010 by John Snyder

All rights reserved. No portion of this book may be reproduced in any fashion, print, facsimile, or electronic, or by any method yet to be developed, without express permission of the copyright holder.

For further information, contact the publisher at:

Clerisy Press
PO Box 8874
Cincinnati, OH 45208-0874

www.clerisypress.com

Library of Congress Cataloging-in-Publication Data

Snyder, John, 1951-
    Angels journal : year by year & day by day with the Los Angeles Angels since 1961 /
      By John Snyder.
      p. cm.
  ISBN-13: 978-1-57860-388-6
  ISBN-10: 1-57860-388-9
  1. Los Angeles Angels (Baseball team)--History. I. Title.

GV875.A6S69 2010
796.357'640979496--dc22

                                              2010003033

Distributed by Publishers Group West
Edited by Jack Heffron
Cover designed by Steven Sullivan and Scott McGrew
Interior designed by Mary Barnes Clark

Cover photo by AP Photo/Eric Risberg

Back cover: Photos courtesy of Jeff Emerson/finalshot.com (Jim Fregosi) and WikiCommons (Vladimir Guerrero)

Photos on the following pages appear courtesy of the Topps Company, Inc.: 18, 38, 50, 89, 121, 135, 149, 161, 182, 210

Photos on the following pages appear courtesy of Jeff Emerson/finalshot.com: 67, 76, 85, 157, 192, 153

Photos on the following pages appear courtesy of Shutterstock.com: 242, 274, 331, 338

Photos on the following pages are drawn from Wikicommons.com: 292, 302, 311, 325, 331

About the Author

John Snyder has a master's degree in history from the University of Cincinnati and a passion for baseball. He has authored fifteen books on baseball, soccer, hockey, tennis, football, basketball, and travel and lives in Cincinnati.

Acknowledgments

This book is part of a series that takes a look at Major League Baseball teams. The first was *Redleg Journal: Year by Year and Day by Day with the Cincinnati Reds Since 1866*, the winner of the 2001 Baseball Research Award issued by *The Sporting News* and SABR. That work was followed by *Cubs Journal: Year by Year and Day by Day with the Chicago Cubs Since 1876*, *Red Sox Journal: Year by Year and Day by Day with the Boston Red Sox Since 1901*, *Cardinals Journal: Year by Year and Day by Day with the St. Louis Cardinals since 1882*, *Indians Journal: Year by Year and Day by Day with the Cleveland Indians Since 1901*, *Dodgers Journal: Year by Year and Day by Day with the Brooklyn and Los Angeles Dodgers Since 1884*, *White Sox Journal: Year by Year and Day by Day with the Chicago White Sox Since 1901*, and *Twins Journal: Year by Year and Day by Day with the Minnesota Twins Since 1961*. Each of these books is filled with little-known items that have never been published in book form.

Greg Rhodes was my co-author on *Redleg Journal*, in addition to publishing the book under his company's name Road West Publishing. While Greg did not actively participate in the books about the Cubs, Red Sox, Cardinals, Indians, Dodgers, White Sox, Twins, or Angels he deserves considerable credit for the success of these books because they benefited from many of the creative concepts he initiated in *Redleg Journal*.

The idea for turning *Redleg Journal* into a series of books goes to Richard Hunt, president and publisher of Emmis Books and its successor company Clerisy Press, and editorial director Jeff Heffron.

And finally, although they should be first, thanks to my wife, Judy, and sons Derek and Kevin, whose encouragement and support helped me through another book.

Contents

LOS ANGELES ANGELS DAY BY DAY

Introduction: Los Angeles, The Pacific Coast League,
and the Original Angels 6

1961–1969 9

1970–1979 71

1980–1989 141

1990–1999 204

2000–2009 271

Los Angeles, the Pacific Coast League and the Original Angels

Los Angeles and Orange Counties have experienced major league baseball since 1958 with the arrival of the Dodgers from Brooklyn. The Angels were created as an expansion team in October 1960, and began play in Los Angeles in 1961. The Angels moved to Anaheim in 1966. Minor league baseball was played in Los Angeles in the Pacific Coast League from 1903 through 1957. The three clubs that played in the league in Los Angeles were the original Los Angeles Angels (1903–57), Vernon Tigers (1909–25) and Hollywood Stars (1926–35 and 1938–57).

Los Angeles Angels

The Angels were one of six charter members of the Pacific Coast League along with clubs from Oakland, Portland, Sacramento, San Francisco and Seattle. From 1903 through 1925, the Angels played at 15,000-seat Washington Park (also known as Chutes Park) at Hill and Eighth Streets in downtown Los Angeles.

The Los Angeles Angels franchise was purchased in 1921 by chewing gum magnate William Wrigley, Jr., who also owned the Chicago Cubs. Wrigley built a new ballpark at 42nd Place and Avalon Boulevard in what is now South Central Los Angeles. Known as Wrigley Field, it held 22,000 fans, opened in September 1925 and was modeled after Wrigley Field in Chicago.

The Los Angeles version of Wrigley Field was used by the Angels until 1957 when the franchise passed out of existence after the Dodgers moved to West Coast. Wrigley Field was a major league venue for one season in 1961 when the major league Angels played there. The ballpark was also the site of the 1959 television series *Home Run Derby* and served as the backdrop for several feature films over a 40-year period. Wrigley Field was demolished in 1966.

The Angels won the PCL regular season title in 1903, 1905, 1907, 1908, 1916, 1921, 1926, 1933, 1934, 1947 and 1956. Notable players included Steve Bilko, Chuck Connors, Gene Mauch, Jimmie Reese, Bill Sarni, Jigger Statz and Dixie Upright.

Vernon Tigers

The Vernon Tigers existed in the PCL from 1909 through 1925. Vernon was, and still is, a small town located about 13 miles southeast of downtown Los Angeles. A baseball franchise settled there because in 1909 it was one of only two communities in Los Angeles County in which the sale of alcohol was legal. The other was Venice, where the Tigers played home games in 1913 and 1914.

Vernon is one of the most unusual municipalities in the United States. In 2000, it had a population of only 91, but some 46,000 were employed by businesses within its borders. Vernon won the league pennant in 1919 and 1920 when the franchise was owned by Hollywood silent-film star Fatty Arbuckle. The beginning of the end came just before the title run of 1920 when the Prohibition amendment passed and barred the sale of alcohol nationwide. Without the enticement of alcohol at the ballpark, few were willing to travel to Vernon to watch baseball. After the close of the 1925 season, the franchise was transferred to San Francisco, where it became known as the Mission Reds.

Hollywood Stars

The first of two versions of the Hollywood Stars existed from 1926 through 1935. The franchise moved from Salt Lake City and filled the void left by the Vernon Tigers. The Stars played not in Hollywood but at Wrigley Field as tenants of the Angels. Because of declining attendance, the Hollywood club moved to San Diego at the end of the 1935 season, but not before winning the pennant in 1929 and 1930.

Los Angeles had only one PCL franchise in 1936 and 1937, while the San Francisco Bay area had three with the San Francisco Seals, San Francisco Mission Reds and Oakland Oaks. In 1938, the Mission club, which was formerly the Vernon Tigers, moved to Hollywood. This time the club played near Hollywood on Beverly Boulevard in the Fairfax district of Los Angeles at 13,000-seat Gilmore Field. Today, the site is the parking lot at CBS Television City.

The principal owner of the Stars was Bob Cobb, who also owned the Brown Derby Restaurant and for whom the Cobb salad is named. He was married to actress Gail Patrick. Stock in the club was sold to many Hollywood celebrities, including Gene Autry and William Frawley. (Autry would later become the principal owner of the major league Angels from the team's inception in 1960 until his death in 1998.) Many movie and television stars regularly attended the Stars' games. The second version of the Stars won the PCL pennant in 1949 when it was a farm club of the Brooklyn Dodgers.

The Road to Major League Status

The states of California, Oregon and Washington had 2.4 million people in 1900—3.2 percent of the U.S. population. By 1950, the population figure reached 15.2 million, which comprised ten percent of United States residents. That year, the 16 major league franchises were located in just ten cities, none of them west of St. Louis or south of Washington, DC. From north to south, Pacific Coast League teams in 1950 were located in Seattle, Portland, Sacramento, San Francisco, Oakland, Hollywood, Los Angeles and San Diego.

PCL owners believed that the league had a sufficient population base to be considered a third major league. By 1946, they banded together as a group to request major league status from the National and American Leagues. They agreed that either all of them or none of them would become major league franchises.

The AL and NL repeatedly denied the PCL's request to become a third major league, believing that only Los Angeles and San Francisco had the population necessary to be considered as major league cities. There was also a concern that the talent level in the PCL was far below that of the AL and NL and that none of the Pacific Coast League ballparks were up to major league standards.

Cracks in the coalition of PCL teams began to surface around 1953 when Los Angeles and San Francisco city officials desired to be included as part of the National and American Leagues. California's two largest major league cities wanted to test their mettle against clubs from New York and Chicago, not Sacramento and Portland.

Also in 1953, the first shift of a major league franchise since 1903 took place when the Braves moved from Boston to Milwaukee. The move succeeded beyond anyone's wildest dreams. After drawing 281,278 fans in Boston in 1952, the Braves attracted 1,826,397 in Milwaukee in 1953. At the end of the 1953 season, the St. Louis Browns moved to Baltimore and were renamed the Orioles. At the close of the 1954 campaign, the Philadelphia Athletics were relocated to Kansas City. But even after the moves, the majors had no franchises south of Washington DC, or west of the state of Missouri.

The city of Los Angeles began courting the Dodgers as early as 1953. At a meeting of major league owners in August of that year, Dodgers owner Walter O'Malley said that he had received a letter from a prominent Los Angeles resident "who is a leader in politics and is well fixed financially" inquiring about the club moving from Brooklyn to the West Coast. "The man whose name I cannot reveal," added O'Malley, "assured me that if the Brooklyn club were transferred to Los Angeles, a large commodious stadium would be built for it."

For the next three years, O'Malley tried to convince the city of New York to give him land in downtown Brooklyn and in exchange, he would build a stadium on the site with his own money. The Dodgers played at aging Ebbets Field, opened in 1913, which had a capacity of only 32,000 and almost no parking facilities. The New York Giants also wanted the city to construct a stadium in Manhattan to replace the Polo Grounds, which was built in 1911.

O'Malley and Giants owner Horace Stoneham grew more and more frustrated as New York politicians moved slowly on their requests for new ballparks for their clubs. The turning point came in October 1956 when O'Malley visited Los Angeles for the first time in his life and was taken on a helicopter tour of the city with county supervisor Kenneth Hahn. The Dodger owner was shown the site in Chavez Ravine that Hahn had touted for a new stadium. O'Malley called it an "ideal location." Stoneham announced that the Giants would be moving to San Francisco in August 1957 effective at the end of the season. O'Malley transferred his franchise to Los Angeles in October.

It would be 1960 at the earliest, however, before a new ballpark could be built at Chavez Ravine. (Legal difficulties delayed the opening of Dodger Stadium until 1962.) O'Malley housed his club temporarily at Memorial Coliseum. Attendance in 1958, the first year in Los Angeles, was 1,845,556, more than the club had ever drawn in Brooklyn. The club won the World Series in 1959 and topped two million in attendance, a figure that was exceeded again in 1960.

Because of the success of the Dodgers, the American League also wanted a piece of the action in Los Angeles. The circuit had eight clubs from its inception in 1901 and decided to expand to ten clubs by placing another team in Los Angeles as a rival to the Dodgers. Our story begins with baseball's first expansion.

THE STATE OF THE ANGELS

In their inaugural season in 1961, the Angels were 70–91, which is the best first-year won-lost record of baseball's 14 expansion teams to date. The Angels followed with an 86–76 ledger in 1962 but were unable to sustain the momentum. The club posted only two more winning seasons during the 1960s in 1964 (82–80) and 1967 (84–77). It would be 1978 and 1979 before the Angels put together consecutive winning campaigns. Overall, the Angels were 685–770 over the course of the decade, a winning percentage of .471. American League pennant winners were the Yankees (1960, 1961, 1962, 1963 and 1964), Twins (1965), Orioles (1966 and 1969), Red Sox (1967) and Tigers (1968).

THE BEST TEAM

The Angels were the surprise team in baseball during the 1962 season with 86 wins and 76 losses in only their second season.

THE WORST TEAM

The 1968 Angels fell to 67–95 and finished eighth in a ten-team league after winning 84 games during a promising 1967 season.

THE BEST MOMENT

The Angels were in first place in the American League on July 4, 1962.

THE WORST MOMENT

Only a month after making his major league debut, pitcher Dick Wantz died of brain cancer at the age of 25. It was the first of many deaths to befall Angels players over the years, most recently Nick Adenhart in 2009.

THE ALL-DECADE TEAM • YEARS W/ANGELS

Buck Rodgers, c	1961–69
Don Mincher, 1b	1967–68
Bobby Knoop, 2b	1964–69
Paul Schaal, 3b	1965–68
Jim Fregosi, ss	1961–71
Rick Reichardt, lf	1964–70
Albie Pearson, cf	1961–64
Lee Thomas, rf	1961–64
Dean Chance, p	1961–66
George Brunet, p	1964–69
Ken McBride, p	1961–63
Bob Lee, p	1964–66

Leon Wagner, who played for the Angels from 1961 through 1963, was one of the best three outfielders on the club during the 1960s but played left field and Reichardt gets the nod at that position. First base, right field and third base were problem areas throughout most of the decade.

THE DECADE LEADERS

Batting Avg:	Albie Pearson	.275
On-Base Pct:	Albie Pearson	.379
Slugging Pct:	Rick Reichardt	.406
Home Runs:	Leon Wagner	91
RBI:	Jim Fregosi	431
Runs:	Jim Fregosi	565
Stolen Bases:	Jose Cardenal	71
Wins:	Dean Chance	74
Strikeouts:	Dean Chance	857
ERA:	Dean Chance	2.83
Saves:	Bob Lee	58

THE HOME FIELD

The Angels played in three ballparks during the first six years of their existence. The club played at Wrigley Field, which held only 20,500 fans, in 1961. Wrigley was previously used by the minor league Angels of the Pacific Coast League from 1925 through 1957. The Angels shared Dodger Stadium with the Dodgers from 1962 through 1965 as tenants of Walter O'Malley, the owner of both the Dodgers and the ballpark. It was referred to as Chavez Ravine during Angels home games. After drawing only 603,510 fans in 1961, the Angels attracted 1,144,063 in 1962, but that was much less than the Dodgers' attendance figure of 2,755,184 that same season. The Angels had trouble competing with the Dodgers in the Los Angeles market and signed an agreement in August 1964 with officials in Anaheim to build a new stadium for the club. It opened in 1966. The Angels drew only 566,727 fans in 1965. The first season in Anaheim, the club led the American league in attendance with a total of 1,400,321. It would be 1977, however, before the Angels drew that many fans again, and 1982 before the club would top the AL in attendance again.

THE GAME YOU WISHED YOU HAD SEEN

Rookie sensation Bo Belinsky pitched a no-hitter against the Orioles on May 5, 1962 at Chavez Ravine.

THE WAY THE GAME WAS PLAYED

Baseball was played in new cities and ballparks during the 1960s with franchise shifts and expansion from 16 teams to 24, with the Angels being one of the eight additional franchises. American League baseball was played for the first time in Southern California, Minnesota, Oakland and Seattle. The expansion of the strike zone in 1963 brought about a decline in offense during the 1960s until the owners lowered the mound for the 1969 season. The league ERA dipped to 2.98 in 1968, the only time it has been lower than 3.00 since 1918.

THE MANAGEMENT

Gene Autry was the original owner of the Angels, a role he held until his death in 1998. Fred Haney was the first general manager and continued in the post until he retired in 1968. Haney was followed by Dick Walsh, who was general manager from 1967 through 1971. Bill Rigney was the first field manager. He led the club for eight full seasons and part of a ninth before being fired in May 1969. Rigney was replaced by Lefty Phillips (1969–71).

THE BEST PLAYER MOVE

The best player move was the selection of Jim Fregosi from the Red Sox in the expansion draft. The best trade brought Leon Wagner and two others plus cash from the Cardinals for Al Cicotte in January 1961.

THE WORST PLAYER MOVE

The worst trade sent Jose Cardenal to the Indians for Chuck Hinton in November 1967.

1960

August 2 — At an historic meeting in Chicago's Conrad-Hilton Hotel, a four-man expansion committee of the National and American Leagues votes unanimously to expand by admitting four new clubs into the major leagues. The additions would increase each major league from eight teams to ten. Eight teams had existed in each league since 1901. The aim was to accomplish expansion by 1962 at the latest.

> *In 1960, there were American League teams in Baltimore, Boston, Chicago, Cleveland, Detroit, Kansas City, New York and Washington. National League clubs were located in Chicago, Cincinnati, Los Angeles, Milwaukee, Philadelphia, Pittsburgh, St. Louis and San Francisco.*

August 12 — New York Yankees co-owner Dan Topping tells Baseball Commissioner Ford Frick that Los Angeles should be one the two American League franchises. Topping reasoned that if the National League could place a second team in New York, the American League should be able to place a franchise in Los Angeles.

October 17 — The National League votes with "unanimous enthusiasm" to expand to ten teams with the addition of franchises in New York and Houston. Both were scheduled to begin playing in 1962.

October 26 — On the day before the Lakers play their first game in Los Angeles, the American League votes to expand from eight to ten teams with the two new organizations to field teams in 1961. Calvin Griffith, owner of the Washington Senators, was given permission to move his franchise to Minneapolis-St. Paul. A new club for Washington, also named the Senators, was approved. The second franchise was to be located in Los Angeles. The ownership groups for the Washington and Los Angeles clubs were to be decided upon at a later date. Hank Greenberg seemed to have the inside track on owning the Los Angeles franchise. A Hall of Fame first baseman during a major league career that covered the 1930s and 1940s, mostly with the Tigers, Greenberg was the general manager of the Indians during much of the 1950s. In 1960, he owned 20 percent of the Chicago White Sox. Greenberg's partners in Los Angeles were to be Ralph Kiner, another former Hall of Fame player, and San Diego banker C. Arnholdt Smith. There were less than four months remaining before the start of spring training, giving the two new teams little time to prepare. Schedules were increased from 154 games to 162.

> *Dodgers owner Walter O'Malley was less than thrilled with the idea of sharing Los Angeles with an American League team. The Dodgers moved to L.A. after the end of the 1957 season. O'Malley said he hoped to get his own problems "in pioneering the territory" and in "building our stadium behind us before the relatives moved in." O'Malley also had an extreme dislike for Smith, whose brother led an unsuccessful campaign to stop O'Malley from acquiring the land to build Dodger Stadium. The Dodgers had played at Memorial Coliseum since 1958. They had one more season left at the massive stadium before Dodger Stadium was scheduled to open in 1962.*

NOVEMBER 17 Nine days after John Kennedy defeats Richard Nixon in the presidential election, Hank Greenberg tells American League president Joe Cronin that he is not interested in heading the new Los Angeles franchise in the American League. A day later, Charlie Finley, a 43-year-old Gary, Indiana, insurance executive, announced that he was interested in purchasing the new club. Finley had previously made unsuccessful attempts to purchase the Kansas City Athletics, Detroit Tigers and Chicago White Sox.

> *Finley would purchase the Athletics in January 1961. He moved the club to Oakland at the end of the 1967 season and led the A's to three consecutive world championships beginning in 1972. Finley sold the franchise in 1981.*

NOVEMBER 22 As a result of the objections of Walter O'Malley and his fellow National League owners regarding the establishment of an American League franchise in Los Angeles, the American League offers a compromise in which each league would field nine clubs in 1961, with an inter-league schedule. Washington would be the ninth AL club with Los Angeles being added in 1962. The National League turned down the offer.

DECEMBER 7 The American and National League agree to an amicable solution to the expansion problem. The new Los Angeles club, nicknamed the Angels, would be permitted to begin play in 1961 with 20,500-seat Wrigley Field as the home ballpark. The new team also entered into a deal with the Dodgers to share Dodger Stadium from 1962 through 1965. A five-man syndicate, headed by 53-year-old Gene Autry, were the owners of the Angels. Autry was named chairman of the board. The club president was 46-year-old Bob Reynolds, who was a partner in Autry's broadcasting empire. Reynolds, a two-time All-American football player at Stanford, played all 60 minutes as a tackle in the Rose Bowl games of 1934, 1935 and 1936. Reynolds also played in the NFL with the Detroit Lions for two seasons.

> *Autry gained fame during the 1930s, 1940s and 1950s as a "singing cowboy." So diverse was Autry's portfolio, that he is the only celebrity with five stars on the Hollywood Walk of Fame. Along Hollywood Boulevard, there are stars honoring Autry for his work in radio, television, motion pictures, live theater and recording. He also built a fortune with sound investments. By the time he purchased the Angels, he owned radio and television stations, a motion picture production facility, a cattle ranch, a resort hotel in Palm Springs, and the Gene Autry Western Heritage Museum. In 1960, Walter O'Malley's Dodgers chose not to renew their radio contract with Autry's radio station KMPC, and Autry became interested in purchasing the Angels. He figured that if he owned the club he could broadcast the games on his own station. Autry would be the principal owner of the Angels until his death in 1998, but unfortunately he failed to live long enough to see the club reach the World Series.*

DECEMBER 8 The Angels hire 62-year-old Fred Haney as general manager.

> *Haney had a long career in baseball as a player, broadcaster and field manager, but he never worked in the front office until hired by the Angels. He was an infielder with four clubs from 1922 through 1929 and was well known to Southern California baseball fans as a player with the original Pacific Coast League Angels and with the Hollywood Stars. He was a radio announcer with the Stars from 1943 through 1948 and as manager from 1949 through 1952, guiding*

the club to two pennants. As a major league manager, he experienced both the best and worst of times, losing over 100 games with the 1939 Browns and the 1953 and 1954 Pirates before leading the Milwaukee Braves to National League pennants in 1957 and 1958, and a World Series title in 1957. Haney was fired by the Braves after narrowly missing a third straight NL crown in 1959. He was the general manager of the Angels until retiring near the end of the 1967 season.

December 12 The Angels hire 41-year-old Bill Rigney as field manager. Gene Autry originally tried to hire Casey Stengel, who turned him down. Stengel had been fired by the Yankees two months earlier after winning his tenth pennant in 12 years. Stengel became manager of the Mets in 1962.

As a player, Rigney was an infielder with the New York Giants from 1946 through 1953. He managed the Giants in both New York and San Francisco from 1956 through 1960. He was The Sporting News *manager of the year in 1962 after the Angels finished a surprising third in only the second season of their existence. That proved to be the highlight during his tenure as Angels manager. The club had three winnings seasons in eight full campaigns before he was fired in May 1969.*

December 14 The Angels and the Washington Senators take part in baseball's first expansion draft. The eight existing American League teams submitted a pool of 15 players from their 25-man roster. Of those 15, seven had to have been on the 25-man roster prior to September 1, 1960. The Angels picked 30 players, at a total cost of $2,150,000. The best players taken in the draft were Jim Fregosi, Dean Chance, Albie Pearson, Buck Rodgers, Ken McBride, Earl Averill, Eli Grba, Ted Bowsfield, Ron Hunt, Steve Bilko and Fred Newman. With the anticipation of playing in their first season at cozy Wrigley Field, the Angels loaded up on power hitters. Given the fact that Fred Haney didn't become general manager until just six days before the draft, the Angels did an amazingly effective job in selecting what little talent the other AL clubs made available.

   The Expansion Draft

The following is a list of the 30 players taken by the Angels in the expansion draft, held on December 14, 1960. In parenthesis following the player's name is the club from which he was drafted, his age at the time of the draft, and his position.

Ken Aspromonte (Cleveland, 29, 2b)
Aspromonte had a career year in 1960, hitting .288 with ten home runs. He was the Angels starting second baseman at the start of the 1961 season but hit only .223 in 67 games before being traded back to the Indians. His younger brother Bob was chosen by Houston in the National League expansion draft in October 1961.

Earl Averill (Chicago, 29, c)
Averill's father, also named Earl, carved out a Hall of Fame career as an outfielder from 1929 through 1941. He played 11 of those seasons with the Indians. The younger Earl Averill hit 21 homers with a .266 batting average in 323 at-bats with the Angels in 1961, but faded dramatically afterward and was traded to the Phillies at the end of the 1962 season. Averill collected a total of 44 home runs over his seven-year career.

Julio Becquer (Minnesota, 28, 1b)
A native of Cuba, Becquer was the only Latin player on the Angels Opening Day roster in 1961. He was also the only minority taken by the club in the

expansion draft. No African-American players were selected. Becquer was hitless in eight at-bats as an Angel before being traded back to the Twins.

Steve Bilko (Detroit, 32, 1b)
Standing six-foot-one and weighing around 260 pounds, Bilko was already a cult hero in Los Angeles from his days in the minors when drafted by the Angels. He played in the majors with the Cardinals and Cubs from 1949 through 1954 but was a regular for only one season. The Cubs sent him to their Los Angeles Angels farm club in the Pacific Coast League where he hit batted .330 with 148 home runs in three seasons from 1955 through 1957. The popular television character Sgt. Bilko played by Phil Silvers on *The Phil Silvers Show* was named after Steve Bilko because he was series creator Nat Hiken's favorite player. Bilko played for the Dodgers briefly in 1958, thereby becoming the first player to play for both of the two major league teams based in Los Angeles. In two seasons with the major league Angels, Bilko batted .282 with 28 home runs in 458 at-bats.

Jerry Casale (Boston, 27, p)
Casale lasted only 13 games with the Angels and was 1–5 with a 6.54 ERA.

Bob Cerv (New York, 34, of)
After 18 games and a .158 batting average with the Angels, Cerv was traded back to the Yankees.

Dean Chance (Baltimore, 19, p)
The Angels took a flyer on several untested young players like Chance in the expansion draft, and it paid off. As a 21-year-old rookie in 1962, he was 14–10. Chance blossomed in 1964 by winning the Cy Young Award with a 20–9 record, a 1.65 ERA and 11 shutouts. Expectations were high, but he never evolved into a consistent winner. Throwing from an unorthodox, twisting windup, Chance never looked at the plate once he received the signal from his catcher and would turn his back fully toward the hitter in mid-windup before spinning and unleashing the pitch. He slipped to 15–10 in 1965 and 12–17 in 1966 and began to berate his teammates for their poor play behind him. He was traded to the Twins before the start of the 1967 season. Chance averaged 265 innings per season from 1963 through 1968, and after winning 16 games as a 27-year-old in 1968, he accumulated only 18 more big league victories.

Tex Clevenger (Minnesota, 28, p)
Clevenger made 12 relief outings with the Angels before being dealt to the Yankees.

Bob Davis (Kansas City, 27, p)
Davis never pitched a game for the Angels.

Jim Fregosi (Boston, 18, ss)
Fregosi was the youngest player chosen by the Angels in the expansion draft, but he turned out to the best of the bunch. In 1960, he played at the Class D level (today's equivalent of low Class A). Fregosi made his big league debut in 1961, was the Angels starting shortstop from 1963 through 1971, and was named to six All-Star teams. He played in 1,429 games for the club with 5,244 at-bats, 691 runs, 1,408 hits, 219 doubles, a club record 70 triples, 88 home runs and 546 RBIs. At the end of the 1971 season, he was traded to the Mets for Nolan Ryan and three others. As a manager, Fregosi led the Angels to their first postseason appearance in 1979. His statistics are worthy of Hall of Fame consideration when compared to many shortstops enshrined at Cooperstown. However, he spent most of his career on an Angels team with a low profile nationally, played in ballparks that favored the pitcher, and his peak years were during the 1960s, which was dominated by pitching. He was also on the wrong end of the Nolan Ryan trade. After being dealt to the Mets, Fregosi went into a sharp decline while Ryan became a baseball icon.

Ned Garver (Kansas City, 34, p)
Garver had a 20–12 record with a 1951 St. Louis Browns team that was 52–102. By 1961, however, he was nearly finished and had an 0–3 record and a 5.59 ERA with the Angels.

Aubrey Gatewood (Detroit, 22, p)
Gatewood reached the majors in 1963 and was 8–9 in three seasons with the Angels.

Eli Grba (New York, 26, p)
Grba was the first player selected in the expansion draft and was the Angels Opening Day starter, posting a 7–2 win over the Orioles.

He was 11–13 in 1961 and 20–24 in three seasons with the club.

Ken Hamlin (Kansas City, 25, ss)
In his only season as an Angel, Hamlin batted .209 in 91 at-bats.

Ken Hunt (New York, 26, of)
Hunt batted .255 with 25 homers and 84 RBIs in 1961 but struck out 120 times and led AL outfielders in errors. After 1961, he played three seasons with the Angels and Senators and batted a paltry .167 with seven home runs in 269 at-bats. His downturn coincided with a back injury that occurred while flexing his bat behind his back in the on-deck circle.

Ted Kluszewski (Chicago, 36, 1b)
With the Reds during the 1950s, Kluszewski was one of the most feared power hitters in the game. He cut off the sleeves of his uniform to show off his prodigious muscles and belted 171 home runs in four seasons from 1953 through 1956. Slowed by a back injury, Kluszewski was about done by 1961 but still had enough left to hit 15 homers in 263 at-bats with the Angels.

Gene Leek (Cleveland, 24, 3b)
Leek hit only .221 in 213 at-bats over two seasons with the Angels.

Jim McAnany (Chicago, 24, of)
McAnany was dealt to the Cubs during spring training in 1961.

Ken McBride (Chicago, 25, p)
McBride was an All-Star in each of the Angels first three seasons and was the starter in the 1963 Midsummer Classic, but back and neck troubles, suffered in an auto accident in 1964, wrecked what appeared to be a promising career.

Ron Moeller (Baltimore, 22, p)
Moeller walked 83 batters in $112^{2/3}$ innings in 1961 and posted a 4–8 record and a 5.83 ERA.

Fred Newman (Boston, 18, p)
Newman gave the Angels two effective seasons with a record of 13–10 in 1964 and 14–16 in 1965, both with earned run averages under 3.00.

He pitched $260^{2/3}$ innings as a 23-year-old in 1965, however, and was never again effective. Newman was only 25 when he threw his last big league pitch two years later.

Albie Pearson (Baltimore, 26, of)
At five-foot-five and 140 pounds, Pearson was the smallest player in the majors throughout his career. He gave the Angels three excellent seasons as a lead-off hitter and center fielder. He hit .288 with an on-base percentage of .420 in 1961 and then led the AL in runs with 115 in 1962. Pearson batted .304 in 1963, but recurring back spasms restricted his play after that season and eventually ended his career. After an attempt at a pro golfing career, he became a radio evangelist in California and Nevada.

Buck Rodgers (Detroit, 22, c)
Rodgers played his entire nine-year big league career with the Angels and was the club's starting catcher from 1962 through 1969. As a rookie in 1962, he caught 155 games. Rodgers later managed the Angels from 1991 through 1994.

Don Ross (Baltimore, 22, inf)
Ross never played a game at the major league level.

Ed Sadowski (Boston, 29, c)
Sadowski was a weak-hitting backup catcher for three seasons with the Angels.

Bob Sprout (Detroit, 19, p)
Sprout made his big league debut as a 19-year-old on September 27, 1961, and pitched four innings as a starting pitcher. He proved to be one of the few players in history whose career in the majors ended as a teenager. Sprout never pitched in another game.

Faye Throneberry (Minnesota, 29, of)
Throneberry lasted only 24 games with the Angels and hit just .194.

Red Wilson (Cleveland, 31, c)
Wilson retired rather than cast his lot with the expansion Angels. Ted Bowsfield was later named as Wilson's replacement. A pitcher, Bowsfield was 20–16 in two seasons with the Angels.

Eddie Yost (Detroit, 34, 3b)
With the Senators and Tigers, Yost led the AL six times in walks and twice in on-base percentage. Saddled with playing on teams that were mediocre at best, he never received the credit he deserved. Yost drew 1,614 career walks. Through 2009, there have been 26 players with at least 1,400 career base on balls. Among those, 23 are eligible for the Hall of Fame. Yost is the only one of those 23 who has not been elected. In fact, when placed on the Hall of Fame ballot in 1968, he failed to receive a single vote from the 340 voters who participated that year. Yost was all but through by the time he donned an Angel uniform, however. Although he drew 80 walks, Yost batted just .215 with three homers in 317 at-bats over two seasons.

1961

Season in a Sentence
Many predicted during spring training that the Angels wouldn't win more than 40 games, but the club silenced the critics with 70 victories.

Finish • Won • Lost • Pct • GB
Eighth   70   91   .435   38.5

Manager
Bill Rigney

Stats

Stats	Angels	AL	Rank
Batting Avg:	.245	.256	9
On-Base Pct:	.331	.329	4
Slugging Pct:	.398	.395	7
Home Runs:	189		2
Stolen Bases:	37		8
ERA:	4.31	4.02	9
Errors:	192		10
Runs Scored:	744		4
Runs Allowed:	784		8

Starting Lineup
Earl Averill, c
Steve Bilko, 1b
Ken Aspromonte, 2b
Eddie Yost, 3b
Joe Koppe, ss
Leon Wagner, lf
Ken Hunt, cf
Albie Pearson, rf-cf
Lee Thomas, rf-1b
George Thomas, lf-3b
Ted Kluszewski, 1b
Rocky Bridges, 2b-ss

Pitchers
Ken McBride, sp
Eli Grba, sp
Ted Bowsfield, sp-rp
Ron Moeller, sp
Tom Morgan, rp
Art Fowler, rp
Ryne Duren, rp-sp
Jim Donohue, rp
Ron Kline, rp

Attendance
603.510 (ninth in AL)

Club Leaders
Batting Avg:	Albie Pearson	.288
On-Base Pct:	Albie Pearson	.420
Slugging Pct:	Leon Wagner	.517
Home Runs:	Leon Wagner	28
RBI:	Ken Hunt	84
Runs:	Albie Pearson	92
Stolen Bases:	Albie Pearson	11
Wins:	Ken McBride	12
Strikeouts:	Ken McBride	180
ERA:	Ken McBride	3.65
Saves:	Art Fowler	11

JANUARY 26   The Angels trade Al Cicotte to the Cardinals for Leon Wagner, Ellis Burton, Cal Browning and cash.

At the time of the trade, Wagner was a 26-year-old outfielder who hit .220 with nine homers in 227 at-bats with the Giants and Cardinals the previous two seasons. He suddenly blossomed with the Angels. In three seasons in Los Angeles, Wagner was named to two All-Star teams while hitting .279 and clubbing 91 homers. His nickname was "Daddy Wags" and for many years he owned a clothing store with the slogan "Buy Your Rags at Daddy Wags." Wagner was also a professional actor and had a role in Bingo Long Traveling All-Stars and Motor Kings, *about a black barnstorming team. Cicotte was a journeyman pitcher on the skids. He had a record of 2–6 with a 5.20 ERA over the remainder of his career.*

January 31   The Angels purchase Tom Morgan from the Twins.

Nicknamed "Plowboy" because of his stooped walk, Morgan had a two-year run of success out of the Angels bullpen. In 1961, he was 8–2 with ten saves and a 2.36 ERA. Morgan's relief partner in 1961 was 38-year-old Art Fowler, who pitched four seasons with the Angels and had an unusual career. He had a brother named Jesse, who was 23 years and eight months older and pitched in the majors in 1924. It is the largest age difference between brothers in major league history. Art made his big league debut in 1954 with the Reds at the age of 31. He was 41 when he hurled his last game in 1964. Fowler was also a pitching coach under Billy Martin with the Twins, Tigers, Rangers, Yankees and Athletics between 1969 and 1988.

February 24   The Angels open their first training camp in Palm Springs, California. The club was headquartered at the Desert Inn. In 1963, Gene Autry purchased the Holiday Inn and renamed it the Gene Autry Hotel. The facility subsequently became the spring training headquarters for the club.

March 1   Former President Dwight Eisenhower visits the Angels training camp. His term as president ended just six weeks earlier. After joking with the players on the field, Eisenhower sat in the dugout and watched a five-inning intra-squad game.

March 11   The Angels play their first exhibition game and beat the Cubs 8–3 at Palm Springs. Dwight Eisenhower was scheduled to throw out the ceremonial first pitch but decided to go fishing instead. Entertainer Dinah Shore agreed to act as a substitute for Eisenhower but was caught in traffic on the way to the game. Palm Springs mayor Frank Bogert threw out the first pitch, but once Shore arrived, the ceremonies were conducted all over again.

The radio and television announcers for the Angels in 1961 were Don Wells, Bob Kelley and Steve Bailey. Wells announced games for the White Sox from 1953 through 1960. Kelley and Bailey were veteran Los Angeles reporters. Kelley announced Angels games for only a year and Bailey for just two. Wells remained with the club until 1972. The games on radio were carried on KMPC, which was owned by Gene Autry. A total of 20 games were televised in 1961 over KHJ-TV.

April 10   The Angels purchase Ron Kline from the Cardinals.

April 11   The Angels play their first regular season game in franchise history and defeat the Orioles 7–2 on a harsh and windy day in Baltimore. The starting lineup consisted of Eddie Yost (3b), Ken Aspromonte (2b), Albie Pearson (rf), Ted Kluszewski (1b), Bob Cerv (lf), Ken Hunt (cf), Fritz Brickell (ss), Del Rice (c), and Eli Grba (p). The Angels scored three runs in the first inning off Milt Pappas on a two-out walk to Pearson and back-to-back homers by Kluszewski and Cerv. Four runs were added in the second for a 7–0 lead, the last three on another home run by Kluszewski. Grba pitched a complete game, allowing six hits. Brickell made the first two errors in Angels history on a single play in the second inning when he booted a ground ball and then threw wildly to first. His father died only two days earlier.

Due to a postponement because of rain and two off days, the Angels didn't play again until April 15. The club was scheduled to open the season with a 13-game road trip through Baltimore, Boston, New York, Detroit and Chicago, but only eight games were played due to bad weather. After winning the first game, the Angels lost the next eight contests.

Bill Rigney managed the Angels throughout most of the 1960s, supplying veteran leadership to the young team.

April 15   The Angels suffer their first loss, dropping a 3–0 decision to the Red Sox in Boston. Jerry Casale was the losing pitcher. Eddie Yost became the first Angel to be ejected for arguing a call in the eighth inning. It was only the second ejection for Yost in 16 years in the majors.

Gene Autry selected navy blue and red as the uniform colors for the Angels. The home whites featured "Angels" written in arched fancy red lettering outlined in blue. The road shirts used the same lettering style with "Los Angeles" across the front. The caps were blue with an interlocking "L" and "A" in red outlined in white. A unique addition was a white "halo" stripe around the tops of the caps to portray the team's "heavenly origins."

April 17   On the day after the failed Bay of Pigs invasion of Cuba, Albie Pearson hits the first pinch-hit home run in Angels history in the eighth inning of a 3–2 loss to the Red Sox in Boston. Tom Morgan became the first Angel pitcher to allow a home run when Gary Geiger connected in the seventh.

April 20   The Angels play their first double-header, losing 7–5 and 4–2 to the Yankees in New York.

1960s

APRIL 23   The Angels play their first extra-inning game and lose 3–2 to the Tigers in 11 innings in the second game of a double-header in Detroit. The Tigers won the opener 3–1.

APRIL 27   The Angels play their first home game and lose 4–2 to the Twins before 11,931 at Wrigley Field. Earl Averill drove in both runs with a home run in the second inning. Eli Grba was the starting and losing pitcher. With the game played on a Thursday afternoon, the crowd was far below expectations. Among those who attended were Baseball Commissioner Ford Frick, Ty Cobb, Casey Stengel, Groucho Marx and Buster Keaton. Cobb threw out the ceremonial first pitch. The legendary ballplayer, whose career lasted from 1905 through 1928, died less than three months later on July 17 at the age of 74.

> *Attendance was a problem at 20,500-seat Wrigley Field all season. There was parking for only 900 cars in car-conscious Los Angeles. As a new team with few marquee players, the club also had difficulty attracting fans away from the more glamorous Dodgers, who moved to Los Angeles in 1958. The Dodgers attracted 1,804,250 in 1961, which led the majors. Among the 18 big league clubs that season, the Angels ranked 16th, outdrawing only the Washington Senators, another first-year expansion team, and the Philadelphia Phillies, who had a record of 47–107 and endured a 23-game losing streak in July and August.*

APRIL 28   Despite making five errors, the Angels win their first game in Los Angeles and break an eight-game losing streak by defeating the Twins 6–5 in 12 innings at Wrigley Field. Minnesota scored in the top of the 12th for a 5–4 lead. Ken Hamlin tied the score with a home run. After two singles and an intentional walk to load the bases, Ken Hunt was hit by a Bill Pleis pitch to drive in the winning run.

> *The home run was the only one that Hamlin hit as a member of the Angels.*

APRIL 30   Tom Morgan records the first save in Angels history by closing out a 6–4 win over the Athletics in the first game of a double-header at Wrigley Field. Kansas City game two 3–2.

> *Wrigley Field was a home run haven in 1961. It was 340 feet down the left-field foul line, 338 to right field, and 410 feet to center field, but the power alleys were only 345 feet from home plate. There were 248 home runs hit at the ballpark in 82 home games and 121 in 80 Angels road games. The 248 homers was a major league record which stood until 271 were struck at Coors Field in Denver in 1996. The Angels hit 122 homers at home and 67 during away contests. The pitching staff surrendered a league-high 126 homers at home and a league-low 54 on the road. The club finished first in the AL in runs scored at home (447) and last in the circuit on road runs (297). The Angels had a 46–36 record at home and were 24–55 (with one tie) away from Los Angeles. In 1962, the club moved into Chavez Ravine, an extreme pitcher's park. In four seasons at that spacious venue, the Angels connected for only 142 home runs at home, but 284 on the road. Over the same four seasons in the same ballpark, the Dodgers struck 141 homers at home and 266 on the road.*

MAY 3   Trailing 6–1, the Angels score a run in the seventh inning, two in the eighth and three in the ninth to down the Orioles 7–6 at Wrigley Field. The Angels were still down 6–4 with two out in the ninth and no one on base when Ted Kluszewski homered, Ken Hunt singled, and Earl Averill connected for a two-run, walk-off homer.

MAY 8 Three days after Alan Shepard becomes the first American in space, the Angels trade Tex Clevenger and Bob Cerv to the Yankees for Lee Thomas, Ryne Duren and Johnny James.

> *This proved to be an excellent trade as Thomas helped the club as a four-year starter. He hit 24 homers in 1961 and 26 more in 1962. Duren was the prototype fireballing relief pitcher. In 1958 and 1959 with the Yankees, he had a 1.95 ERA and allowed only 89 hits with 185 strikeouts in 152 1/3 innings. Duren scared the life out of hitters not only as a result of occasional wildness but because of his vision problems. He peered toward the plate with bottle-thick glasses and sometimes enhanced the effect by throwing warm-up tosses to the screen. With the Angels, Duren's control problems were more than occasional. In two seasons with the club, he walked 132 batters in 170 1/3 innings and had an 8–21 record and a 4.86 ERA. Duren's life was also spinning out of control of the diamond because of alcoholism. He chronicled his problems in an autobiography entitled* The Comeback. *He went on the become director of the Stoughton Community Hospital in Wisconsin and worked to control alcohol advertising through a program called SMART (Stop Marketing Alcohol on Radio and Television).*

MAY 9 Jerry Casale becomes the first pitcher in Angels history to hit a home run with a blast off Ike Delock in the second inning of an 8–7 win over the Red Sox at Wrigley Field.

MAY 12 Twins pitcher Pedro Ramos and Angels hurler Eli Grba homer off each other in the fifth inning of a 5–4 Angels loss in Minnesota. Grba went deep off Ramos in the top of the fifth with one out. Ramos returned the favor on a Grba offering leading off the bottom half. Ramos also hit a two-run single against Grba in the sixth.

MAY 18 Ryne Duren strikes out four batters in the seventh inning of a 6–4 loss to the White Sox at Wrigley Field. Duren was able to accomplish the feat because Roy Sievers swung and missed a pitch that eluded catcher Del Rice for a passed ball. Duren also fanned Minnie Minoso, J. C. Martin and Sammy Esposito.

MAY 23 Ken McBride pitches the first shutout in Angels history by defeating the Indians 9–0 at Wrigley Field on a three-hitter.

JUNE 6 Lee Thomas hits the first grand slam in Angels history with a blast off Milt Pappas in the second inning of a 7–3 victory in the first game of a double-header in Baltimore. The Orioles won the second tilt 3–0.

> *The Angels were the only American League team located west of Kansas City, which led to scheduling problems. From May 30 through June 18, the club endured a road trip through Washington, Cleveland, Baltimore, Boston, New York, Chicago and Kansas City. To make up for April rainouts, the Angels played six double-headers and 26 games in 20 days. Over those 26 games, Los Angeles posted a record of 8–18.*

JUNE 9 Ryne Duren strikes out seven batters in a row during a 5–3 win over the Red Sox in the second game of a double-header at Fenway Park. Duren set down Frank Malzone in the first inning, Pete Runnels, Jim Pagliaroni and Don Buddin in the second, and Mike Fornieles, Chuck Schilling and Gary Geiger in the third. Boston won the first game 5–3.

The Angels hit the low point of the season on June 16 with a record of 21–42. The club was 49–49 the rest of the way.

JUNE 18 — Del Rice stars in a 12-inning, 5–3 win over the Athletics in Kansas City. Rice hit a pinch-hit homer in the ninth inning to tie the contest at 3–3, remained in the lineup as a catcher, and smacked a two-run homer in the 12th.

JUNE 19 — The Angels purchase Joe Koppe from the Cardinals.

JUNE 26 — Albie Pearson opens the first inning with a homer off Whitey Ford, but the Angels lose 8–6 to the Yankees at Wrigley Field. It was the first lead-off homer in Angels history.

JUNE 28 — Ryne Duren strikes out 12 batters in eight innings during a 5–3 win over the Yankees at Wrigley Field. Duren also drove in the first two Angels runs with a two-out single in the sixth inning that put the club into the lead 2–1. Albie Pearson followed with a three-run homer.

JULY 6 — The Angels edge the Twins 12–11 at Metropolitan Stadium in Bloomington, Minnesota. The Twins led 8–7 at the end of the second inning. Lee Thomas belted a three-run homer in the eighth to tie the score 11–11. Albie Pearson drove in the winning run in the ninth with a two-out single.

Angels pitchers led the AL in strikeouts in 1961 with 973 and walks by issuing 713. Angels batters also led the league in strikeouts by accumulating 1,068, which at the time was a major league record, and they topped the American League in drawing walks with 681. The small dimensions and poor lighting at Wrigley Field contributed to both anomalies as there were far more walks and strikeouts at Angels home games than on the road.

JULY 15 — Ed Sadowski pokes a home run in the 12th inning to defeat the Indians 6–5 in Cleveland.

Ken McBride was the only Angel selected for the AL All-Star team in 1961. There were two games played that season (a situation that existed from 1959 through 1962), and McBride didn't appear in either of them.

JULY 19 — Lee Thomas hits a two-run, walk-off homer in the ninth inning to defeat the Twins 2–1 in the second game of a double-header at Wrigley Field. Minnesota won the opener 6–0.

JULY 21 — The Angels collect 20 hits and clobber the Senators 16–5 at Wrigley Field. Both teams left 15 men on base.

JULY 23 — Tom Satriano becomes the first minor league product originally signed by the Angels to play for the club. He was retired as a pinch hitter during a 7–6 loss to the Senators at Wrigley Field. Satriano made his debut straight off the campus of the University of

Southern California without playing in the minor leagues. He played for the Angels as a catcher and utility infielder from 1961 through 1969.

Satriano's daughter Gina, who was born in 1965, became the first female to play in the California Little League system after successfully winning a lawsuit that permitted her to participate. She later pitched for the Colorado Silver Bullets, a professional women's team that toured the United States during the 1990s, and she became a Deputy District Attorney in Los Angeles County.

July 25   Trailing the Tigers 4–3 with two out in the ninth at Wrigley Field, the Angels score twice for a 5–4 victory. Ed Sadowski drove in the tying run and Eddie Yost the game-winning run, both with singles.

July 30   The Angels use five homers to power past the Indians 8–6 at Wrigley Field. Leon Wagner and George Thomas each connected for two homers and Ed Sadowski for one.

August 10   The Angels sell Ron Kline to the Tigers.

August 13   On the day in which construction of the Berlin Wall commences, shortstop Joe Koppe hits a grand slam off Frank Funk in the seventh inning to spark an 8–7 win over the Indians in Cleveland. The blow was struck with the club trailing 5–3.

August 15   Albie Pearson hits a two-out, two-run double in the ninth inning to defeat the Senators 8–7 in Washington.

Of the players on the 1961 Opening Day roster Albie Pearson played for the Angels longer than anyone, staying on the club until 1966. Jim Fregosi was the last of the expansion picks to play for the club. He was traded to the Mets after the end of the 1971 season. Fregosi began the 1961 campaign in the minors.

August 16   The Angels lose an excruciating 3–2 decision to the Senators in Washington. The Angels led 2–1 with two out in the ninth and Washington runners Marty Keough on second base and Bud Zipfel on first. Jim King hit a routine grounder to third baseman Eddie Yost for what should have been the final out, but Yost threw wildly to second on an attempted force play, allowing Keough to score. Right fielder Albie Pearson retrieved the ball and made an errant throw to third trying to nab Zipfel, who then trotted home with the winning run.

August 22   The Angels draw 19,930 fans to Wrigley Field, the largest home crowd of the first season, and defeat the Yankees 4–3.

The Angels averaged crowds of 18,507 for nine games against the Yankees at Wrigley Field in 1961, and 6,620 for the other clubs in the AL.

August 29   After the Orioles score in the top of the 11th for a 5–4 lead, Joe Koppe and Steve Bilko homer in the bottom half for a 6–5 Angels win in the second game of a double-header at Wrigley Field. The Angels won the opener by the same 6–5 score.

September 4   The Athletics score 11 runs in the fifth inning and defeat the Angels 13–7 in Kansas City.

SEPTEMBER 5	Lee Thomas ties a major league record with nine hits in a double-header, although the Angels lose twice to the Athletics in Kansas City. In the opener, Thomas collected four singles and a double in five at-bats. In game two, Thomas became the first Angel to hit three homers in a game and added a single in six at-bats during a 13–12 defeat. He also drove in eight runs. Thomas's first homer was a solo shot in the third inning off Lew Krausse. He added a grand slam off Krausse to cap a seven-run sixth inning that tied the score 9–9. A three-run homer facing Bill Fischer in the eighth put the Angels ahead 12–11, but the A's scored twice in the ninth on a two-out, walk-off homer by Bobby Del Greco off Ken McBride for the win.

> *Thomas had an amazing streak from September 1 through September 10 in which he picked up 23 hits, including five home runs, three doubles and a triple, in 39 at-bats.*

SEPTEMBER 9	George Thomas hits a grand slam off Frank Baumann in the fifth inning of a 6–2 win over the White Sox at Wrigley Field.
SEPTEMBER 28	Leon Wagner drives in eight runs during a 13–4 thrashing of the Senators at Wrigley Field. Wagner doubled in a run in the first inning, hit a sacrifice fly in the third and a two-run double in the fifth off Dick Donovan. He capped his big day with a grand slam facing Johnny Klippstein in the eighth.

> *Wagner closed out the 1961 season with home runs in each of the last four games. Overall, he collected 11 hits in 17 at-bats over those four contests, scored nine runs and drove in 16.*

SEPTEMBER 29	Buck Rodgers hits a grand slam off Barry Latman in the third inning of a 6–4 win over the Indians at Wrigley Field. It was Rodgers' first major league home run.
OCTOBER 1	Wrigley Field, home to the minor league Angels from 1925 through 1957 and the major league Angels in 1961, hosts its last professional baseball game. The Angels defeated the Indians 8–5 before a crowd of 9,868 to win their 70th game.

> *The 70 wins by the Angels is still a first-year expansion record, followed by the 1969 Royals (69–93), 1993 Rockies (67–95), 1998 Diamondbacks (65–97), 1962 Houston Colts (64–96), 1969 Seattle Pilots (64–98), 1977 Mariners (64–98), 1993 Marlins (64–98), 1998 Devil Rays (63–99), 1961 Senators (61–100), 1977 Blue Jays (54–107), 1969 Expos (52–110), 1969 Padres (52–110), and 1962 Mets (40–120).*

> *Wrigley Field was torn down in 1966. The site is currently used as Gilbert Lindsay Park, a public playground, and the Theresa Lindsay Senior Center. A baseball diamond is located at the corner of East 41st Place and South San Pedro Street.*

NOVEMBER 27	The Angels draft Bo Belinsky from the Orioles organization and Felix Torres from the Phillies.

1962

Season in a Sentence

In only their second season, the Angels amaze the baseball world by taking first place on July 4 and finishing in third with a record of 86–76.

Finish • Won • Lost • Pct • GB

Third   86   76   .531   10.0

Manager

Bill Rigney

Stats   Angels • AL • Rank

Batting Avg:	.250	.255	6
On-Base Pct:	.325	.325	5
Slugging Pct:	.380	.394	8
Home Runs:	137		7
Stolen Bases:	46		5
ERA:	3.70	3.97	2
Errors:	175		10
Runs Scored:	718		5
Runs Allowed:	706		5

Starting Lineup

Buck Rodgers, c
Lee Thomas, 1b-rf
Billy Moran, 2b
Felix Torres, 3b
Joe Koppe, ss
Leon Wagner, lf
Albie Pearson, cf
George Thomas, rf
Earl Averill, c

Pitchers

Bo Belinsky, sp
Ken McBride, sp
Eli Grba, sp
Ted Bowsfield, sp
Don Lee, sp
Dean Chance, sp-rp
Tom Morgan, rp
Jack Spring, rp
Art Fowler, rp
Ryne Duren, rp

Attendance

1,144,063 (fourth in AL)

Club Leaders

Batting Avg:	Billy Moran	.290
On-Base Pct:	Albie Pearson	.360
Slugging Pct:	Leon Wagner	.500
Home Runs:	Leon Wagner	37
RBI:	Leon Wagner	107
Runs:	Albie Pearson	115
Stolen Bases:	Albie Pearson	15
Wins:	Dean Chance	14
Strikeouts:	Dean Chance	145
ERA:	Dean Chance	2.96
Saves:	Tom Morgan	9

APRIL 2   Six weeks after John Glenn becomes the first American to orbit the earth in space, the Angels play the Dodgers for the first time and win 6–5 before a sellout crowd of 5,181 at Palm Springs, California, that includes former President Dwight Eisenhower.

The Angels and Dodgers played each other for the first time in Los Angeles in 1963 for another exhibition game. The annual Freeway Series of preseason exhibitions began in 1969. The two clubs began playing during the regular season in 1997.

APRIL 9   The Angels sign Joe Nuxhall as a free agent.

Nuxhall became the youngest player in modern major league history when he made his debut with the Reds at the age of 15 in 1944. He lasted only five games with the Angels.

APRIL 10   The Angels open the season with a 2–1 loss to the White Sox in Chicago. The game ended on a two-out, walk-off single by Sherm Lollar off Joe Nuxhall in the ninth inning.

> *Dodger Stadium opened the same day with a 6–3 Reds win over the Dodgers before 52,564. When the Angels played at the facility, it was called Chavez Ravine.*

April 12   Leon Wagner homers off Joe Horlen in the ninth inning to down the White Sox 1–0 in Chicago. Ken McBride pitched the shutout. It was the first 1–0 win in club history.

April 13   The Angels-Twins game in Minnesota is postponed by a six-inch snowfall.

April 17   The Angels play their first game at Chavez Ravine and lose 5–3 to the Athletics before 18,416.

> *Dodger Stadium/Chavez Ravine was the only privately financed stadium built for baseball between 1923 and 2000. It was unique for its time with 50,000 seats in four multi-colored tiers (yellow, light orange, turquoise and sky blue) with another 6,000 in the outfield pavilions. It was the first major league stadium with "dugout boxes," which put fans on the same level as the players. The two outfield scoreboards, measuring 75 feet by 34 feet, were the largest anywhere in 1962. The most unique features of the ballpark were the terraced parking lots, the only ones of their kind, which allowed fans to park at the same level as their seats. The setting added to the experience of attending a game at Chavez Ravine, which was nestled in the tree-lined Elysian Park hills. The dimensions were 330 feet down each foul line and 406 feet to center field with 380-foot power alleys.*

April 19   After the Athletics score two runs in the top of the 11th for a 4–2 lead, the Angels respond with two in their half and two more in the 12th to win 6–4 at Chavez Ravine. Billy Moran ended the game with a two-out, two-run, walk-off homer.

> *A second baseman, Moran came into the season with three homers and a .242 batting average in 447 career at-bats over three seasons with the Indians and Angels. He was the surprise player of 1962, with 17 home runs and a .282 average in 160 games and 659 at-bats at the age of 28. Moran's bubble soon burst, however, and he was back to a utility role two years later and out of the majors by 1965.*

May 5   In only his fourth major league game, 25-year-old Bo Belinsky pitches the first no-hitter in Angel history and defeats the Orioles 2–0 at Chavez Ravine. Belinsky was part of the Orioles organization until he was drafted by the Angels during the previous offseason. He faced 34 batters, struck out nine, walked four, and nicked two others with pitches. Belinsky loaded the bases in the fourth with one out on two walks and an error by third baseman Felix Torres, but he pitched out of the jam. In the ninth, Belinsky struck out Jackie Brandt, retired Gus Triandos on a ground out from shortstop Joe Koppe to first baseman Steve Bilko, and induced Dave Nicholson to pop up to Torres.

May 6   Lee Thomas collects five hits, including a double, in six at-bats during a 15–7 win over the Orioles at Chavez Ravine.

> *The Angels drew 1,144,063 fans in 1962, well shy of the Dodgers attendance of 2,755,184, which was a major league record that stood until 1977.*

Bo

At the time the Angels selected Bo Belinsky from the Orioles in the Rule 5 in November 1961, few in Los Angeles had ever heard of him. His won-lost record in the minors was 32–35. By the following May, Belinsky was nationally known with victories in his first five starts, including a no-hitter. But he was known best for dating Hollywood celebrities and for his outrageous quotes. In the early sixties, he was the most photographed and interviewed player in baseball.

Belinsky reported to spring training nine days late in 1962 despite having never pitched a big league game and holding a tenuous hold on a roster spot. He told manager Bill Rigney he was tired after playing in a pool tournament in his hometown of Trenton, New Jersey. Once in Palm Springs, Belinsky called a poolside news conference to complain about his contract. He pitched well enough in exhibition games to make the starting rotation, however, and after five starts had a 5–0 record and a 1.72 ERA. Start number four was a no-hitter against the Orioles on May 5.

Belinsky made more news off the field than he did on it. Eager reporters flocked around him because he was also good with a quote. He was seen socially with J. Edgar Hoover, Walter Winchell, Frank Sinatra and Hugh Hefner. Bo dated the likes of Ann-Margaret, Connie Stevens, Doris Duke, Juliet Prowse, Tina Louise and Mamie Van Doren. He was engaged to Van Doren for a year beginning in April 1963. Belinsky also made guest appearances on TV series such as *77 Sunset Strip*, *Surfside Six* and *Dakota*.

Belinsky's star faded when he stopped pitching well. After the 5–0 start as a rookie in 1962, he finished the season at 10–11 with a 3.56 ERA and 122 walks in 187 1/3 innings. In 1963, he was 2–9, and his earned run average soared to 5.75, earning him a trip back to the minors. He rebounded in 1964 compiling a 9–8 record and a 2.86 ERA for the Angels but was suspended in August for slugging a sportswriter more than twice his age (see August 14, 1964).

The Angels traded Belinsky to the Phillies in December 1964. He pitched ineffectively for the Phillies (1965–66), Astros (1967), Pirates (1969) and Reds (1970) before his career ended with a 28–51 record. No one in baseball history has spent as long in the spotlight as Belinsky with so poor a performance.

Later, Belinsky married and divorced *Playboy* Playmate of the Month Jo Collins, then heiress Jane Weyerhauser. He eventually overcame alcohol addiction and became a born-again Christian. He died in Las Vegas from cancer at the age of 64 in 2001.

MAY 11 Bo Belinsky extends his record to 5–0 only five games into his major league career with a 4–2 decision over the White Sox at Chavez Ravine.

Belinsky's 5–0 record was accompanied by a 1.72 ERA. Over the remainder of the 1962 season, he was 5–11 with an earned run average of 4.00.

MAY 20 The Angels sweep the Red Sox 5–3 and 1–0 at Fenway Park. Bo Belinsky pitched a two-hitter in the second game. The only Boston hits were a single by Pete Runnels in the first inning and a double from Bob Tillman in the fourth. Lee Thomas drove in the lone run with a single in the third.

Thomas batted .290 with 26 homers and 104 RBIs in 1962.

MAY 22 The Angels collect only one hit off four Yankees pitchers in 12 innings and lose 2–1 in New York. The Angels scored in the first inning off Whitey Ford when Albie Pearson walked, stole second, moved to third on a groundout, and scored on Leon Wagner's sacrifice fly. Ford was lifted for a pinch hitter in the bottom of the seventh. The only

Los Angeles hit was a single by Buck Rodgers with one out in the ninth off Jim Coates. Bud Daley pitched the 10th and 11th for the Yanks, and Bob Turley the 12th. Elston Howard drove in the winning run with a sacrifice fly. Angels pitchers tied a major league record by issuing seven intentional walks, four of them to Roger Maris.

> *Buddy Blattner replaced Bob Kelley on the Angels broadcasts in 1962. A former infielder in the majors from 1946 through 1949, Blattner called Angels games for seven seasons with Don Wells. Blattner was also an accomplished table tennis player, winning the men's doubles at the age of 16 in 1936. He was inducted into the U.S. Table Tennis Association Hall of Fame in 1979.*

May 29   The Angels trade Jim Donohue to the Twins for Don Lee.

June 1   The Angels draw 51,584 for a 6–2 loss to the Yankees at Chavez Ravine. It was the first time that the Angels had a home crowd above 20,000. Marilyn Monroe, who died two months later, participated in pre-game ceremonies.

> *The smallest crowd for any of the nine Yankee games at Chavez Ravine in 1962 was 34,133. The largest crowd for a non-Yankee game was 25,386. The Yanks accounted for 35 percent of the Angel attendance in 1962.*

June 6   A sacrifice fly by pinch hitter Tom Burgess in the ninth inning accounts for the only run of a 1–0 win over the White Sox at Chavez Ravine. Ken McBride pitched the shutout.

June 8   In his first game as a member of the Angels, Don Lee pitches a two-hitter to defeat the Athletics 7–1 at Chavez Ravine. The only Kansas City hits were a single by Jerry Lumpe in the second inning and a double from Joe Azcue in the sixth.

June 10   The Angels sweep the Athletics 14–6 and 6–5 at Chavez Ravine. Billy Moran drove in six runs in the opener on a home run, double, single, and bases-loaded walk.

> *Earl Averill reached base in 17 consecutive plate appearances from June 3 through June 10 on seven hits (four singles, two doubles, and a home run), eight walks, an error and a fielder's choice. The official major league record is 16 by Ted Williams in 1957. Williams holds the mark instead of Averill because errors and fielder's choices go into the box score as outs.*

June 24   Home runs by Joe Koppe and Billy Moran in the ninth inning beats the Twins 7–6 in the second game of a double-header in Minnesota. The Angels also won the opener 3–2 in ten innings.

June 26   Earl Wilson of the Red Sox beats the Angels 2–0 with a no-hitter in Boston. Wilson recorded five strikeouts and walked four. It was the first no-hitter ever thrown against the Angels. Lee Thomas accounted for the final out with a fly ball to center fielder Gary Geiger. Bo Belinsky, who pitched a no-hitter of his own on May 5, was the losing pitcher.

June 28   The Angels score seven runs in the second inning and rout the Red Sox 19–7 in Boston.

July 1	Albie Pearson is hitless in 11 at-bats during a double-header against the Yankees in New York. The Angels lost 6–3 and won 12–5. Reliever Art Fowler helped himself in game two with a pair of two-run singles.
	Despite the bad day, Pearson led the American League in runs with 115 in 1962. He drew 95 walks and struck out only 36 times.
July 4	The Angels continue to shock the baseball world by taking first place with a 4–2 and 4–1 sweep of the Senators in Washington.
	The Angels had a record of 45–34. The club dropped out of first two days later but remained in contention for the top spot for another two months.
July 10	Lee Thomas, Leon Wagner and Billy Moran are the Angels first participants in an All-Star Game. Moran was the starter at second base and collected a single in three at-bats. Wagner started in left field and was hitless in four at-bats. Thomas was retired as a pinch hitter. The National League won 3–1 at D. C. Stadium in Washington. It was the first of two All-Star Games played in 1962.
July 14	The Angels hit five home runs but lose 9–8 in ten innings to the Yankees at Chavez Ravine. The homers were struck by Albie Pearson, Lee Thomas, Felix Torres, Earl Averill and Ed Sadowski. A win would have put the Angels back into first place.
July 17	Ken McBride pitches the Angels to a 1–0 win over the Tigers at Chavez Ravine. Lee Thomas drove in the lone run with a single in the fourth inning.
July 20	Trailing 3–0, the Angels explode for eight runs in the fifth inning and defeat the Indians 8–5 at Chavez Ravine. The big blow was a three-run homer by Lee Thomas.
July 21	Ken McBride extends his winning streak to ten games by defeating the Indians 4–0 at Chavez Ravine.
	The victory gave McBride an 11–3 record. A rib injury soon surfaced, however, and he didn't win another game all year. McBride finished the season at 11–5.
July 23	The Angels edge the Orioles 6–5 in 14 innings. Felix Torres drove in the winning run with a single.
July 29	After falling behind 8–5, the Angels score seven unanswered runs over the final three innings to outslug the Tigers 12–8 in the second game of a double-header in Detroit. The Tigers won the opener 7–6.
July 30	In the second of two All-Star Games played in 1962, Leon Wagner collects three hits in four at-bats, including a home run off Art Mahaffey in the fourth inning, to lead the AL to a 9–4 win at Wrigley Field.
	Wagner finished the season with 37 homers, 107 RBIs and a .268 batting average.
August 6	Prior to a 5–2 win over the Red Sox in Boston, Art Fowler is hit in the head with a batted ball while chatting with a fan during batting practice. Fowler pitched only

two more games over the remainder of the season, and never regained the sight in his left eye.

AUGUST 10 Dean Chance pitches 11 shutout innings to defeat the Twins 1–0 at Chavez Ravine. The lone run scored on three consecutive singles by Steve Bilko, Buck Rodgers and Leon Wagner.

AUGUST 17 Leon Wagner hits a grand slam in the tenth inning to defeat the Senators 4–3 in the first game of a double-header at Chavez Ravine. The Angels completed the sweep with a 3–2 victory in game two.

AUGUST 28 Lee Thomas, Leon Wagner and Buck Rodgers hit consecutive homers off Moe Drabowsky in the fourth inning of a 10–5 win over the Athletics in Kansas City. It was one of two homers for Wagner. Felix Torres also hit a home run for the Angels giving the club a total of five in the game.

SEPTEMBER 3 Trailing 5–0, the Angels erupt for two runs in the eighth inning and four in the ninth to defeat the Yankees 6–5 in the second game of a double-header in New York. Albie Pearson hit a two-run homer in the eighth. In the ninth, Buck Rodgers doubled in a run, Leo Burke connected for a two-run single, and crossed the plate on a bunt and a single from George Thomas. The Yankees won the opener 8–2.

SEPTEMBER 4 Trailing 4–0, the Angels score six runs in the seventh inning and defeat the Yankees 7–6 in New York.

The Angels were 40–41 at home and 46–35 on the road in 1962.

SEPTEMBER 10 Dean Chance pitches a one-hitter to defeat the Twins 5–0 at Metropolitan Stadium. The only Minnesota hit was an infield single by Zoilo Versalles with one out in the eighth inning.

After a 9–0 triumph over the Twins on September 11, the Angels were in second place, only four games behind the first-place Yankees. The Angels lost 12 of their last 16 games, however, to drop out of the race. Nonetheless, the club finished with an 86–76 record. Among the 14 expansion teams in baseball history, the Angels are one of only two with a winning record in either of their first two seasons. The Diamondbacks were 100–62 in season two in 1999. Unlike the Diamondbacks, who won the World Series in 2001, the Angels were unable to sustain the momentum. The 1962 club outscored the opposition by only 718–706 and led the AL in errors with 175. It was also led by free spirits like Bo Belinsky, Dean Chance, Ryne Duren, Art Fowler and Leon Wagner, none of whom managed to produce consistently throughout their careers.

SEPTEMBER 13 Ed Kirkpatrick makes his major league debut and grounds out as a pinch hitter during a 5–4 loss to the Athletics at Chavez Ravine.

Kirkpatrick was only 17 when he made his big league debut and is the youngest player in Angels history. He was signed by the club out of high school in June 1962 and batted .375 with 12 homers in 64 games that season in the minors at San Jose and Quad Cities. Kirkpatrick was hitless in six at-bats over three games for the Angels in 1962. A catcher and outfielder, he didn't play a full season in the majors until 1966 and never developed into the star he was predicted to be, but he fashioned a 16-year big league career, seven of them as an Angel.

SEPTEMBER 22 — Leon Wagner belts a two-run, walk-off homer in the 11th to defeat the Indians 6–4 at Chavez Ravine. Lee Thomas sent the game into extra innings with a two-out single in the ninth to deadlock the contest at 4–4.

SEPTEMBER 30 — On the last day of the season, 19-year-old Bobby Darwin is the starting pitcher and allows six runs, four of them earned, in $3^{1}/_{3}$ innings of a 6–1 loss to the Indians in the second game of a double-header in Cleveland. The Indians also won the opener 4–3.

With San Jose in the California League 1962, Darwin struck out 202 batters and walked 149 in 202 innings. He didn't play in another game in the majors until 1969 when he appeared in three contests with the Dodgers. He was converted into an outfielder and hit 65 home runs for the Twins from 1972 through 1974.

OCTOBER 26 — While the nation's nerves are frazzled by the Cuban missile crisis, the Angels purchase Bob Turley from the Yankees.

NOVEMBER 30 — The Angels trade Ted Bowsfield to the Athletics for Dan Osinski.

DECEMBER 11 — The Angels trade Earl Averill to the Phillies for Jacke Davis.

1963

Season in a Sentence
After finishing a surprising third in 1962, the Angels take a nosedive into ninth place.

Finish • Won • Lost • Pct • GB
Ninth   70   91   .435   34.0

Manager
Bill Rigney

Stats   Angels • AL • Rank
Batting Avg: .250   .247   6
On-Base Pct: .309   .312   7
Slugging Pct: .354   .380   8
Home Runs: 95   9 (tie)
Stolen Bases: 43   7
ERA: 3.52   3.63   5
Errors: 163   9
Runs Scored: 597   9
Runs Allowed: 660   5

Starting Lineup
Buck Rodgers, c
Charlie Dees, 1b
Billy Moran, 2b
Felix Torres, 3b
Jim Fregosi, ss
Leon Wagner, lf
Albie Pearson, cf
Lee Thomas, rf-1b

Pitchers
Ken McBride, sp
Dean Chance, sp
Don Lee, sp
Bob Turley, sp-rp
Julio Navarro, rp
Art Fowler, rp
Jack Spring, rp
Dan Osinski, rp-sp

Attendance
821,015 (sixth in AL)

Club Leaders
Batting Avg: Albie Pearson .304
On-Base Pct: Albie Pearson .402
Slugging Pct: Leon Wagner   .456
Home Runs: Leon Wagner   26
RBI: Leon Wagner   90
Runs: Albie Pearson 92
Stolen Bases: Albie Pearson 17
Wins: Ken McBride   13
                Dean Chance   13
Strikeouts: Dean Chance   168
ERA: Dean Chance   3.19
Saves: Julio Navarro 12

APRIL 9   The Angels open the season with a 4–1 win over the Red Sox before 21,864 at Chavez Ravine. All four Los Angeles runs scored in the fourth inning, three of them on a home run by Lee Thomas. Ken McBride pitched a complete game four-hitter.

Ten different players started in right field for the Angels in 1963. Thomas was team leader in starts at the position with only 37.

APRIL 13   Three Angels pitchers combine to allow only three hits in 15 innings to outlast the White Sox 1–0 at Chavez Ravine. Ken McBride had a no-hitter in progress until Dave Nicholson and J. C. Martin singled in the eighth. Those were the only two hits surrendered by McBride in 11 innings. Dan Osinski gave up a single to Joe Cunningham in two innings of work. Julio Navarro hurled two hitless innings. Ed Kirkpatrick, who was only 18 years old, drove in the winning run with a walk-off, pinch-hit single. The game also marked the first time that brothers played in the same game for the Angels. Bob Sadowski pinch-hit and played third base. Ed Sadowski was a pinch runner.

APRIL 16   In the first game after a 15-inning 1–0 victory, the Angels lose 11–10 in 13 innings versus the Twins in Minnesota. The Angels scored two runs in the 11th and one in the 13th but couldn't hold the leads. Bill Rigney used nine pitchers during the contest.

APRIL 17   In the first game after the Angels use nine pitchers, Don Lee pitches a three-hit complete game to defeat the Twins 4–0 in Minnesota.

APRIL 23   Jim Fregosi hits a home run in the tenth inning to defeat the Senators 5–4 in Washington.

Playing in his first full season in the majors at the age of 21, Fregosi batted .287 with nine home runs.

APRIL 25   Leon Wagner belts two homers during a 7–5 win over the Tigers in Detroit.

APRIL 26   Leon Wagner collects five hits, including two homers and a double, in six at-bats against the Orioles in Baltimore. His fifth hit was a single in the 13th inning, which drove in the winning run in the Angels 4–3 victory. It also was the second game in a row in which Wagner hit two home runs. The four homers were struck in a span of six plate appearances.

Wagner finished the season with a .291 batting average, 26 homers and 90 RBIs. He had one of the most extreme home-road splits in major league history. At home, Wagner had only two homers, 19 runs batted in, a .261 batting average and .310 slugging percentage. In away games, he belted 24 homers and drove in 71 runs with a .315 batting average and .581 slugging percentage. As a team, the Angels hit 24 homers at Chavez Ravine and 71 on the road.

APRIL 29   Trailing 8–5, the Angels score six runs in the seventh inning and outslug the Senators 13–8 at Chavez Ravine.

MAY 1   George Thomas hits a grand slam off Ralph Terry in the first inning of a 5–3 win over the Yankees at Chavez Ravine.

Angels home attendance fell more than 300,000 to 821,015 in 1963. The nine games against the Yankees attracted 290,318, 35 percent of the total.

MAY 6   Albie Pearson hits a two-run, walk-off double in the ninth inning to defeat the Twins 5–4 at Chavez Ravine.

Pearson batted .304 and scored 92 runs in 1963. He drew 92 walks and struck out only 37 times.

MAY 22   Lee Thomas is hit by a pitch from Gary Bell with the bases loaded in the 12th inning to bring across the winning run of a 7–6 decision over the Indians at Municipal Stadium. The Angels led 6–0 in the fourth inning before letting Cleveland back into the game.

MAY 25   The Angels send Bo Belinsky to Hawaii in the Pacific Coast League. He had a 1–7 record and a 6.39 ERA. Before being sent down, the Angels tried rooming Belinsky with Albie Pearson, a devout Baptist, on road trips, but Pearson spent most nights alone as Belinsky explored the nightlife. Bo hesitated going back to the minors and didn't report to the Hawaii club until mid-July. He didn't return to the Angels until September.

1960s

June 4 — Dan Osinski pitches a three-hitter to defeat the White Sox 1–0 at Chavez Ravine. The lone run scored on a single by Lee Thomas in the second inning.

June 5 — The Angels score seven runs in the sixth inning and beat the White Sox 8–2 in the second game of a double-header at Chavez Ravine. Chicago won the opener 3–0.

June 10 — The Angels rout the Athletics 13–3 in Kansas City.

June 12 — Bob Turley pitches a one-hitter to defeat the White Sox 5–0 in the second game of a double-header at Comiskey Park. The only Chicago hit was a single by Pete Ward in the sixth inning. Chicago won the first game 3–1.

June 15 — The Angels send George Thomas, Frank Kostro and cash to the Tigers for Paul Foytack.

June 19 — Jim Fregosi hits a three-run, walk-off homer in the ninth inning to defeat the Athletics 4–2 at Chavez Ravine. Dan Osinski pitched a two-hitter. The only Kansas City hits were a single by Gino Cimoli in the second inning and a home run from Bobby Del Greco in the sixth.

June 21 — The Angels edge the Senators 1–0 at Chavez Ravine. Bob Perry drove in the lone run with a sacrifice fly in the sixth inning. Dean Chance (8 1/3 innings) and Julio Navarro (two-thirds of an inning) combined on the shutout.

June 28 — Leon Wagner hits two homers and two singles and drives in four runs in five at-bats during an 8–3 win over the Tigers in the first game of a double-header in Detroit. The Tigers won the first contest by the same 8–3 score.

> *The Angels peaked on June 29, holding a record of 41–38. The club was 29–53 the rest of the way to finish at 70–91. It was the same mark the club posted in their first season in 1961.*

July 9 — Albie Pearson collects a double and a single in four at-bats during a 5–3 American League loss in the All-Star Game at Municipal Stadium in Cleveland. Ken McBride was the AL starting pitcher and allowed three runs in three innings.

> *McBride had a record of 12–7 on July 25 but finished the season at 13–12.*

July 12 — The Angels extend their losing streak to ten games with a 4–3 defeat at the hands of the Yankees at Chavez Ravine.

July 17 — Paul Foytack (eight innings) and Art Fowler (one inning) combine to shutout the Indians 1–0 in the second game of a double-header at Chavez Ravine. The Angels also won the opener 7–2.

July 20 — Billy Moran collects four hits and scores four runs in four at-bats during an 11–2 thrashing of the Tigers at Chavez Ravine.

July 27 — The Angels sign Jimmy Piersall following his release by the Mets.

Piersall suffered a nervous breakdown as a rookie with the Red Sox in 1952 and spent six weeks in the violent ward at Westborough State Hospital in Massachusetts, during which he received shock therapy. He battled his way back and played in 151 games for the Sox in 1953 and batted .272. Piersall wrote a book called Fear Strikes Out, *co-authored with Al Hirshberg and published in 1955, about his battle with mental illness. It was made into a movie, with Anthony Perkins portraying Piersall, in 1957. Although he continued to struggle with manic depression, Piersall's big league career lasted until 1967. He played for the Angels for five seasons, mainly as a spare outfielder and pinch hitter, and hit .279 in 545 at-bats.*

JULY 28   Only a day after joining the Angels, Jimmy Piersall becomes engaged in a pushing match with home plate umpire Bill Kinnamon while protesting a strike call in the ninth inning of a 5–4 win over the Red Sox in Boston. Piersall was ejected and later suspended for four games.

JULY 29   The Angels score eight runs in the third inning and wallop the Indians 11–0 at Municipal Stadium. Dean Chance pitched a two-hitter and fanned 12 batters. The only Cleveland hits were singles by Fred Whitfield in the seventh inning and Woodie Held in the eighth.

JULY 31   Paul Foytack allows four consecutive homers in the sixth inning of a 9–5 loss to the Indians during the second game of a double-header in Cleveland. After retiring the first two batters in the inning, Foytack allowed homers to Woodie Held, opposing pitcher Pedro Ramos, Tito Francona and Larry Brown. Brown hit an 0–2 pitch for his first major league homer. Foytack surrendered the four homers to the 8-9-1-2 hitters in the batting order. Cleveland also won the opener 1–0.

Foytack volunteered to pitch in relief two days after throwing seven innings in a start. The only other major league pitcher to allow four straight homers is Chase Wright of the Yankees against the Red Sox in a nationally televised game on ESPN on April 22, 2007. At the time, Foytack was 76 years old and was watching and NBA playoff game. He switched to the Yankees-Red Sox clash during a commercial, saw the first of the four homers that Wright gave up, then went back to basketball and missed the last three home runs that tied his record.

AUGUST 1   The Angels purchase Bob Lee from the Pirates.

AUGUST 3   The Angels beat the White Sox 6–5 in a 16-inning marathon at Chavez Ravine. A single by Jimmy Piersall in the ninth sent the game into extra innings. Billy Moran's walk-off single brought home the winning run.

Piersall collected eight hits in his first 16 at-bats with the Angels.

AUGUST 23   The Angels score seven runs in the seventh inning and clobber the Senators 17–0 in Washington. Ken McBride pitched the shutout. Lee Thomas tied an American League record for first basemen by participating in six double plays. Felix Torres tied a record for third basemen by starting six twin killings.

SEPTEMBER 6   Nine days after Martin Luther King, Jr. makes his famous "I Have a Dream" speech in Washington, Albie Pearson is hit by a pitch from Ted Bowsfield with the bases loaded to force home the winning run in the 14th inning of a 4–3 decision over the Athletics at Chavez Ravine. Billy Moran sent the game into extra innings with a homer in the ninth.

SEPTEMBER 10 The Angels allow the Red Sox to score four runs in the ninth to tie the score 5–5 but survive to win 6–5 in the tenth at Chavez Ravine. Lee Thomas drove in the winning run with a single.

SEPTEMBER 12 The Angels sell Ken Hunt to the Senators.

SEPTEMBER 19 A "crowd" of only 476, the smallest home attendance figure in club history, watches the Angels beat the Orioles 7–2 at Chavez Ravine. The game was played on a Thursday afternoon on what was originally an open date. It was rescheduled because a twi-night double-header was rained out two days earlier.

DECEMBER 2 Ten days after the assassination of President John Kennedy, the Angels trade Leon Wagner to the Indians for Joe Adcock and Barry Latman. On the same day, the Angels drafted Bobby Knoop from the Braves organization.

> *Wagner was the only power threat in the Angels lineup, but the club soured on him after he hit just .229 with seven homers in 271 at-bats after July 1 and refused to change his free-swinging batting style. Over the next three years in Cleveland, he belted 82 home runs. Adcock, who was 36 years old at the time of the trade, picked up some of the slack with 53 home runs for the Angels in three seasons as a platoon first baseman. Ironically, Adcock became manager of the Indians in 1967 but was fired after one season in part because he insisted on platooning Wagner in tandem with Rocky Colavito. A native of Los Angeles, Latman was 7–11 in two seasons with the Angels. Knoop was the Angels starting second baseman from 1964 through 1968, and won the Gold Glove award in 1966, 1967 and 1968.*

1964

Season in a Sentence
Helped by an 11-game winning streak in June and a Cy Young season from Dean Chance, the Angels finish two games above .500 and leap to fifth place after finishing ninth in 1963.

Finish • Won • Lost • Pct • GB
Fifth   82   80   .506   17.0

Manager
Bill Rigney

Stats   Angels • AL • Rank
Stat	Angels	AL	Rank
Batting Avg:	.242	.247	8
On-Base Pct:	.304	.315	9
Slugging Pct:	.344	.382	10
Home Runs:	102		10
Stolen Bases:	49		6
ERA:	2.91	3.63	2
Errors:	138		7 (tie)
Runs Scored:	544		10
Runs Allowed:	551		2

Starting Lineup
Buck Rodgers, c
Joe Adcock, 1b
Bobby Knoop, 2b
Felix Torres, 3b
Jim Fregosi, ss
Willie Smith, lf-rf
Albie Pearson, cf
Lu Clinton, rf
Jimmy Piersall, lf-cf
Tom Satriano, 3b-1b-c
Bob Perry, cf
Vic Power, 1b-3b
Ed Kirkpatrick, lf

Pitchers
Dean Chance, sp
Fred Newman, sp
Bo Belinsky, sp
Ken McBride, sp
Bob Lee, rp
Bob Duliba, rp
Dan Osinski, rp
Barry Latman, rp-sp
Don Lee, rp

Attendance
760,439 (seventh in AL)

Club Leaders
Batting Avg:	Jim Fregosi	.277
On-Base Pct:	Jim Fregosi	.369
Slugging Pct:	Jim Fregosi	.463
Home Runs:	Joe Adcock	21
RBI:	Jim Fregosi	72
Runs:	Jim Fregosi	86
Stolen Bases:	Jim Fregosi	8
Wins:	Dean Chance	20
Strikeouts:	Dean Chance	207
ERA:	Dean Chance	1.65
Saves:	Bob Lee	19

APRIL 10   Two months after the Beatles appear for the first time on *The Ed Sullivan Show*, the Anaheim City Council votes unanimously to build a stadium for the Angels by the start of the 1966 season. The Angels signed a 35-year lease to occupy the facility on August 8. The contractor was Del Webb, part owner of the Yankees and head of a construction company bearing his name. The stadium was planned to accommodate 45,000 fans with parking for 12,000 cars. The 157-acre site was on State College Boulevard between Katella Avenue and Orangewood Avenue previously used as citrus groves. Katella also passed by the Disneyland amusement park, a mile and a half to the west. The proposed ballpark was easily accessible from the Santa Ana (I-5), Riverside (SR 91), Orange (SR 57), Costa Mesa (SR 55) and Garden Grove (SR 22) freeways. In 1964, Anaheim was identified by most Americans as the home of Disneyland, which opened in 1955. Prior to the 1950s, Anaheim was a largely rural community. At that point, it was best known for a running joke on Jack Benny's radio program involving a train station track announcement voiced by Mel Blanc in which he said: "Train leaving on Track Five for Anaheim, Azusa and Cucamonga." Blanc would repeat the phrase with increasing desperation, then ask, "Doesn't anyone want to go to Anaheim, Azusa or Cucamonga?" In 1953, the population of Anaheim was 20,000, many of whom were transplants from the Midwest and Southwest.

The population exploded due to Disneyland and the suburban sprawl that advanced in a southerly direction from Los Angeles, about 30 miles to the north. Fruit and vegetable fields were giving way to housing tracts and industrial development at a dizzying pace. The new residents were attracted by the cleaner air and open spaces. In 1964, Orange County was the fastest growing area of the country. The city of Anaheim had about 155,000 residents amid an expanse of housing tracts, shopping centers, fast food stands, freeways, factories and motels. Per capita income was among the nation's highest. Surrounding Orange County boomed from a population of 216,734 in 1950 to 1,420,386 in 1970 and passed the three million mark in 2005. The Angels made the move because of these population trends, an unsatisfactory lease arrangement with the Dodgers at Chavez Ravine, and difficulties in attracting fans in the Los Angeles market. From 1961 through 1963, the Dodgers drew 7,098,036 fans compared to 2,568,588 for the Angels. In 1964, the Angels won more games (82) than the Dodgers (80), but were outdrawn 2,228,751 to 760,439. The nine home games against the Yankees comprised 33 percent of the Angels attendance. Even though the Angels drew about a fourth of the fans who paid their way into Dodger Stadium/Chavez Ravine, they had to pay for 50 percent of the maintenance and received none of the parking revenue. The Angels also had to pay half of the cost of washing windows at the stadium even though the team offices were located in a windowless basement. Team owner Gene Autry hoped his club could carve out its own niche and fan base in fast-growing Orange County.

Long Beach was among the localities under consideration for a new stadium for the Angels, but negotiations broke down in part because the city inside the city insisted the club be called the Long Beach Angels. Club ownership wanted a more regional designation, and just prior to the move to Anaheim, the Los Angeles Angels became the California Angels (see September 3, 1965).

APRIL 13   After President Lyndon Johnson throws out the ceremonial first pitch, the Angels defeat the Senators 4–0 on Opening Day in Washington. Ken McBride (6⅓ innings) and Julio Navarro (2⅔ innings) combined on a brilliant one-hitter. The only Washington hit was a double by opposing pitcher Claude Osteen in the third inning. McBride was relieved after walking three straight batters. In his debut with the Angels, Joe Adcock collected three hits, including a double, in four at-bats.

APRIL 21   The Angels lose the home opener 6–4 to the Tigers before 13,640 at Chavez Ravine.

APRIL 22   The Angels score two runs in the ninth inning to defeat the Tigers 3–2 at Chavez Ravine. Jim Fregosi drove in the tying run with a double and scored on a single by Lee Thomas.

APRIL 28   The Angels trade Julio Navarro to the Tigers for Willie Smith.

Playing for Syracuse in the International League in 1963, Smith batted .380 and had a 14–2 record with a 2.11 ERA as a pitcher. The Angels traded for him with the idea of using him as a pitcher and pinch hitter, but became intrigued by his hitting abilities. By June, Smith was a starting outfielder and batted .301 with 11 homers in 359 at-bats. He hit .261 in 136 games in 1965 but tailed off considerably afterward. From 1966 through the end of his career in 1971, Smith had a .219 average in 828 at-bats with four clubs.

May 13	The Angels score seven runs in the second inning and shut out the Athletics 9–0 at Chavez Ravine. Barry Latman pitched the shutout.
May 15	The Angels release Art Fowler and Paul Foytack.
May 23	With the Angels trailing 5–4, Bobby Knoop hits a grand slam in the sixth inning off Bill Stafford to spark a 9–5 win over the Yankees in New York.
May 24	In the first inning against the Yankees in New York, Billy Moran doubles in two runs and scores on a Tom Satriano double to account for all three runs of a 3–0 victory. Dean Chance pitched the shutout.

Dean "The Dream" Chance produced one of the great pitching seasons in American League history in 1964.

Chance came into the 1964 season as a 22-year-old with a lifetime record of 27–30. He spent much of the early part of the season pitching out of the bullpen and didn't earn a spot in the starting rotation until mid-May. Chance was 5–5 at the All-Star break. From July 11 through September 25, a span of 72 Angels games, he had a record of 15–3 with eight shutouts and a 1.18 ERA in 160 innings. He finished the season 20–9 along with a 1.65 earned run average and 11 shutouts. The only other major league pitchers with 11 or more shutouts since 1916 are Sandy Koufax, who had 11 in 1963, and Bob Gibson with 13 in 1968. Chance's earned run average was the lowest in the majors since 1943. The terrific season earned him the Cy Young Award at a time when it was granted to only one pitcher in the majors.

June 2	Dean Chance strikes out 15 batters, pitches a two-hitter, and defeats the Red Sox 1–0 at Chavez Ravine. The only Boston hits were singles by Dick Stuart in the sixth inning and Felix Mantilla in the ninth. The lone run scored on a double by Lee Thomas in the fourth.

Chance was the winning pitcher in five complete-game 1–0 decisions in 1964, which tied a major league record.

June 4	The Angels trade Lee Thomas to the Red Sox for Lu Clinton.

JUNE 5	In his first game with the Angels, Lu Clinton collects three hits, including a homer, in four at-bats during a 3–2 win over the Yankees at Chavez Ravine.
	The Angels outfield was in a state of flux all season. Clinton led the club in outfield starts with 83.
JUNE 6	Dean Chance pitches 14 shutout innings, allows only three hits, and strikes out 12, but the Angels lose 2–0 to the Yankees in 15 innings at Chavez Ravine. Chance had a no-hitter in progress until Roger Maris singled in the seventh. The other New York hits off Chance were singles by Tony Kubek in the 12th and Johnny Blanchard in the 13th. The Yanks scored twice in the 15th off Willie Smith and Dan Osinski. Elston Howard drove in both runs with a double. Jim Bouton (13 innings) and Bill Stafford (two innings) pitched for the Yankees. The Angels left 14 runners on base.
	In back-to-back starts on three days' rest, Chance pitched 23 shutout innings while allowing five hits and fanning 27 batters. Against the pennant-winning Yankees in 1964, he made five starts and pitched 50 innings while surrendering just one run and 14 hits.
JUNE 8	Willie Smith pinch-hits in the seventh inning, plays right field in the seventh and eighth, and pitches in the eighth, during a 6–3 loss to the Indians in Cleveland.
JUNE 10	Jim Fregosi drives in six runs on a home run, two doubles and a single in leading the Angels to an 11-inning, 7–4 win over the Indians in the first game of a double-header in Cleveland. The Angels completed a sweep with a 5–3 triumph in the second tilt.
	Fregosi was batting .362 on June 14 and earned a spot as the starting shortstop on the AL All-Star team. He finished the season with a .277 average and 18 home runs.
JUNE 11	As part of a three-team deal, the Angels trade Billy Moran and Frank Kostro to the Indians and receive Vic Power and Lenny Green from the Twins.
	Power was a stylish, exuberant and showboating first baseman who caught the ball with a wide-sweeping motion. He won seven consecutive Gold Gloves from 1958 through 1964 and was named to four AL All-Star teams between 1955 and 1960 while playing for the Athletics and Indians. His career was winding down by the time in played with the Angels, however, and he retired at the end of the 1965 campaign.
JUNE 14	Vic Power homers in his debut with the Angels, a 6–4 loss to the Tigers in the second game of a double-header in Detroit. The Tigers also won the opener 6–5.
JUNE 16	Ed Kirkpatrick hits a two-run homer in the tenth inning to defeat the Senators 7–5 in Washington.
	The Angels came into the game with a 24–37 record. The victory started an 11-game winning streak.
JUNE 23	A two-run homer by Willie Smith in the eighth inning accounts for both runs of a 2–0 win over the Senators at Chavez Ravine. Dean Chance pitched the shutout.

JUNE 24 The Angels sign outfielder Rick Reichardt from the University of Wisconsin for a then-record bonus of over $200,000. An outstanding athlete, Reichardt also played as a halfback and wide receiver on the football team and led the Big Ten in receptions as a junior in 1963. Many NFL scouts were projecting him as a first round draft choice.

At the time, high school and college baseball players were available to every major league team and could sign with the highest bidder. The bonus granted to Reichardt, and other amateur players, led the owners to institute a draft. The first draft took place on June 8, 1965. Reichardt looked as though he might live up to expectations when he hit .288 with 16 homers in only 89 games in 1966 before illness forced the removal of a kidney in August. He played for the Angels until 1970 and in the majors until 1974 and closed his career with a .261 average and 116 home runs in 997 games.

JUNE 26 The Angels sweep the Athletics 1–0 and 6–0 in a double-header at Chavez Ravine. The pair of shutout victories extended the Angels winning streak to 11 games. Bo Belinsky (eight innings) and Bob Duliba (one inning) combined on the first game shutout. Bobby Knoop drove in the lone run with a sacrifice fly in the sixth inning. Bob Meyer (six innings) and Bob Lee (three innings) hurled the game-two shutout.

As a 26-year-old in his first season in the majors, Lee was brilliant out of the bullpen in 1964 with a 6–5 record, 19 saves and a 1.51 ERA in 64 games and 137 innings. He continued to be effective in 1965 when he compiled a 9–7 mark with 23 saves and a 1.92 earned run average in 69 games and 131 1/3 innings. The stress of pitching that many relief innings over two seasons, however, likely led to the downturn in his career beginning in 1966. He was out of the majors by 1968.

JULY 2 On the day of the passage of the Civil Rights Act, prohibiting racial discrimination in employment and places of public accommodation, Willie Smith breaks a 6–6 tie with a grand slam off Stu Miller in the ninth inning, leading to a 10–6 win over the Orioles in Baltimore.

The Angels scored only 230 runs and allowed 226 in 81 home games in 1964. On the road, they scored 314 and gave up 325.

JULY 3 Lu Clinton and Joe Adcock hit back-to-back homers in the tenth inning to defeat the Red Sox 5–3 in Boston.

JULY 7 Jim Fregosi is the American League leadoff batter in the All-Star Game and starts things off with a single against Don Drysdale, but the AL loses 7–4 at Shea Stadium in New York.

JULY 9 Bo Belinsky pitches a two-hitter to defeat the White Sox 3–0 at Chavez Ravine. The only Chicago hits were singles by Ron Hansen in the fifth inning and Jerry McNertney in the sixth.

JULY 11 Joe Adcock's homer off Fred Talbot in the fourth inning accounts for the only run of a 1–0 victory over the White Sox at Chavez Ravine. Dean Chance pitched the shutout.

JULY 12 A pair of walk-off hits beats the Twins 2–1 and 3–2 in a double-header at Chavez Ravine. Jimmy Piersall's single in the ninth inning drove across the game-winner in the opener. A single by Buck Rodgers in the tenth won the second contest.

July 15	The Angels sweep the Tigers 5–4 and 1–0 in a double-header at Chavez Ravine. Bob Perry's homer off Phil Regan in the eighth inning accounted for the lone run in the second game. Dean Chance pitched the shutout and struck out 12.
July 17	The Angels win 1–0 with a home run for the second game in a row, downing the Twins in Minnesota. The homer was struck by Felix Torres off Dick Stigman in the second inning. Fred Newman (seven innings) and Bob Lee (two innings) combined on the shutout.
July 18	Jim Fregosi homers in the 13th inning to beat the Twins 3–2 in Minnesota.
July 19	Dean Chance pitches his third consecutive shutout, beating the Twins 4–0 in the second game of a double-header in Minnesota. The Angels also won the opener 8–6.
July 21	In the first game of a double-header in Chicago, Felix Torres drives in both runs of a 2–0 win over the White Sox with a single in the fourth inning and a homer in the sixth, both off John Buzhardt. Bo Belinsky (six innings) and Bob Lee (three innings) combined on the shutout. The Angels completed the sweep with a 3–2 triumph in game two.
July 25	After scoring just eight runs over their previous six games, the Angels wallop the Athletics 18–2 in Kansas City. Willie Smith collected five hits, including a homer and a triple, in five at-bats.
July 28	Jim Fregosi becomes the first Angel to hit for the cycle in leading the club to a 3–1 win over the Yankees at Chavez Ravine. Facing Stan Williams, Fregosi doubled in the first inning, homered in the third, and tripled in the sixth. Fregosi completed the cycle with a single against Hal Reniff in the eighth. Dean Chance pitched a two-hitter, allowing only a single to Clete Boyer in the third inning and a homer to Mickey Mantle in the seventh.

In home games in 1964, Chance was 11–3 with a 1.07 ERA.

August 4	In Baltimore, the Angels score all five runs of a 5–0 win over the Orioles in the fourth inning.
August 5	Dean Chance (six innings) and Bob Lee (three innings) combine to defeat the Orioles 1–0 in Baltimore. Jim Fregosi drove in the lone run with a single in the third inning.
August 9	The Senators score five runs in the ninth inning off Bob Lee and Bob Duliba to beat the Angels 6–5 at Chavez Ravine.
August 14	Dean Chance pitches a two-hitter to defeat the Senators 7–0 in the second game of a double-header in Washington. The only hits off Chance were singles by Don Zimmer in the fifth inning and Don Blasingame in the sixth. The Senators won the opener 7–3.

On the same day, the Angels suspended Bo Belinsky after he slugged a 64-year-old sportswriter. The incident occurred at a Washington hotel after the club had arrived for a four-game series. Braven Dyer, a writer for the Los Angeles Times, *had written a story that Belinsky planned to retire from baseball.*

Belinsky objected and called Dyer to threaten him with bodily harm. A former college football star, Dyer refused to back down from the challenge and went to Belinsky's room. Once there, the pitcher slugged the writer and knocked him unconscious. Dyer suffered from double vision, swelling under his left ear, where six stitches were taken, and a blackened right eye. After the suspension ended, Belinsky was sent to the Angels Hawaii farm club but refused to report. He was traded to the Phillies in December.

AUGUST 18 Dean Chance pitches a two-hitter to beat the Tigers 1–0 in the first game of a doubleheader in Detroit. It was Chance's second consecutive two-hit shutout. He allowed only singles to Gates Brown in the first inning and Al Kaline in the sixth. Vic Power accounted for the only run with a homer in the second inning off Fred Gladding. It was one of only three Los Angeles hits. The Tigers won the second game by the same 1–0 score.

On the same day, the Angels purchased George Brunet from the Athletics. From 1953 through 1964, Brunet played for 14 minor league and five major league clubs. He settled in with the Angels and played for the club until 1969, although usually in hard luck because of a lack of offense. Despite earned run averages around the league average, he was 54–69 as an Angel and twice led the AL in losses with an 11–19 record in 1967 and 13–17 in 1968. The 19 defeats is a club record he shares with Clyde Wright (11–19 in 1973), Frank Tanana (14–19 in 1974) and Kirk McCaskill (10–19 in 1991).

AUGUST 27 Joe Adcock hits his 300th career homer during a 7–1 win over the Athletics in Kansas City. The milestone was struck in the second inning off Diego Segui.

Athletics owner Charlie Finley signed the Beatles for a September 17 concert at Municipal Stadium, and to publicize the event, dressed himself and the grounds crew in Beatles wigs. Angels outfielder Jimmy Piersall went one better and wore one of the wigs to the plate.

AUGUST 31 Groundbreaking ceremonies take place at Anaheim Stadium. The first spades were turned over by Anaheim Mayor Chuck Chandler and Angels owner Gene Autry. Los Angeles Mayor Sam Yorty was also on hand, along with bands, balloons and all of the Disney characters, including Mickey Mouse.

SEPTEMBER 5 George Brunet (seven innings) and Bob Lee (two innings) combine forces to defeat the Orioles 1–0 in Baltimore.

On the same day, the Angels sold Lenny Green to the Orioles.

SEPTEMBER 7 Dean Chance strikes out 12 batters and beats the Red Sox 4–1 in the first game of a double-header at Chavez Ravine. The Angels won with only two hits, scoring twice in the third on four walks and a sacrifice fly. The two hits were collected in the eighth on a single by Joe Adcock and an inside-the-park homer from Buck Rodgers. The Angels also won the second game 4–3 in 11 innings. In his first major league plate appearance, Jack Hiatt drove in the winning run with a pinch-hit, walk-off single.

SEPTEMBER 9 The Angels send Vic Power and cash to the Phillies for Marcelino Lopez.

Lopez looked like a gem after posting a 14–13 record and a 2.92 ERA as a 21-year-old in 1965, but never came close to posting those numbers again. The Angels bought Power back from the Phillies in another transaction on November 30.

SEPTEMBER 11 Bob Lee's season comes to an end when he breaks his hand slugging a heckling sailor during a 3–0 loss to the Red Sox in Boston.

A group of sailors sat in the bleachers harassing the occupants of the Angels bullpen. One reached into the enclosure and took a swing. Lee squared off and threw at least two punches, one of which broke two bones in his hand.

SEPTEMBER 15 Dean Chance pitches a two-hitter to defeat the Yankees 7–0 at Yankee Stadium. The only New York hits were singles by Bobby Richardson in the fourth inning and by opposing pitcher Al Downing in the sixth.

SEPTEMBER 22 Fred Newman shuts down the White Sox to win 1–0 at Chavez Ravine. The lone run scored on a Willie Smith single in the third inning.

SEPTEMBER 25 Dean Chance records his 20th win of the season with a 1–0 decision over the Twins at Chavez Ravine. The lone run scored in the eighth when Bob Perry tripled and scored on a wild pitch.

SEPTEMBER 26 In his first major league start, Bill Kelso throws a shutout to defeat the Twins 2–0 at Chavez Ravine. Kelso made eight prior relief appearances and allowed five runs in $10^{2/3}$ innings.

Kelso pitched in 119 big league games, and made only two starts. The other one was nearly three years later on July 16, 1967, and he allowed four runs in $6^{1/3}$ innings during a 5–1 loss to the Twins in Minnesota.

OCTOBER 4 Seven days after the release of the Warren Commission, which declared that Lee Harvey Oswald acted alone in the assassination of John Kennedy, the Angels win 3–0 in a game against the Twins in Minnesota, which was called after six innings by rain on the final day of the season. The victory gave the Angels a winning record for the 1964 campaign.

NOVEMBER 21 Two weeks after Lyndon Johnson defeats Barry Goldwater in the presidential election, the Angels trade Jack Hiatt to the Giants for Jose Cardenal.

Cardenal was only 21 as the Angels starting center fielder in 1965 and was the club's first legitimate base-stealing threat. He was a three-year regular with the Angels before being traded to the Indians.

DECEMBER 3 The Angels trade Bo Belinsky to the Phillies for Rudy May and Costen Shockley.

The Angels were happy to find a club that would take Belinsky off their hands. After leaving the Angels, he had a record of 7–23 over five seasons with four different clubs. May played for the Angels in 1965 and again from 1969 through 1974. He showed flashes of brilliance but never developed consistency. He was traded to the Yankees in 1974 with a lifetime record of 51–76.

1965

Season in a Sentence
During their last year at Chavez Ravine, the Los Angeles Angels become the California Angels and continue to alternate losing and winning seasons.

Finish • Won • Lost • Pct • GB
Seventh   75   87   .463   27.0

Manager
Bill Rigney

Stats   Angels • AL • Rank
Stats	Angels	AL	Rank
Batting Avg:	.239	.242	7
On-Base Pct:	.297	.311	10
Slugging Pct:	.341	.369	10
Home Runs:	92		10
Stolen Bases:	107		3
ERA:	3.17	3.46	4
Errors:	123		3
Runs Scored:	527		10
Runs Allowed:	569		2

Starting Lineup
Buck Rodgers, c
Joe Adcock, 1b
Bobby Knoop, 2b
Paul Schaal, 3b
Jim Fregosi, ss
Willie Smith, lf
Jose Cardenal, cf
Albie Pearson, rf
Lu Clinton, rf
Vic Power, 1b

Pitchers
Fred Newman, sp
Dean Chance, sp
Marcelino Lopez, sp
George Brunet, sp-rp
Rudy May, sp-rp
Bob Lee, rp
Aubrey Gatewood, rp

Attendance
566,727 (ninth in AL)

Club Leaders
Batting Avg:	Jim Fregosi	.277
On-Base Pct:	Jim Fregosi	.337
Slugging Pct:	Willie Smith	.423
Home Runs:	Jim Fregosi	15
RBI:	Jim Fregosi	64
Runs:	Jim Fregosi	66
Stolen Bases:	Jose Cardenal	37
Wins:	Dean Chance	15
Strikeouts:	Dean Chance	164
ERA:	Fred Newman	2.93
	Marcelino Lopez	2.93
Saves:	Bob Lee	23

APRIL 12   The scheduled season opener against the Indians at Chavez Ravine is rained out.

APRIL 13   On Opening Day, the Angels lose 7–1 to the Indians before 11,278 at Chavez Ravine.

In their last season in Los Angeles, the Angels drew only 566,727 fans, nearly two million fewer than the 2,553,577 the Dodgers attracted to the same ballpark.

APRIL 14   In only his second game with the Angels, Jose Cardenal collects four hits, including a home run and a double, during a 4–3 victory over the Yankees at Chavez Ravine. Cardenal led off the first inning with his first big league home run. It was struck off Whitey Ford.

Cardenal hit .250 with 11 home runs and 37 stolen bases for the Angels in 1965. Jim Fregosi was the club's top player with a .277 average and 15 home runs.

APRIL 18   In his major league debut, Rudy May allows only one hit over nine innings of a 13-inning, 4–1 loss to the Tigers at Chavez Ravine. May held Detroit hitless until Jake Wood doubled with one out in the eighth inning. Wood scored on an error by second baseman Bobby Knoop. The Tigers scored three times in the 13th off Bob Lee and George Brunet.

MAY 3
Dean Chance pitches the Angels to a 1–0 victory over the Red Sox at Chavez Ravine.

After a 20–9 record and a 1.65 ERA in 1964, Chance was 15–10 accompanied by a 3.15 earned run average in 1965.

MAY 4
Costen Shockley hits a grand slam off Dave Morehead in the fifth inning of a 7–1 win over the Red Sox at Chavez Ravine.

The homer was Shockley's first as an Angel. A first baseman, he struck only three career homers and had a .197 batting average in 142 at-bats.

MAY 13
Angels pitcher Dick Wantz dies at the age of 25 from a brain tumor.

Wantz made his major league debut on Opening Day and allowed two runs in an inning of work. Subsequently, he was stricken by severe headaches and the tumor was discovered. He died in a hospital in Inglewood, California, the day after undergoing surgery.

MAY 21
The Angels edge the White Sox 1–0 at Chavez Ravine. Fred Newman (eight innings) and Bob Lee (one inning) combined on the shutout. Bobby Knoop drove in the lone run with a single in the eighth inning.

The Angels scored only 521 runs in 1965 to rank last in the AL for the second year in a row.

MAY 28
George Brunet pitches a two-hitter to defeat the Orioles 3–1 in the first game of a double-header at Memorial Stadium. The only Baltimore hits were a single by Jackie Brandt in the first inning and a double from Bob Johnson in the eighth. The Orioles won game two 3–0.

JUNE 8
In the first amateur draft, the Angels select first baseman Jim Spencer from Andover High School in Glen Burnie, Maryland, in the first round.

Spencer spent 15 years in the majors, six of them with the Angels beginning in 1968, and won two Gold Gloves, but never developed into a star because of deficiencies at the plate. He had a .250 career batting average and .387 slugging percentage. Other future major leaguers drafted and signed by the Angels in 1965 were Joe Henderson (fifth round), Clyde Wright (sixth), Marty Pattin (seventh), Jarvis Tatum (16th) and Doug Griffin (21st).

JUNE 12
The Angels score six runs in the second inning and trounce the Yankees 13–3 at Chavez Ravine.

JUNE 30
Fred Newman pitches a two-hitter to defeat the Twins 5–0 at Chavez Ravine. The only Minnesota hits were singles by Jerry Kindall in the second inning and Don Mincher in the eighth.

JULY 6
The Angels trade Don Lee to the Astros for Al Spangler.

JULY 9	Marcelino Lopez pitches a two-hitter to defeat the Indians 2–0 in the second game of a double-header at Chavez Ravine. The only Cleveland hits were a double by Larry Brown and a single from Chuck Hinton. The Angels also won the opener 4–3.
JULY 10	Fred Newman (eight innings) and Bob Lee (one inning) combine to defeat the Indians 1–0 at Chavez Ravine. The lone run scored on a single by Vic Power in the first inning.

Power had an unusual season in 1965. He led the Angels in games played at first base with 107, but he started only 30 of them. Power was a late-inning defensive replacement 77 times, usually for Joe Adcock or Costen Shockley.

JULY 11	Dean Chance records the Angels third consecutive shutout, beating the Indians 2–0 at Chavez Ravine.

The Angels shut out the opposition for 34 straight innings over five games.

JULY 20	Paul Schaal delivers a two-out, two-run single in the tenth inning that beats the Twins 2–0 in Minnesota. George Brunet pitched the complete-game shutout and allowed only four hits.
JULY 30	A free-for-all erupts over a beanball battle in the eighth inning of a 9–2 win over the Red Sox at Chavez Ravine. In the sixth, Boston hurler Dave Morehead hit Jose Cardenal, and in turn, Morehead was plunked by Dean Chance. In the eighth, Morehead hit Jim Fregosi with a pitch and was relieved by Arnold Earley, who struck Bob Rodgers with his first delivery to the plate. Rodgers rushed the mound and grabbed Earley around the neck and pummeled him. Both benches emptied, and fights broke out all over the field. Many players suffered painful bruises, scrapes and spike wounds.
AUGUST 9	Dean Chance pitches a two-hitter to defeat the Indians 9–0 at Municipal Stadium. The only Cleveland hits were singles by Billy Moran in the first inning and Chuck Hinton in the third.

Chance set an American League record by striking out in 11 consecutive plate appearances over five games from July 24 through August 13. He was one of the worst hitters in big league history. His career batting average of .066 in 662 at-bats is the lowest of any player with at least 500 at-bats. He had only two extra-base hits, both doubles, for a "slugging" percentage of .069. Chance also struck out 420 times.

AUGUST 11	Riots begin in the Watts section of Los Angeles. The civil unrest lasted six days and claimed 34 lives.
AUGUST 18	The Angels purchase Jack Sanford from the Giants.
AUGUST 31	Batting second in the lineup, Albie Pearson homers in the first inning off Bill Stafford to account for the only run of a 1–0 win over the Yankees at Chavez Ravine. Dean Chance pitched the shutout.

The home run proved to be the last of the 33 that Pearson struck during his major league career.

1960s

SEPTEMBER 3   In anticipation of the move to Anaheim, the franchise changes its name from the Los Angeles Angels to the California Angels. "In the last five years we have been the only American League club in the state of California," said club president Bob Reynolds. "We have had people from all over the state become Angels fans."

The Angels caps were changed from a monogram with an interlocking "L" and "A" to one with an interlocking "C" and "A." At the same time, the socks were changed from navy blue to red.

SEPTEMBER 4   Dean Chance strikes out 14 batters during a 4–1 win over the Athletics at Chavez Ravine.

Dean is Chance's middle name. His first name is Wilmer.

SEPTEMBER 8   Bert Campaneris plays all nine defensive positions for the Athletics during a 13-inning, 5–3 Angels victory in Kansas City. He had to leave the game in the ninth inning while playing as a catcher following a collision at home plate with Ed Kirkpatrick.

SEPTEMBER 9   The Angels sell Lu Clinton to the Indians.

SEPTEMBER 15   A walk-off single by Buck Rodgers in the 14th inning beats the White Sox 2–1 in the second game of a double-header at Chavez Ravine. Chicago won the opener 8–1.

The Dodgers and Angels shared Dodger Stadium/Chavez Ravine from 1962 through 1965. Other teams to play at the same ballpark for at least one full season were the New York Giants and Yankees at the Polo Grounds (1913–22), the St. Louis Browns and Cardinals at Sportsman's Park (1920–53), the Philadelphia Athletics and Phillies at Shibe Park (1938–54), and the New York Mets and Yankees at Shea Stadium (1974–75).

SEPTEMBER 20   The Angels draw only 945 fans for a 4–2 loss to the Orioles at Chavez Ravine. The game was played on a Monday afternoon on what was originally an open date in the schedule because of rainouts on September 18 and 19.

The Angels had the youngest team in the American League in 1965. The youngsters included Rudy May (20), Ed Kirkpatrick (20), Jose Cardenal (21), Marcelino Lopez (21), Paul Schaal (22), Rick Reichardt (22), Jim Fregosi (23), Fred Newman (23), Dean Chance (24), Aubrey Gatewood (26), Bobby Knoop (26), Willie Smith (26) and Buck Rodgers (26).

SEPTEMBER 22   The Angels play at home at Chavez Ravine for the last time and sweep the Red Sox 10–1 and 2–0 before 3,353. George Brunet pitched a two-hitter in the second tilt. The only Boston hits were singles by Tony Horton in the third inning and Mike Ryan in the fifth.

The Angels were 46–34 at home and 29–53 on the road in 1965. Marcelino Lopez was 10–3 in Los Angeles and 4–10 on the road. Dean Chance had an 11–1 record at home and 4–9 in away games. In 1964 and 1965, Chance was 22–4 at Chavez Ravine.

SEPTEMBER 29   A crowd of only 409 watches a 2–1 loss to the Red Sox in Boston. It is the smallest attendance figure ever for an Angels regular season game.

NOVEMBER 29   The Angels sign Lew Burdette as a free agent and draft Willie Montanez from the Cardinals organization.

> *Montanez was 18 years old when he made his major league debut with the Angels on Opening Day in 1966. He was returned to the Cardinals in May 1966. Montanez didn't play in the big league again until 1970 but had a 14-year career as a first baseman.*

NOVEMBER 30   The Angels sign Frank Malzone as a free agent.

DECEMBER 2   The Angels trade Dick Simpson to the Orioles for Norm Siebern.

1966

Season in a Sentence

In their first season in Anaheim, the Angels lead the American league in attendance but finish in sixth place with a losing record.

Finish • Won • Lost • Pct • GB

Sixth   80   82   .494   18.0

Manager

Bill Rigney

Stats   Angels • AL • Rank

Batting Avg:	.232	.240	9
On-Base Pct:	.301	.306	5
Slugging Pct:	.354	.369	8
Home Runs:	122		8
Stolen Bases:	80		3
ERA:	3.56	3.44	7
Errors:	136		4
Runs Scored:	604		6
Runs Allowed:	643		6

Starting Lineup

Buck Rodgers, c
Norm Siebern, 1b
Bobby Knoop, 2b
Paul Schaal, 3b
Jim Fregosi, ss
Rick Reichardt, lf
Jose Cardenal, cf
Ed Kirkpatrick, rf
Jay Johnstone, lf
Joe Adcock, 1b
Tom Satriano, c-3b

Pitchers

Dean Chance, sp
George Brunet, sp
Marcelino Lopez, sp
Fred Newman, sp
Clyde Wright, sp-rp
Bob Lee, rp
Lew Burdette, rp
Minnie Rojas, rp
Jack Sanford, rp

Attendance

1,400,321 (first in AL)

Club Leaders

Batting Avg:	Jose Cardenal	.276
On-Base Pct:	Jim Fregosi	.325
Slugging Pct:	Jose Cardenal	.399
Home Runs:	Bobby Knoop	17
RBI:	Bobby Knoop	72
Runs:	Jim Fregosi	78
Stolen Bases:	Jose Cardenal	24
Wins:	George Brunet	13
Strikeouts:	Dean Chance	180
ERA:	Dean Chance	3.08
Saves:	Bob Lee	16

JANUARY 15   The Angels purchase Ed Bailey from the Cubs.

MARCH 5   The Major League Players Association hires Marvin Miller to be the new executive director of the organization. Miller formally took office on July 1, 1966. Under Miller's leadership, the association would take action that led to a revolution in player-owner relations, including free agency by 1976.

APRIL 9   The Angels open Anaheim Stadium with a 9–3 exhibition loss to the Giants before a crowd of 40,735.

A month-long strike delayed construction. Later, picketing by nonunion construction caused a four-day stoppage. A crew of 250 worked until 2:30 a.m. every day during the final week to get the ballpark ready. On April 10, which was Easter Sunday, the Angels defeated the Giants 6–5 in another exhibition game, with Jim Fregosi hitting a walk-off homer in the tenth inning. Attendance was 23,061.

APRIL 12   On Opening Day, the Angels lose 3–2 to the White Sox in 14 innings in Chicago. Tom McCraw drove in the winning run with a single off George Brunet. Joe Adcock homered in the losing cause.

APRIL 14   Solo homers by Bobby Knoop in the third inning and Jackie Warner in the ninth beats the White Sox 2–1 in Chicago.

Warner's homer was the first of his career, and it came in his second big league game. He started fast as a rookie in 1966 with 19 hits in his first 55 at-bats (.345) but was only 7-for-68 afterward (.103) and was back in the minors in July.

APRIL 19   The Angels play their first regular season game at Anaheim Stadium and lose 3–1 to the White Sox before 31,660. The start of the game was delayed for 20 minutes by a broken water main that flooded one of the city's main thoroughfares and created a massive traffic jam. The first pitch: Marcelino Lopez to Tommie Agee, who grounded out to shortstop Jim Fregosi, with first baseman Joe Adcock making the put out. Fregosi collected the first hit with a double in the first off Tommy John. Rick Reichardt provided the first home run, run scored and RBI with a blast off John in the second. Agee homered in the sixth to tie the score 1–1. Chicago scored twice in the eighth for the victory.

Anaheim Stadium was roughly modeled after Dodger Stadium. In 1966, the three-tiered stadium, built at a cost of $24 million, held 43,250 and was completely open beyond the outfield fences except in the right and left-field corners. Playing field dimensions were 333 feet down each foul line, 370 feet to the power alleys, and 404 feet to center field. Anaheim Stadium was a pitcher's park throughout the 1960s and 1970s. It was known as the "Big A" because of the A-frame scoreboard beyond the left-field fence that rose 230 feet and was visible from the five freeways that served the stadium. A giant gold-colored halo topped the scoreboard that was erected by Standard Oil of California in exchange for advertising considerations. In 2009, Anaheim Stadium was the fourth oldest in baseball, after Fenway Park (1912), Wrigley Field (1914) and Dodger Stadium (1962).

APRIL 20   The Angels win their first game at Anaheim Stadium with a 12-inning, 4–3 decision over the White Sox. Joe Adcock drove in the winning run with a walk-off single. Ed Sukla was the winning pitcher. It was the last of his three major league victories.

After drawing just 566,727 in Los Angeles in 1965, the Angels led the AL in attendance in 1966 with a figure of 1,400,321. The Angels drew fewer fans than six of the ten National League clubs, however, including the Dodgers, who attracted 2,617,029.

April 30 — Trailing 9–3, the Angels explode for 12 runs in the eighth inning and defeat the Red Sox 16–9 in Boston. There were 11 California hits in the big inning, including three homers, a triple and two doubles. Eight runs scored after two were out. Joe Adcock drove in the first run with a single. Rick Reichardt hit two home runs, both with a man on base. Bobby Knoop contributed a double and a two-run homer. Jim Fregosi brought three home with a bases-loaded double. Jackie Warner drove in two on a sacrifice fly and a single.

Fregosi played in every game in 1966 and batted .252 with 32 doubles and 13 homers. Double-play partner Knoop missed just one contest and led the AL in triples with 11. Jose Cardenal stole 24 bases.

May 1 — The Angels and Red Sox combine for nine double plays during a 6–1 California win in the first game of a double-header in Boston. Bobby Knoop set a major league record (since tied) by participating in all six Angels' twin killings. Jim Fregosi tied a record for shortstops by starting five double plays. The Angels turned two more double plays in the second contest but lost 9–1.

May 4 — The Angels wallop the Athletics 13–2 at Anaheim Stadium. Buck Rodgers contributed four hits, including a triple and a double, and drove in five runs.

May 5 — Fred Newman (six innings) and Bob Lee (three innings) combine to defeat the Athletics 1–0 at Anaheim Stadium. Norm Siebern drove in the only run with a single in the first inning.

May 7 — The Angels draw their largest crowd in their first season at Anaheim Stadium, and lose 3–1 to the Yankees before 42,851.

Injuries marred the career of "Bonus Baby" outfielder Rick Reichardt, who did give Angels' fans many thrills during his years with the team.

May 11	After the Senators score in the top of the tenth, the Angels respond with two in their half to win 7–6 at Anaheim Stadium. The rally consisted of a triple by Bobby Knoop, a single and stolen base from Rick Reichardt and a single by Paul Schaal.
May 31	Jose Cardenal collects five hits, including a home run, in eight at-bats, but the Angels lose 7–5 to the Indians in 17 innings at Anaheim Stadium. Rick Reichardt contributed to the defeat by striking out six times, to tie a major league record, in eight plate appearances.
June 7	In the first round of the amateur draft, the Angels select shortstop Jim DeNeff from Indiana University.

> *DeNeff never reached the majors. Among those drafted and signed in the regular phase of the 1966 draft, only Bruce Christensen (17th round), Randy Brown (18th round) and Steve Hovley (35th round) played in the big leagues. The Angels did better in the secondary draft of previously drafted players who did not sign with their original club. The secondary draft was held each year in both January and June from 1966 through 1985. In the secondary draft in 1966, the Angels drafted and signed Vern Geishert in the second round in January and Andy Messersmith in the first round and Ken Tatum in the second in June.*

June 8	George Brunet pitches a two-hitter to defeat the White Sox 1–0 at Anaheim Stadium. The only Chicago hits were a single by J. C. Martin in the second inning and a double from Ken Berry in the third.
June 11	The Angels score a run in the ninth inning and another in the 14th to defeat the Athletics 4–3 at Anaheim Stadium. Jimmy Piersall drove in the winning run with a single.
June 24	The Angels edge the Orioles 5–4 in 14 innings at Anaheim Stadium. Tom Satriano drove in the winning run with a single.
July 3	The Angels score seven runs in the second inning, the last three on a homer by Jim Fregosi, and defeat the Indians 10–2 in the first game of a double-header in Cleveland. The Angels completed the sweep with a 4–3 victory in the second contest.
July 6	George Brunet walks ten batters, but allows only three hits in $9^{1}/_{3}$ innings and is the winning pitcher in a ten-inning, 1–0 decision over the Tigers in Detroit. Jack Sanford nailed down the save by retiring the only two batters to face him. Buck Rodgers drove in the winning run with a single.
July 20	Three pitchers combine on a two-hitter to beat the Red Sox 1–0 in ten innings in the second game of a double-header at Fenway Park. Dean Chance walked eight in eight innings, but held Boston hitless after a single by Tony Conigliaro in the second inning. After Chance walked the first two batters to face him in the ninth, Minnie Rojas retired three batters in a row. Buck Rodgers gave California a 1–0 lead with a single in the top of the tenth. Jack Sanford gave up a double to Mike Ryan in the bottom half, but nailed down the save. The Red Sox won the opener 6–1 behind a two-hitter by Jose Santiago.

JULY 22	Lew Burdette records the 200th win of his career with a two-inning relief stint during a 6–4 decision over the Yankees at Anaheim Stadium.
JULY 28	Troubled by intense headaches and dizzy spells, Rick Reichardt is sidelined by what turns out to be a congenital kidney ailment. After seeking treatment at the Mayo Clinic in Rochester, Minnesota, he underwent an operation to remove his right kidney two weeks later. With the exception of one plate appearance on October 2, Reichardt didn't play again in 1966.
AUGUST 2	Trailing 5–1, the Angels score two runs in the eighth inning, two in the ninth, and one in the 11th to defeat the Yankees 6–5 at Anaheim Stadium. Joe Adcock hit a two-run homer in the eighth. Jay Johnstone and Jim Fregosi each contributed run-scoring singles in the ninth. Paul Schaal won the contest with an inside-the-park homer in the 11th. Schaal broke his finger on the play sliding into catcher Jake Gibbs.

> *Johnstone was a 20-year-old rookie in 1966. He played five seasons with the Angels at the start of a 20-year career in which he played primarily as a spare outfielder and pinch hitter. He accumulated enough plate appearances to qualify for the batting title in only season—1969. He also earned a reputation as a flake who kept his teammates entertained with his clubhouse pranks.*

AUGUST 23	Dean Chance pitches a three-hitter to defeat the Yankees 1–0 in New York. The lone run scored in the fourth inning on Paul Schaal's single.
AUGUST 26	Jay Johnstone belts a walk-off homer in the ninth inning to down the Athletics 5–4 at Anaheim Stadium.
AUGUST 27	The Angels score two runs in the ninth inning and one in the 11th to defeat the Athletics 6–5 at Anaheim Stadium. The Angels were down 5–3 and had two out and no one on base in the ninth when Jim Fregosi, Norm Siebern, Buck Rodgers and Bobby Knoop connected for four consecutive singles. Paul Schaal brought across the winning run in the 11th by drawing a bases-loaded walk.
AUGUST 30	Bobby Knoop sets a major league record for putouts by a second baseman in a nine-inning game with 12 during a 7–6 loss to the Red Sox at Anaheim Stadium.
SEPTEMBER 3	Jim Fregosi and Paul Schaal both steal home in a six-run seventh inning to help defeat the Senators 7–6 at Anaheim Stadium. With two out and the Angels leading 3–2, Fregosi swiped home and Joe Adcock took second base in a double steal with Schaal at bat. Schaal walked, moved to third on Tom Satriano's single, and then stole home in another double steal with Satriano taking second. Washington scored four runs in the ninth before the Angels pulled out the victory.
SEPTEMBER 10	The Angels score seven runs in the fifth inning and defeat the Indians 9–2 in Cleveland.
SEPTEMBER 12	Jim Fregosi hits a grand slam off Wally Bunker in the fifth inning of a 6–5 win over the Orioles in Baltimore. Fregosi also doubled in a run in the first.
SEPTEMBER 18	Jim Fregosi collects hits in his last four plate appearances with two doubles and two singles during a 5–3 win over the Red Sox in Boston.

September 19   Jim Fregosi extends his streak of consecutive hits to eight with singles in his first four plate appearances during an 11–9 loss to the Orioles in Baltimore.

September 23   Marcelino Lopez pitches a three-hit shutout and strikes out 12 batters to defeat the Orioles 2–0 at Anaheim Stadium. The Angels didn't collect a hit off Steve Barber, who pitched the first five innings, or against Frank Bertainia until Charlie Vinson doubled in two runs with two out in the seventh inning after Jose Cardenal and Bobby Knoop walked. The double was Vinson's first major league hit. He made his debut four days earlier.

A first baseman, Vinson finished his career with only four hits and a .182 batting average.

September 30   Dean Chance pitches a two-hitter to defeat the Indians 2–0 at Anaheim Stadium. The only Cleveland hits were singles by Rocky Colavito in the second inning and Joe Azcue in the fifth. Jose Cardenal drove in both runs with a single in the third.

October 2   In the last game of the season, 21-year-old Jorge Rubio strikes out 15 batters in only his fourth major league start and beats the Indians 2–0 at Anaheim Stadium. Bobby Knoop drove in both runs with a triple in the eighth inning.

The win was Rubio's second, and last, in the majors and his only complete game. He pitched only three more games, all in 1967, and was 0–2 with a 3.60 ERA. He was sent back to the minors and then was traded to the Reds after the 1967 season. Despite his great potential, he never made it back to the major leagues.

October 13   The Angels sell Willie Smith to the Indians.

November 28   The Angels draft Rickey Clark from the Tigers organization.

December 2   The Angels trade Dean Chance and Jackie Hernandez to the Twins for Jimmie Hall, Don Mincher and Pete Cimino.

Chance alienated most of his teammates by blaming them for his 12–17 record in 1966. He rebounded in 1967 in Minnesota by posting a 20–14 mark and league-leading totals in innings (283 2/3), starts (39) and complete games (18). The workload took a toll, however. He posted a 16–16 record in 1968 and was only 18–19 over the remainder of his career, which ended in 1970 when he was only 29 years old. Mincher gave the Angels an excellent season in 1967 with a .273 average and 25 homers but was beaned early in the 1968 season by Sam McDowell and suffered from dizzy spells all year. Mincher was selected by the Seattle Pilots in the expansion draft at the end of the season. Hall also gave the Angels one good year before declining.

December 14   The Angels trade Norm Siebern to the Giants for Len Gabrielson.

December 15   The Angels trade Bob Lee to the Dodgers for Nick Willhite.

1967

Season in a Sentence
After falling 12 games below .500, the Angels win 34 of 46 in June and July and help destroy the pennant hopes of the Twins and Tigers during the final week of the season.

Finish • Won • Lost • Pct • GB
Fifth   84   77   .522   7.5

Manager
Bill Rigney

Stats

Stats	Angels	AL	Rank
Batting Avg:	.238	.236	5
On-Base Pct:	.298	.303	5
Slugging Pct:	.349	.351	6
Home Runs:	114		7
Stolen Bases:	40		9
ERA:	3.19	3.23	3
Errors:	111		1
Runs Scored:	567		5
Runs Allowed:	587		2 (tie)

Starting Lineup
Buck Rodgers, c
Don Mincher, 1b
Bobby Knoop, 2b
Paul Schaal, 3b
Jim Fregosi, ss
Rick Reichardt, lf
Jose Cardenal, cf
Jimmie Hall, rf
Jay Johnstone, cf
Bubba Morton, rf
Tom Satriano, 3b

Pitchers
George Brunet, sp
Jim McGlothlin, sp
Rickey Clark, sp
Jack Hamilton, sp
Minnie Rojas, rp
Bill Kelso, rp
Pete Cimino, rp

Attendance
1,317,713 (4th in AL)

Club Leaders
Batting Avg:	Jim Fregosi	.290
On-Base Pct:	Don Mincher	.367
Slugging Pct:	Don Mincher	.487
Home Runs:	Don Mincher	25
RBI:	Don Mincher	76
Runs Scored:	Don Mincher	81
Stolen Bases:	Jose Cardenal	10
Wins:	Three tied with	12
Strikeouts:	George Brunet	165
ERA:	Rickey Clark	2.59
Saves:	Minnie Rojas	27

APRIL 11   Three months after the first Super Bowl, in which the Green Bay Packers defeated the Kansas City Chiefs 35–10 at Memorial Coliseum in Los Angeles, the Angels beat the Tigers 4–2 before 17,839 in the season opener at Anaheim Stadium. George Brunet allowed only three hits and lost a shutout when Gates Brown belted a two-run homer with two out in the ninth. In his Angels debut, Don Mincher hit a home run and two singles in four at-bats. Jim Fregosi was three-for-three with a stolen base. California governor Ronald Reagan, who was elected to the office in November 1966, threw out the ceremonial first pitch.

Mincher collected ten hits, including three home runs and three doubles, in his first 16 at-bats with the Angels.

APRIL 14   Minnie Rojas retires all nine batters he faces during the seventh, eighth and ninth innings of a 10–1 win over the Indians at Anaheim Stadium.

A native of Cuba, Rojas didn't make his major league debut until the age of 32 with the Angels in 1966. During the 1967 campaign, he was 12–9 with 27 saves and a 2.52 ERA in 71 games and 121 2/3 innings. He was shut down in July during the 1968 season because of a sore arm and spent the 1969 campaign in the minors.

His comeback was cut short in the spring of 1970 in a horrific auto accident in Florida. Rojas was paralyzed, and the crash killed his two daughters. His wife and son survived. Rojas died in Los Angeles in 2002 at the age of 68.

APRIL 16 Trailing 4–0, the Angels score two runs in the eighth inning, two in the ninth and one in the tenth to defeat the Orioles 5–4 in the first game of a double-header at Anaheim Stadium. Paul Schaal hit a two-run homer in the eighth to start the comeback. With two out in the ninth, Jose Cardenal and Don Mincher walloped back-to-back home runs. In the tenth, Buck Rodgers singled, went to second on a sacrifice, and scored on Jim Fregosi's walk-off single. In the second tilt, Steve Barber held the Angels hitless until Fregosi doubled with one out in the ninth. Barber retired the next two hitters to close out a one-hitter and a 3–0 Baltimore victory.

Fregosi hit .290 with 171 hits and nine home runs in 1967.

APRIL 20 The Angels close out a 4–3 loss to the Tigers in Detroit with some horrible execution in the ninth inning. Rick Reichardt was picked off second on a throw from catcher Bill Freehan for the first out. Tom Satriano, batting with Jimmie Hall on first base and Don Wallace on third, swung and missed with two strikes on a hit-and-run play. Freehan threw to second attempting to retire Hall running from first, but shortstop Roy Oyler cut off the throw and fired home and Wallace was tagged out coming in from third.

APRIL 21 Jim Fregosi hits a two-out, two-run homer in the ninth inning to defeat the Indians 6–5 in Cleveland.

APRIL 22 In his major league debut, Rickey Clark pitches four shutout innings of relief and is the winning pitcher in an 11–4 decision over the Indians in Cleveland.

Clark was 12–11 with a 2.59 ERA as a 21-year-old rookie in 1967. He fell sharply to 1–11 in 1968, however, and finished his career in 1972 with a record of 19–32.

MAY 2 Jim McGlothlin pitches a three-hitter and strikes out 11 to defeat the Red Sox 3–2 at Anaheim Stadium.

MAY 6 The Angels trade Cotton Nash to the White Sox for Bill Skowron.

Nash was signed by the Angels in 1964 after starring in both baseball and basketball at the University of Kentucky. He played in the NBA with the Lakers and Warriors during the 1964–65 season and averaged 3.0 points per game. Nash also played for the Kentucky Colonels of the ABA in 1967–68. He never played for the Angels, and after being dealt by the club, appeared in 13 games with the White Sox and Twins over three seasons.

MAY 7 Jim McGlothlin pitches a two-hitter to defeat the Senators 5–0 at Anaheim Stadium. The only Washington hits were doubles by Fred Valentine in the fourth inning and Eddie Brinkman in the fifth.

MAY 10 The Angels receive five intentional walks from the Yankees during a 3–2 win at Anaheim Stadium. The five walks were issued to Jim Fregosi, Jimmie Hall,

Rick Reichardt, Bobby Knoop and Paul Schaal. In the ninth, Jose Cardenal tripled, Fregosi and Hall were walked intentionally, and Rick Reichardt drove in the winning run with a single.

May 14   A home run by Bill Skowron off Gary Peters in the second inning is the only Angels hit during a 3–1 loss to the White Sox in the second game of a double-header at Comiskey Park. It came only eight days after the White Sox traded Skowron. Chicago also won the opener 4–2.

> *The Angels scored only nine runs in eight games between May 8 and May 16.*

May 27   Prior to a 3–1 loss to the White Sox at Anaheim Stadium, the Angels honor Jimmy Piersall with a special night. Piersall and his family were showered with gifts, including a $1,000 bond for each of his nine children.

May 28   Jim McGlothlin shuts out the White Sox 5–0 at Anaheim Stadium.

June 2   A two-run double by Paul Schaal in the fifth inning accounts for the only two runs of a 2–0 victory over the Senators in Washington. Jim McGlothlin pitched his second consecutive shutout.

> *McGlothlin tied for the AL lead in shutouts in 1967 with six while going 12–8 with a 2.96 ERA. He pitched five of the shutouts in a span of nine starts from May 7 through June 22. During that stretch, he had an ERA of 0.79 in $79^1/_3$ innings, and pitched 36 consecutive scoreless innings. McGlothlin also pitched in the 1967 All-Star Game. He was traded to the Reds in November 1969 and died of leukemia at the age of 32 in 1975.*

June 6   The Angels lose 16–4 and 11–1 to the Orioles in a double-header at Anaheim Stadium. Curt Blefary hit three homers in the first game. The pair of defeats sent to Angels reeling to a 20–32 record. The club rebounded and won 34 of the next 46 to vault into the pennant race. On July 25, the Angels were 54–44, in third place, and 2½ games out of first.

> *On the same day, the Angels selected catcher Mike Nunn from Smith High School in Greensboro, North Carolina, in the first round of the amateur draft. Nunn never reached the majors. Those drafted and signed by the Angels who reached the big leagues were Tom Murphy (first round of the January secondary draft), Dave LaRoche (fifth round of the January draft) and Greg Washburn (first round of the June secondary draft). The Angels also picked Dave Kingman out of high school in the second round of the regular phase, but he opted not to sign and attended the University of Southern California instead. He signed with the Giants in 1970.*

June 7   Jim McGlothlin pitches his third shutout in a row, beating the Orioles 2–0 at Anaheim Stadium.

June 10   Jose Cardenal drives in both Angels runs of a 2–0 win over the Tigers at Anaheim Stadium with a home run in the sixth inning and a single in the seventh. Clyde Wright (seven innings) and Minnie Rojas (two innings) combined on the shutout.

June 11	Jim Fregosi hits a three-run, walk-off homer in the ninth inning to defeat the Tigers 6–4 at Anaheim Stadium.
June 14	Buck Rodgers hits a two-run, walk-off single in the ninth inning to defeat the Indians 3–2 at Anaheim Stadium.
June 15	The Angels trade Marcelino Lopez and Tom Arruda to the Orioles for Woodie Held, and then swap Jack Sanford and Jackie Warner to the Athletics for Roger Repoz.
June 16	In his first game with the Angels, Woodie Held hits a home run in the ninth inning to break a 1–1 tie against his former Orioles teammates to lift his new club to a 2–1 victory in the first game of a double-header in Baltimore. Held also hit a two-run homer in the second game, a 5–3 California win. He had been hitless in his last 22 at-bats entering the twin bill.
June 19	Rick Reichardt smacks a two-run homer off Mickey Lolich in the eighth inning to drive in the only runs of a 2–0 triumph over the Tigers in Detroit. Clyde Wright ($7^2/_3$ innings) and Minnie Rojas ($1^1/_3$ innings) combined on the shutout.
June 25	Rick Reichardt hits a two-out, inside-the-park grand slam off Blue Moon Odom in the first inning to account for all four Angels runs during a 4–3 win over the Athletics in Kansas City.
July 5	The Angels edge the Red Sox 4–3 in a thrilling contest at Anaheim Stadium. In the top of the ninth, ex-Angel George Thomas hit a two-out, two-run homer off George Brunet to give Boston a 3–2 advantage. In the bottom half, Jim Fregosi led off with a single and Don Mincher followed with a two-run, walk-off homer.
July 11	The All-Star Game is played before 46,039 at Anaheim Stadium, and the National League wins 2–1 in 15 innings in the longest Mid-Summer Classic in history. It was also the first primetime telecast in All-Star history, although the game began at 4:15 p.m. California time. All three runs scored on home runs. Richie Allen of the Phillies started the scoring with a homer in the second off Twins hurler, and ex-Angel, Dean Chance. Brooks Robinson of the Orioles homered in the fifth facing Cubs ace Ferguson Jenkins. Tony Perez of the Reds capped the evening with his 15th-inning blast off Catfish Hunter, who hurled five innings. All three who homered played third base. Jim McGlothlin pitched scoreless ball in the fourth and fifth. Don Mincher singled in his only at-bat, and Jim Fregosi was one-for-four. The 15-inning marathon stood alone as the longest in the history of the All-Star Game until it was matched in 2008 when the American League won 4–3 at Yankee Stadium.
	Future Hall of Famers on the rosters of the two clubs included Hank Aaron, Ernie Banks, Lou Brock, Rod Carew, Orlando Cepeda, Roberto Clemente, Don Drysdale, Bob Gibson, Catfish Hunter, Ferguson Jenkins, Al Kaline, Harmon Killebrew, Mickey Mantle, Juan Marichal, Willie Mays, Bill Mazeroski, Tony Perez, Brooks Robinson, Frank Robinson, Tom Seaver and Carl Yastrzemski. Pete Rose was also among the All-Stars.
July 23	The Angels defeat the Twins 2–1 at Anaheim Stadium. California swept all three games of the series again Minnesota on July 21, 22 and 23 by 2–1 scores. The game was played on the first day of riots in Detroit, which left 43 dead over an eight-day period.

JULY 30	Trailing 2–0, the Angels erupt for nine runs in the seventh inning and beat the Senators 10–2 in the second game of a double-header in Washington. Eight of the runs scored off Joe Coleman before a batter was retired as ten in a row reached base on four singles, a triple, two walks, a hit batsman and an error. The Senators won the first contest 11–1.
AUGUST 2	The Angels score twice in the ninth inning to defeat the Yankees 5–4 in New York. Jose Cardenal tripled in the first run and scored on a single by Woodie Held.
AUGUST 7	Trailing 4–1, the Angels explode for seven runs in the eighth inning and beat the Yankees 8–4 at Anaheim Stadium. All six hits in the inning were singles.
	On the same day, the Angels purchased Curt Simmons from the Cubs.
AUGUST 9	In his first game with the Angels, Curt Simmons scatters ten hits and pitches a complete-game shutout to defeat the Yankees 7–0 at Anaheim Stadium.
	Simmons was acquired at the age of 39 in his 20th year in the majors. The August 9 victory was his 192nd in the majors. As an Angel, he was 2–1 with a 2.60 ERA in 14 games, four of them starts.
AUGUST 11	Jim McGlothlin pitches the Angels to a 1–0 win over the Red Sox at Anaheim Stadium.
AUGUST 13	The Angels defeat the Red Sox 3–2 at Anaheim Stadium to tighten the closest race in American League history.
	At the end of the day, the Angels were in fourth place, but just 1½ games behind the first-place Twins. Only 2½ games separated the top five teams in the league. The White Sox were second, the Tigers third and the Red Sox in fifth. The Angels lost their next seven games, however, to drop out of contention. The other four clubs battled until the final week.
AUGUST 18	In one of the worst tragedies in baseball history, Red Sox outfielder Tony Conigliaro is beaned by Angels pitcher Jack Hamilton in the fourth inning of a 3–2 Boston win at Fenway Park. Conigliaro was hit in the face, which knocked him unconscious, caused a severe hemorrhage of his nose, broke his cheekbone, and sent bone fragments into his eye. He was carried off the field on a stretcher before being sent to the hospital.
	Conigliaro missed the rest of the 1967 season and all of 1968. He returned in 1969 but had problems with his eyesight for the remainder of his career. He became a member of the Angels shortly after the end of the 1970 campaign (see October 11, 1970).
AUGUST 20	The Angels take an 8–0 lead over the Red Sox in the fourth inning of the second game of a double-header at Fenway Park, but wind up losing 9–8. Boston also won the opener 12–2.
AUGUST 23	The Angels collect 25 hits and wallop the Indians 16–5 in Cleveland. The hits consisted of 20 singles, two doubles, a triple and two homers. Rick Reichardt hit a grand slam

off Ed Connolly during a seven-run, fourth inning. Jim Fregosi was four-for-four on three singles and a double and scored four runs.

AUGUST 26   After being held hitless through the first five innings by Tom Phoebus, the Angels erupt for five runs in the sixth to overcome a 4–0 deficit and defeat the Orioles 5–4 in Baltimore. The first five batters in the inning reached base. Jimmie Hall drove in two runs with a single and Don Mincher belted a three-run homer.

SEPTEMBER 2   The Angels outlast the Indians to win 1–0 in 12 innings at Anaheim Stadium. Bubba Morton drove in the winning run with a two-out triple. George Brunet pitched 11 shutout innings and allowed only four hits but wound up with a no decision. Minnie Rojas pitched the 12th and earned the victory.

> *The Angels were 53–30 at home and 31–47 on the road in 1967. They were 23 games above .500 at Anaheim Stadium despite outscoring the opposition only 288–276.*

SEPTEMBER 8   Rickey Clark pitches a two-hitter to defeat the Senators 4–0 in Washington. The only hits off Clark were singles by Cap Peterson in the fifth inning and Fred Valentine in the seventh.

SEPTEMBER 24   The Angels play the Athletics in Kansas City for the last time, and win 2–1.

> *The Athletics moved to Oakland at the end of the 1967 season.*

SEPTEMBER 29   The game between the Angels and Tigers in Detroit is postponed by rain, which forced the teams to play double-headers on each of the last two days of the season.

> *At the end of the day, the Twins led both the Red Sox and Tigers by one game in the standings. The Angels kept the Twins from wrapping up the title by winning two of three during a series in Minnesota on September 25, 26 and 27.*

SEPTEMBER 30   After the Tigers win the first game of a double-header in Detroit 5–0, the Angels rally to win the second tilt 8–6. The Tigers led 6–2 before the Angels put six runs on the board in the eighth. Tom Satriano tied the score with a single. Jim Fregosi broke the deadlock with a two-out, two-run single.

> *The Red Sox defeated the Twins 6–4 in Boston. Heading into the final day of the season, Boston and Minnesota were tied for first place with Detroit one-half game back. The Tigers needed to sweep the Angels in a double-header on October 1 to have a shot at the pennant.*

OCTOBER 1   The Angels lose the first of two at Detroit 6–4, but eliminate the Tigers from the pennant race with an 8–5 victory in the second tilt. The Red Sox defeated the Twins 5–3 to take sole possession of first place. The final out was recorded just after the second clash between the Angels and Tigers began. Had Detroit won that contest, a playoff between the Red Sox and Tigers would have taken place the following day. The Red Sox gathered around the radio in the clubhouse to listen to the Angels-Tigers game and celebrated when the final out was recorded at 7:43 p.m. Boston time. It was the first pennant for the Red Sox since 1946 and came after a season in which they finished in ninth place.

OCTOBER 18   The American League formally approves the transfer of the Athletics from Kansas City to Oakland. The move was enthusiastically approved by the Angels, who now had a rival in California. From the club's inception in 1961 through 1967, the Angels were the only AL club located west of Kansas City. At the same time, expansion from 10 teams to 12 was sanctioned, beginning in 1969. Another team was placed in Kansas City, and named the Royals. The other was in Seattle, the third AL team on the west coast and nicknamed the Pilots. The National League added San Diego and Montreal as expansion teams in May 1968. This gave California five major leagues teams. There were none in the state until the Giants and Dodgers moved west at the end of the 1957 season.

NOVEMBER 29   The Angels trade Jose Cardenal to the Indians for Chuck Hinton.

> *The Angels made a horrible exchange with Cleveland. After leaving California, Cardenal was a starting outfielder for four different clubs over the next nine years. Hinton played one season with the Angels and batted .195 in 116 games.*

1968

Season in a Sentence
In the wake of a winning season in 1967, optimism is high heading into 1968, but it evaporates quickly and the Angels lose 95 games.

Finish • Won • Lost • Pct • GB
Eighth (tie)   67   95   .414   36.0

Manager
Bill Rigney

Stats	Angels	AL	Rank
Batting Avg:	.227	.230	8
On-Base Pct:	.287	.297	8
Slugging Pct:	.318	.339	8
Home Runs:	83		8
Stolen Bases:	62		8
ERA:	3.43	2.98	9
Errors:	156		10
Runs Scored:	498		9
Runs Allowed:	615		9

Starting Lineup
Buck Rodgers, c
Don Mincher, 1b
Bobby Knoop, 2b
Aurelio Rodriguez, 3b
Jim Fregosi, ss
Rick Reichardt, lf
Vic Davalillo, cf
Roger Repoz, rf-cf
Tom Satriano, c
Chuck Hinton, 1b-rf
Paul Schaal, 3b

Pitchers
George Bruney, sp
Jim McGlothlin, sp
Sammy Ellis, sp-rp
Rickey Clark, sp
Tom Murphy, sp
Andy Messersmith, sp
Tom Burgmeier, rp
Marty Pattin, rp
Clyde Wright, rp-sp

Attendance
1,025,956 (fifth in AL)

Club Leaders
Batting Avg:	Rick Reichardt	.255
On-Base Pct:	Rick Reichardt	.328
Slugging Pct:	Rick Reichardt	.421
Home Runs:	Rick Reichardt	21
RBI:	Rick Reichardt	73
Runs:	Jim Fregosi	77
Stolen Bases:	Vic Davalillo	17
Wins:	George Brunet	13
Strikeouts:	Jim McGlothlin	135
ERA:	George Brunet	2.86
Saves:	Minnie Rojas	6

April 9 — The season opener against the Yankees in New York is postponed to avoid conflict with the funeral of Dr. Martin Luther King, Jr., who was murdered in Memphis on April 4.

Because of postponements, the Angels played their first six games in five different cities, traveling from New York to Cleveland, Baltimore, Washington and Anaheim.

April 10 — The Angels open the season with a 1–0 loss to the Yankees in New York. Frank Fernandez drove in the only run of the game with a homer off George Brunet in the second inning. Mel Stottlemyre pitched the shutout for the Yanks.

In a year dominated by the pitchers, such low-scoring games were common. There were only 6.8 runs scored in the average American League game in 1968, breaking the record 6.9 runs per game set in 1909. The Angels scored only 498 runs in 162 games. Rick Reichardt was the club's top offensive producer with a .255 batting average and 21 home runs. Jim Fregosi led the AL in triples with 13.

April 17 — The Angels lose 3–2 to the Yankees in the home opener before 20,068 at Anaheim Stadium. The only California runs came on a homer with a man on base by Rick Reichardt with one out in the ninth inning.

April 24 — Clyde Wright pitches a two-hitter to defeat the Senators 6–1 at Anaheim Stadium. The only Washington hits were singles by Hank Allen in the first inning and Paul Casanova in the seventh.

May 4 — Roger Repoz drives in six runs during a 7–2 win over the Tigers in Detroit with a pair of three-run homers in the third and sixth innings.

May 6 — Angels right fielder Bubba Morton hits his first major league home run since 1962 during a 5–1 loss to the White Sox at Anaheim Stadium.

May 10 — George Brunet hurls a two-hitter to defeat the Twins 3–0 in the first game of a double-header at Anaheim Stadium. The only Minnesota hits were singles by Jackie Hernandez in the fifth inning and Cesar Tovar in the sixth. The Twins won the second tilt 6–5.

May 15 — The Angels defeat the White Sox 4–2 at County Stadium in Milwaukee. The White Sox played nine "home" games in Milwaukee in 1968 and eleven more in 1969.

May 20 — Jim Fregosi hits for the cycle during an 11-inning 5–4 victory over the Red Sox at Anaheim Stadium. The cycle was completed in reverse order. Fregosi homered in the first inning and tripled in the third off Jose Santiago. After being retired in the fifth facing Santiago, the Angels shortstop doubled against Sparky Lyle in the eighth. Fregosi was intentionally walked in the ninth by Lyle, and then capped the evening with a walk-off single off Gary Waslewski in the 11th. It was only the second time that an Angel batter hit for the cycle. Fregosi was also the first on July 28, 1964.

May 28 — In conjunction with the expansion to 12 teams, American League owners vote to split the league into two divisions along with a postseason playoff to determine the champion beginning with the 1969 season. The Angels were placed in the Western Division with Chicago, Kansas City, Minnesota, Oakland and Seattle.

May 31	The Angels play the Athletics in Oakland for the first time and win 3–0 in 12 innings. The California runs scored on a single by Buck Rodgers, a sacrifice, an intentional walk, and a three-run homer with two out by Roger Repoz. Chuck Dobson pitched all 12 innings for the A's. Sammy Ellis (eight innings), Minnie Rojas (two innings) and Clyde Wright (two innings) combined on the shutout.
June 6	On the day Robert Kennedy dies from bullet wounds inflicted the previous day at the Ambassador Hotel in Los Angeles, the Angels erase a 3–0 deficit by scoring seven runs in the seventh inning and go on to defeat the Orioles 8–6 in Baltimore.
June 7	In the first round of the amateur draft, the Angels select pitcher Lloyd Allen from Selma High School in Selma, California.
	Allen had a seven-year major league career in which he posted an 8–25 record. He was 8–15 with the Angels from 1969 through 1973. The only other future major leaguers drafted and signed by the Angels in 1967 were Tom Bradley (seventh round) and Harvey Shank (tenth round).
June 8	The Angels-Yankees game in New York is postponed because of a national day of mourning declared by President Lyndon Johnson in honor of Robert Kennedy.
June 13	Paul Schaal is struck behind the ear on a pitch from Jose Santiago during a 4–2 win over the Red Sox in Boston. The Angels lost the second game 5–1. Making his major league debut, Andy Messersmith entered the game with the bases loaded in the ninth inning and gave up a walk-off grand slam to Ken Harrelson.
	Schaal played only two more games all year, both in August as a pinch hitter.
June 15	The Angels score two runs in the ninth inning and one in the tenth to defeat the Senators 5–4 at Anaheim Stadium. Jim Fregosi tied the score 4–4 with a two-out, two-run triple. Rick Reichardt provided the game-winner with a walk-off homer.
	On the same day, the Angels traded Jimmie Hall to the Indians for Vic Davalillo.
June 17	Jim Fregosi hits a walk-off homer in the 12th inning to defeat the Yankees 2–1 at Anaheim Stadium.
June 23	Jim Fregosi belts another walk-off homer, this one in the ninth inning to beat the Orioles 3–2 at Anaheim Stadium.
June 28	The Angels edge the Senators 1–0 in 11 innings in the second game of a double-header in Washington. Rick Reichardt drove in the lone run with a double. Jim McGlothlin (nine innings) and Marty Pattin (two innings) combined on the shutout. The Angels also won the opener 4–3.
July 9	Jim Fregosi leads off the All-Star Game with a double, but the American League collects only two more hits and loses 1–0 at the Astrodome in Houston.
July 15	The Angels collect only three hits but beat the Tigers 4–0 at Anaheim Stadium. Jim Fregosi hit a two-run homer in the third inning, and Aurelio Rodriguez added another one in the fourth.

Rodriguez played third base for the Angels from 1967 through 1970. The club had hoped the Mexican native would bring crowds across the border, but the anticipated attendance boost never happened. Rodriguez was killed in Detroit at the age of 52 in 2000 when he was run over by a car whose driver suffered a stroke. At the time, Rodriguez was visiting friends in the city. In a bizarre coincidence, there have been three players in major league history named Aurelio, and all three died in auto accidents between the ages of 44 and 53. The other two were Aurelio Lopez and Aurelio Monteagudo. Lopez and Monteagudo died in their native Mexico.

JULY 19 — Roger Repoz hits a two-run homer in the sixth inning for the only runs of a 2–0 triumph over the White Sox in Chicago. George Brunet pitched the shutout.

JULY 20 — The Angels trade Woodie Held to the White Sox for Wayne Causey.

Causey spent only nine days with the Angels and was hitless in 11 at-bats before being sold to the Braves.

AUGUST 4 — Vic Davalillo collects five hits, including a double, in six at-bats during a 12–6 win over the Red Sox in Boston.

AUGUST 9 — Marty Pattin faces only two batters and hits both with pitches during the seventh inning of a 3–0 loss to the Orioles in Baltimore. Pattin plunked Mark Belanger and Frank Robinson. Three batters later, Dennis Bennett hit Brooks Robinson with a pitch. In addition, Angels starter Bill Harrelson hit Don Buford with an offering leading off the first inning.

AUGUST 11 — Rick Reichardt drives in six runs with a triple and two singles during an 11–1 win over the Orioles in Baltimore. Tom Satriano collected five hits, including a homer and two doubles, in five at-bats.

AUGUST 20 — Clyde Wright pitches $6^{1}/_{3}$ innings of hitless relief during a 7–2 win over the Orioles at Anaheim Stadium. Rickey Clark was the starting pitcher and allowed just one hit, a single by Mark Belanger in the third inning, but was relieved because of an arm injury.

AUGUST 27 — One day after the start of the Democratic National Convention in Chicago, an event marred by violent confrontations between anti-war demonstrators and police, Bill Harrelson ($5^{2}/_{3}$ innings) and Andy Messersmith ($3^{1}/_{3}$ innings) combine on a one-hitter to beat the Yankees 2–0 in New York. Harrelson allowed only a single to Joe Pepitone in the sixth, but he relieved because he walked six hitters.

Messersmith pitched mainly out of the bullpen as a rookie in 1968, and allowed just 44 hits in $81^{1}/_{3}$ innings. In 1969 and 1970 he led the AL in lowest opponents' batting average while posting records of 16–11 and 11–10. He was 20–13 in 1971 and earned a spot on the All-Star team. He was dealt to the Dodgers after slipping to 8–11 in 1972.

SEPTEMBER 4 — The Angels set a team record with seven pinch hitters during a 9–5 loss to the Indians at Anaheim Stadium. The seven were Tom Egan, Buck Rodgers, Winston Llenas, Chuck Hinton, Vic Davalillo, Bubba Morton and Jim McGlothlin.

SEPTEMBER 6	In his first major league start, Andy Messersmith pitches a two-hitter to defeat the Red Sox 4–0 at Anaheim Stadium. He had made 23 relief appearances with the Angels prior to the start. The only Boston hits were singles by Joe Foy in the seventh inning and Mike Andrews in the eighth.
SEPTEMBER 7	General manager Fred Haney announces his retirement.
	Haney was the club's original general manager. He was hired in December 1960.
SEPTEMBER 23	The Angels hire 42-year-old Dick Walsh as general manager. A native of Los Angeles, he was in the Dodgers organization in both Brooklyn and L.A. from 1948 through 1966, rising to a position of vice president. Walsh also served as commissioner of the North American Soccer League. He was general manager of the Angels until 1971.
SEPTEMBER 28	The Angels are held hitless by Jack Fisher of the White Sox until Roger Repoz singles with one out in the seventh to drive in the lone run of a 1–0 victory at Anaheim Stadium. Marty Pattin (seven innings) and Jim McGlothlin (two innings) combined on the shutout.
OCTOBER 8	The Angels trade Jack Hamilton to the Indians for Eddie Fisher.
OCTOBER 15	The Angels lose Don Mincher, Marty Pattin and Steve Hovley to the Seattle Pilots and Paul Schaal and Tom Burgmeier to the Kansas City Royals in the expansion draft.
	Pattin proved to be a loss. He won 110 big league games after leaving the Angels and before his career ended in 1980.
DECEMBER 2	A month after Richard Nixon defeats Hubert Humphrey in the presidential election, the Angels draft Pedro Borbon from the Cardinals organization.
DECEMBER 12	The Angels trade Ed Kirkpatrick and Dennis Paepke to the Royals for Hoyt Wilhelm.
	A future Hall of Famer, Wilhelm was 46 years old at the time of the trade. He was 4–4 with ten saves and a 2.47 ERA in 44 games in his only season with the club.

1969

Season in a Sentence

With high hopes of a vast improvement over the debacle of 1968, the Angels stumble out of the gate with an anemic offense and fire Bill Rigney in May as attendance drops drastically for the third year in a row.

Finish • Won • Lost • Pct • GB

Third   71   91   .438   26.0

Managers

Bill Rigney (11–28) and Lefty Phillips (60–63)

Stats

Stats	Angels	AL	Rank
Batting Avg:	.230	.246	12
On-Base Pct:	.298	.321	12
Slugging Pct:	.319	.369	12
Home Runs:	88		12
Stolen Bases:	54		9 (tie)
ERA:	3.54	3.62	6
Errors:	135		5
Runs Scored:	528		12
Runs Allowed:	652		6

Starting Lineup

Joe Azcue, c
Jim Spencer, 1b
Sandy Alomar, 2b
Aurelio Rodriguez, 3b
Jim Fregosi, ss
Rick Reichardt, lf
Jay Johnstone, cf
Bill Voss, rf
Roger Repoz, cf-lf

Pitchers

Andy Messersmith, sp
Tom Murphy, sp
Rudy May, sp
Jim McGlothlin, sp
George Brunet, sp
Ken Tatum, rp
Eddie Fisher, rp
Hoyt Wilhelm, rp

Attendance

755,388 (ninth in AL)

Club Leaders

Batting Avg:	Jay Johnstone	.270
On-Base Pct:	Jim Fregosi	.361
Slugging Pct:	Jim Fregosi	.381
	Jay Johnstone	.381
Home Runs:	Rick Reichardt	13
RBI:	Rick Reichardt	68
Runs:	Jim Fregosi	78
Stolen Bases:	Sandy Alomar	18
Wins:	Andy Messersmith	16
Strikeouts:	Andy Messersmith	211
ERA:	Andy Messersmith	2.52
Saves:	Ken Tatum	22

APRIL 3   The Dodgers play at Anaheim Stadium for the first time and win 4–2 over the Angels in an exhibition game.

> *On the same day, the Angels purchased Bo Belinsky from the Cardinals organization. Belinsky never received a second chance to pitch for the Angels, however. He was 12–5 with a 2.82 ERA at the club's Class AAA farm club in Hawaii and was sold to the Pirates in July.*

APRIL 4   The Angels trade Chuck Hinton to the Indians for Lou Johnson.

APRIL 7   The Angels sign Dick Stuart as a free agent.

APRIL 8   The Angels participate in the first ever game by the Seattle Pilots and lose 4–3 before an Opening Day crowd of 11,930 at Anaheim Stadium. The Pilots scored all four of their runs in the first inning off Jim McGlothlin, who retired only one of the seven batters to face him. Tommy Harper, the first batter in Seattle's major league history, doubled. Mike Hegan followed with a home run. Jim Fregosi homered in the losing cause.

The Pilots lasted only one season in Seattle. The franchise moved to Milwaukee in April 1970 and was renamed the Brewers. Seattle later received another expansion team, named the Mariners, which began play in 1977.

APRIL 25   The Angels play the Royals for the first time and win 6–3 at Municipal Stadium in Kansas City.

Dick Enberg joined Don Wells in the Angels broadcast booth in 1969, replacing Buddy Blattner. Enberg was 34 and had a following in the area as the voice of the Los Angeles Rams and UCLA basketball. He was the announcer for the Angels from 1969 through 1978 and again in 1985. After each Angels victory, he would wrap up his broadcast with "And the halo shines tonight." Enberg joined NBC in 1975 and was part of the network for 25 years covering football, baseball, golf, tennis, horse racing, boxing and the Olympics. He was best known for his signature phrase "Oh, my."

APRIL 29   The Angels play in Seattle for the first time and lose 1–0 to the Pilots at Sicks Stadium.

MAY 1   Tom Satriano is hit by a pitch from Lew Krausse with the bases loaded in the tenth inning to force in the winning run of a 3–2 win over the Athletics at Anaheim Stadium.

MAY 2   The Royals play at Anaheim Stadium for the first time and sweep the Angels 9–4 and 3–2 in a double-header.

MAY 4   Bob Oliver of the Royals collects six hits, including a homer and a double, in six at-bats during a 15–1 win over the Angels at Anaheim Stadium.

MAY 14   Jim McGlothlin (six innings) and Hoyt Wilhelm (three innings) combine to shut out the Senators 1–0 at Anaheim Stadium. A bases-loaded walk to Bubba Morton in the sixth inning accounted for the winning run.

On the same day, the Angels traded Bobby Knoop to the White Sox for Sandy Alomar and Bob Priddy. Alomar was the Angels starting second baseman until 1973 and made the All-Star team in 1970. He also played in 648 consecutive games from 1969 through 1973.

MAY 16   Yankees pitcher Fritz Peterson retires the last 19 batters to face him and beats the Angels 2–1 in New York. Bobby Murcer ended the contest with a two-out, two-run double.

MAY 17   Yankees pitcher Stan Bahnsen retires the first 19 batters to face him and beats the Angels 6–0 in New York. Over two games, 38 consecutive Angels batters were retired. Jim Fregosi broke the string with a single.

MAY 18   A walk-off homer by Joe Pepitone of the Yankees off Hoyt Wilhelm in the ninth inning beats the Angels 1–0 in the second game of a double-header in New York. The Yankees won the opener 3–1.

From May 7 through May 25, the Angels scored just 30 runs in 17 games.

MAY 25   The Angels extend their losing streak to ten games with a 10–0 decision at the hands of the Tigers in Detroit.

The early season losing streak sent attendance plummeting. After drawing 1,400,321 in the first season in Anaheim in 1966, the Angels attracted 1,317,713 in 1967, 1,025,956 in 1968 and 758,388 in 1969.

MAY 27   With the club holding a record of 11–28, the Angels fire Bill Rigney as manager and replace him with 50-year-old Lefty Phillips. Later that evening, the Angels broke their ten-game losing streak with a 2–1 victory over the Indians at Anaheim Stadium.

Rigney was the original manager of the Angels. He was hired in December 1960. Rigney later managed the Twins (1970–72) and Giants (1976). His Minnesota club won the Western Division title in 1970. Phillips was a minor league player for only five games in 1939 with Bisbee in the Arizona League before an arm injury ended his career. After serving in World War II, he became a scout with the Reds, Browns and Dodgers while working a full-time job at the Pacific Electric Railway in Los Angeles. He became the pitching coach with the Dodgers from 1965 through 1968. The 1965 and 1966 clubs reached the World Series. Phillips received his appointment with the Angels despite having never managed in the minors or majors. He was hired by general manager Dick Walsh because of their close relationship when both worked for the Dodgers. Phillips managed the Angels until 1971 to a record of 222–225.

Shortstop Jim Fregosi was the team's biggest star in the 1960s, a team leader who produced many clutch hits through the years.

MAY 28   In his major league debut, Ken Tatum pitches one inning of perfect relief and strikes out two during a 5–4 triumph over the Indians at Anaheim Stadium.

Tatum was a starter in the minors but was converted into a relief pitcher once he reached the big leagues. He proved to be a find in 1969 by allowing only one run over 28 innings in his first 18 games and won the closer's job over seasoned veterans Hoyt Wilhelm and Eddie Fisher. By the end of the season, Tatum had a 7–2 record and 22 saves with an ERA of 1.36 in 45 games and 86 1/3 innings. After an effective season in 1970, he was traded to the Red Sox in a blockbuster deal that brought Tony Conigliaro to Anaheim.

May 30   The Angels trade Vic Davalillo to the Cardinals for Jim Hicks.

June 5   With the fifth pick in the first round of the amateur draft, the Angels select shortstop Alan Bannister from Kennedy High School in Buena Park, California.

Bannister opted not to sign with the Angels and attended Arizona State University instead. He was drafted by the Phillies in 1973, and had a 12-year career as a utility player. Those drafted and signed by the Angels in 1969 who reached the big leagues were Rudy Meoli (fourth round) and Andy Hassler (25th round).

June 11   The Angels outlast the Orioles 7–5 in 14 innings in Baltimore. Tom Satriano drove in the winning runs with a two-out, two-run single. Both clubs scored once in the 11th.

June 15   The Angels trade Tom Satriano to the Red Sox for Joe Azcue.

June 16   The Angels are embarrassed by consecutive double steals in the first inning of an 8–2 loss to the Twins at Metropolitan Stadium. With Joe Azcue catching in his first game with the club and Tom Murphy pitching, Rod Carew stole third and Tony Oliva second in a double steal with Harmon Killebrew batting. Before Killebrew completed his plate appearance, Carew swiped home and Oliva third. Killebrew then singled to score Oliva.

June 17   The Angels score six runs in the sixth inning and wallop the Twins 13–1 in Minnesota.

June 23   Sandy Alomar leads off the first inning with an inside-the-park homer off Dick Woodson to spark a 5–2 win over the Twins at Anaheim Stadium.

The home run was the first of Alomar's career, and it came in his 805th major league at-bat. He made his debut with the Milwaukee Braves in 1964. Alomar didn't homer again until July 26, 1970. He finished his 15-year career with 13 home runs in 4,760 at-bats.

July 4   Jay Johnstone hits a grand slam off Gary Bell in the eighth inning of a 7–3 win over the White Sox in the first game of a double-header at Comiskey Park. Chicago won the second contest 3–1.

July 14   George Brunet pitches a two-hitter to defeat the Royals at Anaheim Stadium. The only Kansas City hits were a single by Jackie Hernandez in the fourth inning and a double from Bob Oliver in the fifth. Jay Johnstone drove in both runs with a homer in the sixth.

July 25   Five days after Neil Armstrong becomes the first man to walk on the moon, Andy Messersmith pitches a two-hitter to defeat the Yankees 6–0 at Anaheim Stadium.

The only New York hits were doubles by Jerry Kenney in the first inning and Jake Gibbs in the eighth.

Messersmith started the season 0–5, but finished with a 16–11 record, 211 strikeouts in 250 innings and a 2.52 ERA. The starting rotation of Messersmith, Tom Murphy, Rudy May and Jim McGlothlin were known as the "M Squad." None was older than 25.

JULY 27	Rick Reichardt drives in all five runs of a 5–4 victory over the Yankees at Anaheim Stadium. Reichardt hit a three-run homer in the third inning and a home run with a man on base in the fifth.
JULY 29	Jay Johnstone hits a walk-off homer in the ninth inning to down the Red Sox 4–3 at Anaheim Stadium.
JULY 31	The Angels sell George Brunet to the Pilots.
AUGUST 8	A two-run double by Aurelio Rodriguez in the ninth inning beats the Red Sox 7–6 in Boston.
AUGUST 11	Tom Egan is beaned by an Earl Wilson pitch in the seventh inning of a 3–1 win over the Tigers in Detroit.

Egan suffered a broken jaw and never regained full sight in his right eye. He returned to play in 1970 but was never more than a reserve catcher and retired in 1975 with a .200 career batting average in 373 games.

AUGUST 17	On the third day of the Woodstock Music Festival, the Angels use five homers to beat the Indians 7–6 at Anaheim Stadium. Rick Reichardt hit two of them. The others were struck by Bubba Morton, Jim Spencer and Billy Cowan. Cowan's blast was as a pinch hitter in the eighth inning with a man on base and erased a 6–5 deficit.
AUGUST 21	Sandy Alomar has a hand in both runs of a 2–0 victory over the Orioles at Anaheim Stadium. Alomar doubled and scored in the first inning and drove in a tally with a single in the fourth. In his first major league start, Steve Kealey pitched the shutout for his first win.

Kealey made four previous relief appearances in the big leagues and allowed six runs in eight innings. He pitched four seasons in the minors and made only one start with Idaho Falls in Rookie ball in 1966. The August 21, 1969, game was one of only four starts during Kealey's 139-game career over six seasons with the Angels and White Sox from 1968 through 1973. It was his lone victory as a starting pitcher.

AUGUST 27	The Angels score a run in the ninth inning and three in the tenth to defeat the Senators 4–1 in Washington. Jim Fregosi led off the ninth with a home run. Rick Reichardt provided the winning margin with a three-run triple with two out in the tenth.

Fregosi hit .260 with 12 homers in 1969.

SEPTEMBER 4 — The Angels collect only two hits off Tommy John but win 1–0 over the White Sox at Anaheim Stadium. Rudy May (7 1/3 innings) and Ken Tatum (1 2/3 innings) combined on the shutout.

SEPTEMBER 6 — Billy Cowan hits a walk-off homer in the 12th inning to beat the White Sox 2–1 at Anaheim Stadium. Cowan entered the game as a pinch hitter in the tenth and remained in the lineup as a first baseman.

SEPTEMBER 8 — The Angels trade Hoyt Wilhelm and Bob Priddy to the Braves for Mickey Rivers and Clint Compton.

Rivers played for the Angels from 1970 through 1975, although he didn't nail down a job as a regular in center field until 1974. A one-of-a-kind personality, Rivers mystified everyone with his baffling monologues. As an Angel, he hit .280, twice led the AL in triples, and stole 126 bases, but with only five homers and 120 walks in 1,663 at-bats.

SEPTEMBER 10 — The Royals use 27 players during an 11–4 loss to the Angels at Anaheim Stadium. Andy Messersmith pitched a complete game and faced 20 different hitters.

SEPTEMBER 15 — The Angels collect only three hits but win 4–0 over the White Sox in Chicago. All four runs scored in the seventh inning. Bill Voss tripled in three of the tallies and scored on a passed ball. Jim McGlothlin (six innings) and Ken Tatum (three innings) combined on the shutout.

SEPTEMBER 19 — The Angels score three runs in the ninth inning to defeat the Athletics 7–6 at Anaheim Stadium. Bill Voss tied the game with a two-run single. The winning run crossed the plate on an error.

SEPTEMBER 28 — Roger Repoz hits a two-run homer in the 11th inning for a 6–4 lead, and the Angels survive an Athletics uprising in the bottom half to win 6–5 in Oakland.

NOVEMBER 25 — The Angels trade Jim McGlothlin, Pedro Borbon and Vern Geishert to the Reds for Alex Johnson and Chico Ruiz.

Johnson came to the Angels with a reputation as a head case. He had previously played for the Phillies, Cardinals and Reds, and wore out his welcome quickly at all three stops. Johnson was moody, sullen and uncommunicative, often failed to hustle, had confrontations with teammates and was downright hostile to the press. On one occasion, he dumped coffee grounds into the typewriter of a reporter. In addition, he was one of the worst defensive outfielders in the majors. There was no doubt, however, that Johnson could hit. In 1970 he won the AL batting title, but his unstable personality disrupted the team in 1971 and once again he was sent packing. McGlothlin gave the Reds one good season. Borbon was a workhorse out of the Cincinnati bullpen for most of the 1970s. He pitched at least 120 innings of relief in six consecutive seasons beginning in 1972, and pitched in the World Series in 1972, 1975 and 1976.

THE STATE OF THE ANGELS

The Angels posted winning records in 1962, 1964, 1967 and 1970, but each of those years was followed by a losing season. In 1976, the club finished below .500 for the sixth straight campaign with one of the youngest teams in the AL. That year, players and owners agreed on a plan in which players could declare themselves free agents after six years in the majors. The agreement transformed the Angels, as Gene Autry threw many of his considerable millions into the free agent market. Between the 1976 and 1977 seasons, the Angels signed Don Baylor, Bobby Grich and Joe Rudi, then added Lyman Bostock the following year. Rod Carew was acquired via a trade in 1979. With the help of these star-quality athletes, the Angels put together back-to-back winning seasons for the first time in 1978 and 1979. The club won the AL West in 1979 to reach the postseason. Overall, the Angels were 781–831, a winning percentage of .484, ranking ninth among the 12 AL teams operating throughout the 1970s. American League champions during the 1970s were the Orioles (1970, 1971 and 1979), Athletics (1972, 1973 and 1974), Red Sox (1975) and Yankees (1976, 1977 and 1978). AL West champs outside of Anaheim were the Twins (1970), Athletics (1971, 1972, 1973, 1974 and 1975) and Royals (1976, 1977 and 1978).

THE BEST TEAM

Managed by Jim Fregosi, the Angels were 88–74 in 1979 and won the AL West before losing to the Orioles in the ALCS.

THE WORST TEAM

The 1974 team was 68–94 and finished last in the division.

THE BEST MOMENT

The Angels clinched their first pennant and postseason appearance on September 25, 1979.

THE WORST MOMENT

Lyman Bostock was murdered in Gary, Indiana, on September 23, 1978. It was one of many tragedies befalling the club during the 1970s. Chico Ruiz, Bruce Heinbechner and Mike Miley all died in auto accidents between 1972 and 1977.

THE ALL-DECADE TEAM • YEARS W/ANGELS

Brian Downing, c	1978–90
Jim Spencer, 1b	1968–73
Sandy Alomar, 2b	1969–74
Ken McMullen, 3b	1970–72
Jim Fregosi, ss	1961–71
Don Baylor, lf	1977–82
Mickey Rivers, cf	1970–75
Leroy Stanton, rf	1972–75
Frank Robinson, dh	1973–74
Nolan Ryan, p	1972–79
Frank Tanana, p	1973–80
Clyde Wright, p	1966–73
Andy Messersmith, p	1968–72

Ryan and Robinson are in the Hall of Fame. Fregosi was also on the 1960 All-Decade Team. Following his departure, finding a capable individual to man the shortstop position was a problem for the Angels well into the 1980s. Third baseman Carney Lansford (1978–80) was another impact player on the club during the 1970s.

THE DECADE LEADERS

Batting Avg:	Don Baylor	.269
On-Base Pct:	Don Baylor	.347
Slugging Pct:	Don Baylor	.480
Home Runs:	Don Baylor	105
RBI:	Don Baylor	313
Runs:	Don Baylor	310
Stolen Bases:	Sandy Alomar	121
Wins:	Nolan Ryan	138
Strikeouts:	Nolan Ryan	2,416
ERA:	Andy Messersmith	2.95
Saves:	Dave LaRoche	61

THE HOME FIELD

Anaheim Stadium began to be transformed in 1979, when it was completely enclosed in anticipation of the move of the Rams from Los Angeles to Anaheim, beginning with the 1980 season. Capacity was increased from 43,550 to 64,593. The Angels set an attendance record of 1,755,386 in 1978, then shattered it with a figure of 2,523,575 in 1979.

THE GAME YOU WISHED YOU HAD SEEN

Nolan Ryan pitched the third of his seven career no-hitters on September 28, 1974 against the Twins. He also struck out 15.

THE WAY THE GAME WAS PLAYED

Speed and defense were more prominent during the 1970s than in any decade since the lively ball was introduced in 1920. Stolen bases per team in the American League rose from 72 in 1970 to 107 in 1979, while home runs declined from 146 in 1970 to 94 in 1976 before surging upward at the end of the decade. The designated hitter rule was introduced in the AL in 1973.

THE MANAGEMENT

Gene Autry was the owner of the Angels from the club's inception in 1960 until his death in 1998. General managers were Dick Walsh (1969–71), Harry Dalton (1971–77) and Buzzie Bavasi (1977–84). There were nine field managers, beginning with Lefty Phillips (1969–71), and followed by Del Rice (1972), Bobby Winkles (1973–74), Whitey Herzog (interim 1974), Dick Williams (1974–76), Norm Sherry (1976–77), Dave Garcia (1977–78) and Jim Fregosi (1978–81).

THE BEST PLAYER MOVE

In the best trade in club history, the Angels dealt Jim Fregosi to the Mets on December 10, 1971 for Nolan Ryan, Leroy Stanton, Don Rose and Francisco Estrada.

THE WORST PLAYER MOVE

The Angels swapped Mickey Rivers and Ed Figueroa to the Yankees in December 1975 for Bobby Bonds.

1970

Season in a Sentence
Spurred by an improved offense behind Alex Johnson, the Angels win 15 more games than the previous season.

Finish • Won • Lost • Pct • GB
Third 86 76 .531 12.0

Manager
Lefty Phillips

Stats   Angels • AL • Rank
Batting Avg:	.251	.250	5
On-Base Pct:	.307	.322	12
Slugging Pct:	.363	.379	8
Home Runs:	114		10
Stolen Bases:	69		7
ERA:	3.48	3.71	5
Errors:	127		4
Runs Scored:	631		9
Runs Allowed:	630		5

Starting Lineup
Joe Azcue, c
Jim Spencer, 1b
Sandy Alomar, 2b
Ken McMullen, 3b
Jim Fregosi, ss
Alex Johnson, lf
Jay Johnstone, cf
Roger Repoz, rf-cf
Tom Egan, c

Pitchers
Clyde Wright, sp
Tom Murphy, sp
Andy Messersmith, sp
Rudy May, sp
Tom Bradley, sp
Ken Tatum, rp
Eddie Fisher, rp

Attendance
1,077,741 (5th in AL)

Club Leaders
Batting Avg:	Alex Johnson	.329
On-Base Pct:	Alex Johnson	.370
Slugging Pct:	Alex Johnson	.459
	Jim Fregosi	.459
Home Runs:	Jim Fregosi	22
RBI:	Alex Johnson	86
Runs:	Jim Fregosi	95
Stolen Bases:	Sandy Alomar	35
Wins:	Clyde Wright	22
Strikeouts:	Rudy May	164
ERA:	Clyde Wright	2.83
Saves:	Ken Tatum	17

APRIL 7 The Angels open the season with a 12–0 win over the Brewers at County Stadium. It was the first ever American League game in Milwaukee. Only four days earlier, the Seattle Pilots moved to Milwaukee and were renamed the Brewers. The Braves previously played in the Wisconsin city from 1953 through 1965. Andy Messersmith pitched the Opening Day shutout and struck out 11. There were no home runs among the 14 California hits. Aurelio Rodriguez was 3-for-5.

The Angels began the season with wins in their first five games by outscoring the Brewers and the Royals 42–16.

APRIL 11 Alex Johnson drives in all six runs of a 6–3 win over the Royals in Kansas City. Johnson hit three-run homers in the first and sixth innings, both off Wally Bunker.

In his first season with the Angels, Johnson won the AL batting title with a .329 average along with 202 hits and 14 home runs. He was the first player in franchise history to top the 200-hit plateau and is the only player in franchise history to lead the league in batting average.

APRIL 14 The Angels lose the home opener 3–1 to the White Sox before 18,229 at Anaheim Stadium.

Dave Niehaus and Jerry Coleman joined Dick Enberg and Don Wells in the Angels broadcast booth in 1970. Niehaus was an Angels announcer until 1976. He also did games for the Los Angeles Rams, Los Angeles Lakers and UCLA football and basketball. In 1977, Niehaus became the first announcer for the expansion Seattle Mariners and became enormously popular in the Pacific Northwest. Coleman played for the Yankees for nine seasons from 1949 through 1957. Eight of those clubs reached the World Series. He was an announcer for the Angels for two years. In 1972, Coleman became the lead announcer for the Padres.

APRIL 18   Bill Voss drives in five runs with one official at-bat during a 7–1 win over the Royals at Anaheim Stadium. Voss hit a sacrifice fly in the first inning, walked in the third, belted a grand slam off Wally Bunker in the fifth and walked again in the seventh.

APRIL 20   The Angels play the Brewers at Anaheim Stadium for the first time, and win 5–4 in ten innings. Roger Repoz drove in the winning run with a walk-off single.

APRIL 27   The Angels trade Aurelio Rodriguez and Rick Reichardt to the Senators for Ken McMullen.

APRIL 28   In his first game with the Angels, Ken McMullen hits a three-run homer, but the Yankees win 7–5 in New York.

MAY 11   Seven days after four students are killed at Kent State University, Ray Culp of the Red Sox strikes out the first six batters to face him, but the Angels survive to win a 16-inning marathon 2–1 at Anaheim Stadium. The winning run scored on a double by Jarvis Tatum and a single from Sandy Alomar. Tom Murphy (eight innings), Ken Tatum (four innings), Paul Doyle (three innings), Eddie Fisher (two-thirds of an inning) and Dave LaRoche (one-third of an inning) combined to allow only six hits. It was LaRoche's major league debut, and he was the winning pitcher after inducing Carl Yastrzemski to pop up to Alomar at second with two runners on base.

MAY 12   Trailing 5–2, the Angels score four runs in the ninth inning to stun the Red Sox 6–5 at Anaheim Stadium. The Angels were still behind 5–4 with two out when Billy Cowan delivered a two-run, walk-off single. Cowan entered the game as a pinch hitter in the eighth and remained in the lineup as a center fielder.

On May 15, the Angels had a 22–10 record and a one-game lead in the AL West.

MAY 16   In his major league debut, Angels reliever Harvey Shank pitches three shutout innings during an 11–4 loss to the Athletics in Oakland. Despite the performance, Shank never pitched another game and ended his career with a perfect ERA of 0.00.

MAY 19   Rudy May pitches a two-hitter to defeat the White Sox 3–0 at Comiskey Park. The only Chicago hits were singles by Ken Berry in the second inning and Walt Williams in the ninth.

JUNE 4   In the first round of the amateur draft, the Angels select outfielder Paul Dade from Nathan Hale High School in Seattle, Washington.

Dade never fulfilled his promise, hitting .270 with ten homers during a 439-game major league career over six seasons. Other future big leaguers drafted and signed by the Angels in 1970 were Dan Briggs (second round), John Balaz (fifth round), Dick Lange (seventh round), Doug Howard (eighth round), Sid Monge (24th round) and Morris Nettles (second round of the secondary phase in January).

JUNE 9   After the Orioles score twice in the ninth inning to tie the score 5–5 in Baltimore, the Angels respond with two tallies in the 11th to win 7–5. Ken McMullen broke the 5–5 deadlock by leading off the 11th with a home run before a California insurance run.

JUNE 19 Alex Johnson loses his temper in spectacular fashion during a 5–2 loss to the Brewers at Anaheim Stadium. He argued a strike call by umpire Bill Kunkel loud and long, then slashed a run-scoring single. After touching first base, he headed back to the plate to berate Kunkel. When Lefty Phillips attempted to push Johnson away from Kunkel, the outfielder charged first base umpire Bill Haller. Then Johnson turned his wrath on third base arbiter Ed Runge and bounced his batting helmet off Phillips' ankle. Ejected from the game, Johnson heaved a lead-weighted bat out of the dugout, barely missing the Angels bat boy.

JUNE 21 The Angels win a 6–5 thriller in ten innings over the Brewers at Anaheim Stadium. Sandy Alomar drove in a run with a single with two out in the ninth to tie the score 4–4. After Milwaukee scored in the top of the tenth, California responded with two runs in their half. Jay Johnstone ended the game with a bases-loaded, two-run double.

JUNE 24 Mel Queen (six innings) and Eddie Fisher (three innings) combine on a two-hitter to defeat the White Sox 2–1 at Anaheim Stadium. The only Chicago hits were a single by Syd O'Brien and a double from Duane Josephson in the fourth inning.

Queen was a pitcher for the Angels from 1970 through 1972. He made his major league debut with the Reds as an outfielder in 1964 and switched to pitching in 1966. His father, also named Mel, pitched in the majors from 1942 through 1952.

JUNE 25 Clyde Wright drives in four runs during a 7–3 win over the White Sox at Anaheim Stadium.

Wright came into the 1970 season as a 29-year-old with a 21–24 career record. He was only 1–8 with a 4.10 ERA in 1969. That offseason, he pitched winter ball for Ponce in the Puerto Rican League, a club managed by Jim Fregosi, and straightened himself out. In a remarkable turnaround, Wright posted a 22–12 mark and a 2.83 earned run average in 260$^{2/3}$ innings in 1970.

JUNE 26 The Angels pull off the first triple play in club history in the fifth inning of a 5–4 win over the Royals in Kansas City. With runners on first and second, Amos Otis grounded to third baseman Chico Ruiz, who stepped on third base and threw to second baseman Sandy Alomar, who in turn, retired Otis with a toss to first baseman Billy Cowan.

Resigned to his career as a utility player, Ruiz sat on custom-made cushions on the bench.

JUNE 27   Sandy Alomar extends his hitting streak to 22 games with a sixth-inning double during a 2–0 loss to the Royals in Kansas City.

Alomar collects 31 hits in 99 at-bats for an average of .313 during the streak.

JULY 1   Greg Garrett is the winning pitcher without throwing a pitch in a 4–3 win over the Brewers in Milwaukee. Garrett entered the contest with California trailing 2–1 and two out in the sixth. He proceeded to pick Tommy Harper off first base and was lifted for a pinch hitter in the top of the seventh when the Angels scored three times to take the lead.

JULY 3   Clyde Wright pitches a no-hitter to defeat the Athletics 4–0 at Anaheim Stadium. The no-hitter came after he was inducted into the NAIA Hall of Fame in pre-game ceremonies on the basis of his college career at Carson-Newman, which is located in his hometown of Jefferson City, Tennessee. Wright threw 98 pitches to 29 batters, walked three and struck out one. Reggie Jackson came close to breaking up the no-hitter in the seventh inning when he backed up center fielder Jay Johnstone to within two feet of the wall in a home run bid. In the ninth, Wright walked Frank Fernandez, retired Bert Campaneris on a line drive to shortstop Jim Fregosi, and induced Felipe Alou to hit into a double play that went from Fregosi to second baseman Sandy Alomar to first baseman Jim Spencer.

In his first year as a full-time starter, Clyde Wright notched 22 victories in 1970 at the age of 29. He followed that success with two more quality seasons for the Angels.

Alomar's son, Sandy Jr., was the catcher for the 1997 American League champion Indians. Clyde's son Jaret Wright was a pitcher on that team. In the World Series that season, Cleveland played the Florida Marlins—a team that featured Felipe Alou's son Moises.

JULY 10 — Andy Messersmith strikes out 13 batters during a 2–1 win over the Twins at Anaheim Stadium.

JULY 14 — Clyde Wright is the losing pitcher in the All-Star Game, played at Riverfront Stadium in Cincinnati, after being involved in the most famous play in the history of the Midsummer Classic. Entering the contest with the score 4–4, Wright retired the side in the 11th and the first two hitters in the 12th before Pete Rose singled. Billy Grabarkewitz also singled. Jim Hickman followed with the third one-base hit in a row, and Rose came steaming around third and barreled over catcher Ray Fosse to score the winning run for a 5–4 NL victory.

JULY 17 — Clyde Wright pitches a complete game shutout, and the Angels rout the Senators 10–0 in Washington.

JULY 26 — With President Richard Nixon in attendance, the Angels take a thrilling 11-inning, 11–10 decision from the Senators at Anaheim Stadium. Jarvis Tatum drove in the winning run with a double.

JULY 28 — Angels catcher Tom Egan commits five passed balls and an error during a 6–5 loss to the Yankees at Anaheim Stadium. Three of the passed balls occurred with knuckleballer Eddie Fisher on the mound. Egan was taken out of the game for a pinch runner in the bottom of the eighth.

AUGUST 18 — The Angels explode for nine runs in the eighth inning and wallop the Indians 12–1 at Anaheim Stadium.

AUGUST 25 — Trailing 4–0, the Angels score two runs in the seventh inning, two in the ninth and two in the 11th to defeat the Tigers 6–4 in the first game of a double-header in Detroit. Jim Fregosi broke the 4–4 tie with a sacrifice fly between doubles by Jim Spencer and Alex Johnson. In the second game, the Angels rallied again with six tallies in the ninth to win 10–6. Fregosi tied the score with a two-run single. Four batters later, Jay Johnstone hit a grand slam off Lerrin LaGrow.

Fregosi hit .278 with 22 homers in 1970.

AUGUST 30 — Nine home runs by nine different players on the two teams highlights a 10–9 win over the Indians at Municipal Stadium. Homers by the Angels came from Sandy Alomar, Alex Johnson, Jay Johnstone, Ken McMullen and Bill Voss. Cleveland home runs were struck by Graig Nettles, Vada Pinson, Ray Fosse and Chuck Hinton. The Angels broke an 8–8 tie in the eighth inning when Sandy Alomar singled, moved to second on a bunt and scored on consecutive wild pitches by Dennis Higgins.

Alex Johnson's younger brother Ron gained 1,027 yards as a running back for the New York Giants in 1970. He topped that with 1,182 yards in 1972.

AUGUST 31 — The Angels purchase Tony Gonzalez from the Braves.

SEPTEMBER 3   Rookie Tom Bradley pitches the Angels to a 1–0 win over the Royals at Anaheim Stadium.

The victory put the Angels in second place, only three games behind the first-place Twins. The Angels lost their next nine games, however, to drop out of the race. The strong showing through Labor Day boosted attendance from 758,388 in 1969 to 1,077,741 in 1970.

SEPTEMBER 9   Alex Johnson becomes only the third player in the history of Comiskey Park, a facility opened in 1910, to homer into the center-field bleachers, but the Angels lose 3–1 to the White Sox in the second game of a double-header, called after eight innings by rain. The Angels also lost the opener 11–4.

SEPTEMBER 15   Trailing 3–0, the Angels erupt for five runs in the ninth inning and beat the Twins 5–3 in Minnesota. Three runs scored after two were out on a single by Ken McMullen and a two-run double from pinch hitter Tony Gonzalez. Right-handed batter Tommie Reynolds originally went to the plate to bat for lefty-swinger Jay Johnstone, but after the Twins switched to southpaw Ron Perranoski, California manager Lefty Phillips sent Reynolds back to the bench and Gonzalez to the plate.

SEPTEMBER 16   Clyde Wright wins his 20th game of the season with a 5–1 decision over the Twins in Minnesota.

OCTOBER 1   On the last day of the season, Alex Johnson wins the batting title in one of the closest races in history, and the Angels come from behind to defeat the White Sox 5–4 in 13 innings at Anaheim Stadium. After Chicago scored in the top of the 13th, the Angels rallied for two in their half. Bill Cowan drove in a run with a double and scored on a pinch-hit single by Mel Queen.

Heading into the day, Carl Yastrzemski had an average of .3286 and had 12 hits in his last 20 at-bats. Johnson's average was .3273, after collecting 18 hits in his previous 46 at-bats. The Red Sox played their last game on September 30. Lefty Phillips put Johnson into the lead-off spot in the batting order for the only time in 1970 to give him as many plate appearances as possible. After grounding out in his first at-bat, Johnson picked up two hits to pass Yastrzemski and was taken out of the game and replaced by Jay Johnstone. Johnson's final average was .3289 to .3286 for Yastrzemski.

OCTOBER 11   The Angels trade Ken Tatum, Doug Griffin and Jarvis Tatum to the Red Sox for Tony Conigliaro, Ray Jarvis and Jerry Moses.

Conigliaro was on a track for Cooperstown until August 18, 1967 when a pitch from Jack Hamilton of the Angels slammed into his face. The day after the injury, doctors predicted that Conigliaro would be playing again in two weeks. But within days it became apparent that the damage caused by the beaning was much more serious when his eyesight failed to return to normal. The accident caused a severe hemorrhage of his nose, broke his cheekbone, and sent bone fragments into his eye, which caused a hole in his retina. Conigliaro was declared legally blind. He missed the rest of the 1967 season and all of 1968. Tony returned in 1969 when the eye made a remarkable recovery and by 1970 appeared to be back to where he was before the injury, when he clubbed

36 homers and drove in 116 runs. Conigliaro was from the Boston area, adored by Red Sox fans, and his brother Billy was a teammate. He was angry over leaving the city, especially after owner Tom Yawkey promised him he wouldn't be traded, but he figured southern California was the next best place to go. With his darkly handsome good looks, Conigliaro had designs on a singing and acting career and rented a home in Newport Beach, where he was a neighbor of Raquel Welch. He enrolled in an acting class and was seen at several of L.A.'s hottest night clubs. It wasn't a good trade for either club. Conigliaro's eye troubles intensified and affected his depth perception, and he hit only .222 with four homers in 266 at-bats for the Angels in 1971 before retiring (see July 11, 1971). Moses never developed into anything more than a second-string catcher, and Jarvis never played another major league game. Ken Tatum failed to develop into the closer the Red Sox envisioned while battling injuries and Fenway Park's cozy dimensions. Jarvis Tatum (no relation to Ken) didn't play a game with the Sox. Griffin became Boston's starting second baseman, but in seven seasons with the Sox, he hit only .248 with seven homers in 2,081 at-bats.

NOVEMBER 30   The Angels trade Jay Johnstone, Tom Egan and Tom Bradley to the White Sox for Ken Berry, Syd O'Brien and Billy Wynne.

Johnstone had 15 years ahead of him in the majors and helped several clubs as an extra outfielder and pinch hitter. Bradley gave the White Sox a pair of 15-win seasons before arm troubles developed. The Angels received next to nothing in return. Berry was one of the best defensive outfielders of the era, but hit only .266 with 11 home runs in 1,122 at-bats over three seasons in California.

DECEMBER 15   The Angels trade Greg Garrett to the Reds for Jim Maloney.

Maloney came to the Angels at the age of 30 with three no-hitters and a lifetime record of 134–81. He missed almost all of the 1970 season with a ruptured Achilles tendon and never recovered. Maloney had an 0–3 record as a member of the Angels.

1971

Season in a Sentence
Alex Johnson, Jim Fregosi and Tony Conigliaro are expected to carry the offense, but Johnson is suspended for the remainder of the season in June; Conigliaro retires in July; and Fregosi slumps badly with an ailing foot.

Finish • Won • Lost • Pct • GB
Fourth   76   86   .469   25.5

Manager
Lefty Phillips

Stats

Stats	Angels	AL	Rank
Batting Avg:	.231	.247	11
On-Base Pct:	.288	.317	12
Slugging Pct:	.329	.364	10
Home Runs:	96		10
Stolen Bases:	72		6
ERA:	3.10	3.46	3
Errors:	131		8
Runs Scored:	511		12
Runs Allowed:	576		4

Starting Lineup
John Stephenson, c
Jim Spencer, 1b
Sandy Alomar, 2b
Ken McMullen, 3b
Jim Fregosi, ss
Tony Gonzalez, lf
Ken Berry, cf
Roger Repoz, rf
Tony Conigliaro, rf
Mickey Rivers, cf
Syd O'Brien, ss
Alex Johnson, lf

Pitchers
Andy Messersmith, sp
Clyde Wright, sp
Tom Murphy, sp
Rudy May, sp
Lloyd Allen, rp
Dave LaRoche, rp
Eddie Fisher, rp
Mel Queen, rp

Attendance
926,373 (sixth in AL)

Club Leaders
Batting Avg:	Sandy Alomar	.260
On-Base Pct:	Ken McMullen	.312
Slugging Pct:	Ken McMullen	.395
Home Runs:	Ken McMullen	21
RBI:	Ken McMullen	68
Runs:	Sandy Alomar	77
Stolen Bases:	Sandy Alomar	39
Wins:	Andy Messersmith	20
Strikeouts:	Andy Messersmith	179
ERA:	Andy Messersmith	2.99
	Clyde Wright	2.99
Saves:	Lloyd Allen	15

APRIL 6   The Angels open the season with a 4–1 loss to the Royals before 24,434 at Anaheim Stadium. Clyde Wright was the starting and winning pitcher.

The Angels sported new uniforms in 1971, replacing a design that was essentially unchanged from 1961 through 1970. The graphics were entirely overhauled, with "Angels" written in modern, san serif, lowercase lettering across the front of the shirts in scarlet with a navy blue border and a gold halo cocked over the left side of the "a." Uniform numbers appeared on the front for the first time. The caps, which previously featured an interlocking "C" and "A," were navy blue with a red lowercase "a" outlined in white. The large white halo, which had been part of the cap since 1961, was not part of the redesign. There was also a shoulder patch design with a red silhouette shape of the state of California encircled by another halo and with a small star in the lower corner of the "map" in the approximate location of Anaheim. In 1972, the lower case "a" on the cap was changed to an upper case "A" with a halo around the top, emulating the Anaheim Stadium scoreboard. In 1973, the lower case "a" on the uniform front was likewise changed to an upper case "A" identical to that on the cap.

APRIL 21	Rudy May strikes out 13 batters in nine innings, but the Angels lose 4–2 in a 13-inning affair against the Athletics at Anaheim Stadium.
APRIL 24	Roger Repoz hits a walk-off grand slam with one out in the ninth inning off Dick Hall to beat the Orioles 7–4 at Anaheim Stadium. The Angels loaded the bases on singles by Alex Johnson and Tony Conigliaro, a bunt by Jim Fregosi and an intentional walk to Ken McMullen.

> *In 1970, Johnson, Conigliaro and Fregosi combined to hit .292 with 72 home runs and 284 RBIs. In 1971, the trio combined for a .237 average, 11 home runs and 69 RBIs. Not surprisingly, the Angels' run production dropped from 631 in 1970 to 511 in 1971.*

APRIL 26	The Angels collect only five hits, but defeat the Indians 8–0 at Anaheim Stadium. Rudy May pitched the shutout.
APRIL 29	Jim Fregosi is diagnosed with plantar neuroma in his right foot. An operation was performed in July, after he batted .160 during the month of June.

> *Through the 2009 season, Fregosi ranks fourth in franchise history in games (1,429), fifth in at-bats (5,244), first in triples (70), fifth in runs (691), fifth in hits (1,408), fifth in doubles (219), fifth in total bases (2,112), fifth in walks (558) and eighth in RBIs (546).*

MAY 7	Syd O'Brien hits a two-run homer in the 11th inning to beat the Indians 4–2 in Cleveland.
MAY 15	With the Angels trailing 4–2 and runners on first and third and none out in the ninth against the Twins in Minnesota, three consecutive pinch hitters strike out facing Tom Hall. The three pinch hitters who failed in the clutch were Billy Cowan, Ken Berry and Jim Fregosi.
MAY 20	Clyde Wright pitches the Angels to a 1–0 win over the Twins at Anaheim Stadium. Jerry Stephenson drove in the lone run with an eighth-inning single.

> *Acquired from the Giants in November 1970, Stephenson was a 30-year-old catcher who won the starting job by collecting 25 hits in his first 61 at-bats for the Angels through May 23, an average of .410. Over the remainder of the season, he hit .165 in 218 at-bats to finish at .219.*

MAY 26	Jim Fregosi hits a two-run homer in the 11th inning to beat the Athletics 7–5 in Oakland.
JUNE 8	In the first round of the amateur draft, the Angels select pitcher Frank Tanana from Catholic Central High School in Redford, Michigan.

> *Tanana reached the majors at the age of 20 in 1973. From 1975 through 1978 with the Angels, he was 68–40 on clubs that lost more often then they won, made three All-Star teams, led the AL in strikeouts in 1975 and earned run average in 1977. But he averaged 259 innings per season over five years beginning in 1974, and the workload at such a young age led to shoulder*

problems and robbed him of his devastating fastball. Tanana struggled for a few years before being traded by the Angels to the Red Sox after the end of the 1980 season. He was able to carve out a long career as a finesse pitcher, however, and his big-league career didn't end until 1993. Tanana's final record was 240–236. Other future major leaguers drafted and signed by the Angels in 1971 were Ron Jackson (second round), Billy Smith (third round), and in the January secondary draft, Bob Allietta in the first round and Jerry Remy in the eighth.

JUNE 15   Trailing 4–1, the Angels score two runs in the eighth inning and two more in the ninth to defeat the Red Sox 5–4 at Anaheim Stadium. Syd O'Brien won the game with a two-run, walk-off homer.

JUNE 26   The Angels suspend Alex Johnson for the remainder of the season "for failure to give his best efforts in the winning of games."

JUNE 27   The Angels break open a scoreless tie with seven runs in the sixth inning and beat the White Sox 12–3 in the second game of a double-header in Chicago. The Angels also won the opener 2–1.

The Case of Alex Johnson

After winning the AL batting title and finishing eighth in the Most Valuable Player Award voting in 1970, Alex Johnson was suspended four times and fined 29 times by the Angels in 1971. The fourth suspension lasted from June 26 until the end of the season. Staging a curious rebellion, he was at the center of a complex drama that dragged on for months. Johnson filed a grievance with the help of the Major League Players Association and subsequently won back pay on the basis of his emotional instability. A ruling, handed down by an impartial arbitrator, was without precedent in baseball. The club owners were advised that a player suffering from an emotional disturbance must be treated no differently than one who has a physical ailment and that such a player, instead of being disciplined or suspended, be placed on the disabled list, which entitles him to full salary and benefits during the length of his disablement. The Angels were ordered to pay Johnson $29,970, which was his salary from June 26 through the end of the season.

Despite his success on the field, warning signs were apparent during the 1970 campaign when Johnson was fined several times for failing to run out ground balls and not giving full effort in the field. The situation worsened in 1971. Johnson's troubles began in spring training when manager Lefty Phillips removed him in the eighth inning of a March 20 exhibition game against the Athletics in Mesa, Arizona, for failing to run out a ground ball and for lackadaisical play in the field. Earlier, Johnson positioned himself in the shadow of a light tower. He followed the moving shadow throughout the hot day, ignoring the normal defensive alignments against the hitters and jogging after balls hit in his direction.

From that point through June, Johnson was fined 29 times, a total of $3,750, for various infractions on the field. Phillips insisted he could have fined Johnson every day. "For every time I fined him," Phillips said, "I looked the other way eight times. When a guy keeps calling someone obscene names for three or four months, it's going to have a reaction. I can't overlook the way he talks to his fellow players. He won't accept criticism from the other players, the coaches or the manager."

The first benching took place on May 15 for failing to hustle in a game against the Brewers in Anaheim. He was benched again six days later for the same reason. On May 23, he was taken out of a game once more for running at half speed both in the outfield and on the base paths during a 13–0 to the White Sox at home. Phillips called a clubhouse meeting the next day and told the players that Johnson would never play for the club again as long as he was manager. General manager Dick Walsh failed to support Phillips, however, and ordered that Johnson be restored to the lineup. In his first game back, on May 26, Johnson collected three hits and scored the winning run in a 12-inning, 7–5 triumph over the Athletics in Oakland.

Johnson's troubles were far from over, however. He was taken out of a 2–1 loss to Oakland at Anaheim Stadium on June 4 for failing to run out a ground ball. Johnson was kept on the bench for the next four games.

Johnson and Chico Ruiz were pinch hitters during a June 13 loss to the Senators in Anaheim. Instead of remaining on the bench until the end of the game, both went into the locker room separately. Johnson later claimed that Ruiz pulled a gun from the top shelf of his locker and threatened him. Ruiz denied owning a gun. Johnson had no witnesses to back up his story. But *Los Angeles Times* columnist John Hall called the Angels clubhouse "an armed camp ready to explode" and insisted that reports of guns were not exaggerated. The paper said that three California players had been carrying guns or knives.

From June 15 through June 24, Johnson didn't miss an inning and had a ten-game hitting streak. During a series against the Royals, however, he made three errors and misplayed a single into a triple.

Walsh announced on June 26 that he had suspended Johnson for the remainder of the season "for failure to give his best efforts with the club." The outfielder's absence was not lamented by teammates, many of whom wondered why it took so long for management to suspend him. Four days later, however, Marvin Miller, director of the Players Association, filed a grievance on Johnson's behalf. Miller contended that Johnson should undergo a "psychiatric evaluation so we could learn all the facts." Walsh replied that he was "not interested," and that as far as he was concerned, Johnson was "merely defying and challenging his authority." Johnson reluctantly agreed to consult a psychiatrist after being persuaded to do so by Miller and Dick Moss, the attorney for the Players Association.

Johnson's hearing was held before a three-man arbitration panel on August 28 in Anaheim and August 31 in his hometown of Detroit, where he underwent the psychiatric counseling. During the hearing, Walsh admitted that Ruiz pulled a gun on Johnson, but concealed the fact to protect Ruiz. Also, Johnson admitted to failing to hustle, blaming his teammates. He claimed he had "justifiable reasons for not being in the spirit of playing properly. There was indifference on the whole team working together. It felt the game wasn't being played properly–so my taste just wasn't there." Johnson also charged that many of his problems stemmed from his poor relationship with reporters. "I rejected them because of what they wrote about me," Johnson said, "and the more I rejected them, the worse they wrote about me."

The arbitrators ruled in Johnson's favor on September 28. The two psychiatrists who examined Johnson expressed the view that with appropriate treatment, he would be able to resume his career. Gene Autry was livid. "It's getting so an owner needs permission from Miller if he only wants to say hello to a player. The next time I have a player who doesn't hustle, I'll close down the park."

Johnson was traded to the Indians in a deal involving five players on October 5. Phillips was fired the next day. And Walsh was dismissed as general manager by owner Gene Autry even though Walsh had four years remaining on a seven-year contract.

JULY 2   Rickey Clark pitches a two-hitter to beat the Athletics 1–0 at Anaheim Stadium. The only Oakland hits were singles by Larry Brown with two out in the seventh inning and Rick Monday in the eighth. The gem was only Clark's second start of the season after being recalled from Salt Lake City in the Pacific Coast League. The lone run scored on a walk-off single in the ninth by Ken McMullen.

JULY 9   The Angels lose 1–0 in a 20-inning marathon in Oakland. Rudy May started and allowed only three hits in 12 innings and struck out 13. He pitched no-hit ball over his last seven innings on the mound and surrendered only one hit over the last ten frames. Eddie Fisher followed May and gave up only two hits in five innings from the 13th through the 17th. The lone run of the game scored on a two-out single in the 20th by Angel Mangual off Mel Queen, who pitched shutout ball in the 18th and 19th. Vida Blue started for the A's and struck out 17 batters in 11 innings. In all, the Angels struck out 26 times off four pitchers. There were 43 strikeouts combined by the two clubs. Billy Cowan tied a major league record by striking out six times while going 0-for-8. Tony Conigliaro was hitless in eight at-bats and fanned five times. He was ejected in the 19th inning for arguing after being called out on strikes on an attempted bunt. Conigliaro flipped his batting helmet high in the air, swung his bat at it and knocked it about 60 feet down the first-base line. It proved to be his last game with the Angels and his last in the majors until 1975.

JULY 10   Just hours after the 20-inning loss to the Athletics, Tony Conigliaro calls a press conference at 5:15 a.m. in the lobby of an Oakland hotel and announces his retirement. "I just can't see the ball," Conigliaro said. "I have no depth perception in the left eye. This is no sudden decision. I'm going home." Tests showed the functional ability of the eye had decreased in the previous 13 months. Manager Lefty Phillips was unsympathetic, stating that Conigliaro was "ready for the insane asylum." Phillips added that "apparently his lack of success has been bothering him. The easiest way out is to quit." Conigliaro later advised the Angels he wanted to be placed on the disabled list and paid for the remainder of the season. He filed a grievance and won the case.

> *Conigliaro tried a comeback with the Red Sox in 1975, but retired again after hitting .123 in 57 at-bats. He then went into television, working at stations in Providence, San Francisco and Boston. Tragedy continued to haunt Conigliaro when he suffered a massive heart attack at the age of 37 in 1982. He was in a coma for four months and needed around-the-clock care from nurses for the rest of his life, which ended in 1990.*

JULY 18   Ken McMullen hits a two-out, two-run, walk-off homer in the ninth inning to down the Indians 3–1 at Anaheim Stadium.

JULY 20   Tommie Reynolds hits a two-run double with two out in the eighth inning to account for both runs of a 2–0 win over the Tigers at Anaheim Stadium. Andy Messersmith pitched a three-hit shutout.

> *Without Johnson and Conigliaro, the Angels outfield was in flux during much of the season. Roger Repoz led Angels outfielders in starts with 82.*

AUGUST 1   After pitching six shutout innings of relief, Lloyd Allen gives up a home run in the 16th to Jim Northrup of the Tigers for a 4–3 loss at Anaheim Stadium.

AUGUST 6   Roger Repoz hits a two-run homer in the sixth inning to account for both runs of a 2–0 triumph over the Twins at Anaheim Stadium. Andy Messersmith twirled a three-hit shutout.

August 15	The Angels play the Senators in Washington for the last time and win 4–3 in ten innings.

After the season ended, the Senators moved to Arlington, Texas, midway between Dallas and Forth Worth and were renamed the Texas Rangers. With Washington no longer fielding a big-league club, Richard Nixon adopted the Angels as his hometown team. After his term as President ended with his resignation in 1974, Nixon moved to San Clemente and became an Angels season-ticket holder.

Andy Messersmith won 20 games in 1971 and proved to be a valuable pitcher for the Angels during his five years with the team.

August 24	Jim Spencer hits a two-run, walk-off homer in the ninth inning to beat the Senators 2–1 at Anaheim Stadium. The blast was only the third hit by the Angels off Pete Broberg. Clyde Wright pitched a two-hitter for California. The only Washington hits were singles by Tim Cullen in the fifth inning and Dave Nelson in the ninth.
August 27	Andy Messersmith ($7^{2}/_{3}$ innings) and Lloyd Allen ($1^{1}/_{3}$ innings) combine on a shutout to defeat the Red Sox 1–0 at Anaheim Stadium.
September 9	The Angels score twice in the ninth inning and one in the 13th to defeat the Brewers 3–2 at Anaheim Stadium. The two runs in the ninth crossed the plate on a triple by Mickey Rivers. The game ended on a home run by Billy Parker, who was making his major league debut. The homer was also his first hit. Parker started the game at second base.

Parker didn't hit another homer in the majors until September 10, 1972. He had only three home runs in 252 career at-bats over three seasons, all with the Angels.

SEPTEMBER 28   Andy Messersmith picks up his 20th win of the season with a 6–2 decision over the Twins in Minnesota.

Messersmith was 20–13 in 1971 with a 2.99 ERA in 276 2/3 innings. He started the season 10–11, then went 10–2 with a 1.64 ERA in a span of 54 days starting on August 6.

OCTOBER 5   The Angels trade Alex Johnson and Jerry Moses to the Indians for Vada Pinson, Frank Baker and Alex Foster.

Following his well-chronicled troubles during the 1971 season, Johnson played five more years in the majors with four clubs and posted on-base and slugging percentages near or below the league averages. Pinson hit over .300 four times for the Reds between 1959 and 1965, but he was 33 years old when acquired by the Angels, and his days as a productive, everyday player were over.

OCTOBER 7   The Angels fire Lefty Phillips as manager after a season in which the team was torn by dissension, with Alex Johnson at the center of the storm. He remained in the organization as a scout, but died on June 12, 1972 at the age of 52 following a bout with asthma.

OCTOBER 20   The Angels fire Dick Walsh as general manager. He never worked in baseball again. Walsh was the director of the Los Angeles Convention center from 1974 through 1998.

OCTOBER 27   The Angels hire 43-year-old Harry Dalton as executive vice president and general manager. Dalton was general manager of the Orioles from 1966 through 1971 and built a club that won four American League pennants in 1966, 1969, 1970 and 1971 and two world championships in 1966 and 1970. The titles were achieved in large part because of brilliant trades made by Dalton, which brought the likes of Frank Robinson, Don Buford and Mike Cuellar to Baltimore. Dalton wasn't able to come close to duplicating that kind of success in California, however. In six years at the helm, he guided the Angels to six losing seasons.

NOVEMBER 30   The angels trade Dave LaRoche to the Twins for Leo Cardenas.

Cardenas was named to five All-Star teams during his career, but was well past his prime and played only one season with the Angels. LaRoche came back to the club in another trade in 1977.

DECEMBER 7   The Angels hire 49-year-old Del Rice as manager. Rice had a 17-year playing career as a catcher. His last big season, in 1961, was spent with the Angels. He was a coach with the club from 1962 through 1966 and with the Indians in 1967. Rice spent four seasons as a manager in the California minor league system and in 1971 led Salt Lake City, the club's top farm club, to the Pacific Coast League title. Despite a clever nickname (the club was called Del's Angels), he lasted only one year as manager of the parent club, however, and was fired after a 75–80 record in 1972.

1970s

December 10 — The Angels trade Jim Fregosi to the Mets for Nolan Ryan, Leroy Stanton, Don Rose and Francisco Estrada.

At the time of the trade, Fregosi was only 29 and was the last of the original Angels acquired in the 1960 expansion draft. He suffered through a horrible season in 1971 after he developed a tumor in his foot that required surgery. Both the Angels and Mets gambled on Fregosi's future health. He was dealt for four prospects. In 1972, Fregosi was moved from shortstop to third base and hit .232 with five homers in 340 at-bats. He was never again a regular in the lineup before his playing career ended in 1978 with an appointment as manager of the Angels. Meantime, Ryan developed into one of the greatest pitchers in baseball history. When acquired by the Angels, he was just shy of his 25th birthday and had a 29–38 lifetime record and a 3.38 ERA over five seasons and had never developed any consistency, largely due to control problems. He struck out 493 batters in 510 innings, but also walked 344. In 1971, Ryan started the season 8–4, then lost ten of his next 12 decisions. Citing his troubles in New York, he said, "I was looking behind myself all the time and expecting something bad to happen, because it always had. Maybe there are just some people who can't deal with success." The Mets spent several years trying to unlock his considerable talent and finally gave up. Once in California, Ryan suddenly lived up to his awesome potential when given a regular spot in the rotation for the first time, making the trade one of the most lopsided ever. Over eight seasons with the club, he was 138–121, a winning percentage of .533 on a club that finished below .500 six times, and was named to five All-Star teams. He led the AL in strikeouts seven times, with a big-league record of 383 in 1973. It was one of five seasons in which Ryan fanned 329 batters or more. There were four games in which he fanned 19 batters. He also topped the circuit in lowest opponents' batting average five times, shutouts in three, and innings pitched and complete games once each. Overall, Ryan completed 156 of his 288 starts with the Angels, four of them no-hitters, and compiled 40 shutouts. He struck out 2,416 batters in 2,181$^1/_3$ innings and had a 3.07 ERA. Ryan won 21 games in 1973 and 22 in 1974 and had 19 victories in two others. Leroy Stanton also had a measure of success in Anaheim. He was the Angels starting right fielder for four years.

1972

Season in a Sentence
The arrival of Nolan Ryan fails to compensate for an offense that scores the fewest runs in the league for the third time in four years, and attendance drops to the lowest point since the move to Anaheim.

Finish • Won • Lost • Pct • GB
Fifth   75   80   .484   18.0

Manager
Del Rice

Stats

Stats	Angels	AL	Rank
Batting Avg:	.242	.239	5
On-Base Pct:	.291	.306	10
Slugging Pct:	.330	.343	9
Home Runs:	78		10
Stolen Bases:	57		9
ERA:	3.06	3.06	7
Errors:	114		3
Runs Scored:	454		12
Runs Allowed:	533		6

Starting Lineup
Art Kusyner, c
Bob Oliver, 1b
Sandy Alomar, 2b
Ken McMullen, 3b
Leo Cardenas, ss
Vada Pinson, lf
Ken Berry, cf
Leroy Stanton, rf
Jim Spencer, 1b-lf

Pitchers
Nolan Ryan, sp
Clyde Wright, sp
Rudy May, sp
Andy Messersmith, sp
Rickey Clark, sp
Lloyd Allen, rp
Eddie Fisher, rp

Attendance
744,190 (eighth in AL)

Club Leaders
Batting Avg:	Vada Pinson	.275
On-Base Pct:	Ken McMullen	.335
Slugging Pct:	Bob Oliver	.436
Home Runs:	Bob Oliver	19
RBI:	Bob Oliver	70
Runs:	Sandy Alomar	65
Stolen Bases:	Sandy Alomar	20
Wins:	Nolan Ryan	19
Strikeouts:	Nolan Ryan	329
ERA:	Nolan Ryan	2.28
Saves:	Lloyd Allen	6

FEBRUARY 9   Chico Ruiz, who played for the Angels in 1970 and 1971, dies in an auto accident near San Diego, California. He was traveling at 75 to 80 miles per hour when his car veered off US 395 at the Carmel Mountain exit north of the city and struck a signpost. Ruiz was released by the Angels at the end of the 1971 season and was signed as a free agent by the Royals. A native of Cuba, he had received his American citizenship just two weeks before his death.

APRIL 6   The Angels' scheduled season opener against the Twins in Minnesota is canceled by baseball's first players' strike. The Angels' first seven games were eliminated by the labor action, which began on April 1 and ended on April 13.

APRIL 15   The Angels win 1–0 over the Rangers in the strike-delayed opener before 13,916 at Anaheim Stadium. It was also the first game in the history of the Texas Rangers franchise. Andy Messersmith pitched a two-hitter, allowing only singles to Hal King leading off the seventh inning and Toby Harrah in the eighth. The lone run scored in the ninth. The Angels loaded the bases on two walks and an error before Sandy Alomar scored on a wild pitch by Dick Bosman.

The club had a problem drawing fans to the ballpark all year with the lingering effects of the strike and a disappointing year in 1971. The 1972 club got off to a bad start (11–21 on May 23) and had trouble scoring runs. The final attendance figure was 744,190, the second lowest in club history. The only year with a lower box office was 1965, when the Angels attracted 566,727 in their last season at Chavez Ravine.

APRIL 18 — Nolan Ryan pitches his first game for the Angels and hurls a shutout to win 2–0 over the Twins at Anaheim Stadium. He also had a hand in both runs by reaching on a force-out and scoring in the fifth inning and by driving in a run with a single in the sixth.

Ryan was 19–16 with a 2.28 ERA in 284 innings in 1972. He led the AL in shutouts (nine), strikeouts (329), lowest opponent's batting average (.171) and complete games (20 in 39 starts), walks (157) and wild pitches (18). At Anaheim Stadium, Ryan had a 13–8 record with a 1.07 earned run average and 220 strikeouts in 176$^{1}/_{3}$ innings.

APRIL 21 — The Angels participate in the first American League game ever played in the state of Texas and lose 7–6 to the Rangers at Arlington Stadium in Arlington.

APRIL 26 — Vada Pinson plays in his 2,000th career game and collects three hits, two of them doubles, during a 3–1 win over the Brewers in Milwaukee.

MAY 5 — Nolan Ryan strikes out 14 batters and pitches a three-hit shutout to defeat the Brewers 4–0 at Anaheim Stadium.

On the same day, the Angels traded Tom Murphy to the Royals for Bob Oliver.

MAY 6 — Andy Messersmith pitches a two-hitter to defeat the Brewers 2–0 at Anaheim Stadium. The only Milwaukee hits were a pair of singles by Rick Auerbach in the third and ninth innings. Vada Pinson scored both runs, one of them on a home run in the sixth inning.

Fire-baller Nolan Ryan dominated the American League during his eight years with the Angels in the 1970s. He led the league in strikeouts seven times, hurled four no-hitters, twice won 20 games and twice won 19.

MAY 7   Bob Oliver homers in his first game with the Angels, but the Brewers win 5–2 at Anaheim Stadium.

MAY 16   The Angels sign Steve Barber as a free agent following his release by the Braves.

MAY 24   In his second major league game and first with the Angels, starting pitcher Don Rose homers on the first pitch thrown to him and is the winning pitcher in a 6–5 decision over the Athletics in Oakland. The homer was struck off Diego Segui.

> *Rose never hit another home run or won another game during his brief big-league career. He made his major league debut with the Mets on September 15, 1971 and came to the Angels in the same trade that brought Nolan Ryan to the club. Rose finished his career with a 1–4 record and a 4.14 ERA in 19 games, four of them starts. He had ten career at-bats.*

JUNE 6   In the first round of the amateur draft, the Angels select shortstop Dave Chalk from the University of Texas.

> *Chalk was the Angels' starting shortstop from 1974 through 1978 and was named to two All-Star teams. Other future major leaguers drafted and signed by the Angels in 1972 included Bruce Bochte (second round), Dave Machemer (fourth round), Dave Collins (first round of the secondary phase in June) and Tom Donohue (first round of the secondary phase in January).*

JUNE 10   The Angels trade Roger Repoz to the Orioles for Jerry Davanon.

JUNE 17   On the day of the break-in of Democratic Party National Committee headquarters at the Watergate complex in Washington, Rudy May strikes out 12 batters in seven innings, but the Angels lose 3–2 to the Tigers at Anaheim Stadium.

JUNE 23   Nolan Ryan pitches a two-hitter to beat the Athletics 2–1 in Oakland. The only hits off Ryan were a home run by Reggie Jackson in the first inning and a single from Dave Duncan in the seventh.

JUNE 27   The Angels pull off a triple play in the fourth inning of a 3–1 victory over the Twins in Minnesota. With Harmon Killebrew the base runner on third base and Steve Braun on second, Jim Nettles hit a fly ball to Jim Spencer in left field. Killebrew faked toward home, and Spencer fired the ball to Ken McMullen at third base. McMullen spotted Braun off the bag at second and threw to second baseman Sandy Alomar for the second out. Alomar threw to shortstop Leo Cardenas, who tagged Killebrew standing off the base. Spencer started the triple play in only his third career game as an outfielder.

JULY 1   Nolan Ryan strikes out 16 batters during a 5–3 triumph over the Athletics at Anaheim Stadium. Ryan fanned seven batters in the first three innings.

JULY 5   Winston Llenas delivers a two-out, pinch-hit, walk-off single in the ninth inning to beat the Brewers 1–0 at Anaheim Stadium. Llenas was batting for Nolan Ryan, who pitched the complete game shutout.

July 8	The Angels outlast the Red Sox 4–3 in 16 innings at Anaheim Stadium. California scored three runs in the sixth inning to tie the score 3–3. Lloyd Allen, Rickey Clark, Eddie Fisher and Steve Barber combined to shut out Boston over the final 14 innings. Sandy Alomar drove in the winning run with a two-out single.
July 9	Nolan Ryan strikes out 16 batters, walks only one, and surrenders just one hit to defeat the Red Sox 3–0 at Anaheim Stadium. After walking lead-off batter Tommy Harper and giving up a one-out single to Carl Yastrzemski in the first, Ryan closed out the inning by striking out Reggie Smith and Rico Petrocelli. In the second, Ryan fanned Carlton Fisk, Bob Burda and Juan Beniquez on the minimum nine pitches. He proceeded to set down Sonny Siebert, Tommy Harper and Doug Griffin in the third to run his streak to eight consecutive strikeouts. It was only the beginning. Ryan retired the last 26 batters to face him.
July 16	Nolan Ryan pitches a two-hitter to down the Brewers 1–0 in the first game of a double-header at County Stadium. The only Milwaukee hits were singles by ex-Angel Tommie Reynolds in the fourth and seventh innings. The Angels collected only three hits off Jim Colborn. The lone run scored in the third inning on a sacrifice fly by Vada Pinson. The Brewers won the second tilt 2–1.

> *The Angels scored only eight runs in eight games from July 16 through July 22. California finished last in the AL in runs in 1969, 1971 and 1972. Lack of patience at the plate was a contributing factor. The club finished last in drawing walks four consecutive seasons from 1969 through 1972.*

July 22	Steve Barber (seven innings) and Eddie Fisher (two innings) combined to defeat the Yankees 1–0 in the first game of a double-header in New York. Pinch hitter Andy Kosco drove in the lone run with a sacrifice fly in the eighth inning. The Yanks won the second contest 7–1.
July 27	Nolan Ryan strikes out 14 batters and pitches a two-hitter to defeat the Rangers 5–0 at Anaheim Stadium. Ryan fanned 11 batters in the first five innings. He had a no-hitter in progress until Larry Biittner doubled with two out in the eighth. Jim Mason singled with two out in the ninth.
July 28	The Angels trade Syd O'Brien and Joe Azcue to the Brewers for Paul Ratliff and Ron Clark.
July 30	Bob Oliver hits a walk-off homer leading off the 11th inning to beat the Royals 4–3 at Anaheim Stadium.
July 31	Nolan Ryan commits three errors in a 1–0 loss to the Royals at Anaheim Stadium. In the first inning, Ryan made his first error by throwing past first base on a pick-off attempt of Amos Otis. In the fourth, Ryan walked Otis, then threw wildly again to first on a pick-off attempt. Otis reached third on the play, then stole home for the lone run of the game. In the fifth, Ryan made his third error on yet another attempted pick off at first base, this time with Freddie Patek on the bag. Ryan had a no-hitter in progress until Steve Hovley led off the eighth with a single. It was the only hit that Ryan surrendered in eight innings of work.

AUGUST 4	Vada Pinson collects five singles in six at-bats during a ten-inning, 6–5 win over the Royals in Kansas City. His fifth hit drove in the winning run.
AUGUST 10	Rudy May strikes out 16 batters and pitches a four-hitter to beat the Twins 3–1 at Anaheim Stadium.
AUGUST 17	Leroy Stanton collects four hits, including two homers, in four at-bats during a 4–2 victory over the Indians in Cleveland.
	On the same day, the Angels traded Eddie Fisher to the White Sox for Bruce Kimm and Bruce Miller.
AUGUST 20	The Angels lose a tough 11–9 decision to the Tigers in Detroit. Trailing 2–0, the Angels erupted for nine runs in the fourth inning. Vada Pinson led off the frame with a home run. The other eight hits in the inning were all singles, two of them by Sandy Alomar. But the Tigers scored eight times in the sixth to take a 10–9 lead and added an insurance run in the seventh.
	The Angels were held scoreless for 11 straight innings over two games before the nine-run eruption and for eight consecutive innings over two contests afterward.
AUGUST 22	Bob Oliver has a hand in both runs of a 2–0 triumph over the Orioles in Baltimore. Oliver contributed a sacrifice fly in the third inning and doubled and scored in the seventh. Nolan Ryan pitched the shutout and struck out 11.
AUGUST 27	Nolan Ryan pitches a 12-inning complete game to defeat the Indians 1–0 at Anaheim Stadium. The lone run scored on a sacrifice fly by pinch hitter Winston Llenas, who was batting for Ryan. It was the second time in 1972 that Llenas saved a shutout for Ryan with a walk-off RBI as a pinch hitter. The other one was on July 5.
SEPTEMBER 2	A two-run homer by Bob Oliver off Jim Palmer in the first inning holds up for a 2–0 win over the Orioles at Anaheim Stadium. Rudy May pitched a three-hit shutout.
SEPTEMBER 5	Andy Messersmith pitches a ten-inning, complete game to beat the Orioles 1–0 at Anaheim Stadium. The lone run scored on a walk-off single by Ken Berry.
	The Angels allowed only eight runs in 87 innings over nine games from August 27 through September 3.
SEPTEMBER 7	The Angels play at Municipal Stadium in Kansas City for the last time and lose 6–0 to the Royals.
SEPTEMBER 8	Clyde Wright homers during a 9–4 win over the White Sox in the second game of a double-header at Comiskey Park. It was the last home run by an Angels pitcher before the passage of the designated hitter rule. Chicago won the opener 5–1.
	Wright was 18–11 with a 2.98 ERA in 1972.
SEPTEMBER 12	Nolan Ryan strikes out 15 batters, but loses 3–0 to the Rangers at Anaheim Stadium. The only hit by the Angels off Texas pitcher Bill Gogolewski was a double by Billy Parker with two out in the eighth inning.

SEPTEMBER 14	Clyde Wright pitches a two-hitter to beat the Rangers 4–0 at Anaheim Stadium. The only Texas hits were singles by Joe Lovitto in the sixth inning and Ted Ford in the ninth.
SEPTEMBER 15	Rudy May pitches an 11-inning shutout to beat the White Sox 1–0 at Anaheim Stadium. The lone run scored on a two-out, walk-off single from Leo Cardenas.
SEPTEMBER 29	The Angels collect only two hits, both in the second inning, but beat the Twins 2–1 at Anaheim Stadium. The pair of California runs scored in the second off Jim Perry on a single by Leroy Stanton, a walk and a two-out triple by Jack Hiatt.
SEPTEMBER 30	Nolan Ryan strikes out 17 batters during a 3–2 victory over the Twins at Anaheim Stadium. Ryan allowed two Minnesota runs in the ninth inning and ended the game by striking out Rick Renick with runners on second and third.

The Angels won six in a row from September 24 through September 30 despite scoring only 14 runs. The pitching staff allowed only seven tallies and the Angels won five times by one run.

OCTOBER 4	On the last day of the season, Nolan Ryan fails in his attempt to win his 20th game of the season by dropping a 2–1 decision to the Athletics at Anaheim Stadium.
OCTOBER 11	The Angels fire Del Rice as manager and replace him with 42-year-old Bobby Winkles.

Winkles never played in the majors. After six seasons in the Chicago White Sox system from 1954 through 1959, he became the coach at Arizona State University. When he arrived, the school had just started playing at the varsity level, but he quickly built the program and won NCAA championships in 1965, 1967 and 1969 with players like Reggie Jackson, Rick Monday, Sal Bando and Larry Gura. Winkles was the first manager whose only previous managerial experience was in college since Hugo Bezdek in 1917. Winkles became a coach with the Angels in 1972 and took a $10,000 cut in salary from what he was receiving at Arizona State for a shot at the majors. He was hired in part because of his college experience. It was believed that Winkles could bridge the generation gap and help bring order to the chaotic Angels clubhouse. He bucked the changing times, however, by instituting strict hair and dress codes. Winkles also added yoga relaxation exercises to the Angels training routine. In addition, he was the first manager in major league baseball to require his players to stretch their muscles before workouts. None of the innovations translated to winning games, however. As manager of the club, Winkles was 109–127 before being fired in July 1974. Rice never managed another big-league club.

NOVEMBER 28	Three weeks after Richard Nixon wins reelection by defeating George McGovern in the presidential election, the Angels trade Andy Messersmith and Ken McMullen to the Dodgers for Frank Robinson, Bill Singer, Billy Grabarkewitz, Mike Strahler and Bobby Valentine.

Both teams gained some short-term benefit from the trade. Messersmith was 8–11 for the Angels in 1972 after winning 20 games in 1971. In three seasons with the Dodgers, Messersmith was 53–30, including a 20–6 mark in leading the club to the World Series in 1974. At the end of the 1975 season, Messersmith *was declared a free agent by arbitrator Pete Seitz in an historic decision that led to free agency for all players with at least six years in the majors. Messersmith signed with the Braves, but, largely due to a heavy workload inflicted on him by the Dodgers (614 regular season innings in 1974 and 1975), he was ineffective in Atlanta. General manager Harry Dalton traded for Robinson in December 1965 when Dalton headed the Orioles organization, and Robinson played in four World Series in Baltimore. Robinson came to the Angels as a 37-year-old with 522 career home runs and had the worst season of his career in 1972, his only year as a Dodger. He gave the Angels two excellent seasons as a designated hitter and, like Messersmith, was destined to make history. The Angels traded Robinson to the Indians in September 1974, and a few weeks later, Cleveland made him major league baseball's first African-American manager. Singer won 20 games for the Angels in 1973, but pitched $315^{2}/_{3}$ innings and declined sharply afterward. Grabarkewitz came to the Angels with a history of injuries and hit only .163 in 61 games. Valentine was only 22 and was considered to be one of the most talented young players in the game, but he too was injury-prone. On May 17, 1973, Valentine broke his leg crashing into the wall at Anaheim Stadium and was never fully recovered.*

DECEMBER 10 The American League votes to adopt the designated hitter rule on a three-year experimental basis. Under the new rule, the designated hitter replaced the pitcher in the batting order unless otherwise noted before the game. The rule was adopted permanently by the AL in 1975, but to this day, the NL has declined to go along with the change.

1973

Season in a Sentence

Nolan Ryan wins 21 games, strikes out 383 batters and pitches two no-hitters; Bill Singer is a 20-game winner; and Frank Robinson clouts 30 homers—but the Angels finish with a losing record again.

Finish • Won • Lost • Pct • GB

Fourth   79   83   .488   15.0

Manager

Bobby Winkles

Stats

Stats	Angels	AL	Rank
Batting Avg:	.253	.259	11
On-Base Pct:	.317	.328	9
Slugging Pct:	.348	.381	12
Home Runs:	93		12
Stolen Bases:	59		10
ERA:	3.53	3.82	4
Errors:	156		9 (tie)
Runs Scored:	629		11
Runs Allowed:	657		5

Starting Lineup

Jeff Torborg, c
Mike Epstein, 1b
Sandy Alomar, 2b
Al Gallagher, 3b
Rudy Meoli, ss
Vada Pinson, lf
Ken Berry, cf
Al Oliver, rf-3b-1b
Frank Robinson, dh
Leroy Stanton, rf
Tom McCraw, 1b
Richie Scheinblum, rf

Pitchers

Nolan Ryan, sp
Bill Singer, sp
Clyde Wright, sp
Rudy May, sp
Dave Sells, rp
Steve Barber, rp

Attendance

1,058,206 (seventh in AL)

Club Leaders

Batting Avg:	Frank Robinson	.266
On-Base Pct:	Frank Robinson	.372
Slugging Pct:	Frank Robinson	.489
Home Runs:	Frank Robinson	30
RBI:	Frank Robinson	97
Runs:	Frank Robinson	85
Stolen Bases:	Sandy Alomar	25
Wins:	Nolan Ryan	21
Strikeouts:	Nolan Ryan	383
ERA:	Nolan Ryan	2.87
Saves:	Dave Sells	10

MARCH 24   The Angels brawl with the Giants during a 14–4 exhibition game defeat in Palm Springs. The day before, during a 6–1 loss to San Francisco, Nolan Ryan hit Willie McCovey in the back with a pitch. McCovey moved threateningly toward Ryan and both benches emptied but order was quickly restored. In the fourth inning of the March 24 contest, Tito Fuentes of the Giants was struck by a pitch from Clyde Wright and the two tangled. Wright wound up with a three-inch cut on his forehead. Moments later, another fight broke out between Angels catcher Jack Hiatt and Giants manager Charlie Fox. In yet another battle, San Francisco's Dave Kingman had California coach Johnny Roseboro in a chokehold before coach Tom Morgan pried Kingman loose. The intervention of the police were necessary to help quell the disturbance.

Frank Robinson missed ten days of action during spring training after he broke a toe climbing out of the press box.

APRIL 2   The Angels trade Leo Cardenas to the Indians for Tommy McCraw and Bob Marcano.

APRIL 6	The Angels open the season by defeating the Royals 3–2 before 27,240 at Anaheim Stadium. President Richard Nixon threw out the ceremonial first pitch along with Major David Luna, who was a prisoner of the North Vietnamese for six years. Luna pitched for Orange High School, located less than three miles from Anaheim Stadium. Eighteen other former prisoners of war were also in attendance. Frank Robinson, in his first plate appearance with the Angels, homered in the second inning. Bobby Valentine, also in his first game with the club, tripled in a run in the third inning and scored on a single. Nolan Ryan pitched seven shutout innings before allowing two tallies in the eighth. He struck out 12 batters. It was also the first Angels regular season game in which the designated hitter was used. Tom McCraw was the California DH and batted fifth in the order. McCraw moved to left field defensively in the ninth inning.

On the same day, the Angels signed Ron Perranoski as a free agent.

APRIL 10	In his first game with the Angels, Bill Singer strikes out ten batters and beats the Twins 4–2 at Anaheim Stadium.

Don Drysdale replaced Don Wells on the Angels broadcasts in 1973. A future Hall of Famer, Drysdale pitched for the Dodgers from 1956 through 1969. He announced Angels games until 1981. Wells had been with the club since its inception in 1961. He continued to do sports and general news for KFWB radio in Los Angeles until retiring in 1988, when he moved to Switzerland. Wells died there in 2002.

APRIL 14	The Angels trade Bruce Miller to the Giants for Al Gallagher.

Gallagher's full name was Alvin Mitchell Edward George Patrick Henry Gallagher. He was nicknamed "Dirty Al" because his uniform always seemed to be caked with dirt.

APRIL 18	Nolan Ryan strikes out 14 batters and defeats the Twins 3–2 in Minnesota.
APRIL 24	Trailing 5–0, the Angels score four runs in the sixth inning, one in the ninth, and one in the tenth to defeat the Orioles 6–5 at Anaheim Stadium. Frank Robinson hit a three-run homer in the sixth in his first game against the Orioles since they traded him in 1971. Jim Spencer drove in the winning run with a single.
APRIL 25	Bill Singer pitches the Angels to a 1–0 win over the Orioles at Anaheim Stadium. Bobby Valentine drove in the run with a single off Dave McNally in the eighth inning.
MAY 2	Nolan Ryan throws 205 pitches during a 12-inning, 5–3 win over the Tigers in Detroit.
MAY 4	Rudy May pitches a two-hitter to defeat the Orioles 1–0 at Memorial Stadium. The only Baltimore hits were a single by Brooks Robinson in the second inning and a double from Bobby Grich in the ninth. The lone run scored on back-to-back doubles by Frank Robinson and Bob Oliver off Dave McNally in the seventh inning. It was McNally's second 1–0 loss to California in a span of ten days.

Robinson was by far the Angels best hitter in 1973. He batted .266 with 30 home runs and 97 RBIs. Robinson played in 127 games as a designated hitter and 17 in the outfield.

MAY 5 — For the second day in a row, an Angels pitcher throws a two-hitter to beat the Orioles at Memorial Stadium. This time it was Bill Singer in a 3–1 victory. Both Baltimore hits were triples by Al Bumbry leading off the first inning and Rich Coggins in the fourth.

MAY 14 — The Angels play at Royals Stadium in Kansas City for the first time and win 3–2 in ten innings.

MAY 15 — Nolan Ryan pitches the first of his seven career no-hitters, beating the Royals 3–0 in Kansas City. He walked three and struck out 12. In his previous start, on May 11, Ryan allowed five runs in one-third of an inning in a 7–4 loss to the White Sox at Anaheim Stadium. Shortstop Rudy Meoli helped preserve the no-hitter by catching a pop fly by Gail Hopkins in short left field with his back to the plate. In the ninth, Ryan set down Freddie Patek on a foul fly to first baseman Jim Spencer, struck out Steve Hovley and induced Amos Otis to hit a fly ball to right fielder Bob Oliver. Oliver also hit a two-run homer in the first inning.

Sandy Alomar was the second baseman in both of Ryan's no-hitters in 1973. Sandy's son Roberto made the last out in Ryan's seventh no-hitter in 1991 when Roberto played for the Blue Jays and Ryan for the Rangers.

MAY 17 — Bobby Valentine breaks his leg by running into the center-field wall at Anaheim Stadium while chasing a home run drive by Dick Green in the second inning of a 3–0 loss to the Athletics. Leaping for the ball, Valentine caught his spikes in the wall as he descended. The leg was broken in two places.

The injury occurred four days after Valentine's 23rd birthday, and he was carrying a .302 batting average in 32 games. Valentine didn't play again in 1973. The accident left his leg misshapen, and he was never again the same player. Over the remainder of his career, which ended in 1979, Valentine batted .251 with seven home runs in 900 at-bats.

MAY 19 — Nolan Ryan strikes out 12 batters and beats the Rangers 9–1 at Anaheim Stadium.

MAY 20 — The Angels trade Jim Spencer and Lloyd Allen to the Rangers for Mike Epstein, Rich Hand and Rick Stelmaszek.

MAY 22 — Sandy Alomar's playing streak of 648 games comes to an end when he misses a 6–2 loss to the White Sox in Chicago. It was the first time that Alomar had failed to play since joining the Angels on May 14, 1969.

MAY 24 — Nolan Ryan strikes out 13 batters, but loses 4–1 to the White Sox in Chicago.

MAY 31 — Trailing 5–0, the Angels score three runs in the fifth inning and four in the eighth to defeat the Red Sox 7–6 in Boston. Still down 6–3 in the eighth, Frank Robinson drove in a run with a single, and Bob Oliver followed with a three-run homer.

June 5	In the first round of the amateur draft, the Angels select outfielder Billy Taylor from Windsor Forest High School in Savannah, Georgia.
	Taylor never advanced past the Class A level. In what has been the worst draft in franchise history, the only future big leaguers chosen and signed by the Angels in 1973 were Pat Kelly (third round) and Mike Overy (second round of the secondary phase in January). Kelly and Overy combined to play in only eight games in the majors.
June 9	Rudy May pitches a two-hitter, but loses 1–0 to the Brewers at Anaheim Stadium. May had a no-hitter in progress until Ollie Brown homered in the fifth inning.
June 16	Richie Scheinblum homers in his first game with the Angels, a 5–2 victory over the Yankees at Anaheim Stadium. He was acquired in a trade with the Reds the previous day.
	Scheinblum hit .328 in 77 games for the Angels in 1973, but played fly balls like they were hand grenades. His horrible defense play prompted a trade to the Royals the following season.
June 19	A three-run pinch-hit home run by Winston Llenas off Wilbur Wood in the seventh inning provides all of the Angels runs in a 3–1 win over the White Sox in Chicago.
	Actor Kurt Russell played six games for the Angels Class AA affiliate in El Paso in 1973. He had nine hits in 16 at-bats when hit in the shoulder by an opposing player in a play at second base. The collision tore Russell's rotator cuff and ended his baseball career.
June 22	The Angels use five singles and a sacrifice bunt to score three runs in the ninth inning and beat the Twins 4–3 in Minnesota. Sandy Alomar drove in the go-ahead tally.
June 23	Mike Epstein hits a two-run homer in the 11th inning to beat the Twins in Minnesota.
	Epstein was a social psychology major at the University of California at Berkeley and called himself "Super Jew." He wasn't so super with the Angels, however, batting .206 with 12 homers in 374 at-bats in 1973 and 1974.
June 24	The Angels score three runs in the ninth inning to defeat the Twins 3–0 in Minnesota. The three runs crossed the plate after the first two batters were retired. Winston Llenas broke the 0–0 deadlock with a two-run pinch-single. Clyde Wright ($8^{2}/_{3}$ innings) and Steve Barber (one-third of an inning) combined on the shutout.
June 26	Trailing 5–0, the Angels score four times in the eighth inning and twice in the ninth to defeat the Royals 6–5 at Anaheim Stadium. Frank Robinson hit a three-run homer in the eighth. Ken Berry and Al Gallagher contributed RBI-singles in the ninth.
	The win put the Angels into first place, but the club remained there for only two days. After holding a 39–32 record on June 27, the Angels went 25–43 from July 28 through September 6. The fast start and Nolan Ryan's superlative season did help boost attendance from 744,190 in 1972 to 1,058,206.

1970s

JULY 1	A home run by Frank Robinson off Jim Kaat in the second inning is the only Angels hit in a 2–1 loss to the Twins at Anaheim Stadium.
	Robinson and Vada Pinson both attended McClymonds High School in Oakland. They were also teammates with the Reds from 1958 through 1965.
JULY 6	Trailing 7–1, the Angels stage an incredible six-run rally in the ninth inning only to lose 8–7 in 11 innings to the Indians in Cleveland. All seven California hits in the ninth were singles, and four runs scored after two were out. Leroy Stanton tied the score with a two-run single.
	On the same day, the Angels traded Don Rose and Bruce Christensen to the Giants for Ed Figueroa.
JULY 8	Richie Scheinblum hits a two-run homer in the 11th inning to beat the Indians 5–3 in the second game of a double-header in Cleveland. The Angels also won the opener 10–4.
	Bill Singer was the winning pitcher in the first game. At the 81-game mark, he was 14–4 with a 2.44 ERA in 177 innings. Over the remainder of the year, he was 6–10 with an earned run average of 4.22 to finish at 20–14 with 241 strikeouts. The 315²/₃-inning workload was too much, however. Singer was 7–4 in 108²/₃ innings in 1974, before back surgery in June, and compiled a 7–15 record in 1975.
JULY 10	Leroy Stanton belts three homers, drives in five runs and scores four during an exciting ten-inning, 10–8 triumph over the Orioles at Memorial Stadium. The first homer was struck with no one on base off Jim Palmer in the fourth inning. After singling in the seventh, Stanton hit a two-run homer off Palmer in the ninth. The Angels added two more runs to take an 8–3 lead, but Baltimore put together a five-run rally before a batter was retired in their half to force extra innings. Given another opportunity, Stanton hit a two-run homer off Eddie Watt in the tenth.
	Stanton came into the contest with one homer during the season, and that one was struck on April 20. The three-home run explosion came after 106 homerless at-bats. Stanton finished the year with eight home runs in 306 at-bats.
JULY 15	Nolan Ryan pitches a no-hitter and strikes out 17 batters to beat the Tigers 6–0 in Detroit. He walked four. The pitching performance came two months to the day after he no-hit the Royals in Kansas City. Ryan struck out seven of the first ten batters he faced. Through seven innings, he had struck out 16 Tigers. The major league record at the time was 19. Ryan added a 17th strikeout in the eighth, but fanned no one in the ninth, although he set the side down in order. Shortstop Rudy Meoli handled all three chances in the ninth on a ground out by Mickey Stanley, a soft line drive from Gates Brown, and Norm Cash's popfly. Expressing the futility of the Detroit hitters, Cash went to the plate carrying a table leg from the clubhouse. After Cash took one pitch holding the table leg, umpire Ron Luciano ordered him to get a regulation bat.
JULY 19	In his first start since his no-hitter, Nolan Ryan holds the Orioles without a hit until the eighth inning, but winds up losing 3–1 in 11 innings at Anaheim Stadium.

With one out in the eighth, the no-hitter was broken up by Mark Belanger on a looping short fly to center that just barely fell out of the reach of a charging Ken Berry. It was the only Orioles hit through the first nine innings. Baltimore scored in the first without a hit. Ryan gave up one more base hit in the tenth and another in the 11th before giving way to reliever Dave Sells. Ryan struck out 13 batters in 10 1/3 innings. Mike Cuellar pitched a complete game for the Orioles and fanned 12.

July 28 — The Angels score 18 runs through the first five innings and clobber the Royals 19–8 in Kansas City. There were 21 California hits in the contest. Frank Robinson homered twice and drove in five runs.

August 3 — Bill Singer pitches 11 innings, allows only three hits and strikes out 13, but loses 2–1 to the Athletics at Anaheim Stadium. Singer had a no-hitter in progress until Gene Tenace doubled leading off the eighth. Singer lost the game in the 11th on doubles by Mike Hegan and Bert Campaneris. The two-bagger by Campaneris was a bloop hit that fell in shallow center with two out.

August 7 — Nolan Ryan strikes out 13 batters in nine innings, including eight in a row, and the Angels overcome a 5–1 deficit to defeat the Brewers 6–5 in Milwaukee. From the second though the fifth, Ryan fanned George Scott, John Felske, Ellie Rodriguez, Tim Johnson, Pedro Garcia, John Vukovich, Johnny Briggs and Bob Coluccio in succession. Bob Oliver drove in the winning run with a sacrifice fly.

August 11 — Nolan Ryan strikes out 12 batters in eight innings, but loses 2–1 to the Red Sox in Boston.

August 17 — Nolan Ryan strikes out 13 batters during a 10–2 win over the Tigers at Anaheim Stadium.

August 22 — The Angels take a thrilling ten-inning, 5–4 win over the Brewers at Anaheim Stadium. Frank Robinson tied the game with a two-out double in the ninth. The game-winner was Leroy Stanton's walk-off home run.

August 26 — Bill Singer outduels Luis Tiant to beat the Red Sox 1–0 at Anaheim Stadium. The lone run scored on Leroy Stanton's single in the second inning.

August 29 — Nolan Ryan pitches a one-hitter to defeat the Yankees 5–0 at Anaheim Stadium. The only New York hit was a single by Thurman Munson with one out in the first inning on a short fly to right field, which should have been caught. Second baseman Sandy Alomar and shortstop Rudy Meoli were indecisive about who was going to catch the ball, which fell safely.

September 3 — Nolan Ryan strikes out 12 batters and allows only three hits during a 3–1 win over the Athletics at Anaheim Stadium.

September 11 — Nolan Ryan strikes out 12 batters during a 3–1 victory over the White Sox at Anaheim Stadium.

September 17 — Rudy May pitches a 12 2/3-inning complete game and walks 11 while striking out eight. The Angels lost 3–2 when May walked four, one intentionally, and threw a wild pitch in the 13th.

1970s

SEPTEMBER 23 — Nolan Ryan gives up seven runs and 13 hits, but strikes out 12 and beats the Twins 15–7 in Minnesota. It was his 20th win of the season.

SEPTEMBER 24 — The Angels take an exciting 10–9 win over the Rangers at Anaheim Stadium. California led 6–2 heading into the ninth before Texas scored seven runs to pull ahead 9–6. The Angels countered with four tallies in the bottom of the ninth. The first two in the inning were retired before six in a row reached base. Richie Scheinblum and Charlie Sands drew bases-loaded walks, and Leroy Stanton delivered a two-run, walk-off double.

SEPTEMBER 26 — A walk-off single by Bob Oliver in the ninth defeats the Rangers 5–4 at Anaheim Stadium.

SEPTEMBER 27 — At Anaheim Stadium, Nolan Ryan strikes out 16 batters in 11 innings to break the all-time single-season strikeout record of 382, set by Sandy Koufax with the Dodgers in 1965. In his last start of the season, Ryan entered the contest against the Twins with 367 strikeouts. In the eighth inning, Ryan struck out his 15th batter of the game to tie Koufax. At the same time, the Angels ace suffered a muscle tear in his right thigh. Trainer Freddie Frederico and team physician Dr. Jules Rasinski worked on the leg between innings. Unable to push off the mound because of the injury, Ryan lost his fastball. He failed to strike out a batter in the ninth or tenth. With two out in the 11th, Ryan fanned Rich Reese on three consecutive pitches to pass Koufax with his 383rd strikeout of the year. The Angels won with a walk-off hit for the second game in a row, this time on a double by Richie Scheinblum in the 11th inning to beat the Twins 5–4.

Ryan finished the year with a 21–16 record and a 3.26 record in 326 innings. He completed 26 of his 39 starts, threw four shutouts, and walked 167 batters.

SEPTEMBER 29 — Bill Singer records his 20th win of the season with an 11-inning, 4–3 decision over the Twins at Anaheim Stadium. Winston Llenas drove in the winning run with a two-out, walk-off single.

The Angels had two 20-game winners in 1973 despite a losing record. Ryan and Singer were 41–30. The rest of the staff had a record of 38–53.

SEPTEMBER 30 — On the final day of the season, Frank Tanana pitches a two-hitter to defeat the Twins 3–0 at Anaheim Stadium. It was only the fourth game of Tanana's big-league career. The Minnesota hits were singles by Eric Soderholm in the first inning and Steve Brye in the third.

OCTOBER 22 — Two weeks after Vice President Spiro Agnew resigns due to financial improprieties, the Angels send Clyde Wright, Steve Barber, Ken Berry, Art Kusyner and cash to the Brewers for Ellie Rodriguez, Skip Lockwood, Joe Lahoud, Gary Ryerson and Ollie Brown.

The ten-player trade had little effect on the success of either the Angels or Brewers. Both had losing records for each of the next four seasons. Rodriguez was the best player acquired by the Angels. He was the club's starting catcher for two years.

DECEMBER 5   The Angels trade Andy Hassler and Bruce Heinbechner to the Cubs for Ron Santo.

> *Santo refused to go to the Angels, invoking a new rule that stipulated that a player with at least ten years of service in the majors and five with one club could reject a trade. Santo was the first player to use the regulation. He was dealt to the White Sox two days later.*

1974

Season in a Sentence

A change in managers from Bobby Winkles to Dick Williams and a reshuffling of the roster fails to improve the club and leads to the worst record in the American League.

Finish • Won • Lost • Pct • GB

Sixth   68   94   .420   22.0

Managers

Bobby Winkles (30–44), Whitey Herzog (2–2) and Dick Williams (36–48).

Stats   Angels • AL • Rank

Batting Avg:	.254	.258	9
On-Base Pct:	.318	.323	9
Slugging Pct:	.356	.371	12
Home Runs:	95		11
Stolen Bases:	119		4
ERA:	3.52	3.62	5
Errors:	147		7 (tie)
Runs Scored:	618		12
Runs Allowed:	657		4

Starting Lineup

Ellie Rodriguez, c
Bob Oliver, 1b-3b
Denny Doyle, 2b
Paul Schaal, 3b
Dave Chalk, ss
Bobby Valentine, lf
Mickey Rivers, cf
Leroy Stanton, rf
Frank Robinson, dh
Joe Lahoud, lf-rf
John Doherty, 1b

Pitchers

Nolan Ryan, sp
Frank Tanana, sp
Andy Hassler, sp
Bill Singer, sp
Dick Lange, sp
Skip Lockwood, rp
Ed Figueroa, rp-sp

Attendance

917,269 (10th in AL)

Club Leaders

Batting Avg:	Mickey Rivers	.285
On-Base Pct:	Ellie Rodriguez	.373
Slugging Pct:	Frank Robinson	.461
Home Runs:	Frank Robinson	20
RBI:	Frank Robinson	63
Runs:	Frank Robinson	75
Stolen Bases:	Mickey Rivers	30
Wins:	Nolan Ryan	22
Strikeouts:	Nolan Ryan	367
ERA:	Andy Hassler	2.61
Saves:	Orlando Pena	3

FEBRUARY 23   Two weeks following the kidnapping of Patty Hearst, the Angels trade Vada Pinson to the Royals for Barry Raziano and cash.

MARCH 10   Bruce Heinbechner, a pitcher on the 40-man spring training roster, dies in an auto accident near Palm Springs, California. Driving alone in his 1966 red Porsche, Heinbechner crashed head-on into another vehicle driven by a 21-year-old woman, who was seriously injured. Heinbechner apparently crossed the center line. He was returning to the Angels' hotel, which was about a mile way.

MARCH 28	The Angels sell Ollie Brown to the Brewers.
APRIL 4	The Angels purchase Bill Stoneman from the Expos.
APRIL 5	The Angels open the season with an 8–2 win over the White Sox in Chicago. Bob Oliver collected four hits and Leroy Stanton homered and drove in three runs. Nolan Ryan walked ten batters, but allowed only two runs and four hits in eight innings.

The game-time temperature was 37 degrees. The streaking craze was at it's height, and several fans took a nude romp through the Comiskey Park stands.

APRIL 9	The day after Hank Aaron passes Babe Ruth with his 715th career home run, the Rangers score nine runs in the second inning, seven of them off Nolan Ryan, and beat the Angels 10–2 in the home opener at Anaheim Stadium before 25,241.
APRIL 12	The Angels romp to a 15–1 win over the White Sox at Anaheim Stadium.

The Angels had a 7–2 record on April 15, then lost 54 of their next 79 games.

APRIL 29	Tommy McCraw collects four extra base hits during a 7–2 win over the Red Sox in Boston. All four hits came off the pitches of Luis Tiant on a home run in the second inning, doubles in the fourth and sixth and another homer in the eighth.
APRIL 30	Nolan Ryan strikes out 15 batters during a 16–6 victory over the Red Sox in Boston. Denny Doyle collected five singles in six at-bats.

On the same day, the Angels traded Richie Scheinblum to the Royals for Paul Schaal, who had played previously for the Angels from 1964 through 1968. The Angels had problems at third base throughout the 1974 season. Schaal was the team leader in games started at the position with 44.

MAY 3	The Angels beat the Orioles 2–0 at Anaheim Stadium on solo homers by Bob Oliver in the fourth inning and Tommy McCraw in the seventh, both off Ross Grimsley. Frank Tanana (8^2/$_3$ innings) and Rudy May (one-third of an inning) combined on the shutout.

The Angels converted only 12 of 39 save opportunities in 1974. The club leader in saves was 40-year-old Orlando Pena with three. Pena pitched only four games for the club in 1974 and wasn't acquired until September. In save opportunities, the Angels had a 6.08 ERA in 40 innings.

MAY 4	A walk-off homer by Dave Chalk in the ninth inning beats the Orioles 8–7 at Anaheim Stadium.
MAY 19	Nolan Ryan strikes out 12 batters during a 4–2 victory over the Twins in Minnesota.

Ryan was 22–16 with a 2.89 ERA in 1974. He led the AL in strikeouts (367), walks (202), innings pitched (332^2/$_3$) and lowest opponent's batting average (.190), and completed 26 of his 41 starts. The 367 strikeouts are the fourth highest single season total since the 60-foot, six-inch pitching distance was *established in 1893. The only higher figures were by Ryan, who had 383 the previous season in 1973; 382 by Sandy Koufax with the Dodgers in 1965; and 372 by Randy Johnson as a Diamondback in 2001. Ryan struck out 750 batters in 1973 and 1974, the most ever in back-to-back seasons. The next best is 719 by Johnson in 2000 and 2001.*

May 29   Bobby Valentine dislocates his shoulder during a brawl in the first inning of a 7–5 loss to the Brewers in Milwaukee. Former Angel Clyde Wright threw a pitch that sailed past Valentine's head. Valentine rushed the mound and uncorked a punch. Wright threw Valentine to the ground. Valentine was out of action for two weeks.

June 1   Nolan Ryan pitches a two-hitter to defeat the Tigers 4–1 at Anaheim Stadium. Ryan had a no-hitter in progress until Mickey Stanley and Al Kaline singled in the eighth inning.

June 5   A two-out, two-run homer by Joe Lahoud in the ninth inning beats the Tigers 6–5 in Detroit.

On the same day, the Angels selected shortstop Mike Miley from Louisiana State University in the first round of the amateur draft. As a quarterback, Miley led the 1973 LSU football team to a 9–3 record and a berth in the Orange Bowl, but gave up his senior year of eligibility to pursue a career in baseball. Miley reached the majors in 1975 and batted .176 in 84 games before being killed in an auto accident on January 6, 1977. Other future major leaguers drafted and signed by the Angels in 1974 were Rance Mulliniks (third round), Thad Bosley (fourth round), Stan Cliburn (fifth round), Gary Wheelcock (sixth round), Ralph Botting (seventh round), John Verhoeven (12th round) and John Caneira (first round of the secondary phase).

June 10   The Angels play at Shea Stadium for the first time and lose 7–5 to the Yankees.

The Yankees played home games at Shea Stadium in 1974 and 1975 while Yankee Stadium was being renovated.

June 14   Nolan Ryan strikes out 19 batters in 13 innings, and the Angels defeat the Red Sox 4–3 in 15 innings at Anaheim Stadium. Ryan struck out 13 batters in the first six innings. He also walked ten batters during the contest. Ryan fanned Cecil Cooper six times. Carl Yastrzemski tied the score 3–3 by belting a two-run homer with one out in the ninth inning. Ryan left the game at the end of the 13th inning after throwing 235 pitches. Barry Raziano followed Ryan to the mound and tossed two scoreless innings and recorded the 20th California strikeout. Luis Tiant hurled a complete game for Boston. Denny Doyle drove in the winning run with a walk-off double.

The win was the only one of Raziano's big-league career. In two seasons with the Royals and Angels he was 1–2 with a 6.23 ERA in 21 2/3 innings.

June 15   The Angels sell Rudy May to the Yankees.

May had a record of 51–76 over seven seasons with the Angels. After the trade, he was 101–80 with three clubs through 1983. May had an 18–14 mark with the Orioles in 1974.

1970s

JUNE 23 — Andy Hassler records the first win of his big-league career by defeating the Rangers 10–2 in Arlington.

Hassler began his career in 1971 and started 0–8. He pitched for the Angels in 1971 and from 1973 through 1976 and had a record of 10–36 before being traded to the Royals. In 1975 and 1976, Hassler lost 17 consecutive decisions. He returned to California from 1980 through 1983 as a reliever, and was 11–10.

JUNE 27 — Nolan Ryan pitches a one-hitter to defeat the Rangers 5–0 at Anaheim Stadium. The only Texas hit was a single by Alex Johnson with two out in the first inning. Ryan retired 25 of the last 26 batters to face him, a streak marred only by a walk to Toby Harrah leading off the sixth.

On the same day, the Angels fired Bobby Winkles as manager and replaced him with 45-year-old Dick Williams. Coach Whitey Herzog served as interim manager for four games until Williams could arrive. The club had lost 18 of their previous 24 games. "We're in the entertainment business," explained general manager Harry Dalton, "and I don't think we were entertaining on the field." Winkles cited a rift with Frank Robinson as the reason for his dismissal. Robinson had ambitions to be a major league manager. Williams was a utility player with five clubs from 1951 through 1964 and was kept around because he would do anything to win. His first season as a major league manager was with the Red Sox in 1967. At the age of 38, he took over the Boston franchise, which had eight losing seasons in a row and finished in ninth place in 1966. In his first season with the Sox, he won the AL pennant in a year that will forever be known in New England as the "Impossible Dream." The Red Sox had winning records in both 1968 and 1969, but failed to come close to finishing in first place. Players began to complain that Williams was too tough on them. He was fired in September 1969. Williams' next stop was with the Athletics where he won three consecutive AL West titles from 1971 through 1973 and the World Series in both 1972 and 1973. But angry over interference from owner Charlie Finley, Williams resigned after the end of the 1973 Fall Classic. He took a job as manager of the Yankees, but Finley claimed he had Williams under contract for 1974 and barred the move. Finley allowed the Angels to sign Williams, in part, because he owed Gene Autry a favor. In 1967, when Finley wanted to relocate his franchise from Kansas City to Oakland, Autry helped secure the votes necessary for passage of the move. Williams came to California with a reputation as a sharp, skillful, hard-driving leader, but couldn't revive the Angels. The club lost the first ten games he managed, and he was 147–194 in California before being fired in 1976. Winkles was named as a coach with the Athletics the following day. He managed the A's in 1977 and 1978.

JULY 1 — Dick Williams manages his first game in a California uniform, and the Angels lose 5–3 to the Athletics at Anaheim Stadium.

JULY 8 — The Angels sell Sandy Alomar to the Yankees.

JULY 10 — The Angels extend their losing streak to 11 games with a 9–1 defeat at the hands of the Orioles at Anaheim Stadium. All 11 defeats came at home, ten of them in Dick Williams' first ten games as manager.

Under the more relaxed grooming rules of Dick Williams, Angels players sported mustaches for the first time in club history. Among those with facial hair were Williams himself, along with Denny Doyle, John Cumberland, Luis Quintana, Ed Figueroa, Dick Lange and Charlie Sands.

JULY 12 — The Angels end their 11-game losing streak by beating the Red Sox 7–0 in Boston. Ed Figueroa pitched a ten-hit shutout without striking out a batter.

JULY 13 — The Angels rout the Red Sox 12–1 in Boston.

JULY 17 — Down 5–0, the Angels score four runs in the eighth inning and three in the ninth to defeat the Indians 7–5 in Cleveland. Leroy Stanton drove in four runs during the comeback with two-run singles in both the eighth and ninth.

On the same day, the Angels sold Tommy McCraw to the Indians.

JULY 23 — At Three Rivers Stadium in Pittsburgh, Angels manager Dick Williams manages the American League All-Stars to a 7–2 loss. Williams was given the assignment because he managed the Athletics to the World Series in 1973.

JULY 25 — In only his second major league start, first baseman Bruce Bochte collects four hits in five at-bats during a 2–1 loss to the Royals at Anaheim Stadium.

Bochte had 23 hits in his first 50 big-league at-bats for an average of .460.

JULY 28 — The Angels extend their losing streak at Anaheim Stadium to 15 games with a 5–3 loss to the Twins in the first game of a double-header. The Angels broke the streak with a 12–9 victory in the second tilt.

JULY 31 — Dick Lange ($6^{1}/_{3}$ innings) and Luis Quintana ($2^{2}/_{3}$ innings) combine on a two-hitter in a 14–4 hammering of the White Sox at Anaheim Stadium. The only Chicago hits were a three-run homer by Bill Melton in the fourth inning and a solo home run from Dick Allen in the sixth. The Angels took a 9–4 lead with five runs in the seventh inning and added five more in the eighth.

AUGUST 7 — Nolan Ryan strikes out 13 batters and carries a no-hitter into the ninth inning, only to lose 2–1 to the White Sox at Comiskey Park. Ryan started the ninth by striking out Jorge Orta, but a single to Dick Allen, an error from first baseman Bruce Bochte and singles by Ken Henderson and Bill Sharp led to two Chicago runs and the loss.

AUGUST 12 — Five days after Richard Nixon resigns as President, Nolan Ryan strikes out 19 batters in nine innings and beats the Red Sox 4–2 at Anaheim Stadium. He struck out the side in the eighth inning to give him 17 strikeouts. In the ninth, Ryan fanned Rick Miller with runners on first and third. An error by shortstop Bobby Valentine allowed a run to score before Ryan set down Bernie Carbo for strikeout number 19, which tied the existing major league record for strikeouts in a nine-inning game. With a chance for his 20th strikeout, and runners on second and third and a two-run lead, Ryan recorded the final out by inducing Rick Burleson to hit a fly ball to right fielder Leroy Stanton.

At the time, the only pitchers to fan 19 batters in a nine-inning game were Steve Carlton with the Cardinals in 1969 and Tom Seaver as a Met in 1970. Ryan also struck out 19 against the Red Sox on June 14, 1974, but required 13 innings to do so. He would strike out 19 once more eight days later (see August 20, 1974).

AUGUST 19 — Pinch hitter Winston Llenas hits a sacrifice fly in the ninth inning to defeat the Tigers 1–0 at Anaheim Stadium. Frank Tanana pitched the shutout.

AUGUST 20 — Nolan Ryan strikes out 19 batters in 11 innings, but the Angels lose 1–0 to the Tigers at Anaheim Stadium. Through ten innings, Ryan had a two-hit shutout and 18 strikeouts. With two out in the 11th, Ben Oglivie singled, stole second and scored on Bill Freehan's single. Mickey Lolich pitched a complete game for Detroit.

SEPTEMBER 4 — Andy Hassler walks ten batters and throws a wild pitch while striking out only two, but beats the Athletics 5–2 in Oakland.

SEPTEMBER 8 — On the day President Gerald Ford pardons Richard Nixon, Andy Hassler pitches a one-hitter, but loses 1–0 to the White Sox at Anaheim Stadium. The only Chicago hit was a single by Lee Richard in the third inning, which led to an unearned run.

The Angels were 15–31 in one-run games in 1974.

SEPTEMBER 11 — Nolan Ryan strikes out 15 batters in ten innings and beats the Royals 3–2 at Anaheim Stadium. Bruce Bochte drove in the winning run with a walk-off single.

On the same day, the Angels traded Bob Oliver to the Orioles for Mickey Scott.

SEPTEMBER 12 — The Angels send Frank Robinson to the Indians for Ken Suarez, Rusty Torres and cash. Robinson was the Angels team leader in homers (20) and RBIs (63) in 1974.

On October 3, the Indians named Frank Robinson as manager replacing Ken Aspromonte. With the appointment, Robinson became the first African-American manager in major league history.

SEPTEMBER 15 — Nolan Ryan records his 20th win of the season with a 6–2 decision over the White Sox in Chicago.

SEPTEMBER 18 — Dick Williams starts seven rookies during a 2–0 loss to the Rangers in the second game of a double-header against the Rangers in Arlington. The seven were pitcher Frank Tanana, first baseman John Doherty, shortstop Orlando Ramirez, third baseman Dave Chalk, left fielder John Balaz, center fielder Morris Nettles and right fielder Bruce Bochte. The Angels won the opener 4–1.

SEPTEMBER 28 — Nolan Ryan pitches his third career no-hitter to beat the Twins 4–0 at Anaheim Stadium. He struck out 15 and walked eight. After facing nine batters, Ryan had seven strikeouts and two walks. Seven of the base on balls were issued in Ryan's first 4 1/3 innings. In the ninth, he retired Tony Oliva on a fly ball to centerfielder Morris Nettles, struck out Larry Hisle, walked Harmon Killebrew and fanned Eric Soderholm.

SEPTEMBER 29 — Andy Hassler shuts out the Twins 4–0 at Anaheim Stadium.

October 1   Frank Tanana records the Angels' third shutout in a row, beating the Athletics 2–0 at Anaheim Stadium.

December 2   Bob Reynolds resigns as club president and sells his 20 percent interest in the Angels to Gene Autry. Reynolds had been president since the franchise's inception in December 1960. Reynolds was 60 years old and said that he made the move to "simplify" his life (see February 22, 1975).

On the same day, the Angels traded Bob Heise to the Red Sox for Tommy Harper.

December 3   The Angels trade Skip Lockwood to the Yankees for Bill Sudakis.

1975

Season in a Sentence
The Angels steal 220 bases, more than any major league team since 1916, but hit only 55 home runs and lose 89 games.

Finish • Won • Lost • Pct • GB
Sixth   72   89   .447   25.5

Manager
Dick Williams

Stats   Angels • AL • Rank
Batting Avg: .246   .258   12
On-Base Pct: .321   .328   10
Slugging Pct: .328   .379   12
Home Runs: 55   12
Stolen Bases: 220   1
ERA: 3.89   3.78   7
Errors: 184   11
Runs Scored: 628   11
Runs Allowed: 723   8

Starting Lineup
Ellie Rodriguez, c
Bruce Bochte, 1b
Jerry Remy, 2b
Dave Chalk, 3b
Mike Miley, ss
Dave Collins, lf
Mickey Rivers, cf
Leroy Stanton, rf
Tommy Harper, dh
Morris Nettles, cf-lf
Joe Lahoud, dh-rf

Pitchers
Frank Tanana, sp
Ed Figueroa, sp
Nolan Ryan, sp
Bill Singer, sp
Andy Hassler, sp
Don Kirkwood, rp
Mickey Scott, rp
Dick Lange, rp

Attendance
1,058,163 (eighth in AL)

Club Leaders
Batting Avg: Mickey Rivers   .284
On-Base Pct: Dave Chalk   .353
Slugging Pct: Leroy Stanton   .416
Home Runs: Leroy Stanton   14
RBI: Leroy Stanton   82
Runs: Jerry Remy   82
Stolen Bases: Mickey Rivers   70
Wins: Frank Tanana   16
               Ed Figueroa   16
Strikeouts: Frank Tanana   269
ERA: Frank Tanana   2.62
Saves: Don Kirkwood   7

February 22   Arthur (Red) Patterson becomes president of the Angels, succeeding Bob Reynolds, who resigned in December 1974. Patterson was 65 years old and had been an executive with the Dodgers in both Brooklyn and Los Angeles for 20 years.

April 7   In the season opener, the Angels score twice in the ninth inning to defeat the Royals 3–2 before 24,105 at Anaheim Stadium. The Angels loaded the bases on two singles and a walk before Tommy Harper singled and Bruce Bochte hit a sacrifice fly. Nolan Ryan pitched a complete game and struck out 12.

Dave Chalk bolted out of the gate with 19 hits in his first 35 at-bats for an average of .541. He finished the year batting .273.

APRIL 12 — Leroy Stanton hits a walk-off homer in the tenth inning to defeat the White Sox 4–3 at Anaheim Stadium.

The Angels hit only 55 home runs in 1976, the fewest of any big-league club since 1953. With the exception of the 1981 strike year, the only team with fewer homers in a season since 1975 was the Astros with 49 in 1979. Stanton led the Angels in home runs in 1975 with 14. No one else had more than six. On the other hand, California stole 220 bases, the most of any team since the 1916 St. Louis Browns. Mickey Rivers led the AL with 70. Other base stealing threats included Jerry Remy (34), Dave Collins (24), Morris Nettles (22), Tommy Harper (19) and Stanton (18).

APRIL 26 — Frank Tanana ($6^{2}/_{3}$ innings) and Don Kirkwood ($2^{2}/_{3}$ innings) combine on a one-hitter to defeat the Athletics 1–0 at Anaheim Stadium. The only Oakland hit was a single by Ray Fosse in the sixth inning. The lone run scored in the third on a single by Orlando Ramirez, a stolen base, and a single from Mickey Rivers.

APRIL 29 — The Angels score nine runs in the third inning and clobber the Royals 12–1 in Kansas City. The big blow was a three-run double by Tommy Harper.

APRIL 30 — The Angels score twice in the ninth inning to down the Royals 7–6 in Kansas City. Tommy Harper drove in the tying run with a double and scored on a two-bagger by Bruce Bochte.

MAY 2 — The Rangers score four runs in the ninth inning to defeat the Angels 4–3 at Anaheim Stadium. The rally started when Jeff Burroughs swung and missed on a two-strike pitch from Bill Singer, but reached first base when the ball sailed past catcher Ellie Rodriguez for a wild pitch. The winning run crossed the plate on another wild pitch from Frank Tanana.

MAY 10 — Frank Tanana strikes out 13 batters and pitches a four-hit shutout to beat the Red Sox 2–0 at Anaheim Stadium.

MAY 13 — Nolan Ryan pitches a two-hitter to down the Yankees 5–0 at Anaheim Stadium. The only New York hits were singles by Bobby Bonds and Chris Chambliss in the seventh inning.

MAY 16 — Bobby Grich of the Orioles hits a walk-off homer off Frank Tanana with two out in the ninth inning to defeat the Angels 1–0 in the first game of a double-header in Baltimore. The drive struck the left-field foul pole. The Angels won the second contest 3–2. Tommy Harper drove in all three California runs with a pair of homers, one of which also hit the left-field foul pole.

MAY 18 — Nolan Ryan pitches his second consecutive two-hitter to defeat Orioles 5–1 at Memorial Stadium. The only Baltimore hits were a single by Al Bumbry in the sixth inning and a double from Tommy Davis in the ninth.

MAY 24   The Angels take batting practice in the lobby of the Sheraton Hotel in Boston before losing to Bill Lee and the Red Sox 6–0 at Fenway Park in a contest televised nationally on NBC.

A couple of days earlier, Lee had told reporters that the weak-hitting Angels "could take batting practice in a hotel lobby without breaking a chandelier." Manager Dick Williams decided to go along with the gag. He told his players to report to the lobby at noon instead of the ballpark. With plastic bats and Nerf balls, Williams pitched to Winston Llenas before hotel security officers put an end to the hijinks. Lee pitched the complete game shutout, allowing just four hits. "He popped off," said Williams of Lee, "and embarrassed us."

JUNE 1   Nolan Ryan pitches his fourth career no-hitter with a 1–0 win over the Orioles at Anaheim Stadium. He walked four and struck out nine. Dave Chalk drove in the lone run of the game with a single off Ross Grimsley in the third inning. In the ninth, Ryan retired Al Bumbry on a fly ball to left fielder Winston Llenas, Tommy Davis on a grounder from second baseman Jerry Remy to first baseman Bruce Bochte, and Bobby Grich on a strikeout.

With the no-hitter, Ryan tied Sandy Koufax for most career no-hitters with four. Koufax had his four with the Dodgers in 1962, 1963, 1964 and 1965. Ryan compiled four no-hitters with the Angels. He had two in 1973, one in 1974 and one in 1975. Ryan finished his career with seven no-hitters. He pitched one with the Astros in 1981 and two while playing for the Rangers in 1990 and 1991.

JUNE 3   With the first overall pick in the amateur draft, the Angels select catcher Danny Goodwin from Southern University.

Goodwin is the only player to be selected as the number-one, overall choice twice. He was drafted number one by the White Sox out of Central High School in Peoria, Illinois, but opted instead to attend college. Goodwin had an extremely disappointing career. He played for the Angels in 1975 and again in 1977 and 1978 and in the majors until 1982, and batted .236 with 13 homers in 636 at-bats. Other future major leaguers drafted and signed by the Angels in 1975 were Jim Anderson (second round), Carney Lansford (third round), Floyd Rayford (fourth round), John Flannery (ninth round), Paul Hartzell (tenth round) and Steve Eddy (19th round). In the secondary phase in January, the club picked Willie Aikens (first round), Gil Kubski (also in the first round), Jim Doersey (second round), Derek Botelho (fourth round) and Bobby Clark (fifth round). Lansford and Aikens had productive careers, but the Angels traded each of them before they reached their peak.

JUNE 6   In his first start since pitching a no-hitter, Nolan Ryan allows only two hits and defeats the Brewers 6–0 at Anaheim Stadium. The only Milwaukee hits were singles by Hank Aaron in the sixth inning and George Scott in the eighth. Over two consecutive starts, Ryan pitched 14 consecutive hitless innings.

Through June 6, the Angels played in 53 games and Ryan had a 10–3 record, 102 strikeouts, and a 2.24 ERA in 106²/₃ innings. But a series of injuries curtailed his season. After June 6, Ryan was 4–9 with a 4.82 earned run average, and he was shut down for the season in August. Four bone chips were removed from his pitching arm in October.

JUNE 11 Leroy Stanton hits a grand slam off Bob Reynolds in the eighth inning of a 14–7 victory over the Tigers in the first game of a double-header in Detroit. It was the first grand slam by an Angels batter since 1971. The Tigers won the second contest 5–3.

JUNE 14 Nolan Ryan strikes out 12 batters in eight innings, but the Angels lose 6–4 to the Brewers in Milwaukee.

On the same day, the Angels traded Denny Doyle to the Red Sox for Chuck Ross.

JUNE 15 Leroy Stanton hits a grand slam off Eduardo Rodriguez in the third inning of an 11-inning, 8–7 triumph over the Brewers in the first game of a double-header at County Stadium. It was Stanton's second grand slam in a span of five days. Milwaukee won the second tilt 4–2.

On the same day, the Angels purchased Andy Etchebarren from the Orioles.

JUNE 20 The Angels take a thrilling 12–11 decision from the Rangers in 11 innings at Anaheim Stadium. Texas scored six runs in the first inning, but the Angels battled back to take an 8–7 lead, only to have the opposition tie the score 8–8 in the seventh. The Rangers scored three times in the 11th, and the game appeared to be over. The Angels came off the mat, however, to score four runs in the bottom half for the victory. John Doherty and Morris Nettles started the inning with back-to-back doubles, but with two out, California still trailed 11–9 with runners on first and second. But Rudy Meoli singled in a run, Dave Collins brought home the tying run with a single and the winning run crossed the plate on an error. Collins finished the day with five hits, including a triple and a double, in six at-bats. The Angels collected 20 hits as a team.

The five-hit outburst came in only the 12th game of Collins' career game. He had 23 hits in his first 56 at-bats, an average of .404. Collins finished his rookie season with a .266 average in 93 contests.

JUNE 21 Frank Tanana strikes out 17 batters and beats the Rangers 4–2 in the first game of a double-header at Anaheim Stadium. He recorded his 17 strikeouts in the first eight innings and had a shot at the existing record of 19 for a nine-inning game. Tanana retired the side in order in the ninth, but without a strikeout. Texas won the second tilt 6–5.

The 17-strikeout game was achieved 12 days before Tanana's 22nd birthday. He finished the season with a league-leading 269 strikeouts in 257$^1/_3$ innings. Tanana also had a 16–9 record and a 2.62 ERA.

JUNE 22 Ed Figueroa pitches a two-hitter to defeat the Rangers 1–0 at Anaheim Stadium. The only Texas hits were singles by Lenny Randle in the second inning and Roy Smalley in the ninth. Joe Lahoud drove in the lone run of the game with a single in the fourth.

Figueroa started the season at the Angels Class AAA farm club in Salt Lake City after compiling a 2–8 record as a rookie in 1974. During the 1975 campaign, he was 16–13 with a 2.90 earned run average.

JUNE 23	Bill Singer pitches brilliantly, allowing only one hit in 11 innings, but the Angels lose 1–0 in 13 innings to the Rangers at Anaheim Stadium. Singer surrendered a one-out double in the second inning to Jim Spencer, then pitched 9²/₃ innings of hitless baseball. Singer was relieved by Don Kirkwood. Kirkwood struck out the side in the 12th, but allowed the only run of the contest in the 13th. Steve Hargan (11¹/₃ innings) and Jim Umbarger (1²/₃ innings) combined on the Texas shutout.
	Angels shortstops combined for 51 errors in 1975. The offenders were Mike Miley (19), Orlando Ramirez (16), Billy Smith (13), Rudy Meoli (2) and Ike Hampton (1).
JUNE 30	Frank Tanana strikes out 15 batters and beats the Twins 10–3 in Minnesota.
JULY 15	The Angels trade Dave Sells to the Dodgers for Jim Brewer.
JULY 23	Frank Tanana pitches the Angels to a 1–0 victory over the Orioles in Baltimore. Joe Lahoud drove in the lone run of the game with a single in the first inning.
JULY 30	The Angels score three runs in the ninth inning off Jim Kaat and Goose Gossage without a batter being retired to beat the White Sox 5–4 at Anaheim Stadium. The first run scored on a bases-loaded walk to Joe Lahoud before John Doherty followed with a two-run single.
AUGUST 10	A walk-off double by Leroy Stanton in the ninth inning off ex-Angel Rudy May beats the Yankees 1–0 at Anaheim Stadium. Bill Singer (eight innings) and Mickey Scott (one inning) combined on the shutout.
	Scott was born in Weimar, West Germany in 1947.
AUGUST 13	The Angels sell Tommy Harper to the Athletics.
AUGUST 18	A three-run, walk-off homer by Leroy Stanton with one out in the ninth inning beats the Brewers 5–4 at Anaheim Stadium.
AUGUST 19	The Angels win with a walk-off homer for the second game in a row, this time when Mike Miley connects in the 15th inning to defeat the Brewers 5–4 at Anaheim Stadium. Frank Tanana pitched the first 12 innings.
SEPTEMBER 2	Frank Tanana strikes out 14 batters and beats the Athletics 4–1 at Anaheim Stadium.
	In September, Nolan Ryan made a brief guest appearance on the afternoon soap opera Ryan's Hope. *The program ran on ABC from 1975 through 1989.*
SEPTEMBER 3	Andy Hassler loses his 11th game in a row by dropping a 5–4 decision to the Rangers at Anaheim Stadium.
	Hassler finished the season with a 3–12 record and a 5.94 ERA.
SEPTEMBER 7	Tony Solaita of the Royals hits three homers and a game-winning single in the 11th inning, which beats the Angels 8–7 at Anaheim Stadium. The Angels scored four runs in the ninth to force extra innings.

The Angels had the youngest team in the American League in 1975. The youngsters included Frank Tanana (21), Jerry Remy (22), Dave Collins (22), Mike Miley (22), Andy Hassler (23), Morris Nettles (23), Bruce Bochte (24), Dave Chalk (24), Don Kirkwood (25), Ed Figueroa (26) and Mickey Rivers (26).

SEPTEMBER 15   Bruce Bochte collects five hits, including a triple and a double, in five at-bats, but the Angels lose 7–6 in 12 innings to the Twins in Minnesota.

SEPTEMBER 19   Joe Pactwa (seven innings) and Jim Brewer (two innings) combine on a 12-hit shutout to beat the Twins 1–0 at Anaheim Stadium. Pactwa walked four in addition to giving up nine hits. The lone run scored in the fourth when Mickey Rivers walked, stole second and crossed the plate on a single by Dan Briggs off Bert Blyleven.

The decision was the only one of Pactwa's career. He pitched in only four big-league games and had a 1–0 record.

SEPTEMBER 22   The Angels outlast the White Sox to win 3–0 in 16 innings at Anaheim Stadium. The game was won on a three-run, pinch-hit, walk-off home run by Adrian Garrett. Frank Tanana pitched the first 13 innings and struck out 13 batters. Don Kirkwood completed the shutout with three spotless innings of work.

SEPTEMBER 28   On the final day of the season, four Athletics hurlers combine to pitch a no-hitter and beat the Angels 5–0 in Oakland. A's manager Al Dark used four pitchers because he wanted to set his rotation for the upcoming playoff series against the Red Sox. The quartet that threw the no-hitter were Vida Blue (five innings), Glenn Abbott (one inning), Paul Lindblad (one inning) and Rollie Fingers (two innings). Mickey Rivers made the final out on a grounder to shortstop Dal Maxvill.

DECEMBER 10   The Angels send Bill Singer to the Rangers for Jim Spencer and $100,000. The following day, Spencer was dealt to the White Sox along with Morris Nettles for Bill Melton and Steve Dunning.

DECEMBER 11   The Angels trade Mickey Rivers and Ed Figueroa to the Yankees for Bobby Bonds.

In what is arguably the worst trade in club history, the Angels traded two proven young players for an over-the-hill veteran. Bonds came to the Angels at the age of 29. Over the previous seven seasons with the Giants and Yankees, he averaged 30 homers, 86 RBIs, 40 stolen bases and 115 runs scored per season. Bonds also played in three All-Star Games. The trades for Bonds and Melton (see December 10, 1975) were designed to inject some power into the Angel lineup. In 1975, the two combined to hit 47 home runs. The entire Angels team hit only 55 homers. Bonds had an injury-marred season in 1976 and a great year in 1977 before being traded to the White Sox. Melton went into a steep decline and hit only six homers with a .208 batting average in a California uniform. Sacrificing speed for power failed to work. From 1975 to 1976, home runs increased from only 55 to just 63, while stolen bases fell from 220 to 126 and run production from 628 to 550. Meanwhile, Rivers and Figueroa were valuable components on the Yankee World Series teams of 1976, 1977 and 1978. Rivers batted .312 in 1976 and .326 in 1977. Figueroa was 19–10 in 1976, 16–11 in 1977 and 20–9 in 1978 before being beset with elbow problems.

1976

Season in a Sentence
The Angels fire Dick Williams in July with a record of 39–55, and the club responds over the last 66 games under the gentler approach of Norm Sherry.

Finish • Won • Lost • Pct • GB
Fourth   76   86   .469   14.0
(tie)

Managers
Dick Williams (39–55) and Norm Sherry (37–29)

Stats

Stats	Angels	AL	Rank
Batting Avg:	.235	.256	12
On-Base Pct:	.304	.320	12
Slugging Pct:	.318	.361	12
Home Runs:	63		12
Stolen Bases:	126		6
ERA:	3.36	3.52	5
Errors:	150		8
Runs Scored:	550		12
Runs Allowed:	631		12

Starting Lineup
Andy Etchebarren, c
Bruce Bochte, 1b-lf
Jerry Remy, 2b
Ron Jackson, 3b
Dave Chalk, ss-3b
Dave Collins, lf
Rusty Torres, cf
Bobby Bonds, rf
Tommy Davis, dh
Bill Melton, dh-1b
Mario Guerrero, ss
Dan Briggs, cf-1b
Leroy Stanton, rf-cf-lf
Tony Solaita, 1b

Pitchers
Frank Tanana, sp
Nolan Ryan, sp
Gary Ross, sp
Don Kirkwood, sp
Dick Drago, rp
Mickey Scott, rp
Paul Hartzell, rp-sp
Sid Monge, rp-sp

Attendance
1,006,774 (eighth in AL)

Club Leaders
Batting Avg: Bobby Bonds .265
On-Base Pct: Bruce Bochte .346
Slugging Pct: Bobby Bonds .386
Home Runs: Bobby Bonds 10
RBI: Bobby Bonds 54
Runs: Jerry Remy 64
Stolen Bases: Jerry Remy 35
Wins: Frank Tanana 19
Strikeouts: Nolan Ryan 327
ERA: Frank Tanana 2.43
Saves: Dick Drago 6

FEBRUARY 20   The Angels purchase Ed Herrmann from the Yankees.

Herrmann was expected to be the Angels' starting catcher, but he batted only .174 with two homers before being traded to the Astros in June.

MARCH 3   The Angels trade John Balaz, Dave Machemer and Dick Sharon to the Red Sox for Dick Drago.

MARCH 21   A concert by The Who is staged at Anaheim Stadium.

About 10,000 of the 55,000 in attendance were permitted to sit in the outfield. Some 70 feet of the center-field wall was pushed down by those who couldn't obtain tickets to the event. And days later, marijuana plants began growing along the left-field line and in a large patch in center field. "At first we thought it was weeds," said stadium manager Tom Liegler. "Later we found out we were right." Liegler ordered heavy spraying with herbicides, after issuing orders that nobody besides his most trusted assistants were to work on the project. Many volunteered to work for nothing, but were turned away. Nonetheless, the marijuana thrived. The ultimate solution was to clip it off at about 17 inches, which succeeded it killing the plants.

MARCH 31   The Angels trade Ellie Rodriguez to the Dodgers for Orlando Alvarez and cash.

APRIL 9   The Angels start the season with a 5–2 loss to the Athletics before 30,194 at Anaheim Stadium. Frank Tanana was the starting and losing pitcher.

The Angels lost the first four games of the 1976 season.

APRIL 16   Andy Etchebarren stars in an 11-inning, 7–6 win over the Tigers at Anaheim Stadium. Etchebarren drove in the tying run with a two-out single in the ninth inning and brought home the winning tally with another single in the 11th.

APRIL 19   Frank Tanana strikes out 12 batters during a 9–4 win over the Orioles at Anaheim Stadium. Bobby Bonds collected three hits in his first game with the Angels.

Bonds hit only ten homers and drove in 54 runs for the Angels in 1976, but both figures led the weak-hitting club.

APRIL 20   Nolan Ryan pitches a three-hitter and strikes out 12 to defeat the Orioles 5–0 at Anaheim Stadium.

Ryan was 17–18 with a 3.36 ERA in 284^1/$_3$ innings in 1976. He led the AL in strikeouts (327) and shutouts (seven).

APRIL 26   Frank Tanana strikes out 12 batters and pitches a two-hitter, but the Angels lose 1–0 to the Brewers at County Stadium. The only run came on a home run by Don Money leading off the first inning. The other Milwaukee hit was a single by Robin Yount in the fourth. The Angels collected only three hits off Jim Colborn and Eduardo Rodriguez.

MAY 1   The Angels break a 13-game home losing streak against the Indians with a 6–1 victory. The Angels were 0–6 against Cleveland at Anaheim Stadium in both 1974 and 1975.

MAY 8   The Angels draw 14 walks off five Indians pitchers and win 4–3 in 13 innings at Anaheim Stadium. After the Indians scored in the top of the 12th to move ahead 3–2, the Angels scored in the bottom half on a ground out by Leroy Stanton and scored in the 13th on Stanton's single.

MAY 15   Bobby Bonds hits a grand slam off Pete Redfern in the sixth inning, but the Angels lose 15–5 to the Twins in the second game of a double-header at Anaheim Stadium. Minnesota also won the opener 5–2.

MAY 26   The Angels collect only two hits during an 11-inning, 1–0 loss to the White Sox at Anaheim Stadium. Ken Brett retired the first 23 batters to face him and had a no-hitter in progress until Jerry Remy collected an infield single with two out in the ninth inning. Remy's hit was the result of a controversial scoring decision by official scorer Don Merry of the *Long Beach Independent Telegram*. Jorge Orta, playing third base had trouble picking up Remy's slow roller as it skidded under his glove, and

	most observers thought the play should have been ruled an error. Bill Melton added another single in the tenth. Don Kirkwood was the hard luck loser. He pitched ten shutout innings before allowing a run in the 11th on a two-out single by Bucky Dent.
May 29	The Angels score three runs in the ninth inning to beat the Royals 3–2 in the first game of a double-header at Anaheim Stadium. Ron Jackson hit a two-out, two-run triple to tie the score and crossed the plate on a single by Andy Etchebarren. The Angels completed the sweep with a 7–2 triumph in the second tilt.
May 31	Frank Tanana strikes out 12 batters without a walk and beats the Twins 3–2 in Minnesota.
June 2	The Angels sign Tommy Davis as a free agent.
June 6	The Angels trade Ed Herrmann to the Astros for Terry Humphrey and Mike Barlow.
June 8	The Angels play at remodeled Yankee Stadium for the first time and lose to the Yanks 4–2.

On the same day, the Angels selected outfielder Ken Landreaux from Arizona State University in the first round of the amateur draft. Landreaux was traded to the Twins in February 1979 in the deal that brought Rod Carew to the Angels. Other future major leaguers drafted and signed by the Angels in 1976 were Bob Ferris (second round), Chuck Porter (seventh round), Mike Bishop (12th round), Ken Schrom (17th round), John Harris (29th round) and Danny Boone (second round of the secondary phase). In the January draft, the Angels picked Mark Brouhard (fourth round) and Keith Comstock (fifth round).

June 10	Ron Jackson accounts for both runs of a 2–0 win over the Yankees in New York with a triple in the third inning. Frank Tanana pitched the shutout.

Frank Tanana was 19–10 with a 2.43 ERA and 261 strikeouts in 1976. Only 22 years of age at the start of the season, he pitched $288^{1}/_{3}$ innings and completed 23 of his 34 starts.

June 15	Nolan Ryan pitches a two-hitter to defeat the Brewers 1–0 at Anaheim Stadium. The only Milwaukee hits were singles by Don Money in the first inning and Gary Sutherland in the eighth. Bobby Bonds drove in the lone run of the game with a single in the seventh.
June 17	Gary Ross pitches a two-hitter to defeat the Brewers 2–0 at Anaheim Stadium. The only Milwaukee hits were singles by Darrell Porter in the sixth inning and Von Joshua in the ninth.
June 19	Nolan Ryan strikes out 15 batters during a 5–3 win over the Red Sox at Anaheim Stadium.
June 30	Nolan Ryan is mistakenly put on the lineup card as the starting pitcher against the White Sox in Chicago. By rule, Ryan had to pitch to one batter and induced Chet Lemon to ground out. Ryan gave way to Gary Ross, and the Angels won 2–1 in ten innings.

July 2	Andy Hassler allows only one run in six innings of relief, but is the losing pitcher in a 6–5 defeat at the hands of the Twins in Minnesota.
	The loss was the 17th in a row for Hassler over two seasons. He dropped his last 11 decisions in 1975 and the first six in 1976. Hassler was traded to the Royals on July 5. His losing streak extended to 18 games while in Kansas City before he finally won on August 6.
July 4	On the day the nation celebrates the Bicentennial, Ron Jackson hits a grand slam off Bill Campbell in the seventh inning, but the Angels lose 9–5 to the Twins in the second game of a double-header in Minnesota. The Angels score five runs on only two hits. The opener resulted in a 5–3 California victory.
July 7	Bobby Bonds drives in both runs of a 2–0 win over the Indians at Anaheim Stadium. Bonds homered in the first inning and doubled in the third. Nolan Ryan pitched the shutout.
July 11	Nolan Ryan strikes out 12 batters, but the Angels lose 3–1 to the Orioles at Anaheim Stadium.
July 20	Angels pitcher Dick Drago gives up Hank Aaron's 755th, and last, career home run during a 6–2 Angels loss to the Brewers in Milwaukee.
	Bobby Bonds was standing in right field for the Angels when the ball cleared the wall. Bobby's son Barry would eventually pass Aaron on the all-time home run list in 2006. Barry celebrated his 12th and 13th birthdays while his father played for the Angels.
July 23	With the club holding a record of 39–55, the Angels fire Dick Williams as manager and hire 45-year-old Norm Sherry.
	Team morale had been a problem all year under the hard-driving Williams, who was fired shortly after he nearly came to blows with Bill Melton during a heated argument on the team bus. The Angels were 147–194 under Williams in one full season and parts of two others. He came to California with a winning percentage of .574, three AL pennants and two world championships in six seasons with the Red Sox and Athletics. Williams later managed the Expos (1977–81), Padres (1982–85) and Mariners (1986–88) and reached the World Series again with San Diego in 1984. Sherry was a catcher with the Dodgers and Mets from 1959 through 1963. He was a coach with the Angels in 1970 and 1971, a manager in the farm system from 1972 through 1975, and a coach again in 1976 before his appointment as manager. Over the remainder of the 1976 season, the Angels were 37–29 under Sherry, but he was fired in July 1977 after the club started 39–42.
July 25	Leroy Stanton hits a walk-off grand slam off Steve Foucault in the 11th inning to beat the Rangers 7–3 at Anaheim Stadium. The bases were loaded on a single by Terry Humphrey, a bunt and a ground out that advanced Humphrey to third, and two intentional walks.
August 4	Bruce Bochte collects four hits, including a triple and a double, and scores four runs during a 9–6 win over the Rangers in Arlington.

AUGUST 6	Frank Tanana strikes out 13 batters during a 2–1 win over the Athletics in Oakland.
AUGUST 11	Frank Tanana pitches a two-hitter to defeat the Red Sox 6–0 at Anaheim Stadium. The only Boston hits were singles by Dwight Evans in the second inning and Rick Burleson in the sixth.
AUGUST 18	Nolan Ryan strikes out 17 batters in ten innings of an 11-inning, 5–4 win over the Tigers in Detroit. Dan Meyer hit a two-run homer off Ryan with two out in the ninth inning to tie the score 3–3. Both teams scored in the tenth.
AUGUST 21	Rusty Torres homers in the tenth inning to beat the Yankees 4–3 in New York.
AUGUST 22	The Angels blow an eight-run lead in the ninth inning, but still manage to defeat the Yankees 11–8 in 11 innings in New York. Frank Tanana carried an 8–0 advantage into the ninth and retired the first batter of the inning, but before the third out was recorded, the Yanks scored eight runs in an amazing rally to tie the score. Tanana was relieved after allowing six batters in a row to reach base. John Verhoeven replaced Tanana and gave up a two-run single and a two-run homer. The Angels recovered and scored three runs in the 11th.
AUGUST 27	The Yankees score five runs in the 15th inning to beat the Angels 5–0 at Anaheim Stadium. Frank Tanana pitched the first 13 innings for the Angels and recorded 13 strikeouts. Catfish Hunter (13 innings) and Grant Jackson (two innings) combined on the New York shutout.
SEPTEMBER 3	The Angels trade Ron Farkas to the Cardinals for Mike Easler.
SEPTEMBER 6	Frank Tanana strikes out 15 batters in ten innings, but winds up with a no decision, and the Angels lose 2–1 to the Athletics at Anaheim Stadium.
SEPTEMBER 8	Mike Easler drives in both runs of a 2–0 victory over the Royals in Kansas City with singles in the first and fifth innings. Gary Ross (three innings) and Dick Drago (six innings) combined on the shutout. Ross left the game with none out in the fourth inning after he was struck on the right foot on a liner off the bat of George Brett.
SEPTEMBER 10	Nolan Ryan strikes out 18 batters, walks nine and allows just three hits in defeating the White Sox 3–2 at Comiskey Park. Eleven of the first 14 Chicago outs were recorded on strikeouts. After struggling with his control and surrendering two runs in the fifth, Ryan struck out seven batters in the last three innings, including the final five batters to face him.
SEPTEMBER 12	Designated hitter for the White Sox, Minnie Minoso, age 53, collects a single in the second inning off Sid Monge, and Chicago defeats the Angels 2–1 in ten innings in the first game of a double-header at Comiskey Park. Minoso is the oldest player in major league history to record a base hit. The White Sox also won game two 5–1.
SEPTEMBER 13	The Angels erupt for four runs in the 14th inning to down the Rangers 6–2 in Arlington.
SEPTEMBER 20	Nolan Ryan pitches the Angels to a 1–0 win over the Rangers at Anaheim Stadium. Terry Humphrey drove in the lone run of the game with a double in the sixth inning.

On the same day, the Angels sold Tommy Davis to the Royals.

SEPTEMBER 21   The Angels score twice in the ninth to defeat the Rangers 2–1 at Anaheim Stadium. Ron Jackson led off the inning with a home run. Dave Chalk drove in the winning run with a walk-off single.

SEPTEMBER 29   Nolan Ryan strikes out 11 batters and pitches a two-hitter to defeat the White Sox 3–0 at Anaheim Stadium. The only Chicago hits were singles by Ralph Garr in the first inning and Jim Spencer in the ninth.

OCTOBER 1   Frank Tanana pitches 11 shutout innings and strikes out 14 batters during a 12-inning, 2–0 triumph over the Athletics in Oakland. Dick Drago nailed down the save. Vida Blue pitched a complete game for the A's. Rusty Torres broke the scoreless deadlock with a solo home run with one out in the 12th before the Angels added an insurance run.

OCTOBER 3   In the last game of the season, Nolan Ryan pitches his second consecutive two-hit shutout and beats the Athletics 1–0 in Oakland. Ryan also fanned 14 batters. The only A's hits were singles by Wayne Gross in the fourth inning and Phil Garner in the sixth. Terry Humphrey drove in the lone run of the game with a single in the seventh.

NOVEMBER 14   A week after Jimmy Carter defeats Gerald Ford in the Presidential election, the Angels lose Gary Wheelcock, Dave Collins, Carlos Lopez, Leroy Stanton and Julio Cruz to the Mariners in the expansion draft.

NOVEMBER 16   The Angels sign Don Baylor, most recently with the Athletics, as a free agent.

Free agency was available to major league players for the first time during the 1976–77 offseason. Gene Autry was vehemently opposed to free agency, but once it became a reality, he used it to his advantage to build a winning club by sinking his millions into star players. It immediately paid dividends financially, as the season-ticket base increased from 3,817 in 1976 to 5,879 in 1977. Overall attendance went from 1,006,774 with a club that won 76 games in 1976 to 1,432,633 in 1977 with a 74-game winner. The 1977 figure broke the existing club record of 1,400,321 set in 1966. Baylor was the first player signed by the Angels under the new system. As an outfielder and designated hitter, he gave the Angels six excellent seasons, the best of which was in 1979 when he was the AL MVP. He hit 141 homers as an Angel and was briefly the franchise leader in the category.

NOVEMBER 17   The Angels sign Joe Rudi, most recently with the Athletics, as a free agent.

Rudi was a bust with the Angels, largely due to injuries, and hit only .249 with 57 homers in four seasons.

NOVEMBER 24   The Angels sign Bobby Grich, most recently with the Orioles, as a free agent.

Grich is one of the most underrated second baseman of all time. He failed to attain the recognition he deserved because of a .266 career batting average in 17 seasons from 1970 through 1986 and a failure to appear in the World Series, but he compiled a .371 on-base percentage and belted 224 home runs in addition to winning four Gold Glove awards. Grich grew up as an Angels fan in Southern California and jumped at the chance to sign with the club. But on Valentine's Day in 1977, he hurt his back trying to lift an air conditioner at his apartment in Long Beach. He played only 52 games before undergoing surgery on July 1 for a herniated disk. He struggled again in 1978, but bounced back and played in the All-Star Game in an Angels uniform in 1979, 1980 and 1982. During the strike-shortened 1981 campaign, Grich led the AL in home runs (22) and slugging percentage (.541). He played ten seasons with the Angels.

December 3   The Angels trade Bill Melton to the Indians for Stan Perzanowski.

1977

Season in a Sentence
After signing Bobby Grich, Don Baylor and Joe Rudi as free agents, the Angels enter the year as favorites to win the AL West but unexpected injuries result in a seventh straight losing season.

Finish • Won • Lost • Pct • GB
Fifth   74   88   .457   28.0

Managers
Norm Sherry (39–42) and Dave Garcia (35–46)

Stats   Angels • AL • Rank
Batting Avg: .255   .266   12
On-Base Pct: .323   .330   9
Slugging Pct: .386   .405   10
Home Runs: 131   9
Stolen Bases: 159   3
ERA: 3.72   4.06   4
Errors: 147   10 (tie)
Runs Scored: 675   10
Runs Allowed: 695   5

Starting Lineup
Terry Humphrey, c
Tony Solaita, 1b
Jerry Remy, 2b
Dave Chalk, 3b
Rance Mulliniks, ss
Joe Rudi, lf
Gil Flores, cf
Bobby Bonds, rf
Don Baylor, dh-lf
Ron Jackson, 1b-3b
Mario Guerrero, ss
Thad Bosley, cf
Bobby Grich, ss

Pitchers
Nolan Ryan, sp
Frank Tanana, sp
Paul Hartzell, sp-rp
Ken Brett, sp
Wayne Simpson, sp
Dave LaRoche, rp
Dyar Miller, rp

Attendance
1,432,633 (sixth in AL)

Club Leaders
Batting Avg: Dave Chalk   .277
On-Base Pct: Dave Chalk   .345
Slugging Pct: Bobby Bonds   .520
Home Runs: Bobby Bonds   37
RBI: Bobby Bonds   115
Runs: Bobby Bonds   103
Stolen Bases: Jerry Remy   41
               Bobby Bonds   41
Wins: Nolan Ryan   19
Strikeouts: Nolan Ryan   341
ERA: Frank Tanana   2.54
Saves: Dave LaRoche   13

January 6   Angels shortstop Mike Miley dies in an auto accident near Baton Rouge, Louisiana, at about 2 a.m. Miley missed a curve and the car slammed into a culvert and overturned several times.

January 11   In the January amateur draft, the Angels select Alan Wiggins in the first round and Daryl Sconiers in the third.

1970s

JANUARY 25   The Angels sign Mike Cuellar, most recently with the Orioles, as a free agent.

APRIL 4   The Angels trade Mike Easler to the Pirates for Randy Sealy.

APRIL 6   The Angels participate in the first game in Mariners history and win 7–0 before 57,762 in the Kingdome in Seattle. Jerry Remy led off the first inning by drawing a walk from Diego Segui and scored on a double by Don Baylor, in his California debut. The first Mariners batter was ex-Angel Dave Collins, who struck out. Frank Tanana pitched a complete game, allowing nine hits in the shutout. Playing in his first game with the Angels, Joe Rudi collected three hits, including a homer and a double, and drove in four runs in five at-bats.

APRIL 7   The Angels begin the 1977 season with two shutouts as Nolan Ryan pitches a three-hitter to defeat the Mariners 2–0 in Seattle.

APRIL 8   The Mariners pull off their first victory in franchise history by defeating the Angels 7–6 in Seattle.

APRIL 10   In the fifth game of a season-opening, five-game series against the Mariners in Seattle, Joe Rudi hits a grand slam off Glenn Abbott in the first inning of a 12–5 victory. The slam came after Abbott allowed a single to Bobby Grich, then hit Bobby Bonds and Don Baylor with pitches.

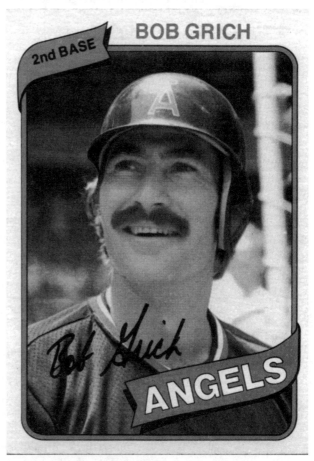

A fan favorite during his ten years with the Angels, beginning in 1977, second baseman Bobby Grich was a consistent performer with a hustling style of play.

> *Rudi looked like money in the bank early in the season. He drove in 27 runs in the first 21 games through April 29. But Rudi broke his hand when struck by a pitch from Nelson Briles on June 26 and didn't play for the rest of the season. Rudi finished the season with a .264 average, 13 homers and 53 RBIs in 64 games. He was leading the AL in runs batted in when hurt.*

APRIL 15   In the home opener, Nolan Ryan pitches a one-hitter to defeat the Mariners 7–0 before 34,654 at Anaheim Stadium. The only Seattle hit was a single by Bob Stinson in the fifth inning. Bobby Grich, Bobby Bonds and Don Baylor each homered. It was the first home run in an Angels uniform for Grich and Baylor.

Bonds batted .264 with 37 homers, 115 RBIs, 103 runs scored and 41 stolen bases in 1977.

APRIL 19   Joe Rudi collects four hits, including a homer, and scores four runs during an 11–2 triumph over the White Sox at Anaheim Stadium.

APRIL 29   Dramatic homers spark an 11-inning, 3–2 win over the Orioles in Baltimore. Joe Rudi homered off Jim Palmer with one out in the ninth to tie the score 2–2, and Don Baylor powered a solo shot facing Dyar Miller in the 11th.

APRIL 30   Nolan Ryan strikes out 13 batters, but the Angels lose 4–3 in ten innings to the Orioles in Baltimore.

MAY 6   Nolan Ryan strikes out 15 batters in $8^{2}/_{3}$ innings, and the Angels defeat the Red Sox 8–4 in Boston.

Ryan was 19–16 with a 2.77 ERA in 1977. He led the majors in complete games (22 in 37 starts), strikeouts (342), walks (204) in 299 innings. The walks total is the second highest in the majors since 1894. The only pitcher to exceed the figure was Bob Feller, who walked 208 in $277^{2}/_{3}$ innings as a 19-year-old with the Indians in 1938.

MAY 8   In his major league debut, Angels centerfielder Gil Flores collects three hits, including a double and a triple, during a 4–3 loss to the Red Sox in Boston.

Flores was a boxer in his native Puerto Rico until he was nearly killed in an auto accident at the age of 16. After recovering from his injuries, Flores switched to baseball.

MAY 10   Nolan Ryan pitches a two-hitter to defeat the Royals 6–1 in Kansas City. Amos Otis collected both Royals hits with a single in the fifth inning and a double in the sixth.

MAY 11   Bobby Bonds, Don Baylor and Ron Jackson hit consecutive homers off Ross Grimsley in the second inning of a 6–0 win over the Orioles at Anaheim Stadium. Frank Tanana pitched the shutout after predicting he would do so prior to the game.

On the same day, the Angels sent Bruce Bochte, Sid Monge and $250,000 to the Indians for Dave LaRoche and Dave Schuler. LaRoche previously played for the Angels in 1970 and 1971. He saved 25 games for the club in 1978. Bochte remained in the majors until 1986 as an effective first baseman for the Indians, Mariners and Athletics. He sat out the entire 1983 season, however, because he was disgusted with the "cold, impersonal attitude on the part of management."

MAY 19   Nolan Ryan strikes out 12 batters and beats the Twins 5–3 at Anaheim Stadium.

MAY 24   Nolan Ryan strikes out 12 batters, walks seven and allows three hits in a 2–1 win over the Tigers in Detroit.

MAY 25	Frank Tanana pitches the Angels' second consecutive three-hitter and beats the Tigers 4–0 in his hometown of Detroit. He struck out 11.
	Al Wisk joined the Angels broadcasting team in 1977 replacing Dave Niehaus. Wisk announced Angels games for three seasons.
MAY 27	The Angels play a regular season game outside of the United States for the first time and win 4–1 over the Blue Jays at Exhibition Stadium in Toronto.
MAY 29	Nolan Ryan strikes out 12 batters for the third start in a row and beats the Blue Jays 3–2 in Toronto.
	Ryan and Frank Tanana were a combined 34–25 in 1977. The rest of the staff was 40–63. The starting rotation was dubbed "Tanana and Ryan and two days of cryin'."
MAY 30	Dennis Eckersley pitches a no-hitter to lead the Indians to a 1–0 win over the Angels in Cleveland. The final out was recorded when Gil Flores struck out. It was the 12th strikeout recorded by Eckersley during the game.
	Tony Solaita, who played for the angels from 1976 through 1978, is the only native of American Samoa ever to play in the major leagues. He was murdered in Tafuna, American Samoa, on February 10, 1990 during a land dispute.
MAY 31	Jerry Remy collects five hits in six at-bats during a ten-inning, 6–5 victory over the Indians in Cleveland. Remy's fifth hit drove in the winning run.
JUNE 7	The Blue Jays play for the first time at Anaheim Stadium and beat the Angels 6–3.
	On the same day, the Angels selected pitcher Rich Dotson from Anderson High School in Cincinnati, Ohio. Dotson was traded by the Angels to the White Sox before making his major league debut in 1979 and went on to career in which he had a record of 111–113. Other future major leaguers drafted and signed by the Angels in 1977 were Brian Harper (fourth round), Rick Steirer (fifth round) and Brad Havens (eighth round).
JUNE 8	Nolan Ryan strikes out 19 batters in ten innings and Bobby Grich hits a walk-off homer in the 13th inning to defeat the Blue Jays 2–1 at Anaheim Stadium. The game was tied 1–1 when Bobby Bonds delivered a two-out, RBI-single in the ninth. Ryan struck out 12 of the first 16 batters to face him and had 18 strikeouts at the end of the ninth. Dave LaRoche followed with three hitless innings of relief. It was the fourth time that Ryan struck out 19 batters in a game. The others were all in 1974 on June 14, August 12 and August 20. The only other pitchers with multiple games of 19 strikeouts or more are Randy Johnson (three) and Roger Clemens (two).
	The dramatic home run was the last plate appearance of the year for Grich. He underwent surgery for removal of a herniated lumbar disc on July 3.
JUNE 10	Frank Tanana pitches a two-hitter to defeat the Indians 1–0 at Anaheim Stadium. The only Cleveland hits were doubles by Buddy Bell in the fifth inning and

Ron Pruitt in the ninth. The lone run scored on a homer by Bobby Bonds off Wayne Garland in the second inning.

> *Tanana finished the season with a record of 15–9, seven shutouts and a league-leading 2.54 ERA in 288 1/3 innings. He completed 14 consecutive starts from April 29 through July 3. Tanana had a 12–5 record and a 1.89 earned run average at that point, but hurling 127 innings in a span of 66 days robbed him of his fastball just as he was reaching his 24th birthday. Tanana didn't make an appearance in 1977 after September 5. He lasted in the majors until 1993, but was never again a dominant strikeout artist.*

JUNE 12   Joe Rudi homers twice and drives in five runs during an 11–4 triumph over the Indians at Anaheim Stadium.

JUNE 13   The Angels trade Dick Drago to the Orioles for Dyar Miller.

JUNE 14   For the second game in a row, Joe Rudi homers twice and drives in five runs to spark the Angels to a 12–9 victory over the Twins in Minnesota. He also picked up a double during the contest. Shortstop Mario Guerrero collected five hits, including a triple and a double, in five at-bats.

JUNE 15   The Angels trade Craig Hendrickson to the Reds for Gary Nolan and send Don Kirkwood, John Verhoeven and John Flannery to the White Sox for Ken Brett.

> *Brett played for ten teams in his 14 years in the majors. His younger brother George played his entire 21 seasons with the Royals. Ken did a Miller Lite commercial after his career was over in which he didn't know what town he was in.*

JUNE 16   Nolan Ryan strikes out 14 batters, but the Angels lose 7–6 to the Twins in Minnesota.

JUNE 19   The Angels score seven runs in the top of the first inning, and it holds up for a 7–0 victory over the Brewers in Milwaukee. The first seven California batters reached base on three singles, a walk and three doubles in that order. Frank Tanana pitched the shutout.

JUNE 23   Bobby Bonds steals four bases and scores four runs during a 10–6 win over the White Sox in Chicago.

JUNE 24   Frank Tanana pitches a ten-inning complete game, but loses 1–0 to the Rangers at Anaheim Stadium on a home run to Ken Henderson.

JUNE 25   Nolan Ryan strikes out 12 batters in 7 1/3 innings, and the Angels score two runs in the ninth to beat the Rangers 3–2 at Anaheim Stadium. Ron Jackson drove in the winning run with a walk-off single in the ninth.

JUNE 26   Ron Jackson delivers a walk-off single for the second game in a row, this time in the 11th to defeat the Rangers 4–3 in the first game of a double-header at Anaheim Stadium. The Angels won the second tilt by the same 4–3 score, although in the conventional nine innings.

June 29	Nolan Ryan strikes out 12 batters and beats the Royals 7–0 at Anaheim Stadium. Center fielder Thad Bosley drove in three runs in his major league debut with a triple and a single. He arrived at the ballpark just 25 minutes before game time after being called up from Class AAA Salt Lake City.
July 11	The Angels fire Norm Sherry as manager and replace him with 46-year-old Dave Garcia. The club also hired hypnotist Arthur Ellen to teach the players the power of positive thinking.

The switch took place with the Angels holding a 39–42 record. A minor league infielder for 20 years, Garcia never played in the majors. He had been a manager in the Angels system in 1974 and a coach with the Indians under Frank Robinson in 1975 and 1976. Garcia returned to the Angels as a coach in 1977. One of his first acts was to hire Robinson as the Angels' batting coach. Garcia managed the Angels to a 35–46 record over the remainder of 1977. He was rehired at the end of the season only after negotiations to bring Gene Mauch to the Angels fell through. Garcia was fired in May 1978 with the club holding a record of 25–21. Sherry never managed another big-league team.

July 14	The Angels pull off a triple play during a 4–1 loss to the Mariners at Anaheim Stadium. With Seattle runners on first and second in the fifth inning, Leroy Stanton grounded to third baseman Ron Jackson, who stepped on third and fired the ball to second baseman Jerry Remy for the force. Remy then threw to first baseman Tony Solaita for the third out.
July 16	Nolan Ryan strikes out 12 batters during a 5–4 win over the Mariners at Anaheim Stadium.

Frank Tanana was scheduled to be the American League starter in the All-Star Game at Yankee Stadium on July 19, but was scratched due to an arm injury. Ryan created a flap when he refused to join the AL squad after being named as Tanana's replacement.

July 23	The Angels complete their second triple play in ten days, but lose 10–4 to the Twins at Metropolitan Stadium. With runners on first and second, Lyman Bostock lined out to shortstop Rance Mulliniks, and outs were records on force-outs on throws from Mulliniks to second baseman Jerry Remy and from Remy to first baseman Tony Solaita.
July 25	Don Baylor hits a grand slam off Paul Mitchell in the first inning of a 9–3 win over the Athletics in Oakland.
August 7	Bobby Bonds homers in his fifth consecutive game during a 6–3 win over the Angels in Anaheim.

Bonds hit eight homers in a span of nine games from August 2 through August 11. He homered against the Yankees in Anaheim on August 2 and 3 and versus the Orioles at home on August 5, 6 and 7. After being held without a home run in the first game of a double-header facing the Royals in Kansas City on August 8, Bonds cleared the wall with a drive in the second contest, then homered against the Red Sox in Boston on August 10 and 11.

AUGUST 19	Nolan Ryan strikes out 13 batters, but walks nine, and the Angels lose 3–1 to the Blue Jays at Anaheim Stadium.
AUGUST 26	Bobby Bonds breaks a 4–4 tie with a two-run homer in the 12th inning, and the Angels defeat the Tigers 7–6 in Detroit.
SEPTEMBER 6	The Angels purchase Dave Kingman from the Padres.

Kingman was sent to the Yankees nine days later for Randy Stein and cash. The Yanks were Kingman's fourth team in 1977. He began the season with the Mets.

SEPTEMBER 8	Don Baylor scores both runs, one of them on a home run in the sixth inning, during a 2–0 win over the White Sox in the first game of a double-header at Anaheim Stadium. Nolan Ryan (6$\frac{1}{3}$ innings) and Dave LaRoche (2$\frac{2}{3}$ innings) combined on the shutout. In the second tilt, the Angels scored three times in the ninth to win 3–2.

The win gave Ryan a 19–13 record, but he lost his last three starts in an attempt at victory number 20.

SEPTEMBER 10	White Sox pitcher Wilbur Wood hits three batters in a row with pitches in the first inning leading to the Angels' first run during a 6–1 triumph at Anaheim Stadium. Wood plunked Dave Kingman, Don Baylor and Dave Chalk.
SEPTEMBER 13	Trailing 7–4, the Angels erupt for eight runs in the seventh inning and down the Rangers 12–7 in Arlington.
SEPTEMBER 16	The Angels purchase Carlos May from the Yankees.
SEPTEMBER 22	Bert Blyleven of the Rangers pitches a no-hitter to beat the Angels 6–0 at Anaheim Stadium. It was the second time in 1977 that the Angels were held without a hit. The first was by Dennis Eckersley. Blyleven walked one and struck out seven. The last out was recorded on a strikeout of Thad Bosley.
OCTOBER 20	Buzzie Bavasi replaces Harry Dalton as general manager.

Following a seventh consecutive losing season, Gene Autry said he was taking control of the franchise. In addition to his title as chairman of the board, Autry also became club president. Red Patterson, who had held the title of president, became the assistant to the chairman of the board and was placed in charge of public relations. Bavasi was 62 at the time of his appointment with the Angels. He had previously been the general manager of the Dodgers from 1950 through 1968 when he resigned to become president of the Padres. Under Bavasi, the Dodgers won eight NL pennants and four World Series. He was unsuccessful in building a winner in San Diego, however. Bavasi was the general manager of the Angels until 1984 and helped the club reach the postseason in 1979 and 1982.

NOVEMBER 21	The Angels sign Lyman Bostock, most recently with the Twins, as a free agent.

Bostock was only 27 when signed by the Angels and appeared to be poised for stardom after batting .323 for Minnesota in 1976 and .336 in 1977. After collecting only two hits in his first 39 at-bats with the Angels in 1978,

> *Bostock donated his first month's salary to charity. He started hitting again and raised his batting average to .296 when he was murdered while sitting in an automobile in Gary, Indiana (see September 23, 1978).*

DECEMBER 5   The Angels trade Bobby Bonds, Thad Bosley and Rick Dotson to the White Sox for Brian Downing, Chris Knapp and Dave Frost.

> *Following the announcement of the deal, the switchboard at the Big-A lit up immediately, and Buzzie Bavasi was deluged with hate mail. In the long run, however, it proved to be one of the best deals in club history. Bonds went into a rapid decline and was out of baseball by 1981. Downing, a native of Anaheim, played 13 seasons for the Angels as a catcher, outfielder and designated hitter. He had an unusually wide, open stance at home plate, facing the pitcher while holding the bat high over his head. He was also one of the first players to devote himself to body building year-round, building both a batting cage and special workout gym at his Southern California home. Downing's impressive physique earned him the nickname of the "Incredible Hulk." Through the 2009 season, Downing ranks third among Angels players in games (1,661), third in at-bats (5,854), third in doubles (282), third in home runs (222), third in RBIs (846), third in runs scored (889), third in hits (1,558) and third in walks (886).*

DECEMBER 8   The Angels trade Jerry Remy to the Red Sox for Don Aase and cash. On the same day, the Angels dealt Pat Kelly and Butch Alberts to the Blue Jays for Ron Fairly.

> *This trade was completed between Buzzie Bavasi and his son Peter, who was the president of the Blue Jays. Fairly hit .217 in 91 games for the Angels in 1978, the last of his 21 seasons in the majors.*

DECEMBER 15   The Angels sell Andy Etchebarren to the Brewers.

DECEMBER 21   The Angels sign Rick Miller, most recently with the Red Sox, as a free agent.

1978

Season in a Sentence
The Angels change managers in mid-season for the third year in a row and achieve a winning season for the first time since 1970 with 87 wins, but the year ends in tragedy with the murder of Lyman Bostock.

Finish • Won • Lost • Pct • GB
Second 87 75 .537 5.0
(tie)

Managers
Dave Garcia (25–21) and Jim Fregosi (62–54)

Stats

Stats	Angels	AL	Rank
Batting Avg:	.259	.261	9
On-Base Pct:	.325	.326	9
Slugging Pct:	.370	.365	11
Home Runs:	108		7
Stolen Bases:	86		9
ERA:	3.65	3.76	8
Errors:	136		6
Runs Scored:	691		7
Runs Allowed:	666		8

Starting Lineup
Brian Downing, c
Ron Jackson, 1b
Bobby Grich, 2b
Carney Lansford, 3b
Dave Chalk, ss
Joe Rudi, lf
Rick Miller, cf
Lyman Bostock, rf-cf
Don Baylor, dh
Ken Landreaux, rf-cf-lf
Ron Fairly, 1b

Pitchers
Frank Tanana, sp
Chris Knapp, sp
Nolan Ryan, sp
Don Aase, sp
Dave Frost, rp
Dave LaRoche, rp
Paul Hartzell, rp
Dyar Miller, rp
Ken Brett, rp

Attendance
1,755,386 (fourth in AL)

Club Leaders
Batting Avg:	Lyman Bostock	.296
On-Base Pct:	Lyman Bostock	.362
Slugging Pct:	Don Baylor	.472
Home Runs:	Don Baylor	34
RBI:	Don Baylor	99
Runs:	Don Baylor	103
Stolen Bases:	Don Baylor	22
Wins:	Frank Tanana	18
Strikeouts:	Nolan Ryan	260
ERA:	Frank Tanana	3.65
Saves:	Dave LaRoche	25

MARCH 25 — The Angels sign Merv Rettenmund, most recently with the Padres, as a free agent.

APRIL 7 — The Angels open the season with a 1–0 win over the Athletics before 28,194 at Anaheim Stadium. Frank Tanana pitched the complete game six-hit shutout. The lone run scored in the sixth inning off Rick Langford on a triple by Terry Humphrey and a single from Rick Miller, who was making his debut with the club.

The Angels drew a then club record of 1,755,386 in 1978. The previous mark was 1,432,633 in 1977.

APRIL 8 — Nolan Ryan strikes out 13 batters in six shutout innings, but the relievers allow four runs and the Angels lose 4–2 to the Athletics at Anaheim Stadium.

APRIL 12 — The Angels explode for eight runs in the first inning and beat the Twins 9–5 at Anaheim Stadium. Rick Miller started the inning with a walk and accounted for the final four runs with a grand slam off Gary Serum.

APRIL 13	The Angels play beat the clock to defeat the Twins 1–0 in 11 innings at Anaheim Stadium. By prior agreement, it was decided that no inning could start after 3:50 p.m. of the Thursday afternoon contest to allow the Twins sufficient time to catch a plane. At 3:55 p.m., with one out in the bottom of the 11th, Joe Rudi smacked a walk-off home run off Tom Johnson. Nolan Ryan went ten innings, allowed only four hits and struck out 12, but earned a no decision. Dave LaRoche pitched the 11th.
	LaRoche was 10–9 with 25 saves and a 2.81 ERA in 59 games and 96 innings in 1978.
APRIL 19	Ron Jackson drives in six runs on two doubles and a single during an 11–2 thumping of the Mariners in Seattle.
APRIL 24	Nolan Ryan strikes out 15 batters in nine innings, but the Angels lose 6–5 in 12 innings to the Mariners in Seattle.
APRIL 29	Nolan Ryan pitches a two-hitter and strikes out 11 to defeat the Blue Jays 5–0 at Anaheim Stadium. The only Toronto hits were a triple by Willie Upshaw in the third inning and a single from Rick Cerone in the seventh.
MAY 5	Nolan Ryan follows his two-hitter with a one-hitter and defeats the Indians 5–0 at Anaheim Stadium. The only Cleveland hit was a single by Duane Kuiper in the sixth inning.
	Ryan was nearly untouchable in his first six starts, allowing only 20 hits in 50 innings while striking out 71. He tailed off afterward, however. Ryan finished the year leading the AL in strikeouts with 260 in 234 2/3 innings, but was 10–13 with an ERA of 3.72.
MAY 6	Merv Rettenmund hits a pinch-hit grand slam off Dennis Kinney in the seventh inning of a 7–3 victory over the Indians at Anaheim Stadium.
MAY 7	The Angels collect 21 hits and clobber the Indians 16–3 at Anaheim Stadium.
MAY 18	Don Baylor hits a grand slam off Ron Schueler in the third inning of a 9–5 win over the White Sox in Chicago.
	Baylor batted .255 with 34 homers, 99 RBIs and 103 runs scored in 1978.
MAY 31	The White Sox break a 1–1 tie by erupting for 11 runs in the fifth inning and pummel the Angels 17–2 in Chicago.
JUNE 2	The Angels hire 36-year-old Jim Fregosi as manager to replace Dave Garcia. Fregosi became the eighth permanent manager of the Angels since 1969, following Bill Rigney, Lefty Phillips, Del Rice, Bobby Winkles, Dick Williams, Norm Sherry and Garcia.
	The Angels were 25–21 at the time of the switch. "We felt the Angels needed motivation," said Gene Autry, "and that Fregosi was the type to fill the bill." It was a homecoming for Fregosi, who played shortstop for the Angels from 1961 through 1971. He was a utility player for the Pirates at the time the Angels hired him as manager. Fregosi's only prior experience as a manager was two seasons

in the Puerto Rican Winter League. He would guide the Angels to their first postseason berth in 1979. Garcia later managed the Indians from 1979 through 1982.

JUNE 6   In the first round of the amateur draft, the Angels select outfielder Tom Brunansky from West Covina High School in West Covina, California.

Brunansky played in 11 games for the Angels in 1981 before being traded to the Twins. He had a 14-year career in the majors. Other future major leaguers drafted and signed by the Angels in 1978 were Dave Engle (third round), Mike Witt (fourth round), and Dan Whitmer (14th round).

JUNE 8   Trailing 7–4, the Angels get a three-run homer from Ron Jackson in the eighth inning and another three-run blast by Don Baylor in the ninth and defeat the Athletics 10–7 in Oakland.

JUNE 17   Ron Guidry strikes out 18 Angels while leading the Yankees to a 4–0 win in New York.

JUNE 21   Leading off the first inning in his first big-league plate appearance, Angels second baseman Dave Machemer homers off Geoff Zahn to spark a 5–2 victory over the Twins in Minnesota.

Machemer never hit another homer during his major league career, which lasted 29 games and 48 at-bats with the Angels and Tigers in 1978 and 1979.

JUNE 26   Richard Nixon attends his first baseball game since leaving the White House in 1974, and the former President watches the Angels lose 4–0 to the Royals at Anaheim Stadium. It was the third game in a row and the fourth in the last five in which the Angels were held without a run.

JUNE 27   With the Angels trailing 4–1, Joe Rudi hits a pinch-hit grand slam off Steve Mingori in the seventh inning to beat the Royals 5–4 at Anaheim Stadium.

JULY 1   Ron Fairly is ejected in an unusual manner in the eighth inning of a 6–3 loss to the Rangers at Anaheim Stadium. Fairly was tagged out after tripping and falling in the base path and, in disgust, picked up a handful of dirt and flung it over his head. Unfortunately, the dirt landed on the head and shoulders of umpire Terry Cooney, who sent Fairly to the clubhouse.

JULY 6   Joe Rudi hits a grand slam off Marty Pattin in the first inning of a 9–5 triumph over the Royals in Kansas City.

JULY 8   The Angels sweep the Mariners 10–5 and 5–0 in a double-header in Seattle to take a two-game lead in the AL West. The Angels had a record of 46–39.

JULY 14   Nolan Ryan strikes out 13 batters in nine innings as the Angels defeat the Blue Jays 3–2 in 12 innings at Anaheim Stadium. Tony Solaita drove in the winning run with a single.

July 24	The Angels outlast the Indians 5–4 in a 16-inning marathon in Cleveland. Don Baylor hit a two-run homer in the 11th, but the Indians came back with two runs in their half. Dave Chalk drove in the winning run with a single.
July 26	Joe Rudi hits a grand slam off Bill Travers in the first inning to spark an 11–9 win over the Brewers in Milwaukee. It was Rudi's third grand slam in a span of 30 days.
August 4	The Angels score seven runs in the third inning and rout the Twins 12–3 in Minnesota.
August 10	The Angels clobber the Athletics 16–5 in Oakland.
August 11	Nolan Ryan pitches a two-hitter to defeat the Mariners 3–1 at the Kingdome. The only Seattle hits were a double by Bruce Bochte in the second inning and a single from Dan Meyer with two out in the ninth.
August 12	Danny Goodwin stars in a ten-inning, 7–5 win over the Mariners in the first game of a double-header at the Kingdome. Goodwin homered with one out in the ninth to tie the score 5–5 in the ninth, then delivered a two-run single in the tenth. Seattle won the second contest 5–3.
August 16	Nolan Ryan strikes out 13 batters, but the Angels lose 4–2 to the Red Sox at Anaheim Stadium.
August 18	Don Baylor hits a walk-off homer in the ninth inning to defeat the Orioles 3–2 at Anaheim Stadium.
August 20	The Angels edge the Orioles 1–0 in a 14-inning marathon at Anaheim Stadium. Don Baylor drove in the lone run of the game with a double. Nolan Ryan (seven innings), Dave LaRoche (five innings) and Tom Griffin (two innings) combined on the shutout. The three allowed seven hits and struck out 16.

The Angels were in first place on August 24, 25 and 26, but dropped back into second behind the Royals during a five-game losing streak which began on the 25th.

September 2	Joe Rudi drives in both runs of a 2–0 win over the Blue Jays in Toronto with a double in the first inning. Frank Tanana pitched the shutout.

Tanana was 11–3 with a 2.52 ERA on June 20 and had pitched 118 innings in the Angels' first 65 games. He finished the season with an 18–12 record, but his ERA increased from 2.54 in 1977 to 3.65 in 1978, while his strikeout rate dropped from 7.65 per nine innings the previous season to 5.16. Due to arm miseries, Tanana pitched only 90 1/3 innings in 1979 and had a record of 22–40 with the Angels, Red Sox and Rangers from 1980 through 1982.

September 3	Chris Knapp pitches a one-hitter to defeat the Blue Jays 3–1 at Exhibition Stadium. The only Toronto hit was a home run by Willie Horton in the second inning.

Knapp was 14–8 in 1978 despite missing three weeks in July and August after he left the club due to dissatisfaction with his contract and management's treatment of him.

SEPTEMBER 7	Trailing 6–0, the Angels explode for seven runs in the sixth inning to down the Rangers 7–6 at Anaheim Stadium. Don Baylor put the Angels within a run at 6–5 with a two-run homer, and after a single by Joe Rudi, Ron Fairly followed with another homer to put California into the lead.
SEPTEMBER 10	The Angels trounce the Royals 13–3 at Anaheim Stadium. Nolan Ryan struck out 13 batters, and Don Baylor contributed a grand slam off Paul Splittorf in the first inning.

> *The win put the Angels only one-half game behind the first-place Royals. The Angels lost six of their next eight games, however, to fall 5½ games behind Kansas City by September 18.*

SEPTEMBER 14	The Angels break open a close game with 13 unearned runs in the ninth and hammer the Rangers 16–1 in Arlington. After the inning started with a fly ball out, 13 batters in a row reached base on seven singles, two doubles, two walks and two errors. The batters who reached during the streak were Brian Downing (twice), Bobby Grich (twice), Dave Chalk (twice), Rick Miller (twice), Carney Lansford, Lyman Bostock, Joe Rudi, Don Baylor and Ron Jackson.
SEPTEMBER 23	Lyman Bostock is killed by a shotgun blast in an automobile driven by his uncle at Fifth and Jackson Streets in Gary, Indiana. He was visiting relatives in the city, which was his hometown. Bostock was the innocent victim of a domestic dispute. The murderer, 31-year-old Leonard Smith, intended to shoot his wife, but instead shot Bostock in the temple with a .410 gauge shotgun. Bostock was sitting in the back seat next to Smith's wife, Barbara, when Smith pulled alongside in another vehicle and fired. Barbara Smith suffered only minor wounds to the face. Bostock was 27 and had a .311 batting average in four big-league seasons, the last of which was spent with the Angels. Earlier in the day, he had two hits in four at-bats during a 5–4 win over the White Sox in Chicago, about 35 miles from Gary.

> *Bostock remains the only major leaguer to be murdered during a season. Smith was tried twice for murder. The first ended in a hung jury. In the second, Smith was found not guilty by reason of insanity. He served only 21 months in custody.*

SEPTEMBER 24	Less than 24 hours following Lyman Bostock's murder, the grieving Angels defeat the White Sox 7–3 in Chicago.
NOVEMBER 21	The Los Angeles Rams sign a contract to play at Anaheim Stadium beginning in 1980. The lease agreement was for 35 years. The Rams had played at Memorial Coliseum since 1946. The Rams were the second pro football team to call Anaheim Stadium home. The first was the Southern California Sun of the World Football League in 1974 and 1975.

> *As a result of the Rams' move, Anaheim Stadium was completely enclosed, increasing capacity from 43,550 to over 64,593. The mezzanine and upper deck were extended completely around the playing field. An elevated bank of bleachers was built in right field, and temporary seats were placed underneath to be used for football games only. Among the additions were new executive boxes, media boxes and a new sound system. The new video board was installed on the facade of the left-center field roof. The Big-A scoreboard was preserved*

and moved to the edge of the stadium parking lot. The enclosure destroyed much of the ambiance of the ballpark, and Angel fans lamented the loss of the views of the distant mountains. The Rams played at Anaheim Stadium from 1980 through 1994, when the club moved to St. Louis. In 1996 and 1997, the stadium was opened up beyond the outfield once again when the football seats were removed.

DECEMBER 3   The Angels sign Jim Barr, most recently with the Giants, as a free agent.

DECEMBER 4   The Angels trade Ron Jackson and Danny Goodwin to the Twins for Dan Ford.

1979

Season in a Sentence
Utilizing the best batting attack in the league, the Angels shatter their previous attendance record and reach the postseason for the first time before losing to the Orioles in the ALCS.

Finish • Won • Lost • Pct • GB
First   88   74   .574   +3.0

AL Championship Series
The Angels lost to the Baltimore Orioles three games to one.

Manager
Jim Fregosi

Stats

Stats	Angels	AL	Rank
Batting Avg:	.282	.270	2
On-Base Pct:	.351	.334	1
Slugging Pct:	.429	.408	3
Home Runs:	164		4
Stolen Bases:	100		6
ERA:	4.34	4.22	9
Errors:	135		8
Runs Scored:	866		1
Runs Allowed:	768		9

Starting Lineup
Brian Downing, c
Rod Carew, 1b
Bobby Grich, 2b
Carney Lansford, 3b
Bert Campaneris, ss
Don Baylor, lf-dh
Rick Miller, cf
Dan Ford, rf
Willie Aikens, dh-1b
Joe Rudi, lf
Jim Anderson, ss

Pitchers
Dave Frost, sp
Nolan Ryan, sp
Jim Barr, sp
Don Aase, sp
Chris Knapp, sp
Frank Tanana, sp
Mark Clear, rp
Dave LaRoche, rp
Mike Barlow, rp

Attendance
2,523,575 (second in AL)

Club Leaders

Batting Avg:	Brian Downing	.326
On-Base Pct:	Brian Downing	.418
Slugging Pct:	Bobby Grich	.537
Home Runs:	Don Baylor	36
RBI:	Don Baylor	139
Runs:	Don Baylor	120
Stolen Bases:	Don Baylor	22
Wins:	Dave Frost	16
	Nolan Ryan	16
Strikeouts:	Nolan Ryan	223
ERA:	Dave Frost	3.57
Saves:	Mark Clear	14

February 3 The Angels trade Ken Landreaux, Dave Engle, Paul Hartzell and Brad Havens to the Twins for Rod Carew.

Carew spent 12 years with the Twins as a second baseman and first baseman. While in Minnesota, he was named to the All-Star team in all 12 seasons, compiled a batting average of .334 and won seven batting titles and MVP award, in addition to leading the league in hits three times, triples twice and runs once. He was 33 at the time of the trade, but was still at the top of his game. Carew batted .388 with 239 hits in 1977 and .333 in 1978 while playing a combined 307 games over those two seasons, but became disgruntled with the tight-fisted fiscal policies and racially insensitive comments of Twins owner Calvin Griffith and demanded a trade. A deal with the Giants was pending, but Carew turned it down to remain in the American League. The Yankees also nearly completed a deal before the Angels stepped in. The deal excited Angels fans who had yet to see their club win a pennant. The day after the trade was announced, the club sold 250 season tickets, including two to former President Richard Nixon. Carew spent the final seven seasons of his career in Anaheim. He was named to six All-Star teams and batted .314. In 1985, he collected his 3,000th career hit and was elected to the Hall of Fame on the first ballot in 1991.

March 27 The Angels sign Willie Davis as a free agent.

April 4 Seven days after the nuclear disaster at Three Mile Island, the Angels open the season with a 5–4 loss to the Mariners in Seattle. Frank Tanana was the starting and losing pitcher. Rick Miller homered and drove in three runs.

Ron Fairly joined the Angels broadcast team in 1979. He remained as an announcer of the club's games until 1986.

April 10 In the home opener, the Angels lose 8–1 to the Twins before 33,171 at Anaheim Stadium.

The Angels had a dramatic increase in attendance during the late 1970s. The club drew 1,006,174 in 1976, 1,432,633 in 1977, 1,755,396 in 1978 and 2,523,575 in 1979.

April 15 Brian Downing collects five hits, three of them doubles, in five at-bats during an 8–1 victory over the Athletics in Oakland.

Downing batted .326 with 12 homers in 1979.

April 21 The Angels extend their winning streak to ten games with a 13–1 thrashing of the Athletics at Anaheim Stadium. Don Baylor hit a grand slam off Bob Lacey during a nine-run fifth inning. Nolan Ryan struck out 12 and pitched a two-hitter. He had a no-hitter in progress until Mitchell Page singled with one out in the eighth inning. Wayne Gross added another single later in the eighth.

The win gave the Angels a record of 12–3 and a two-game lead in the AL West.

MAY 2   The Angels edge the Yankees 1–0 at Anaheim Stadium. Nolan Ryan pitched the shutout. Jim Anderson drove in the lone run with a double off Ron Guidry in the third inning.

> *Ryan led the AL in strikeouts for the seventh time in a span of eight years with 223 in 222$^{2}/_{3}$ innings. He also had a 16–14 record and a 3.60 ERA.*

MAY 4   The Angels trade Dave Chalk to the Rangers for Bert Campaneris.

MAY 8   Joe Rudi hits a grand slam off Chuck Rainey in the first inning of a 10–2 trouncing of the Red Sox at Anaheim Stadium.

> *Despite playing in a pitcher's park, the Angels led the American League in runs scored in 1979 with 866. The club scored 691 runs (seventh in AL), in 1978, 675 (tenth) in 1977 and 550 (12th and last) in 1976. The 1979 run production proved to be a one-year aberration. The Angels scored 698 times in 1980 to rank ninth in the American League.*

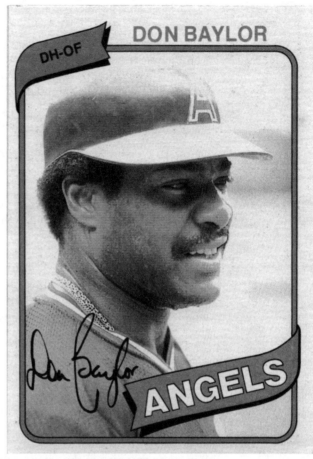

Don Baylor enjoyed a monster year in 1979, giving the Angels lineup a feared power bat.

MAY 13   The Angels score seven runs in the ninth inning, but it's too late to prevent a 12–10 loss to the Yankees in New York. The seven runs crossed the plate before a batter was retired on a double, five singles and a three-run homer by Willie Aikens. During the game, Chris Knapp slipped on the wet mound at Yankee Stadium and injured his back. He was only 25 years of age but was never again the same pitcher. Over the remainder of his career, which ended in 1980, Knapp had a record of 5–16 with a 6.25 ERA.

> *Willie's full name is Willie Mays Aikens after his father's favorite player. Aikens was born on October 14, 1954 in Seneca, South Carolina, just 15 days after Mays made his famous over-the-shoulder catch against the Indians at the Polo Grounds in the World Series.*

MAY 15   Don Baylor hits a walk-off homer in the ninth inning to defeat the Brewers 2–1 at Anaheim Stadium.

May 16	The Angels win with a walk-off hit for the second game in a row when Rod Carew delivers a single in the 11th inning to defeat the Brewers 4–3 at Anaheim Stadium.
May 19	The Angels score seven runs in the first and defeat the White Sox 10–6 at Anaheim Stadium. Carney Lansford drove in the first run of the inning with a lead-off homer and Bobby Grich capped the rally with a three-run blast.

> *In his first two seasons with the Angels, Grich was an extreme disappointment with a .249 batting average and 13 homers in 668 at-bats. In 1979, he lived up to his contract by batting .294 along with 30 doubles, 30 home runs and 101 runs batted in.*

May 20	Nolan Ryan pitches a two-hitter to defeat the White Sox 4–0 at Anaheim Stadium. The only Chicago hits were singles by Chet Lemon in the first inning and Greg Pryor in the third.
May 23	Because of injuries to Brian Downing and Terry Humphrey, infielder Jim Anderson is the starting catcher for a game against the Brewers in Milwaukee. It was the first since high school that Anderson played as a catcher. In the seventh inning, he was unable to handle a pitch from Don Aase which allowed Paul Molitor to score from third base, leading to the only run in a 1–0 loss.
May 30	Nolan Ryan strikes out 12 batters and pitches a three-hitter to defeat the Mariners 3–2 in Seattle.
May 31	Bobby Grich collects four hits, including two homers and a double, and drives in five runs, but the Angels lose 12–10 to the Mariners in Seattle.
June 5	With their first pick in the amateur draft, the Angels select pitcher Mickey Saatzer from Eisenhower High School in Hopkins, Minnesota. He was chosen in the third round. The Angels forfeited their first- and second-round picks due to free agent compensation.

> *Saatzer never reached the majors. The only future big leaguers drafted and signed by the Angels in 1978 were Pat Keedy (fifth round), Darrell Miller (ninth round) and Gary Pettis (sixth round of the January draft).*

June 8	Dan Ford hits a grand slam off John Hiller in the seventh inning of a 6–4 win over the Tigers at Anaheim Stadium.

> *Ford hit .290 with 21 homers, 101 RBIs and 100 runs scored in 1979.*

June 9	Nolan Ryan strikes out 16 batters during a 9–1 win over the Tigers at Anaheim Stadium. He got stronger as the game progressed, fanning 11 over the last five innings.
June 11	The Angels erupt for six runs in the ninth inning to defeat the Indians 9–4 in Cleveland. The first run of the rally scored when Willie Aikens was hit by a pitch with the bases loaded. Brian Downing broke the deadlock with a two-run double.

JUNE 13	The Angels score seven runs in the seventh inning to tie the score 8–8, but wind up losing 9–8 to the Blue Jays in the first game of a double-header in Toronto. Brian Downing hit a grand slam off Dyar Miller. The Angels won the second tilt 10–2.
JUNE 14	Willie Aikens hits a grand slam off Phil Huffman in the first inning of a 10–2 victory over the Blue Jays in Toronto. It was the second game in a row in which the Angels downed the Jays.
JUNE 18	Nolan Ryan pitches a two-hitter to defeat the Rangers 5–0 at Anaheim Stadium. Ryan had a no-hitter in progress until Oscar Gamble singled with one out in the eighth inning. Bill Sample added another single with two out in the ninth. Ryan was a doubtful starter right up until game time because of a pulled calf muscle.
JUNE 19	Bobby Grich extends his hitting streak to 20 games during a 2–1 loss to the Rangers at Anaheim Stadium.
JULY 1	The Angels erupt for ten runs in the eighth inning and pummel the Royals 14–2 in Kansas City. Don Baylor and Dan Ford each homered twice during the game.
JULY 4	For the second time in four days, the Angels score ten runs in an inning, this time in the eighth during a 17–6 triumph over the Athletics at Anaheim Stadium. The seventh, eighth and ninth runs scored on three consecutive bases-loaded walks by Craig Minetto to Jim Anderson, Bobby Grich and Carney Lansford. Lansford finished the day with four runs scored and four hits, including a double. Don Baylor homered for the fourth game in a row.

> *Baylor homered twice against the Royals in Kansas City on July 1 and once each versus the A's on July 2, 3 and 4. He collected eight hits in 14 at-bats over those four games and drove in 14 runs. By the end of the season, Baylor had a .296 batting average, 36 homers, 120 runs, 333 total bases and a league-leading 139 RBIs. He started all 162 games in the fourth slot in the batting order. The tremendous season earned him the AL MVP award.*

JULY 7	The Angels score seven runs in the seventh inning and beat the Orioles 10–1 at Anaheim Stadium. Joe Rudi hit a grand slam off Don Stanhouse.
JULY 9	Nolan Ryan strikes out 12 batters during a 6–0 win over the Red Sox at Anaheim Stadium. The victory also put the Angels into first place. With the exception of one day (August 30), the club was in first for the remainder of the season.
JULY 13	Nolan Ryan loses a no-hitter in the ninth inning before closing out a 6–1 victory over the Yankees at Anaheim Stadium. Thurman Munson led off the ninth by reaching on an error. After Graig Nettles fouled out, Reggie Jackson collected the only New York hit of the game with a single. Munson scored on a sacrifice fly.
JULY 14	The Angels score three runs in the ninth inning and one in the 12th to beat the Yankees 8–7 at Anaheim Stadium. Trailing 7–4, the first two batters in the ninth were retired before Carney Lansford and Dan Ford singled and Don Baylor hit a dramatic three-run homer off the left-field foul pole. Merv Rettunmund drove in the winning run with a single.

JULY 15 — Bobby Grich drives in all five runs during a 5–4 triumph over the Yankees at Anaheim Stadium. He singled in a run in the third inning and collected a two-run double in the seventh. With the Angels still trailing 4–3 with two out in the ninth, Grich clubbed a two-run, walk-off homer.

JULY 17 — In the All-Star Game at the Kingdome in Seattle, Don Baylor collects a double and a single in four at-bats, scores two runs and drives in one, but the American League loses 7–6.

JULY 23 — Joe Rudi hits a grand slam off Dick Drago in the first inning of a 9–2 triumph over the Red Sox in Boston.

Rudi hit three grand slams in both 1978 and 1979.

AUGUST 8 — Despite 21 hits, seven of them for extra bases, the Angels score just eight runs, but it's enough to rout the Athletics 8–1 in Oakland. Dan Ford collected four hits in four at-bats.

AUGUST 10 — Dan Ford hits for the cycle and collects four extra base hits, but the Angels lose 8–6 in 14 innings to the Mariners at Anaheim Stadium. Facing Mike Parrott, Ford doubled in the first inning, singled in the third and homered in the fifth. After making outs in the seventh and ninth, Ford tripled off Byron McLaughlin in the 12th and collected another double against Randy Stein in the 14th.

During the games on August 7, 8 and 10, Ford collected hits in eight consecutive at-bats. He was named "Disco Dan" because he had a financial interest in a disco club.

AUGUST 12 — After being shut out through eight innings, the Angels score four runs in the ninth to stun the Mariners 4–3 at Anaheim Stadium. The inning started with singles by Don Baylor, Willie Aikens and Brian Downing to produce one run. The second scored on a Seattle error. After a walk to Joe Rudi, Rod Carew delivered a two-run, walk-off single for the victory.

AUGUST 25 — The Angels collect 26 hits and rout the Blue Jays 24–2 in Toronto. The runs, hits and margin-of-victory figures are all club records. The Angels scored eight runs in the first inning, three in the second, two in the third, three in the fourth, one in the fifth, five in the sixth and two in the eighth. Don Baylor led the way with eight runs batted in. He hit a grand slam off Balor Moore in the first inning, a run-scoring double facing Jefferson in the third and a three-run homer off Todd in the sixth. Bobby Grich, Dan Ford and Bobby Clark also homered. It was Clark's first big-league home run.

The 24–2 rout was the Angels' only victory in the stretch of nine games. The club lost its previous three games and the next five.

SEPTEMBER 1 — Carney Lansford hits three homers in his first three plate appearances during a 7–4 triumph over the Indians in Cleveland. All three were solo shots off Dan Spillner in the first, third and fifth innings.

SEPTEMBER 14 — The Angels take a four-game lead with 15 contests left on the schedule after defeating the Brewers 8–7 in Milwaukee.

SEPTEMBER 20	The Angels purchase Ralph Garr from the White Sox.
SEPTEMBER 23	The Angels bunch all six of their runs and five of their six hits in the fifth inning of a 6–1 victory over the Rangers at Anaheim Stadium. The win gave California a three-game advantage over the second-place Royals with six contests left on the schedule.
SEPTEMBER 24	The Angels take a four-game lead in the AL West by defeating the Royals 4–3 at Anaheim Stadium. Dan Ford drove in all four runs with a two-run single and two sacrifice flies.
SEPTEMBER 25	The Angels clinch their first division title by defeating the Royals 4–1 at Anaheim Stadium. Frank Tanana pitched a complete game. Former President Richard Nixon was among the 40,631 in attendance on a Tuesday night. He sat next to Gene Autry in a box behind home plate. A foul ball by Bobby Grich in the second inning headed toward Nixon, but it was deflected by a Secret Service agent. Nixon also took part in the clubhouse celebration and was showered with champagne by players. Later, the Angels were guests of Nixon at his San Clemente estate.

The Angels finished the season with a record of 88–74, which was the fifth best in the American League. The club's opponent in the best-of-five Championship Series was the Baltimore Orioles. Managed by Earl Weaver, the Orioles were 102–57 in 1979. The Angels were without the services of pitcher Jim Barr during the playoffs. After the pennant-clinching, Barr went to a local restaurant named The Catch, where a fan was carrying a toilet seat with the slogan "Flush the Royals" along with a picture of Kansas City club owner Ewing Kaufman, who had earlier made disparaging comments about the Angels. Barr punched the toilet seat, believing it was cardboard, only to discover that it was a real toilet seat. Barr suffered a fractured a finger on his pitching hand.

OCTOBER 3	The Angels open the Championship Series with a ten-inning, 6–3 loss to the Orioles at Memorial Stadium in Baltimore. Dan Ford started the scoring with a homer off Jim Palmer in the first inning. After falling behind 3–2, the Angels tied the score in the sixth. Pinch hitter John Lowenstein ended the game with a three-run, walk-off homer off John Montague.

NBC covered the Series on television with Dick Enberg, Wes Parker and Sparky Anderson serving as the announcers.

OCTOBER 4	After falling behind 9–1, the Angels put together a furious rally, but fall short and lose 9–8 to the Orioles in Baltimore. For the second day in a row, Dan Ford homered in the first, but Baltimore scored four in the half, four more in the second and one in the third. California rallied with a run in the sixth, another in the seventh, three in the eighth and two in the ninth. The Angels had the bases loaded when Brian Downing grounded into a force-out to end the game. Carney Lansford collected three hits and drove in three runs in the losing cause.
OCTOBER 5	In the first postseason game ever played at Anaheim Stadium, the Angels score two runs in the ninth to win 4–3 over the Orioles before 43,199. Don Baylor homered in the fourth to give California a 2–1 advantage, but Baltimore tallied in the sixth and seventh to move ahead 3–2. With the Angels facing elimination, Rod Carew doubled with one out in the ninth, and Don Stanhouse replaced Dennis Martinez. After a walk

to Brian Downing, center fielder Al Bumbry dropped Bobby Grich's liner to score Carew. Larry Harlow followed with a double, and Downing raced home with the winning run. Don Aase pitched four innings of relief for the win, the first in the club's postseason history.

OCTOBER 6   The Orioles with the American League pennant by defeating the Angels 8–0 before 43,199 at Anaheim Stadium. Scott McGregor pitched the shutout.

NOVEMBER 16   Two weeks after 63 Americans are taken hostage by militant followers of the Ayatollah Khomeini, the Angels sign Bruce Kison, most recently with the Pirates, as a free agent.

NOVEMBER 19   Nolan Ryan signs a contract with the Astros as a free agent.

A native Texan, Ryan had developed a distaste for Southern California in general and Angels general manager Buzzie Bavasi in particular. With the lure of returning to his home state, there was little the Angels could do to keep him. Ryan was 33 on Opening Day in 1980, but played until he was 46 in 1993. He was a member of the Astros from 1980 through 1988 and the Rangers over the final five seasons of his career. After leaving the Angels, Ryan had a record of 167–133 to finish at 329–292. He also struck out 2,477 more batters for a career record of 5,714 that will likely never be broken. In addition, Ryan hurled three more no-hitters for a total of seven in his career, another mark that will probably stand the test of time.

DECEMBER 5   The Angels sign Freddie Patek, most recently with the Royals, as a free agent.

DECEMBER 6   The Angels trade Willie Aikens and Rance Mulliniks to the Royals for Al Cowens, Todd Cruz and Craig Eaton.

THE STATE OF THE ANGELS

The Angels entered the decade on the heels of their first division title in 1979, but inconsistency and postseason disappointment plagued the club during the 1980s. In part because of Gene Autry's advanced age (he turned 70 in 1977), the Angels spent heavily on free agents during the late 1970s and most of the 1980s in a "win now" mentality while at the same time trading away young players who became stars elsewhere. The Angels fielded the oldest roster in the American League in 1982, 1983, 1984, 1985 and 1986. Autry's dream of seeing the Angels reach the World Series before his death failed to come to fruition. The club had losing records in 1980, 1981, 1983, 1987 and 1988, winning ledgers in 1982, 1985, 1986 and 1989, and finished at .500 in 1984. The postseason appearances of 1979, 1982 and 1986 were each followed by losing campaigns. There were also defeats in the 1982 and 1986 Championship Series, both in agonizing fashion. In 1982, California won the first two contests of the best-of-five series against the Brewers, then lost three in a row. In 1986, the Angels led the Red Sox three games to one and were two out from a World Series berth with a three-run lead only to lose games five, six and seven. Overall, the franchise won 783 games and lost 783 during the decade. The .500 winning percentage ranked seventh among the 14 AL teams. AL champs were the Royals (1980 and 1985), Yankees (1981), Brewers (1982), Orioles (1983), Tigers (1984), Red Sox (1986), Twins (1987) and Athletics (1988 and 1989). AL West champs outside of Anaheim were the Royals (1980, 1984 and 1985), Athletics (1981, 1988 and 1989), White Sox (1983) and Twins (1987).

THE BEST TEAM

The 1982 team became the first club in franchise history to crack the 90-win barrier with a record of 93–69. The 93 wins weren't exceeded again until 2002.

THE WORST TEAM

After winning the AL West in 1979, the Angels sank to 65–95 in 1980. The 95 defeats is a franchise record.

THE BEST MOMENT

Mike Witt pitched a perfect game against the Rangers in Arlington on September 30, 1984. Also, Reggie Jackson hit his 500th homer in 1982, Rod Carew collected his 3,000th hit in 1985 and Don Sutton won his 300th game in 1986, all while wearing Angels uniforms.

THE WORST MOMENT

After leading 5–2 heading into the ninth, the Angels wound up losing game five of the 1986 ALCS 7–6 in 11 innings, then dropped games six and seven as well at Fenway Park.

THE ALL-DECADE TEAM • YEARS W/ANGELS

Bob Boone, c	1982–88
Wally Joyner, 1b	1986–91
Bobby Grich, 2b	1977–86
Doug DeCinces, 3b	1982–86
Dick Schofield, ss	1983–92, 1996
Brian Downing, lf	1979–90
Fred Lynn, cf	1981–84
Dan Ford, rf	1979–81
Reggie Jackson, dh	1982–86
Mike Witt, p	1981–90
Kirk McCaskill, p	1985–91
Geoff Zahn, p	1981–85
Ken Forsch, p	1981–84, 1986

Pitching depth was a problem throughout the 1980s. Right field was a revolving door for most of the first three decades of franchise history. No one played in at least 120 games in right in consecutive seasons until Tim Salmon did it in 1995 and 1996. Other outstanding players during the 1980s were first baseman Rod Carew (1979–85), third baseman Carney Lansford (1978–80), third baseman Jack Howell (1985–91; 1996) and center fielder Gary Pettis (1982–87). Carew and Jackson were elected to the Hall of Fame on the first ballot.

THE DECADE LEADERS

Batting Avg:	Rod Carew	.313
On-Base Pct:	Rod Carew	.387
Slugging Pct:	Doug DeCinces	.463
Home Runs:	Brian Downing	189
RBI:	Brian Downing	674
Runs:	Brian Downing	679
Stolen Bases:	Gary Pettis	186
Wins:	Mike Witt	109
Strikeouts:	Mike Witt	1,269
ERA:	Geoff Zahn	3.64
Saves:	Donnie Moore	61

THE HOME FIELD

Anaheim Stadium was transformed from a baseball-only ballpark into a multi-purpose stadium in 1979 and 1980 when the Rams moved there from Los Angeles. The area behind the outfield walls was enclosed, and capacity was increased from 43,550 to 64,593. With the exception of the strike-shortened 1981 season, the Angels drew at least 2.2 million fans every season during the 1980s with a high of 2,807,360 in 1982.

THE GAME YOU WISHED YOU HAD SEEN

Trailing Roger Clemens and the Red Sox 3–0 on October 11, 1986 in game four of the Championship Series, the Angels scored three runs in the ninth and one in the 11th to win 4–3 at Anaheim Stadium.

THE WAY THE GAME WAS PLAYED

The 1980s had a little something for everybody. Trends that surfaced in the 1970s continued, with teams still emphasizing speed. In 1987, offense spiked in a year that combined the speed of the dead-ball era with the power of the 1950s. AL teams averaged 124 stolen bases and 188 home runs.

THE MANAGEMENT

Gene Autry owned the Angels from the club's inception in December 1960 until his death in 1998. General managers were Buzzie Bavasi (1977–1984) and Mike Port (1984–1991). Field managers were Jim Fregosi (1978–81), Gene Mauch (1981 and 1982), John McNamama (1983 and 1984), Mauch again (1985–87), Cookie Rojas (1988), Moose Stubing (interim in 1988) and Doug Rader (1989–91).

THE BEST PLAYER MOVE

The Angels drafted Tom Salmon in the third round of the amateur draft in June 1989. He made his major league debut in 1992. The best trade brought Doug DeCinces and Jeff Schneider to the Angels in January 1982 for Dan Ford.

THE WORST PLAYER MOVE

The Angels traded Carney Lansford, Mark Clear and Rick Miller to the Red Sox for Rick Burleson and Butch Hobson on December 10, 1980.

1980

Season in a Sentence

In a stunning reversal of form a year after winning the AL West, nearly everything goes wrong in a franchise-record 95-loss season.

Finish • Won • Lost • Pct • GB

Sixth   65   95   .406   31.0

Manager

Jim Fregosi

Stats   Angels • AL • Rank

Stats	Angels	AL	Rank
Batting Avg:	.265	.269	9
On-Base Pct:	.331	.331	8
Slugging Pct:	.378	.399	12
Home Runs:	106		10
Stolen Bases:	91		7
ERA:	4.52	4.03	13
Errors:	134		6
Runs Scored:	698		9
Runs Allowed:	797		13

Starting Lineup

Tom Donohue, c
Rod Carew, 1b
Bobby Grich, 2b
Carney Lansford, 3b
Freddie Patek, ss
Joe Rudi, lf
Rick Miller, cf
Larry Harlow, rf
Jason Thompson, dh-1b
Don Baylor, dh-lf
Dickie Thon, ss-2b
Bobby Clark, cf-lf
Dan Ford, rf
Bert Campaneris, ss

Pitchers

Frank Tanana, sp
Don Aase, sp-rp
Alfredo Martinez, sp
Chris Knapp, sp-rp
Andy Hassler, rp
Mark Clear, rp
Dave LaRoche, rp

Attendance

2,297,327 (second in AL)

Club Leaders

Batting Avg:	Rod Carew	.331
On-Base Pct:	Rod Carew	.396
Slugging Pct:	Rod Carew	.437
Home Runs:	Jason Thompson	17
RBI:	Carney Lansford	80
Runs:	Carney Lansford	87
Stolen Bases:	Rod Carew	23
Wins:	Frank Tanana	11
Strikeouts:	Frank Tanana	113
ERA:	Don Aase	4.06
Saves:	Andy Hassler	10

APRIL 11   Seven weeks after the U.S. Olympic hockey team wins the gold medal in Lake Placid, the Angels clobber the Indians 10–2 before 37,085 on Opening Day at Anaheim Stadium. Joe Rudi homered twice and drove in four runs. Rod Carew collected three hits and stole a base. Dave Frost was the starting and winning pitcher.

Carew hit .331 for the Angels in 1980.

APRIL 16   Don Baylor foils the strategy of Twins manager Gene Mauch in the tenth inning of a 2–1 win at Anaheim Stadium. With runners on first and third and one out, Mauch utilized a five-man infield and two-man outfield, but Baylor hit a game-winning sacrifice fly. The Angels tied the score 1–1 in the ninth on another sacrifice fly by Bobby Grich.

> *Injuries devastated the Angels in 1980. Brian Downing, who batted .326 the previous season, was out from April 20 through September 1 with a broken ankle. His replacements at the catching position were woefully inadequate, batting .200 with five homers. Don Baylor, the AL MVP in 1979, broke his wrist in the first game of the season and didn't hit a home run after the All-Star break. After driving in 101 runs during the title chase in 1979, Dan Ford*

injured his knee during the last week of May and appeared in only 65 games. He saw little urgency in returning to the lineup because the Angels were out of the pennant race, drawing the ire of management. The pitching staff was also patched together because of injuries, mainly to Bruce Kison, Dave Frost and Chris Knapp, and compiled a 4.52 ERA, the second worst in the AL.

APRIL 23   The Angels score seven runs in the ninth inning to cap a 17–0 thrashing of the Twins in Minnesota. Bruce Kison had a no-hitter in progress until Ken Landreaux doubled with one out in the ninth. Kison retired the next two batters to close out a one-hit shutout. The hit by Landreaux was the first in a 31-game hitting streak. The losing pitcher was Terry Felton, who finished his career in 1982 with a record of 0–16. The one-sided victory broke a five-game losing streak in which the Angels scored only eight runs.

Bob Starr joined the Angels broadcast team in 1980. He was an announcer for the club from 1980 through 1989, and after three years with the Red Sox, returned to Anaheim again from 1993 through 1997. Starr also announced games for the Los Angeles Rams from 1979 through 1990.

MAY 14   The Angels break a 4–4 tie with seven runs in the third inning and down the Indians 13–7 in Cleveland. Playing in his first game with the Angels, catcher Dave Skaggs collected three hits, including a home run, and drove in five runs. He was purchased from the Orioles the previous day. The victory broke a six-game losing streak in which the Angels scored only 14 runs.

Skaggs played only 24 games for the Angels, and batted .197 with just one homer and nine RBIs.

MAY 16   The Angels score eight runs in the third inning and trounce the Royals 11–1 in Kansas City.

MAY 26   Eight days after the eruption of Mt. St. Helens in Washington state, the Angels lose a brawl-filled game to the Rangers by a 6–5 score at Anaheim Stadium. In the sixth inning, Texas third baseman Buddy Bell took exception to a pitch up and in from Bruce Kison and charged the mound and both benches emptied. Bell was ejected from the premises. In the seventh, Rangers pitcher Bob Babcock threw a pitch behind the head of Dan Ford and the dugouts cleared again. Babcock was banished by umpire Bill Haller. During the top of the eighth, Kison hit Rangers outfielder Johnny Grubb with a pitch, and players from both clubs stormed the field for a third time in three innings. Kison and Grubb staged a wrestling match on the mound, and after being separated, were sent to their respective clubhouses by the umpires.

MAY 27   The Angels trade Al Cowens to the Tigers for Jason Thompson.

Thompson played 102 games for the Angels and batted .317 with 17 homers. He was traded to the Pirates before the start of the 1981 season.

MAY 28   In his first plate appearance with the Angels, Jason Thompson breaks a 3–3 tie by driving in three runs with a bases-loaded double in the eighth inning, sparking a 7–6 victory over the Rangers at Anaheim Stadium. Batting in the lead-off spot as the designated hitter, Dickie Thon collected five hits, including a double in his five at-bats.

The five-hit outburst came in Thon's first major league game of the 1980 season. He began the year with Salt Lake City in the Pacific Coast League, where he batted .394 in 40 games.

JUNE 3   In the first round of the amateur draft, the Angels select pitcher Dennis Rasmussen from Creighton University.

The Angels traded Rasmussen to the Yankees in 1982. He was 91–77 in a career that lasted from 1983 through 1995. Others drafted and signed by the Angels in 1980 were Mike Brown (seventh round) and Bill Mooneyham (first round of the secondary phase).

JUNE 10   The Angels purchase Andy Hassler from the Pirates.

JUNE 20   The Angels break a nine-game losing streak by collecting 26 hits in a 20–2 clobbering of the Red Sox in Boston. There were seven California runs in the second inning, three in the third, four in the fifth, one in the sixth and five in the eighth. The Angels set a club record with 52 total bases on six homers, a triple, six doubles and 15 singles. Diminutive shortstop Freddie Patek was the unexpected hero with three homers, a double, seven RBIs and four runs scored in six at-bats. Patek doubled off Steve Renko in the second inning, homered against Dick Drago in both the third and fifth, and homered again facing Jack Billingham in the eighth. Patek received a standing ovation from Fenway Park fans following the third blast. Rick Miller, Jason Thompson and Carney Lansford also hit home runs for the Angels.

The Angels didn't hit a single home run in six games before the 20–2 pounding of the Red Sox, or during the four games afterward. Patek hit only five homers in 273 at-bats in 1980. The other two were on June 10 and August 10. The August 10 homer was the last of a career in which Patek homered 41 times in 5,530 at-bats. The three-home-run contest in Boston was the only one in which he homered more than once during his 14 years in the big leagues.

JULY 4   Rick Miller scores both runs of a 2–0 victory over the Brewers in Milwaukee. Don Aase (7⅓ innings) and Mark Clear (1⅔ innings) combined on the shutout.

JULY 6   Ed Halicki (8⅓ innings) and Mark Clear (two-thirds of an inning) combine on a two-hitter to defeat the Brewers 2–0 at County Stadium. The only Milwaukee hits were a single by Cecil Cooper in the first inning and a double from Robin Yount in the ninth. Halicki retired 20 batters in a row from the first through the eighth.

JULY 13   The Angels outlast the Athletics 5–4 in 14 innings at Anaheim Stadium. Bobby Grich drove in the winning run with a single. It was the fifth hit of the night for Grich, who had three singles, a double and a homer in seven at-bats. Andy Hassler (five innings), Mark Clear (four innings) and John Montague (one inning) combined for ten innings of shutout relief.

Grich hit .271 with 14 homers in 1980.

July 27	Bobby Grich drives in six runs during a 7–0 win over the Tigers in Detroit. Grich hit a two-run homer off Bruce Robbins in the second inning and a grand slam off Roger Weaver in the fifth. Alfredo Martinez (6⅔ innings) and Andy Hassler (2⅓ innings) combined on the shutout.
August 6	Trailing 3–1, the Angels score seven runs in the third inning and defeat the Mariners 8–3 at Anaheim Stadium.

The Angels were only 30–51 at Anaheim Stadium in 1980.

August 7	Rod Carew hits a two-run, walk-off homer in the 15th inning to defeat the Twins 4–2 at Anaheim Stadium. Mark Clear (five innings) and Andy Hassler (three innings) combined for eight innings of shutout relief.
August 13	The Angels erupt for six runs in the tenth inning and defeat the Mariners 10–4 in Seattle.
August 22	The Angels score seven runs in the fifth inning and defeat the Yankees 8–4 at Anaheim Stadium.
August 28	The Orioles collect 26 hits and beat the Angels 13–8 in Baltimore.
September 6	The Rams play a regular season game at Anaheim Stadium for the first time and lose 41–20 to the Detroit Lions.
September 20	Trailing 4–0, the Angels score a run in the eighth inning, three in the ninth and two in the tenth to defeat the Rangers 6–4 in Arlington. Rick Miller tied the score with a two-out, two-run single in the ninth. Gil Kubski broke the 4–4 deadlock with a run-scoring one-base hit and scored on Carney Lansford's double.
December 2	A month after Ronald Reagan defeats Jimmy Carter in the Presidential election, the Angels sign Geoff Zahn, most recently with the Twins, as a free agent.

Zahn spent four seasons in the Angels starting rotation. He was 18–8 in 1982.

December 10	Two days after John Lennon is murdered by a deranged fan, the Angels trade Carney Lansford, Rick Miller and Mark Clear to the Red Sox for Rick Burleson and Butch Hobson.

This proved to be a terrible transaction for the Angels. Lansford was only 23 when traded. He won the AL batting title in 1981 by hitting .336 and had an average of .293 over the remainder of his career, which lasted until 1992. Lansford was the Athletics starting third baseman in the World Series in 1988, 1989 and 1990. Clear was an effective reliever for the Red Sox and Brewers through much of the 1980s. The Angels received little in return. Burleson had one good season in California, batting .293 in 1981, before an injury to his throwing arm reduced him to a role as a reserve. Hobson was also beset by injuries and lasted just one season with the Angels.

December 29	The Angels sign Juan Beniquez, most recently with the Mariners, as a free agent.

1981

Season in a Sentence

In a season interrupted by a strike, the Angels fall short of expectations once again and change managers in mid-season for the fifth time in nine years.

Finish • Won • Lost • Pct • GB

*   51   59   .464   *

* Because of the player's strike, the season was split into two halves. In the first half, the Angels finished in fourth place with a 31–29 record and six games out of first. In the second half, the club was 20–30 in seventh place and 8½ games out of first.

Managers

Jim Fregosi (22–25) and
Gene Mauch (29–34)

Stats

Stats	Angels	AL	Rank
Batting Avg:	.256	.256	7
On-Base Pct:	.328	.321	5
Slugging Pct:	.380	.373	6
Home Runs:	97		3
Stolen Bases:	44		10
ERA:	3.70	3.66	7
Errors:	101		13
Runs Scored:	476		3
Runs Allowed:	453		9

Starting Lineup

Ed Ott, c
Rod Carew, 1b
Bobby Grich, 2b
Butch Hobson, 3b
Rick Burleson, ss
Brian Downing, lf
Fred Lynn, cf
Dan Ford, rf
Don Baylor, dh
Juan Beniquez, cf

Pitchers

Ken Forsch, sp
Geoff Zahn, sp
Mike Witt, sp
Steve Renko, sp-rp
Don Aase, rp
Andy Hassler, rp
Jesse Jefferson, sp

Attendance

1,441,545 (third in AL)

Club Leaders

Batting Avg:	Rod Carew	.305
On-Base Pct:	Rod Carew	.380
Slugging Pct:	Bobby Grich	.543
Home Runs:	Bobby Grich	22
RBI:	Bobby Grich	61
Runs	Rod Carew	57
Stolen Bases:	Rod Carew	16
Wins:	Ken Forsch	11
Strikeouts:	Mike Witt	75
ERA:	Ken Forsch	2.88
Saves	Don Aase	11

JANUARY 23   Three days after the Iranians release the American hostages after 14 months in captivity, the Angels trade Frank Tanana, Joe Rudi and Jim Dorsey to the Red Sox for Fred Lynn and Steve Renko.

> *The Angels were able to acquire Lynn, a native of Southern California, because he was involved in a contract dispute with the Red Sox. At the time of the trade, Lynn had played in the All-Star Game each of the previous six seasons, was 29 years old and had a career batting average of .308 with 124 home runs in 828 games. He was an All-Star in three of his four seasons with the Angels, but due to injuries, played far below expectations. In 1981, Lynn injured his knee twice, the second time in the All-Star Game, and batted only .219. He bounced back and hit a combined .281 with 66 home runs in three seasons from 1982 through 1984, but averaged only 132 games per season because of an assortment of ailments. Lynn went to the Orioles as a free agent following the 1984 campaign.*

APRIL 1   Two days after Ronald Reagan is wounded by John Hinckley in an assassination attempt, the Angels trade Jason Thompson to the Pirates for Ed Ott and Mickey Mahler. On the same day, the Angels also traded Dickie Thon to the Astros for Ken Forsch.

> *Forsch was 11–7 with four shutouts and a 2.88 ERA during the strike-shortened season in 1981, and gave the club three solid seasons as a starting pitcher. Thon was only 22 when traded and looked like an emerging star as a shortstop in Houston before he was beaned in a game in 1984. After coming back from the injury, he was never again the same caliber of player.*

APRIL 9 — The Angels open the season with a 6–2 victory over the Mariners in Seattle. Brian Downing hit a grand slam off Glenn Abbott in the first inning. Dan Ford also homered. Geoff Zahn, in his Angels debut, was the starting and winning pitcher.

APRIL 11 — Playing in only his third major league game, Tom Brunansky homers twice and drives in four runs during a 7–4 victory over the Mariners in Seattle.

APRIL 12 — On the day of the launch of the Columbia, the first space shuttle, the Angels score four runs in the ninth inning and defeat the Mariners 8–6 in Seattle. Rod Carew broke the 6–6 tie by stealing home off pitcher Dick Drago and catcher Bud Bulling.

APRIL 13 — The Angels lose the home opener 3–2 to the Athletics before 38,076 at Anaheim Stadium.

APRIL 26 — Mike Witt pitches a two-hitter for a 7–1 win over the Twins in the first game in Minnesota. The only Twins hits were a triple by Roy Smalley in the fourth inning and a homer from John Castino with two out in the ninth. The game was only the third of Witt's career. The Twins won the second contest 5–2. It also marked last time that the Angels played at Metropolitan Stadium in Bloomington.

> *Standing six-foot-seven, Witt was only 20 when he made his major league debut. He pitched for the Angels from 1981 through 1990 and had a record of 109–107. From 1984 through 1987, Witt was 64–44. He pitched the only perfect game in Angels history on September 30, 1984 and was named to the All-Star team in both 1986 and 1987.*

APRIL 29 — Dan Ford fights Athletics catcher Mike Heath during a 6–4 Angels loss in Oakland. Ford homered in the eighth inning, and Heath picked up Ford's bat for evidence of cork. Ford took exception, and after he crossed the plate, he and Heath grappled. Both landed several solid punches before being separated (see September 4, 1981).

MAY 1 — Fred Lynn hits two homers and drives in five runs during a 7–4 win over the Brewers in Milwaukee. Mike Witt allowed four runs in the first inning, then settled down and pitched a complete game.

MAY 4 — Yankees reliever Ron Davis strikes out the last eight Angels batters of a 4–2 New York win at Anaheim Stadium. Davis fanned Ed Ott and Bobby Grich in the seventh inning; Butch Hobson, Rod Carew and Rick Burleson in the eighth; and Dan Ford, Fred Lynn and John Harris in the ninth.

MAY 9 — The Angels trounce the Tigers 15–1 at Anaheim Stadium. Brian Downing had an unusual stat line with four runs scored on one official at-bat. He reached base five times in five plate appearances on a home run, three walks, and by being hit with a pitch.

> *Downing was converted from a catcher to a left fielder during the season. Downing quickly mastered the art of playing the outfield. He didn't make a*

single error in 330 fielding chances in 1982. Downing never caught another game after 1981, and spent the final 11 years of his career in left and as a designated hitter.

May 21 — Doug Rau pitches five shutout innings in a 2–0 victory over the Orioles in Baltimore. Don Aase hurled the final four innings in relief. It was Rau's first big-league win since May 11, 1979, when he pitched for the Dodgers.

After the May 21 win, Rau pitched only one more game before calling it a career with a record of 81–60.

May 28 — Jim Fregosi is dismissed as manager and replaced by 55-year-old Gene Mauch.

Few players in Angels history have been as popular as catcher/outfielder Brian Downing during his 13 years with the team, from 1978 through 1990.

The Angels were 22–25 at the time of the switch. Mauch had previously managed the Phillies (1960–68), Expos (1969–75) and Twins (1976–80). His 1964 Phils are infamous for blowing a 6½-game lead with two weeks remaining, and winding up in second place. Mauch had been hired by the Angels on February 12, 1981 as director of player personnel, and speculation began immediately that he was primed to replace Fregosi. Mauch managed the Angels to division titles in 1982 and 1986, but on both occasions, the club blew a two-game advantage in the Championship Series. Fregosi later managed the White Sox (1986–88), Phillies (1991–96) and Blue Jays (1999–2000). His 1993 club in Philadelphia played in the World Series.

June 3 — Rick Burleson collects five hits, including a double, in five at-bats during a 17–6 hammering of the Blue Jays in Toronto.

June 6 — The Angels rout the Orioles 10–0 at Anaheim Stadium. Ken Forsch pitched the shutout.

June 8 — The Angels score six runs in the eighth inning of a 10–2 thrashing of the Indians at Anaheim Stadium. Fred Lynn accounted for all three outs. He led off the inning by flying out. After eight batters in a row reached base on six singles, a home run and an error, Lynn ended the inning by grounding into a double play.

On the same day, the Angels selected shortstop Dick Schofield from Griffin High School in Springfield, Illinois. He was the son of another big-league infielder, also named Dick Schofield, who played for eight teams from 1953 through 1971. The father and son had remarkably similar careers. The elder Schofield played in 1,321 games, while his son appeared in 1,368 contests from 1983 through 1996. The first Dick Schofield had a batting average of .227 and on-base percentage of .317 and a slugging percentage of .297. The second Dick Schofield, had a batting average of .230, an on-base percentage of .308 and a slugging percentage of .316. He played for the Angels from 1983 through 1992 and again in 1995 and 1996. Other players drafted and signed by the Angels in 1981 who later played in the majors were Devon White (sixth round), Sap Randall (tenth round), Craig Gerber (20th round) and Rick Romanick (first round of the secondary phase in January).

JUNE 11 — In the last game before the players' strike, the Angels defeat the Red Sox 7–2 at Anaheim Stadium.

JUNE 12 — Major League baseball players begin a strike that lasts 50 days and wipes out nearly two months of the 1981 season. The strike reduced the Angels schedule to 110 games.

JULY 19 — At the age of 73, Gene Autry marries 39-year-old Jackie Ellam. Gene's first wife, Ina, died in 1980 after 48 years of marriage. A former banking executive, Jackie took an active role in both the Angels' front office and in her husband's broadcasting empire. A year after Gene's death in 1998, Jackie was named honorary president of the American League.

JULY 31 — Two days after Prince Charles marries Lady Diana Spencer in London, the players and owners hammer out an agreement to end the strike.

AUGUST 6 — The owners vote to split the 1981 pennant race with the winners of the two halves of the season to compete in an extra round of playoffs for the division title.

AUGUST 10 — The Angels open the second half of the season with a 5–4 loss to the Mariners in Seattle. Ironically, the Angels and Mariners also met in the season opener at the Kingdome on April 9.

AUGUST 12 — Bobby Grich hits a three-run homer in the 11th inning to defeat the Mariners 4–1 in Seattle. Grich also provided the first California run with a solo shot in the second.

AUGUST 15 — Bobby Grich collects four hits, two of them homers, in seven at-bats, but the Angels lose 8–7 in 12 innings to the Athletics in Oakland.

AUGUST 19 — Bobby Grich runs his hitting streak to 21 games during a 6–3 win over the Orioles at Anaheim Stadium.

Grich hit five homers in a three-game span on August 12, 14 and 15. He finished the season tied for the league lead in home runs with 22. Grich also hit .304 and drove in 61 runs.

AUGUST 21 — Rod Carew and Dan Ford star in a 12–2 pounding of the Indians at Anaheim Stadium. Carew collected five hits in five at-bats. Ford picked up four hits, including a homer and two doubles, in five at-bats and drove in five runs.

August 22	Dan Ford is in the spotlight again during a ten-inning, 3–2 victory over the Indians at Anaheim Stadium. Ford led off the ninth with a homer to tie the score 2–2, then drove in the winning run in the tenth with a sacrifice fly.
August 25	After the Red Sox score in the top of the tenth, Bobby Grich delivers a two-run, walk-off single in the bottom half for an 8–7 win at Anaheim Stadium. The Angels stole a team-record seven bases. Bert Campaneris swiped second and third as a pinch runner in the eighth inning. Rod Carew stole three bases, and Rick Burleson and Freddie Patek one each.
September 1	The Angels sign Joe Ferguson as a free agent.
September 4	Dan Ford is ejected for using a corked bat in the fourth inning of a 3–1 triumph over the Indians in Cleveland. Ford was later suspended for four games by the American League.

The Angels lost 14 of 15 games between September 5 through September 20.

September 22	The Angels edge the White Sox 1–0 at Anaheim Stadium. Bert Campaneris drove in the lone run of the game with a single in the second inning. Angel Moreno (8 2/3 innings) and Don Aase (one-third of an inning) combined on the shutout. It was Moreno's first big-league victory.

Don Aase didn't pitch after September 22 because he was put out of commission when he sneezed so hard he separated a cartilage in his rib cage.

September 25	The Angels score six runs in the first inning and five in the second, and rout the Blue Jays 11–5 at Anaheim Stadium.
September 26	Rod Carew collects his 2,500th career hit with a single off Juan Berenguer in the third inning of a 6–3 win over the Blue Jays at Anaheim Stadium.
October 3	Bob Johnson of the Rangers hits a walk-off homer off Angel Moreno in the ninth inning to beat the Angels 1–0 in Arlington.
December 6	The Angels purchase Bob Boone from the Phillies.

A graduate of Stanford University with a degree in psychology, Boone was the middle part of baseball's first three-generation family. His father Ray was in the majors from 1948 through 1960. Son Bret played from 1992 through 2005. Bret's younger brother Aaron debuted in 1997 and was still active in 2008 before missing the 2009 season following heart surgery. All four members of the Boone family played in at least one All-Star Game. Bob was a catcher from 1972 through 1990. He caught 2,225 career games, which was the major league record until Carlton Fisk passed him by one game in 1993. Generally a mediocre hitter, Boone won raves for his defensive abilities. He played seven seasons with the Angels and won four Gold Gloves.

December 11	The Angels trade Brian Harper to the Pirates for Tim Foli.

1982

Season in a Sentence
Boosted by several new additions, the Angels win the AL West and take a two games to none lead over the Brewers in the ALCS, only to lose three in a row and blow a chance at the World Series.

Finish • Won • Lost • Pct • GB
First   93   69   .574   +3.0

AL Championship Series
The Angels lost three games to two to the Milwaukee Brewers.

Manager
Gene Mauch

Stats   Angels • AL • Rank

Stats	Angels	AL	Rank
Batting Avg:	.274	.264	3
On-Base Pct:	.347	.328	1
Slugging Pct:	.433	.402	2
Home Runs:	186		2
Stolen Bases:	55		11
ERA:	3.82	4.07	2
Errors:	108		2 (tie)
Runs Scored:	814		2
Runs Allowed:	670		1

Starting Lineup
Bob Boone, c
Rod Carew, 1b
Bobby Grich, 2b
Doug DeCinces, 3b
Tim Foli, ss
Brian Downing, lf
Fred Lynn, cf
Reggie Jackson, rf
Don Baylor, dh
Juan Beniquez, cf-rf
Bobby Clark, rf-cf

Pitchers
Geoff Zahn, sp
Ken Forsch, sp
Steve Renko, sp
Mike Witt, sp
Andy Hassler, rp
Luis Sanchez, rp
Dave Goltz, rp
Bruce Kison, rp-sp

Attendance
2,807,360 (first in AL)

Club Leaders

Batting Avg:	Rod Carew	.319
On-Base Pct:	Rod Carew	.396
Slugging Pct:	Doug DeCinces	.546
Home Runs:	Reggie Jackson	39
RBI:	Reggie Jackson	101
Runs:	Brian Downing	109
Stolen Bases:	Rod Carew	10
	Don Baylor	10
Wins:	Geoff Zahn	18
Strikeouts:	Mike Witt	85
ERA:	Mike Witt	3.51
Saves:	Doug Corbett	8

JANUARY 22   The Angels sign Reggie Jackson, most recently with the Yankees, as a free agent.

Among baseball's most colorful and brashest players, Jackson was one of those rare athletes who was recognized by his first name alone. Before arriving in Anaheim, he played for the Athletics (1967–75), Orioles (1976) and Yankees (1977–81). With those three clubs, Jackson played on six clubs which reached the World Series and was named to 11 All-Star teams. He led the league in home runs three times, slugging percentage three seasons, runs scored twice and RBIs once and had 425 career homers. It was in the World Series where Jackson shined and earned his nickname "Mr. October," particularly in 1977 when he clubbed five home runs, including three in one game against the Dodgers on three straight pitches. The Yankees thought Jackson was washed up, however, after a subpar season in 1981. Without him, it's doubtful the Angels could have reached the postseason in 1982. He led the AL in home runs for the fourth time in his career with 39 and also drove in 101 runs while batting .275. He played five seasons for the Angels, made the All-Star team in three of them and hit 123 home runs.

1980s

JANUARY 28 — The Angels trade Dan Ford to the Orioles for Doug DeCinces and Jeff Schneider.

The Angels pulled off a coup in acquiring DeCinces, who had the best season of his career in 1982 with a .301 batting average, 30 home runs and 97 RBIs. He was the club's starting third baseman for six years.

FEBRUARY 3 — Dave Frost signs a contract with the Royals as a free agent.

APRIL 6 — The Angels open the season with a 3–2 loss to the Athletics in 11 innings in Oakland. The game ended on a bases-loaded walk by Don Aase to Davey Lopes. Ken Forsch went 8 2/3 innings as the California starting pitcher. Reggie Jackson collected three hits in his Angels debut. Brian Downing homered in the fifth inning.

APRIL 8 — The Angels outlast the Athletics 8–6 in 16 innings in Oakland. The A's tied the contest 4–4 in the seventh. There was no more scoring until the 16th when the Angels plated four runs, the first on a lead-off homer by Doug DeCinces. It was his second homer of the game. Oakland countered with two in their half.

APRIL 9 — The Angels play at the Metrodome in Minneapolis for the first time, and lose 2–1 to the Twins.

APRIL 13 — In the home opener, the Angels play 17 innings before the game against the Mariners is suspended with the score tied 3–3 before 33,574 at Anaheim Stadium. The contest was suspended at 1:05 a.m. because of the American League curfew rule. With two out and no one on base in the ninth, Seattle

Reggie Jackson was 36 when he came to Anaheim, but even on the downside of his career he led the league in home runs in 1982 and gave the team a feared bat in the middle of the lineup.

deadlocked the contest 2–2 on two singles and a double by Jim Essian. Both teams scored in the 15th, with the California run crossing the plate on a two-out single by Don Baylor. The game was completed the following day.

APRIL 14   The Angels and Mariners complete their suspended game of the previous night with the Angels prevailing 3–2 in 20 innings. Total playing time over the two days was six hours and six minutes. Bob Boone drove in the winning run with a single. Don Baylor finished the game with five hits, including two doubles, in five at-bats. Rick Burleson set a major league record for most assists by a shortstop in a game with 15. Rod Carew tied American League records for most putouts (32) and most total chances (34) by a first baseman in a game. The 20 innings is tied for the longest in Angels history. The club lost 1–0 to the Athletics in Oakland in 20 innings on July 9, 1971. After the suspended contest was completed, the two clubs played the regularly scheduled game of the day, and the Angels won 2–1 in ten innings. Again, the Mariners tied the score in the ninth on an RBI by Jim Essian. Bobby Grich drove in the winning run with a walk-off double.

APRIL 16   Doug DeCinces hits a two-run, walk-off homer in the ninth inning to beat the Twins 4–2 at Anaheim Stadium. Fred Lynn tied the score 2–2 with a double in the ninth.

Lynn hit .299 with 21 homers in 1982.

APRIL 17   Rick Burleson tears his rotator cuff during a 6–2 win over the Twins before 61,640 at Anaheim Stadium. Burleson didn't play in another major league game until June 30, 1983 and never regained his role as a starting shortstop. The injury also broke up the double play combination of Burleson and Bobby Grich. The Angels didn't have a single double play combo start 100 games together in consecutive seasons between Sandy Alomar and Jim Fregosi in 1969 and 1970 and Adam Kennedy and Orlando Cabrera in 2005 and 2006.

Anaheim Stadium was enclosed with seats beyond the outfield wall in 1980 to accommodate the Los Angeles Rams, but the Angels didn't open those seats for baseball use until 1982. During that season, the club drew a then-record 2,807,360 and led the AL in attendance for the first time since 1966. It also broke the existing American League record, which was 2,633,701, held by the 1980 Yankees. The mark set by the 1982 Angels stood as the AL standard until the Twins drew 3,033,672 in 1988. The 1982 attendance figure also remained the club record until 2003.

APRIL 27   Reggie Jackson plays against the Yankees for the first time and homers off Ron Guidry in the seventh inning of a 3–1 Angels win at Yankee Stadium. The plate appearance began with Yankee fans chanting "Reg-gie! Reg-gie!" After the home run, many were chanting "Steinbrenner sucks" in response to the decision of the Yankees owner to allow Jackson to sign with the Angels. It was Jackson's first homer in a California uniform. It was his 19th game with the club. The contest was called at the end of the seventh due to rain.

The Angels had the oldest team in the American League in 1982 with a roster that included Steve Renko (37), Reggie Jackson (36), Rod Carew (36), Geoff Zahn (36), Ken Forsch (35), Bob Boone (34), Dave Goltz (33), Bobby Grich (33), Don Baylor (33) and Bruce Kison (32).

May 1	Don Baylor hits a two-run homer in the 13th inning to beat the Orioles 6–4 in Baltimore.
May 12	The Angels send Tom Brunansky, Mike Walters and $400,000 to the Twins for Doug Corbett and Ron Wilfong.

> *At the time of the trade, Corbett was one of the top relievers in baseball and was expected to solve the Angels' bullpen problems. He proved to be a disappointment in Anaheim, however, posting a 1–7 record and a 5.05 ERA with the club in 1982, and spent some time in the minors. He recovered and gave the Angels a couple of productive seasons during his five years with the club. Brunansky spent 14 years in the majors as an outfielder, consistently posting batting numbers around the league average.*

May 24	The Angels sign Dave Goltz, most recently with the Dodgers, as a free agent.
May 29	Reggie Jackson hits a walk-off homer in the tenth inning to defeat the Brewers 5–4 at Anaheim Stadium. Bobby Grich tied the score with a two-out single in the ninth.

> *The Angels had six players with 19 or more home runs in 1982. The six were Reggie Jackson (39), Doug DeCinces (30), Brian Downing (28), Don Baylor (24), Fred Lynn (21) and Bobby Grich (19).*

June 4	The Red Sox explode for seven runs in the 11th inning to beat the Angels 11–4 at Anaheim Stadium. Boston scored twice in the ninth to tie the score.
June 7	In the first round of the amateur draft, the Angels select pitcher Bob Kipper from Aurora Central Catholic High School in Aurora, Illinois.

> *Kipper pitched just two games for the Angels in 1985 before being traded to the Pirates. He was 27–37 during his big-league career. Other future major leaguers drafted and signed by the Angels in 1982 were Tony Mack (third round), Kirk McCaskill (fourth round) and Mark McLemore (ninth round).*

June 18	Reggie Jackson collects his 2,000th career hit with a home run off Dennis Lamp in the second inning of a 7–2 win over the White Sox at Anaheim Stadium.
June 21	Rod Carew extends his hitting streak to 25 games during a 10–2 win over the Rangers at Anaheim Stadium. The Angels scored seven runs in the eighth inning.

> *During the 25-game hitting streak, Carew collected 41 hits in 99 at-bats, an average of .414.*

June 26	After the Royals score in the top of the 12th inning, Don Baylor hits a two-run, walk-off homer in the bottom half for a 6–5 victory at Anaheim Stadium.

> *On June 29, the Angels had a record of 45–29 and a three-game lead in the AL West. The club lost the next eight contests, however, to fall three games back of the Royals.*

July 5	Doug DeCinces collects four hits, including a homer and two doubles, in four at-bats, but the Angels lose 8–5 to the Orioles at Anaheim Stadium.

July 9	Geoff Zahn pitches a two-hitter to defeat the Yankees 4–1 at Yankee Stadium. The only New York hits were a triple by Jerry Mumphrey in the fifth inning and a single from Willie Randolph in the sixth.
July 10	The Angels erupt for ten runs in the third inning and beat the Yankees 12–6 at Anaheim Stadium. Reggie Jackson drove in three of the ten tallies with a single and a homer.
July 13	In the All-Star Game at Olympic Stadium in Montreal, Reggie Jackson hits a sacrifice fly in the first inning, but the American League loses 4–1.
July 15	Fred Lynn hits a grand slam off Rick Waits in the third inning of an 8–2 win over the Indians in Cleveland.
July 16	The Angels score ten runs in the sixth inning and trounce the Indians 15–0 in Cleveland. It was the second time the club scored ten runs in an inning in a seven-day span. Rod Carew drove in four of the ten tallies with a triple and a single.
July 27	Bob Boone throws out Rickey Henderson three times on stolen base attempts during a 13-inning, 8–7 win over the Athletics at Anaheim Stadium. Don Baylor drove in the winning run with a walk-off single.
	Boone threw out 64 of the 110 runners who attempted to steal on him in 1982.
July 28	Don Baylor collects two homers, scores four runs, and drives in four during a 13–1 clobbering of the Athletics at Anaheim Stadium.
August 2	The Angels purchase Luis Tiant from Tabasco in the Mexican League.
	Tiant was at least 41 years old when purchased by the Angels (his exact age is open to speculation) and had a 227–170 major league record. He was 2–2 with a 4.04 ERA in six games in Anaheim.
August 3	Doug DeCinces hits three homers in consecutive at-bats and drives in all four California runs during a 5–4 loss to the Twins at Anaheim Stadium. All three homers were struck off Brad Havens in the first, third and fifth innings.
August 6	The Angels score eight runs in the sixth inning and beat the Mariners 11–9 in Seattle. Reggie Jackson hit a grand slam off Ed Vande Berg.
August 8	Doug DeCinces hits three home runs during a 9–5 triumph over the Mariners in Seattle. He also had a three-homer game on August 3. No one in major league history has put together two games of three home runs or more in a shorter time span. DeCinces hit solo homers off Mike Moore in the first and third innings and a two-run shot against Rich Bordi in the eighth.
	In 14 games from July 29 through August 13, DeCinces hit 12 homers and drove in 22 runs and collected 28 hits in all in 56 at-bats for a batting average of .500.
August 11	Don Baylor hits a grand slam off Ron Davis in the seventh inning of a 6–3 victory over the Twins in Minneapolis.

The Angels lineup in 1982 included four former MVPs in Reggie Jackson (1973), Fred Lynn (1975), Rod Carew (1977) and Don Baylor (1979).

AUGUST 17 — The Angels club five homers during a 10–2 triumph over the Red Sox at Anaheim Stadium. The five home runs were struck by Brian Downing, Don Baylor, Fred Lynn, Bobby Grich and Joe Ferguson.

AUGUST 21 — The Angels crush the Tigers 13–1 at Anaheim Stadium.

Dave Goltz missed three weeks in August and September after slicing his finger on an exposed metal screw on a toilet paper dispenser in the Fenway Park clubhouse.

AUGUST 31 — The Angels score seven runs in the fifth inning and hammer the Tigers 11–0 in Detroit. Brian Downing hit two homers, two singles and drove in five runs. One of his homers was a grand slam off Larry Pashnick. Downing's first homer led off the first inning.

On the same day, the Angels traded Dennis Rasmussen to the Yankees for Tommy John. The Angels also purchased John Curtis from the Padres. At the time of the trade, Tommy John was 39 and had a career record of 233-169. He was not only a top-flight pitcher, but made a courageous comeback in 1976 after surgery in which a ligament was transplanted front his right wrist into his left (pitching) elbow. John was the first athlete to undergo the procedure, and it is still known as Tommy John surgery. He won four key games for the Angels in September 1982 and helped the club reach the postseason. John had a 20–30 record for the Angels from 1983 through 1985 before being released.

SEPTEMBER 6 — Brian Downing hits a grand slam off Jerry Koosman in the second inning of an 8–6 win over the White Sox at Anaheim Stadium.

SEPTEMBER 19 — The Angels move into a tie for first place with the Royals by beating the Blue Jays 5–1 at Anaheim Stadium.

SEPTEMBER 20 — The Angels take sole possession of first place with a 3–2 victory over the Royals at Anaheim Stadium.

SEPTEMBER 21 — The Angels take a two-game advantage in the pennant race with a 2–1 decision over the Royals at Anaheim Stadium. Daryl Sconiers drove in the winning run with a pinch-hit, walk-off single in the ninth. It was his first hit of the season, after starting 0-for-8.

In the fourth inning with the score 0–0, Fred Lynn and Brian Downing crashed through the left-field fence while chasing a fly ball off the bat of Amos Otis. The two reached the fence at exactly time and leaped with no regard for their own welfare or each other. The impact was so great the wall gave way. Lynn caught the drive, and the umpires ruled it an out, reasoning that it was the same as tumbling into the seats. Downing, who ducked to avoid colliding with Lynn, wound up on the warning track.

SEPTEMBER 22 — The Angels complete a three-game sweep of the Royals with an 8–5 triumph at Anaheim Stadium. Doug DeCinces hit two homers.

September 27   The Angels beat the Royals 3–2 in Kansas City to extend their lead in the AL West to 4½ games.

The Angels could have clinched the division title with a win in either of the final two games of the series against the Royals in Kansas City, but blew a pair of 4–1 leads and lost 5–4 on September 28, and 6–5 on September 29.

October 2   The Angels clinch the AL West pennant with a 6–4 win over the Rangers at Anaheim Stadium.

The Angels played the Milwaukee Brewers in the best-of-five Championship Series. The Brewers were 23–24 in May when ex-Angels catcher Buck Rodgers was fired as manager and replaced by Harvey Kuenn. The club went 72–43 the rest of the way to finish at 95–67. The Brewers needed a win on the final day of the regular season to finish one game ahead of the Orioles in the AL East.

October 3   In the last game of the season, Gary Pettis hits a walk-off homer in the ninth inning to beat the Rangers 7–6 at Anaheim Stadium. It was his first big-league hit and came in his fifth at-bat. Pettis entered the game as a pinch runner for Fred Lynn in the first inning. Lynn was removed early to rest up for the playoffs.

October 5   The Angels open the Championship Series with an 8–3 win over the Brewers before 64,406 at Anaheim Stadium. Don Baylor drove in five runs. He put the Angels into a 1–0 lead in the first with a sacrifice fly. Milwaukee surged ahead 3–1, but the Angels countered with four tallies in the third. Baylor put California into the lead with a two-run triple, and drove in two more with a single in the fourth. Fred Lynn collected three hits, including a homer in the fifth. Tommy John pitched a complete game.

Baylor drove in ten runs during the five-game series. Lynn collected 11 hits in 18 at-bats for an average of .611.

October 6   The Angels move to within one victory of a World Series berth with a 4–2 victory over the Brewers before 64,179 at Anaheim Stadium. Reggie Jackson hit a long homer over the center-field wall in the third inning. Bruce Kison pitched a complete game.

The 1982 ALCS was carried on television over ABC with Keith Jackson, Jim Palmer and Earl Weaver serving as announcers.

October 8   The Brewers stay alive by beating the Angels 5–3 at County Stadium in Milwaukee. The Angels trailed 5–0 before scoring three in the eighth inning, the first on a lead-off homer by Bob Boone.

The only players to appear in both the 1979 and 1982 Championship Series for the Angels were Don Baylor, Rod Carew, Bobby Clark, Brian Downing, and Bobby Grich.

October 9   The Brewers even the series by defeating the Angels 9–5 in Milwaukee. California trailed 7–1 in the eighth when Don Baylor hit a grand slam off Moose Haas.

Gene Mauch elected to start 39-year-old Tommy John on three days' rest instead of Ken Forsch. Forsch led the Angels in innings pitched in 1982, but was hit hard in his last two regular-season starts, allowing eight runs in 4 1/3 innings. In game four of the ALCS against the Brewers, John surrendered six runs, four earned, in 3 1/3 innings. For game five, Mauch again bypassed Forsch and went with Bruce Kison on three days' rest. Troubled with a blister on his finger, Kison lasted only five innings.

OCTOBER 10   The Angels lose the fifth and deciding game of the ALCS 4–3 to the Brewers in Milwaukee. The Angels scored in the first on a double by Brian Downing and a single from Fred Lynn. The Brewers evened the score 1–1 in their half, but runs in the third and fourth gave the Angels a 3–1 lead. Milwaukee scored in the bottom of the fourth, but the Angels still had a 3–2 advantage in the seventh with reliever Luis Sanchez on the mound. With one out in the seventh, Charlie Moore blooped a single into short right just out of the reach of second baseman Bobby Grich. Jim Gantner singled, but Paul Molitor fouled out. The Angels had a one-run lead and were seven outs from the World Series. Cecil Cooper, a left-handed batter, was next up. Gene Mauch elected to stick with the right-handed Sanchez instead of bringing in southpaw Andy Hassler. Cooper responded with a two-run single for a 4–3 Brewers lead. Ron Jackson led off the California ninth with a pinch-single and moved to second on a bunt by Bob Boone, but Milwaukee reliever Bob McClure induced Brian Downing and Rod Carew to ground out to end the game.

The Brewers went on to lose the World Series in seven games to the St. Louis Cardinals.

OCTOBER 22   Gene Mauch resigns as manager of the Angels.

Mauch resigned in the wake of the bitter setback in the Championship Series. On October 20, Mauch and general manager Buzzie Bavasi held an extensive news conference in which Mauch was offered less than a vote of confidence. "If we had to make a decision today," said Bavasi, "it wouldn't be a good one. By that I mean the atmosphere isn't right. Every time we pick up the papers and see it's the Brewers in the World Series, and every time we think about the money we're losing by not being there, we become disappointed." Mauch would return to manage the Angels once again from 1985 through 1987 and would once again experience a devastating loss in the ALCS—this time to the Red Sox in 1986.

NOVEMBER 1   The Angels name 50-year-old John McNamara as manager.

McNamara never reached the majors as a player, but his leadership skills were recognized when he was a minor league catcher. His first job as a manager was in 1959 when he was only 26, and he led Lewiston, Idaho, to the Northwest League championship. McNamara managed in the majors with the Athletics (1968–69), Padres (1974–77) and Reds (1982–84) before being hired by the Angels. His low-key style didn't click with the veteran club he inherited with the Angels, however, and McNamara had a 151–173 record with the club in two seasons before being replaced by Gene Mauch.

DECEMBER 1   Don Baylor signs a contract with the Yankees as a free agent.

> *Baylor played in the ALCS with five different clubs during the 1970s and 1980s with the Orioles (1973 and 1974), Angels (1979 and 1982), Red Sox (1986), Twins (1987) and Athletics (1988). The Boston, Minnesota and Oakland clubs also reached the World Series, making him the only player ever to appear in the Fall Classic with three franchises over a three-year period.*

1983

Season in a Sentence
The Angels are 30–21 with a five-game lead in the AL West on June 4, but unravel in the second half and win only 70 games.

Finish • Won • Lost • Pct • GB
Fifth (tie)   70   92   .432   29.0

Manager
Gene Mauch

Stats   Angels • AL • Rank
Batting Avg:	.260	.266	12
On-Base Pct:	.321	.328	10
Slugging Pct:	.393	.401	10
Home Runs:	154		5
Stolen Bases:	41		12
ERA:	4.31	4.06	10
Errors:	154		12
Runs Scored:	722		8
Runs Allowed:	779		11

Starting Lineup
Bob Boone, c
Rod Carew, 1b
Bobby Grich, 2b
Doug DeCinces, 3b
Tim Foli, ss
Brian Downing, lf
Fred Lynn, cf
Ellis Valentine, rf
Reggie Jackson, dh-rf
Ron Jackson, 3b-1b
Juan Beniquez, cf-rf-lf
Daryl Sconiers, 1b

Pitchers
Tommy John, sp
Ken Forsch, sp
Geoff Zahn, sp
Bruce Kison, sp-rp
Luis Sanchez, rp
Andy Hassler, rp
John Curtis, rp
Mike Witt, rp-sp

Attendance
2,555,016 (first in AL)

Club Leaders
Batting Avg:	Rod Carew	.339
On-Base Pct:	Rod Carew	.409
Slugging Pct:	Fred Lynn	.483
Home Runs:	Fred Lynn	22
RBI:	Fred Lynn	74
Runs:	Brian Downing	68
Stolen Bases:	Gary Pettis	8
Wins:	Three tied with	11
Strikeouts:	Bruce Kison	83
ERA:	Geoff Zahn	3.33
Saves:	Luis Sanchez	7

JANUARY 21   The Angels sign Ellis Valentine, most recently with the Mets, as a free agent.

APRIL 5   In the season opener, the Angels edge the Brewers 3–2 before 34,177 at Anaheim Stadium. Daryl Sconiers homered. Bruce Kison was the starting and winning pitcher.

APRIL 9   Rod Carew hits a grand slam off Matt Keough in the fifth inning of a 10–2 victory over the Athletics in Oakland.

APRIL 14   The Twins-Angels game in Minneapolis is postponed because of a snow storm. The Angels were unable to reach the city because the airport was closed. Later in the evening, a chunk of ice tore a 20-foot hole in the roof of the Metrodome, causing it to deflate.

APRIL 16	The Angels score seven runs in the fifth inning and defeat the Twins 9–5 in Minneapolis.
APRIL 22	Rod Carew delivers a walk-off single in the 11th inning to defeat the Orioles 6–5 at Anaheim Stadium. It was Carew's fifth hit of the evening. He collected four singles and a double in seven at-bats.

> *At the age of 37, Carew had a spectacular start in 1983 with 48 hits in his first 96 at-bats for an average of .500. From April 21 through May 6, he belted out 33 hits in 57 at-bats. Carew kept his batting average above .400 until July 15. By the end of the season, his average was .339, second best in the American League. It was the 15th year in a row in which Carew batted .300 or better.*

APRIL 27	Fred Lynn and Daryl Sconiers both hit grand slams during a 13–3 win over the Tigers at Anaheim Stadium. Lynn hit his slam off Milt Wilcox in the third inning. Sconiers cleared the bases against Bob James in the seventh.
APRIL 30	Daryl Sconiers hits a three-run, pinch-hit, walk-off homer in the 11th inning to defeat the Red Sox 4–1 at Anaheim Stadium.
MAY 4	The Angels thrash the Orioles 16–8 in Baltimore.
MAY 7	Doug DeCinces hits a homer in the 12th inning to defeat the Tigers 6–5 in Detroit. He also recorded 11 assists to tie an American League record for third basemen. Daryl Sconiers hit a pinch-hit home run in the ninth inning to deadlock the contest at 5–5. It was his second consecutive pinch homer. The other one was on April 30.
MAY 11	The Angels collect only three hits, but two of them are homers, in a 3–1 victory over the Red Sox in Boston. Bobby Clark hit a two-run homer in the second inning and Ellis Valentine contributed a solo shot in the seventh.
MAY 24	After the Yankees score in the top of the tenth, the Angels rally for two runs in the bottom half to win 7–6

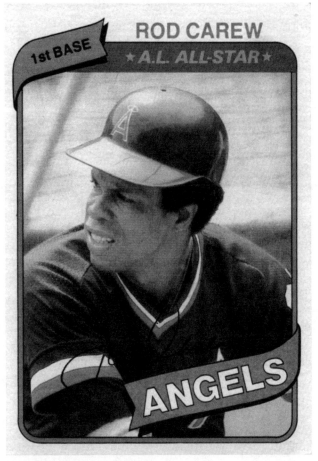

Already an aging superstar when he joined the Angels in 1979, Rod Carew produced seven good years with the team, hitting over .300 in five of them.

at Anaheim Stadium. With two out and no one on base in the tenth, Fred Lynn walked, Ron Jackson was hit by a pitch and Ellis Valentine and Bobby Grich singled to account for the winning tallies.

Grich hit .292 with 16 homers in 1983.

May 28   Daryl Sconiers hits a grand slam off Len Barker in the first inning of a 7–4 win over the Indians in Cleveland.

June 2   The Angels capture a thrilling 9–8 victory over the Yankees in New York. Trailing 7–1, the Angels erupted for six runs in the sixth inning, the last four on a grand slam by Ellis Valentine off Dale Murray. Doug DeCinces broke the 7–7 tie with a two-run homer in the seventh.

The Angels had a 30–21 record and a five-game lead in the AL West on June 4. The club was still tied for first at 44–37 on July 10, but went into a nosedive in the second half, losing 55 of the last 81 games. Age and injuries were contributing factors. The Angels fielded the oldest roster in the American League, and the only two players to appear in more than 120 games were Bob Boone (142) and Rod Carew (129).

June 6   Reggie Jackson hits a grand slam off Bob McClure in the eighth inning, but it's too late to prevent a 9–7 loss to the Brewers in Milwaukee.

On the same day, the Angels selected outfielder Mark Doran in the first round of the amateur draft. Doran never reached the majors, but the Angels did pick up a quality player by choosing Wally Joyner in the third round. Other future big leaguers drafted and signed by the Angels in 1983 were Pat Clements (fourth round) and Ray Chadwick (16th round). The club signed Jack Howell as an undrafted free agent.

June 18   The Angels score four runs in the ninth inning to beat the Blue Jays 7–6 in Toronto. Bobby Grich led off the inning with a home run, and after the next two batters were retired, Rod Carew and Juan Beniquez singled and Reggie Jackson homered.

June 20   The Angels outlast the Rangers 10–9 in 13 innings in Arlington. Doug DeCinces drove in the winning run with a double. Both teams scored twice in the tenth.

June 27   Bruce Kison (seven innings) and Luis Sanchez (two innings) combine on a two-hitter to defeat the Rangers 8–0 in Anaheim. The only Texas hits were a double by Mickey Rivers in the first inning and a single from George Wright in the second.

July 6   At the All-Star Game in the original Comiskey Park in Chicago, Fred Lynn hits a grand slam off Atlee Hammaker of the Giants in the third inning of the American League's 13–3 victory. It was the first grand slam in All-Star history, and it came on the 50th anniversary of the first game, played in 1933. Through 2009, Lynn's slam remains as the only one in All-Star play. Rod Carew contributed two singles and two runs scored in three at-bats.

July 22   Brian Downing's streak of 244 consecutive games without an error in the outfield comes to an end when he misplays a Chet Lemon line drive during a 13–11 loss to the Tigers at Anaheim Stadium.

JULY 30	The Angels score seven runs in the first inning for a 7–0 lead, but wind up losing 13–8 to the Athletics in the first game of a double-header at Anaheim Stadium. The A's also won the second tilt 2–1 in 12 innings.
AUGUST 13	Two benches-clearing brawls erupt in the first inning of a 10–4 win over the Mariners at Anaheim Stadium. Seattle's Brian Clark threw a pitch behind Rod Carew, who stormed to the mound with catcher Rick Sweet in pursuit. After both benches emptied, home plate umpire Ken Kaiser separated Carew and Sweet. Carew and Clark were both ejected. A second scuffle broke out when Rick Burleson left the dugout to go after Clark. Burleson, who was not in the lineup, was also ejected from the premises.
AUGUST 17	Juan Beniquez hits a grand slam off Mike Warren in the seventh inning of a 6–5 triumph over the Athletics in Oakland.
AUGUST 22	The Angels score two runs in the ninth inning and four in the 13th to defeat the Indians 7–3 in Cleveland. Bobby Grich tied the score 3–3 with an RBI-single in the ninth and contributed a two-run double in the 13th.
AUGUST 27	The Angels score three runs in the ninth inning to defeat the Yankees 7–6 at Anaheim Stadium. Juan Beniquez tied the score 6–6 with a two-run single, and Bobby Grich delivered a two-out, walk-off single.
SEPTEMBER 7	Trailing 6–4, the Angels explode for five runs in the ninth inning to defeat the Blue Jays 9–6 in Toronto. Daryl Sconiers put the Angels in the lead with a three-run, pinch-hit double.
SEPTEMBER 10	Holding a 6–1 lead over the White Sox in Chicago, the Angels allow five runs in the ninth inning and one in the 12th to lose 7–6. Three of the runs in the ninth scored after two were out. Harold Baines ended the contest with a home run.
SEPTEMBER 14	The Angels lose 1–0 to the Royals at Anaheim Stadium when reliever Rick Steirer allows a run in the 14th inning. Tommy John pitched 13 shutout innings before giving way to Steirer.
SEPTEMBER 27	Gary Pettis collects four hits, including an inside-the-park homer, in four at-bats during a 7–1 win over the Blue Jays at Anaheim Stadium.
	Pettis played only 22 games in 1983, yet led the Angels in stolen bases with eight. He played for the Angels from 1982 through 1987 and was the club's starting center fielder over the last four seasons. Pettis stole 186 bases in a California uniform, and held the club career record until he was passed by Chone Figgins in 2007. Pettis also won Gold Gloves in 1985 and 1986. He hit only .242 with 13 homers in 584 games as an Angel, however, and was traded to the Tigers after a horrible 1987 campaign in which he batted just .208 with one home run in 394 at-bats.
DECEMBER 7	Six weeks after a bomb rips through a Marine compound in Beirut, Lebanon, killing 241, the Angels send Tim Foli to the Yankees for Curt Kaufman and cash.
DECEMBER 20	The Angels trade Bobby Clark to the Brewers for Jim Slaton.

1984

Season in a Sentence

The Angels lead the AL West for 52 straight days in May, June and July and remain in the pennant race in a weak division well into September despite finishing with a .500 record.

Finish • Won • Lost • Pct • GB

Second 81 81 .500 3.0
(tie)

Manager

John McNamara

Stats   Angels • AL • Rank

Batting Avg:	.249	.264	13
On-Base Pct:	.318	.326	9
Slugging Pct:	.381	.398	12
Home Runs:	150		6
Stolen Bases:	80		9
ERA:	3.96	3.99	8
Errors:	128		6 (tie)
Runs Scored:	696		7
Runs Allowed:	697		7

Starting Lineup

Bob Boone, c
Rod Carew, 1b
Bobby Grich, 2b
Doug DeCinces, 3b
Dick Schofield, ss
Brian Downing, lf
Gary Pettis, cf
Fred Lynn, rf-cf
Reggie Jackson, dh
Juan Beniquez, rf-lf
Ron Wilfong, 2b

Pitchers

Mike Witt, sp
Ron Romanick, sp
Geoff Zahn, sp
Tommy John, sp
Jim Slaton, sp-rp
Luis Sanchez, rp
Doug Corbett, rp

Attendance

2,402,997 (second in AL)

Club Leaders

Batting Avg:	Rod Carew	.295
On-Base Pct:	Rod Carew	.367
Slugging Pct:	Fred Lynn	.474
Home Runs:	Reggie Jackson	25
RBI:	Brian Downing	91
Runs:	Fred Lynn	84
Stolen Bases:	Gary Pettis	48
Wins:	Mike Witt	15
Strikeouts:	Mike Witt	196
ERA:	Geoff Zahn	3.12
Saves:	Luis Sanchez	11

April 2   On Opening Day, the Angels score two runs in the ninth inning to defeat the Red Sox 2–1 before 31,760 at Anaheim Stadium. The Angels loaded the bases on a single by Juan Beniquez and two walks, the second one intentional to Daryl Sconiers with two out. The two California runs crossed the plate when Boston shortstop Jackie Gutierrez threw the ball past first after fielding a ground ball hit by Bob Boone. Ken Forsch pitched a complete game for the Angels.

April 7   Ken Forsch separates his shoulder in a collision with Willie Upshaw during a play at first base in the eighth inning of a 3–1 loss to the Blue Jays at Anaheim Stadium.

Forsch didn't pitch in another game until 1986. After the injury, he played in only ten more major league contests, all in relief, and had a 9.53 ERA in 17 innings.

April 15   The Angels score seven runs in the second inning to take a 10–0 lead, then hang on to defeat the Athletics 12–8 in Oakland. Brian Downing hit a grand slam off Chris Codiroli.

April 20	The Angels collect 20 hits and defeat the Blue Jays 10–6 in 13 innings in Toronto. The 13th inning rally began with three consecutive doubles from Rob Picciolo, Fred Lynn and Doug DeCinces.
	Lynn batted .271 with 23 homers in 1984.
April 24	The Angels edge the Red Sox 8–7 in Boston. Trailing 5–1, Reggie Jackson, Brian Downing and Bobby Grich led off the fourth inning with back-to-back-to-back homers off Oil Can Boyd. The Angels broke a 7–7 tie in the ninth on a double by Jackson and an RBI-single from Downing.
April 28	Gary Pettis hits a grand slam off Dave Beard in the seventh inning of a 10–1 win over the Mariners at Anaheim Stadium..
April 29	The Angels score five runs in the ninth inning to tie the Mariners 6–6, but wind up losing 9–6 in ten innings at Anaheim Stadium. Three of the runs in the ninth scored after two were out on a two-run single by Gary Pettis and another one-base hit from Rod Carew.
May 1	Tommy John (eight innings) and Luis Sanchez (one inning) combine on a two-hitter to defeat the Athletics 4–1 at Anaheim Stadium. John had a no-hitter in progress until Davey Lopes singled with one out in the seventh inning. Rickey Henderson added another single in the eighth. It was also John's 250th major league victory.
May 18	Doug DeCinces hits a home run in the tenth inning to defeat the Yankees 4–3 in New York. The Yanks tied the score 3–3 on a two-out, two-run single by Butch Wynegar off Luis Sanchez.
May 28	Reggie Jackson hits a grand slam off Dennis Rasmussen in the fourth inning of a 6–2 victory over the Yankees at Anaheim Stadium.
May 29	Juan Beniquez collects five hits in five at-bats during a 6–5 triumph over the Yankees at Anaheim Stadium.
	In a five-game span from May 25 through May 29, Beniquez had 14 hits, including two homers and a double, in 21 at-bats. He hit .336 in 354 at-bats in 1984. At Anaheim Stadium, Juan's average was .399 in 203 at-bats. Largely a platoon player, he batted .315 with 19 homers in 1,080 at-bats for the Angels from 1983 through 1985.
June 4	In the first round of the amateur draft, the Angels select catcher Erik Pappas from Mount Carmel High School in Chicago.
	Pappas didn't reach the majors until 1991 as a member of the Cubs. He had 289 big-league at-bats over three seasons and hit .242 with one homer. Other future major leaguers drafted and signed by the Angels in 1984 were Sherman Corbett (third round), Kent Anderson (fourth round), Brian Brady (sixth round), Doug Davis (ninth round), Pete Coachman (11th round), Dante Bichette (17th round) and Doug Jennings (second round of the secondary phase in January). Bichette was the best of the bunch, but was traded by the Angels before reaching his peak.

The Angels also signed Bryan Harvey as an undrafted free agent. Harvey was the club's closer from 1988 through 1992.

June 10   Doug DeCinces scores both runs of a 2–0 win over the Royals in Kansas City. Geoff Zahn pitched the shutout.

The Angels had a problem with tortillas during the 1984 season. Fans in the upper deck began throwing the tortillas around like Frisbees, some of which smacked into the faces of unamused spectators. Some of the tortillas wound up on the playing field. Police began to crack down on the practice in June, and during one contest, 20 fans were kicked out of the stadium. The problem persisted, however. It finally came to an end when the Anaheim City Council passed an ordinance prohibiting the throwing of food. Fans caught in the act now faced a fine of $1,000.

June 12   Mike Witt strikes out 13 batters in $8^1/_3$ innings and the Angels defeat the White Sox 3–2 in ten innings at Anaheim Stadium. Doug DeCinces drove in the winning run with a single.

The Angels had a record of 36–29 and a $4^1/_2$-game lead in the AL West on June 16.

June 14   Bobby Grich is thrown out at second, third and home during a 9–3 win over the White Sox at Anaheim Stadium. In the second inning, he was thrown trying to stretch a single into a double. In the fourth, he was retired attempting to stretch a double into a triple. And in the sixth, Grich was out at home on a bid to score from first base on Rob Picciolo's double.

Picciolo had 119 at-bats as an infielder with the Angels in 1984 and didn't draw a single walk. He walked 25 times on 730 games and 1,680 at-bats over a nine-year career with the Athletics, Brewers and Angels. Picciolo's career on-base percentage was .246.

June 26   The Angels eke out a 14-inning, 3–2 win over the Rangers in Arlington. The winning run scored on a walk to Gary Pettis, a stolen base and a single from Rod Carew. Pettis tied the score 2–2 with a two-out, RBI-single in the ninth.

Darrell Miller, who was a backup catcher for the Angels from 1984 through 1987, had two younger siblings who were basketball icons. Cheryl Miller, who played at USC, was one of the greatest female basketball players of all time. Reggie Miller played 18 seasons as a star in the NBA with the Indiana Pacers from 1987 through 2005. Both Cheryl and Reggie went into careers in television after their playing days were over.

July 1   Brian Downing drives in six runs during a 7–6 triumph over the Brewers in Milwaukee. Downing smacked a pair of three-run homers off Bob McClure in the first inning and Pete Ladd in the seventh.

July 14   Bob Boone hits a walk-off homer in the tenth inning to defeat the Brewers 2–1 at Anaheim Stadium.

July 15	The Angels win on a walk-off hit for the second game in a row when Juan Beniquez singles in the ninth inning to defeat the Brewers 7–6 at Anaheim Stadium.
July 23	Mike Witt strikes out 16 batters during a 7–1 victory over the Mariners at Anaheim Stadium. Witt struck out 11 of the first 17 batters to face him through the first five innings.
July 25	The Angels edge the Mariners 1–0 in ten innings at Anaheim Stadium. Gary Pettis drove in the lone run of the game with a single in the tenth inning off Jim Beattie, who pitched a complete game. Ron Romanick (nine innings) and Luis Sanchez (one inning) combined on the shutout.

Romanick was 12–12 as a 23-year-old rookie in 1984 and had a 14–9 record in 1985, but a 5–8 mark and a 5.50 ERA in 1986 ended his career.

July 30	Juan Beniquez homers in the 12th inning to defeat the Athletics 5–4 in Oakland.
August 2	The Angels erupt for eight runs in the fourth inning to take a 14–0 lead and cruise to a 14–2 win over the Twins at Anaheim Stadium. The first seven California base runners reached in the eight-run inning on five singles and two walks, and seven different players drove in runs.
August 4	The Angels take over first place in the AL West with a 4–2 victory over the Twins at Anaheim Stadium.

The Angels had a record of 56–52 on August 4. The club lost 15 of its next 22 games to fall five games behind the first-place Twins.

August 7	The Angels score two runs in the ninth inning to defeat the Mariners 7–6 in Seattle. Daryl Sconiers doubled in a run, advanced to third on an error and crossed the plate on a sacrifice fly by Fred Lynn.
August 12	Juan Beniquez collects two homers and two singles and drives in four runs in four at-bats during a 10–9 victory over the Athletics at Anaheim Stadium.
August 14	Juan Beniquez collects four hits for the second game in a row with three singles and a double in five at-bats during a 6–4 triumph over the Tigers in the first game of a double-header in Detroit. The Angels scored seven runs in the third inning of game two and won 12–1. All seven runs scored before a batter was retired as eight in a row reached base on a walk, three singles, a double, a triple and a three-run homer by Doug DeCinces.
August 31	Executive vice president and general manager Buzzie Bavasi announces his retirement, effective at the end of the season. Bavasi was 68 and had been employed by the Angels since 1977. He was replaced by 39-year-old Mike Port, who had been the club's vice president and chief administration officer. He had been a part of the Angels front office since 1978. Port was general manager until 1991 and helped put together the team that nearly reached the World Series in 1986.
September 6	The Angels purchase Derrell Thomas from the Expos.

SEPTEMBER 7   The Angels score seven runs in the second inning and rout the White Sox 16–8 in Chicago.

> *Fred Lynn set a club record by driving in runs in ten consecutive games from August 28 through September 8. He drove in 18 runs over those ten contests and collected 18 hits, five of them home runs, in 41 at-bats. Bobby Grich tied a club record with eight consecutive hits over three games from September 14 through September 16 with four singles, two doubles and two home runs. He also reached base in 12 straight plate appearances from September 14 through September 17 with those eight hits plus four walks, two of them intentional.*

SEPTEMBER 17   Reggie Jackson collects his 500th career home run during a 10–1 loss to the Royals at Anaheim Stadium. The milestone was struck off Bud Black in the seventh inning.

SEPTEMBER 21   The Angels overcome a 4–1 deficit in the fourth inning and beat the Rangers 5–4 at Anaheim Stadium. Bobby Grich broke the 4–4 tie with an RBI-single in the eighth.

> *The win gave the Angels a 78–74 record and a spot one-half game behind the first-place Royals. The Angels lost seven of their next eight games, however, to quickly drop out of the race.*

SEPTEMBER 30   On the final day of the regular season, Mike Witt pitches a perfect game and beats the Rangers 1–0 in Arlington. He threw 94 pitches, struck out ten and allowed only four Texas batters to get the ball out of the infield. In the ninth inning, Witt struck out Tom Dunbar on three pitches and retired both Bob Jones and Marv Foley on grounders from second baseman from second baseman Rob Wilfong to first baseman Bobby Grich. The lone run of the contest scored in the seventh on a single by Doug DeCinces, a passed ball and two ground outs. Charlie Hough pitched a complete game for the Rangers. The victory also gave the Angels a record of 81–81 on the 1984 season.

> *Witt finished the season with a 15–11 record, a 3.47 ERA and 196 strikeouts.*

The 27 Outs of Mike Witt's Perfect Game

Mike Witt is the only pitcher in Angels history with a perfect game. He threw it against the Rangers in Arlington on September 30, 1984 for a 1–0 victory on the final day of the regular season. There have been only 15 officially recognized perfect games in major league history since the four-ball, three-strike count was established in 1889. Fourteen of them have occurred during the regular season and one in the postseason, that by Don Larsen of the Yankees in the 1956 World Series against the Dodgers. There have been four since Witt's gem, including one by Kenny Rogers of the Rangers against the Angels on July 28, 1994.

The 27 outs of Witt's perfect game are as follows:

First Inning
Mickey Rivers struck out. Wayne Tolleson flied out to left fielder Brian Downing. Gary Ward grounded out from second baseman Rob Wilfong to first baseman Daryl Sconiers.

Second Inning
Larry Parrish grounded out from shortstop Dick Schofield to Sconiers. Pete O'Brien flied out to center fielder Fred Lynn. George Wright struck out.

Third Inning
Tom Dunbar struck out. Donnie Scott struck out. Curtis Wilkerson grounded out from Schofield to Sconiers.

Fourth Inning
Rivers grounded to Sconiers, who tossed the ball to Witt covering first. Tolleson grounded out Schofield to Sconiers. Ward flied out to right fielder Mike Brown.

Fifth Inning
Parrish grounded out from third baseman Doug DeCinces to Sconiers. O'Brien grounded out from Wilfong to Sconiers. Wright struck out.

Sixth Inning
Dunbar grounded out from Wilfong to Sconiers. Scott struck out. Wilkerson grounded out from Wilfong to Sconiers.

Seventh Inning
Rivers struck out. Tolleson grounded out Wilfong to Sconiers. Ward grounded out Wilfong to Sconiers.

Eighth Inning
Parrish flied out to right fielder Mike Brown. O'Brien struck out. Ward struck out.

Ninth Inning
Tom Dunbar struck out. Bob Jones, pinch-hitting for Scott, grounded out from Wilfong to first baseman Bobby Grich, who replaced Sconiers at first in the eighth inning. Marv Foley, pinch-hitting for Wilkerson, grounded out Wilfong to Grich.

OCTOBER 9   After two seasons at the helm, John McNamara resigns as manager of the Angels. Just nine days later, McNamara was hired to manage the Red Sox, a job he held until July 1988. McNamara was the manager of the Boston team that beat out the Angels in the 1986 ALCS, then lost to the Mets in the World Series. He also managed the Indians in 1990 and 1991 and the Angels again for 50 games in 1996.

OCTOBER 16   The Angels name Gene Mauch as manager of the Angels.

Mauch previously managed the Angels in 1981 and 1982, but resigned at the end of the 1982 season after the club took a two-games-to-none lead in the best of five Championship Series, then lost three in a row to the Brewers. Mauch was replaced by John McNamara, only to turn around and succeed McNamara two years later. The 1985 season was Mauch's 24th as a big-league manager. The Angels were 90–72 and finished just one game behind the Royals in the AL West. The club won the Western Division in 1986 and had a three-games-to-one lead against the Red Sox in the best-of-seven ALCS, then lost three in a row for the second crushing defeat in the postseason in five years. After a 75–87 season in 1987, Mauch resigned again, ending his career as a big-league manager.

DECEMBER 11 Five weeks after Ronald Reagan defeats Walter Mondale in the presidential election, Fred Lynn signs with the Orioles as a free agent.

DECEMBER 13 Don Aase signs with the Orioles as a free agent.

1985

Season in a Sentence
With a team few expect to contend for a pennant, the Angels take a 6½-game lead in July, hold first place for 142 days and wind up one game behind the Royals in the AL West at season's end.

Finish • Won • Lost • Pct • GB
First 90 72 .556 1.0

Manager
Gene Mauch

Stats   Angels • AL • Rank
Batting Avg: .251   .261   14
On-Base Pct: .330   .327   4
Slugging Pct: .386   .406   11
Home Runs: 153   9
Stolen Bases: 106   8
ERA: 3.91   4.15   5
Errors: 112   2
Runs Scored: 732   7
Runs Allowed: 705   5

Starting Lineup
Bob Boone, c
Rod Carew, 1b
Bobby Grich, 2b
Doug DeCinces, 3b
Dick Schofield, ss
Brian Downing, lf
Gary Pettis, cf
Reggie Jackson, rf-dh
Ruppert Jones, dh-of
Juan Beniquez, of-1b
Rob Wilfong, 2b

Pitchers
Mike Witt, sp
Ron Romanick, sp
Kirk McCaskill, sp
Jim Slaton, sp
Donnie Moore, rp
Stew Cliburn, rp
Urbano Lugo, rp-sp

Attendance
2,567,427 (first in AL)

Club Leaders
Batting Avg: Rod Carew   .280
On-Base Pct: Rod Carew   .371
               Brian Downing   .371
Slugging Pct: Reggie Jackson .487
Home Runs: Reggie Jackson 27
RBI: Reggie Jackson 85
Runs: Brian Downing   80
Stolen Bases: Gary Pettis   56
Wins: Mike Witt   15
Strikeouts: Mike Witt   180
ERA: Mike Witt   3.56
Saves: Donnie Moore   31

JANUARY 3   The Angels draft Chuck Finley in the first round of the secondary phase of the amateur draft.

> *Finley was pitching for the University of Louisiana at Monroe when drafted by the Angels. He pitched for the club from 1986 through 1999, made four All-Star teams and had six seasons of 15 wins or more. Finley peaked with 18–9 records in both 1990 and 1991. He is also the all-time career leader in franchise history in wins (165), innings pitched (2,675), and games started (379), and is second in strikeouts (2,151), and fourth in complete games (57) and shutouts (14). Finley was married to actress Tawny Kitaen from 1997 through 2002. While pitching for the Indians, Finley filed for divorce three days after Kitaen was charged with committing domestic violence against him, having beaten him with a stiletto heel while he was driving an automobile.*

JANUARY 14   Bruce Kison signs with the Red Sox as a free agent.

JANUARY 24   The Angels draft Donnie Moore from the Braves organization.

At the time, teams which lost quality free agents could enter a draft in which they could select players from other clubs. The Angels were allowed to participate in 1985 for the loss of Fred Lynn to the Orioles. Each team could protect 26 players and Moore was not among the 26 that the Atlanta organization chose to shield from the draft. He immediately stepped into the closer's role with the Angels, and recorded 31 saves with a 1.92 ERA in 65 games and 103 innings in 1985. Heading into the season, Moore had 28 career saves in nine seasons with the Cubs, Cardinals, Brewers and Braves. Unfortunately, he'll be remembered chiefly for blowing a lead in the game five of the 1986 ALCS against the Red Sox (see October 12, 1986) and his tragic death (see July 18, 1989).

January 30   The Angels sign Ruppert Jones, most recently with the Tigers, as a free agent.

April 9   The Angels open the 1985 season with a 6–2 loss to the Twins before 35,244 at Anaheim Stadium. The score was 1–1 before Minnesota scored three runs in the eighth off Mike Witt.

April 11   The Angels score two runs in the ninth inning and one in the tenth to defeat the Twins 4–3 at Anaheim Stadium. With one out in the ninth, Dick Schofield singled, Jerry Narron doubled, Rod Carew drove in a run on a ground out and Brian Downing singled in the tying tally. In the tenth, a one-out grounder by Bob Boone brought Darrell Miller in from third.

The 1985 season was the first of six that Joe Torre spent in the Angels broadcast booth. He played 18 seasons in the majors with the Braves, Cardinals and Mets from 1961 through 1978, then managed the Mets (1977–81) and Braves (1982–84). Torre's broadcasting career ended in August 1990 when he was appointed manager of the Cardinals, a job he held until 1995. He became manager of the Yankees in 1996 and managed world champions in 1996, 1998, 1999 and 2000, then moved to the Dodgers in 2008.

April 12   Dick Schofield hits a grand slam off Keith Atherton in the ninth inning, but it's much too late to prevent a 15–6 loss to the Athletics in Oakland.

April 23   The Angels collect six homers but allow four during a 14–9 loss to the Athletics at Anaheim Stadium. Reggie Jackson hit two homers for the Angels, with Doug DeCinces, Bobby Grich, Jerry Narron and Dick Schofield accounting for the others. Carney Lansford, Dave Kingman, Dusty Baker and Mike Davis homered for Oakland.

Jackson hit .252 with 27 home runs in 1985.

April 30   The Angels edge the Red Sox 3–2 in 15 innings at Anaheim Stadium. The winning rally consisted four walks by Bob Ojeda. The first was issued to Rod Carew and was followed by a sacrifice from Ruppert Jones, an intentional walk to Doug DeCinces, a ground out that advanced both runners, an intentional walk to Bobby Grich to load the bases and a walk to Dick Schofield.

The Angels were 30–13 in one-run games in 1985.

MAY 15   The Angels score six runs in the ninth inning to defeat the Blue Jays 9–6 in Toronto. With two out in the ninth, the score 6–4, Bill Caudill pitching, and runners on first and second, Brian Downing reached on an error to bring Juan Beniquez across the plate, Ruppert Jones walked, and Jerry Narron hit a pinch-hit grand slam.

MAY 21   Kirk McCaskill (8⅔ innings) and Donnie Moore (2⅓ innings) combine on a four-hitter to defeat the Tigers 2–1 in 11 innings at Anaheim Stadium. Ruppert Jones drove in the winning run with a double.

> *A native of Kapuskasing, Ontario, Canada, McCaskill was an All-American hockey player at the University of Vermont. He was runner-up for the Hobey Baker Award (college hockey's player of the year) in 1981 and played professionally for the Sherbrook Jets of the American Hockey League in 1983–84.*

JUNE 3   With two selections in the first round of the amateur draft, the Angels choose pitcher Willie Fraser from Concordia College and pitcher Mike Cook from the University of South Carolina.

> *Fraser pitched five seasons for the Angels beginning in 1986 and had a 38–40 major league record. Cook was 1–6 over a five-year career, three of those years in a California uniform. Other future major leaguers drafted and signed by the Angels included Bobby Rose (fifth round), Jeff Manto (14th round), and Frank Dimichele (15th round). The club also picked Greg Vaughn in the third round and Bo Jackson in the 20th, but failed to sign either player.*

JUNE 4   The Angels outlast the Orioles 6–5 in 15 innings at Memorial Stadium. Baltimore scored two runs with two out in the ninth to tie the game 5–5. Mike Brown drove in the winning run with a single. Gary Pettis tied a major league record for putouts by a centerfielder with 12.

> *Pettis hit .257 and stole 56 bases, including 22 in a row, in 1985. The photograph on his Topps baseball card that season was actually of Pettis' 14-year-old brother Lynn. Topps fell for the ruse and printed the card.*

JUNE 9   The Angels edge the Royals 1–0 at Anaheim Stadium. Bob Boone drove in the lone run of the game with a single in the fourth inning. Ron Romanick (seven innings) and Donnie Moore (two innings) combined on the shutout.

JUNE 10   Juan Beniquez collects two triples, a double and a single in five at-bats during an 8–1 triumph over the Rangers at Anaheim Stadium.

JUNE 18   The Angels score only seven runs on 20 hits, but it's enough to defeat the Indians 7–3 in Cleveland.

JUNE 19   The Angels release Tommy John.

JUNE 23   The Angels rout the White Sox 11–1 in Chicago.

JUNE 25   The Angels take a thrilling 7–3 win over the Indians in 13 innings at Anaheim Stadium. Bob Boone drove in a run with a one-out single in the ninth to tie the score 2–2.

	After Cleveland scored in the top of the 13th, the first two Angels batters were retired in the bottom half. The next five reached base on a walk by Juan Beniquez, a run-scoring double from Brian Downing, walks to Reggie Jackson and Doug DeCinces and a walk-off grand slam by Ruppert Jones.
JUNE 26	Reggie Jackson hits a grand slam off Bryan Clark in the sixth inning of a 10–6 win over the Indians at Anaheim Stadium.
JULY 5	The Angels clobber the Red Sox 13–4 at Anaheim Stadium.

Red Sox outfielder Rick Miller, who played with the Angels from 1977 through 1980, fought with rowdy fans during the contest. Three unruly fans began to fight with a friend of Miller, prompting him to jump into the stands to enter the fracas. After leaping over the railing and catching one of the fans in a chokehold, Miller evacuated his wife and son, who were sitting nearby, through the clubhouse. Two policemen were injured trying to break up the altercation. Charles Hewes (age 21), Robert Reza (25) and Robert Algarin (22) were placed under arrest.

JULY 8	Doug DeCinces delivers a walk-off single in the 11th inning to defeat the Brewers 3–2 at Anaheim Stadium.
JULY 9	The Angels win with an extra-inning, walk-off hit for the second day in a row when Juan Beniquez singles in the tenth to defeat the Brewers 5–4 at Anaheim Stadium. Brian Downing led off the ninth with a homer to tie the score.
JULY 13	The Angels score two runs in the ninth inning on three singles by pinch-hitters Darrell Miller, Mike Brown and Bob Boone, the final two with two out, to defeat the Blue Jays 4–3 at Anaheim Stadium.
JULY 14	The Angels score three runs in the ninth inning and win with two-out walk-off hits for the second day in a row to defeat the Blue Jays 5–3 at Anaheim Stadium. Bobby Grich tied the score 3–3 with a single and scored on a home run from Brian Downing.
JULY 16	Donnie Moore pitches two perfect innings (the seventh and eighth) during the All-Star Game at the Metrodome in Minneapolis, but the American League loses 6–1.

The Angels had a record of 56–38 and a 6½-game lead in the AL West on July 24. The club held first place continuously from June 21 through September 4.

AUGUST 2	The Angels trade Bob Kipper, Mike Brown and Pat Clements to the Pirates for George Hendrick, John Candelaria and Al Holland.

The Angels traded three prospects for three veterans to help during the pennant race. Candelaria was hampered by injuries during his three years with the Angels, but had a record of 25–11. Hendrick was one of baseball's most underrated players of the late 1970s and early 1980s, but was well past his peak by the time he arrived in Anaheim. He played four seasons with the Angels as a spare outfielder. Holland was effective out of the bullpen during the 1985 stretch run, then went to the Yankees as a free agent.

AUGUST 3	Trailing 4–3 with one out in the ninth inning and Bert Blyleven on the mound for the Twins, Brian Downing doubles and Doug DeCinces homers for a 5–4 victory at Anaheim Stadium.
AUGUST 4	Rod Carew collects his 3,000th career hit with a single off Frank Viola in the third of a 6–5 win over the Twins at Anaheim Stadium.
AUGUST 6	The game between the Angels and Mariners is canceled by a strike of the major league players. The August 7 contest between the two clubs was also called off before the strike was settled on August 8. The two missed games were later made up with double-headers in Seattle, costing the Angels two home dates, which may have made a difference in the close pennant race. The club was 49–30 at home in 1985.
AUGUST 12	The Angels trounce the Twins 12–0 in Minneapolis.
AUGUST 23	The Angels beat the Tigers 7–6 with a stunning comeback by scoring five runs with two out in the ninth inning at Anaheim Stadium. Rick Romanick gave up three runs in the first and three in the second to fall behind 6–0. The Angels picked up two runs in the sixth, but with two outs in the ninth still trailed 6–2 with a runner on first base. Juan Beniquez and Bob Boone walked to load the bases. Dick Schofield singled in two runs to make the score 6–4. Gary Pettis singled in two more to tie the score and went all the way to third base on an error by center fielder Kirk Gibson. After an intentional walk to Rod Carew, Pettis scored the winning run when third baseman Tom Brookens booted Brian Downing's ground ball. Alan Fowlkes (four innings), Al Holland (two innings) and Luis Sanchez (one inning) combined on seven innings of shutout relief.
	The game was Fowlkes' first as a member of the Angels and his first at the major league level since September 8, 1982 when he played for the Giants. Fowlkes pitched only one more big-league game and gave up seven runs in four innings during a 17–3 loss to the Orioles on August 26 at Anaheim Stadium. Eddie Murray paced the Baltimore attack that day with three home runs and nine runs batted in. Murray homered twice off Fowlkes—one of the homers was a grand slam.
AUGUST 27	Jack Howell hits a grand slam off Scott McGregor in the second inning of a 7–3 win over the Orioles at Anaheim Stadium. Howell also had a solo homer against Ken Dixon in the fifth.
AUGUST 30	Reggie Jackson collects his 1,000th career extra base hit with a double off Bob Shirley in the fifth inning of a 4–1 victory over the Yankees in New York.
SEPTEMBER 2	The Angels score nine runs in the fourth inning and trounce the Tigers 11–1 in Detroit. George Hendrick singled and belted a three-run homer during the big inning, and Bob Boone collected both a single and a double.
SEPTEMBER 8	The Angels score two runs in the ninth inning and three in the 11th to defeat the Orioles 7–4 in Baltimore.
SEPTEMBER 9	John Candelaria (eight innings) and Doug Corbett (one inning) combine on a two-hitter for a 7–1 victory over the Royals at Anaheim Stadium. The only Kansas

City hits were a double by Hal McRae in the second inning and a homer from Darryl Motley in the eighth.

SEPTEMBER 10 — The Angels trade Robert Sharpnack and Jerome Nelson to the Athletics for Don Sutton.

Sutton was 40 years old and had 293 big-league victories when acquired by the Angels. He was 28–24 with the club over three seasons and recorded his 300th victory during a 15–11 season in 1986.

SEPTEMBER 13 — Reggie Jackson hits a two-run homer off Charlie Hough in the fourth inning to account for the only two runs of a 2–0 win over the Rangers at Anaheim Stadium. Don Sutton, in his first game with the Angels, pitched seven shutout innings. Stew Cliburn and Donnie Moore each hurled one inning of relief.

Cliburn pitched for the Angels in 1984 and 1985 and again in 1988. His twin brother, Stan, was a catcher and appeared in 54 games for the Angels in 1980.

SEPTEMBER 19 — The Angels move into a tie for first place with the Royals by defeating the White Sox 8–0 in Chicago. John Candelaria pitched the shutout.

SEPTEMBER 22 — The Angels take sole possession of first place by one full game with a 10–9 defeat of the Indians in 12 innings at Anaheim Stadium. Bobby Grich hit a grand slam off Jamie Easterly in the first inning for a 4–3 lead, but Cleveland pulled ahead 8–4 in the top of the fourth. The Angels responded with three runs in the bottom of the fourth and two more in the fifth before the Indians tied the contest in the ninth. The winning run scored on two walks and an error.

SEPTEMBER 28 — The Angels fall back into a tie for first place with a tough 7–5 loss to the Indians in Cleveland. The Angels led 5–0 before the Indians scored five runs in the eighth inning and two in the ninth. Don Sutton pitched the first seven innings, allowing only three hits, but was relieved by Donnie Moore, who gave up the five eighth-inning runs. Four scored with two out, the last three on a home run by Andre Thornton. The contest ended with a two-run, walk-off homer by Jerry Willard off Stew Cliburn.

SEPTEMBER 29 — The Angels beat the Indians 9–3 in Cleveland to pull one game ahead of the Royals in the AL West race.

There were seven games left on the schedule. The next four were against the Royals in Kansas City from September 30 through October 3. The Angels lost the first game 3–1, won the second 4–2, then dropped the final two contests 4–0 and 4–1 to fall one game back.

OCTOBER 4 — The Angels' hope for a pennant are all but dashed with a 6–0 loss to the Rangers in Arlington. The club was two games back with two contests left on the schedule.

OCTOBER 5 — The Angels beat the Rangers 3–1 in Arlington but are eliminated from the pennant race when the Royals defeat the Athletics 5–4 in ten innings in Kansas City.

OCTOBER 6   On the last day of the season, the Angels defeat the Rangers 6–5 in Arlington. Mike Witt, who pitched a perfect game in Arlington in the final game of 1984, struck out 13 batters in seven innings.

There were several oddities during the final fray of 1985. Angels designated hitter, Rufino Linares, hit a three-run homer in the eighth inning for a 6–4 California lead in what would prove to be his final major league plate appearance. The homer was struck off Texas hurler Rick Surhoff, who was playing in his last big-league game. Left fielder Pat Keedy, in his third game and first start, also homered. Keedy would never play another game for the Angels. His brief career consisted of 29 games with the Angels, White Sox and Indians from 1985 through 1989.

NOVEMBER 12   Rod Carew files for free agency.

No one offered Carew a contract, ending his big-league career with a .328 batting average and 3,053 hits. He was elected to the Hall of Fame on the first ballot in 1991.

NOVEMBER 15   The 2½-year-old son of Angels pitcher John Candelaria dies after being in a coma since Christmas Day 1984. He had been in a coma since a swimming pool accident at Candelaria's winter home in Florida.

1986

Season in a Sentence

The season ends in disaster when Angels are three outs from their first World Series berth with a three-run lead against the Red Sox in game five of the ALCS, but blow the advantage, then lose games six and seven as well.

Finish • Won • Lost • Pct • GB

First   92   70   .556   +5.0

AL Championship Series

The Angels lost four games to three to the Boston Red Sox.

Manager

Gene Mauch

Stats

Stats	Angels	AL	Rank
Batting Avg:	.255	.262	9
On-Base Pct:	.337	.330	3
Slugging Pct:	.404	.408	8
Home Runs:	167		7
Stolen Bases:	109		7
ERA:	3.84	4.18	2
Errors:	107		2
Runs Scored:	786		6
Runs Allowed:	684		2

Starting Lineup

Bob Boone, c
Wally Joyner, 1b
Bobby Grich, 2b
Doug DeCinces, 3b
Dick Schofield, ss
Brian Downing, lf
Gary Pettis, cf
Ruppert Jones, rf
Reggie Jackson, dh
Rob Wilfong, 2b
George Hendrick, rf
Rich Burleson, dh-ss

Pitchers

Mike Witt, sp
Kirk McCaskill, sp
Don Sutton, sp
Ron Romanick, sp
John Candelaria, sp
Donnie Moore, rp
Doug Corbett, rp
Terry Forster, rp

Attendance

2,655,872 (first in AL)

Club Leaders

Batting Avg:	Wally Joyner	.290
On-Base Pct:	Brian Downing	.389
Slugging Pct:	Doug DeCinces	.459
Home Runs:	Doug DeCinces	26
RBI:	Wally Joyner	100
Runs:	Gary Pettis	93
Stolen Bases:	Gary Pettis	50
Wins:	Mike Witt	18
Strikeouts:	Mike Witt	208
ERA:	Mike Witt	2.84
Saves:	Donnie Moore	21

JANUARY 28 On the day the space shuttle *Challenger* explodes, killing six astronauts and teacher Christa McAuliffe, Juan Beniquez signs a contract as a free agent with the Orioles.

FEBRUARY 6 Al Holland signs a contract as a free agent with the Yankees.

APRIL 8 The Angels suffer a heartbreaking 8–4 loss in ten innings to the Mariners on Opening Day in Seattle. Bobby Grich led off the game with a home run off Mike Moore, and before the first inning ended, Reggie Jackson smacked a two-run homer. The Angels still led 4–2 heading into the ninth when Jim Presley hit a two-run homer off Donnie Moore to tie the score 4–4. In the tenth, Ken Forsch loaded the bases on a single and two walks, then surrendered a walk-off grand slam to Presley with two out. It was the first time that Forsch pitched a game since separating his shoulder on April 7, 1984.

APRIL 9   In just his second big-league game, Wally Joyner collects three hits, including a home run, in six at-bats during a 9–5 win over the Mariners in Seattle.

A rookie who was just 23 years old at the start of the season with the additional pressure of replacing Rod Carew as the Angels first baseman, Joyner became a fan favorite almost immediately in 1986. Through May 22, he had a .325 batting average in 166 at-bats and 40 games with 15 home runs and 38 RBIs. Thousands of fans waved "Wally World" signs at home games as a salute to Joyner. "Wally World" was a reference to the fictitious amusement park in the 1983 Chevy Chase film National Lampoon's Vacation *and an echo to nearby Disneyland, created by Walt Disney. Joyner was elected as the American League's starting first baseman in the All-Star balloting on a write-in vote, but tapered off in the second half and finished with a .290 average, 22 homers and 100 RBIs. He had a terrific year in 1987, compiling 34 home runs, 117 runs batted in while hitting .285, but failed to live up to his lofty expectations. Joyner played for the Angels from 1986 through 1991 and again in his final season in 2001, but never made another All-Star team after his rookie campaign.*

APRIL 14   The Angels score a run in the eighth inning and another in the ninth to defeat the Mariners 7–6 in the home opener before 37,489 at Anaheim Stadium. Darrell Miller drove in the winning run with a single.

APRIL 16   Ron Romanick pitches a two-hitter to defeat the Mariners 4–0 at Anaheim Stadium. The only Seattle hits were singles by Ivan Calderon in the sixth inning and Gorman Thomas with one out in the ninth.

On the same day, the Angels signed Terry Forster, most recently with the Braves, as a free agent. During the 1985 season, David Letterman called Forster a "fat tub of goo" on his late-night talk show. At first, Forster threatened to tear Letterman limb from limb, but eventually went along with the joke and appeared on the program. Forster even did a workout video called "Fat Is In." He made 41 relief appearances for the Angels in 1986 and had a 3.51 ERA in 41 games and 41 innings.

APRIL 20   The Angels take a thrilling 8–5 win over the Twins at Anaheim Stadium. Minnesota led 4–1 before the Angels scored three times in the eighth inning, the first two on a home run by Doug DeCinces off Bert Blyleven. The Twins took a 5–4 lead in the ninth, but the Angels struck again in the bottom half with four tallies on a single by Rick Burleson, a walk to Ruppert Jones, a run-scoring single from Wally Joyner and a three-run, walk-off home run off the bat of Brian Downing. The last five California runs scored off reliever Ron Davis.

Downing hit .267 with 20 home runs in 1986.

APRIL 22   Kirk McCaskill pitches a two-hitter and strikes out 12 batters to defeat the Athletics 5–1 at Anaheim Stadium. The only Oakland hits were a single by Alfredo Griffin in the third inning and a double from Mickey Tettleton in the sixth.

APRIL 26   The Angels score six runs in the ninth inning to stun the Twins 7–6 in Minneapolis. With Frank Viola on the mound, Brian Downing led off the ninth with a double and scored on a home run from George Hendrick. Ron Davis, who was victimized by a

California rally six days earlier, relieved Viola. Davis surrendered a single to Rob Wilfong and a homer to Ruppert Jones to make the score 6–5. After a walk to Reggie Jackson, Wally Joyner smacked a two-out, two-run homer for the victory.

> *To add to the weird night in Minnesota, the game was delayed for 15 minutes with two out in the bottom of the eighth inning just prior to the Angels' incredible rally when strong winds blew a hole in the Metrodome roof. The rupture caused suspended lights and speakers to sag toward the field while players and fans scurried toward safety. When all 20 blower fans were used to inflate the roof were turned on, the roof rose to its accustomed height of about 175 feet above the field and play resumed.*

May 3 — Reggie Jackson is involved in a fight with a fan at a Milwaukee tavern called Major Goolsby's. Jackson was sitting with three teammates and grappled with 26-year-old Donald Weimer of Racine, Wisconsin, allegedly after Jackson refused to sign an autograph. Weimer was treated at a hospital for bruises to his forehead, a chipped tooth, and a cut on his chin that required four stitches. Milwaukee police refused to press charges against Jackson.

May 16 — The Angels rout the Tigers 11–1 in Detroit.

> *Wally Joyner hit two homers during the contest. He collected six homers in five game stretch against the Brewers, Red Sox and Tigers from May 11 through May 16.*

May 26 — Wally Joyner hits a two-run homer with two out in the ninth to beat the Yankees 8–7 in New York.

May 31 — Kirk McCaskill pitches a two-hitter to defeat the Orioles 2–0 at Memorial Stadium. The only Baltimore hits were a single from Alan Wiggins leading off the first inning and a double by Jim Dwyer leading off the ninth. Gary Pettis drove in both runs with a single in the fifth.

> *McCaskill was 17–10 with a 3.36 ERA and 202 strikeouts in $246^{2}/_{3}$ innings in 1986.*

June 2 — The Angels blow a five-run lead but beat the Yankees 8–7 at Anaheim Stadium. The Angels led 6–1 before the Yanks scored a run in the seventh inning, three in the eighth and two in the ninth for a 7–6 advantage. California rallied with two in the bottom half of the ninth for the victory. Pinch hitter Rick Burleson drove in the tying run with a sacrifice fly, and Brian Downing delivered a walk-off single.

June 3 — With three selections in the first round of the amateur draft, the Angels choose pitcher Roberto Hernandez from the University of South Carolina at Aiken, first baseman Lee Stevens from Lawrence High School in Lawrence, Kansas, and outfielder Terry Carr from Bennett High School in Salisbury, Maryland.

> *The Angels traded Hernandez before he reached the majors in 1991. He went on to play 17 seasons in the big leagues. Stevens played three seasons in California as a reserve first baseman. Carr never reached the majors. Other future big leaguers drafted and signed by the Angels in 1986 were Mike Fetters (second round),*

Paul Sorrento (fourth round), Colby Ward (11th round) and Alan Mills (first round of the secondary phase).

June 9 — Don Sutton throws a two-hitter to defeat the White Sox 3–0 at Comiskey Park. The only Chicago hits were singles by Bobby Bonilla and Scott Bradley in the fifth inning.

June 11 — The Angels survive a five-run White Sox rally in the ninth inning to win 12–11 in Chicago. Highlighting the inconsistency that plagued him throughout his five seasons with the Angels, Doug Corbett pitched shutout ball in the sixth, seventh and eighth innings before surrendering the five tallies in the ninth.

Heading into the contest, the Angels had a record of 28–29 and were four games behind the first-place Rangers in the AL West.

June 16 — The Angels collect only one hit off Charlie Hough, but beat the Rangers 2–1 with two runs in the ninth inning at Anaheim Stadium. Hough went into the ninth with a no-hitter and fanned Ruppert Jones for the first out. Jack Howell went all the way to third base when left fielder George Wright dropped Howell's line drive. Wright came into the game at the start of the inning, replacing Gary Ward for defensive purposes. Wally Joyner broke up the no-hitter and the shutout with a single to score Howell. Joyner moved to second base on a passed ball when Hough's knuckler eluded catcher Orlando Mercado, then scored from second on another passed ball, on which George Hendrick swung and missed for strike three. Joyner advanced two bases because he was running on the 3–2 pitch to Hendrick, and Hough inexplicably failed to cover the plate.

June 18 — Don Sutton wins his 300th career game with a 5–1 decision over the Rangers at Anaheim Stadium.

Sutton finished his career with a record of 324–256. At the end of the 2009 season, he was tied for 14th with Nolan Ryan on the all-time career wins list. Among those whose careers began after 1950, only Roger Clemens, Greg Maddux and Steve Carlton rank ahead of Sutton and Ryan.

June 25 — Kirk McCaskill pitches a one-hitter to defeat the Rangers 7–1 at Arlington Stadium. The lone Texas hit was a home run by Steve Buechele leading off the third inning.

June 28 — In a match-up between the Indians and Angels at Anaheim Stadium, the starting pitchers are 300-game winners Phil Niekro and Don Sutton. Niekro entered the fray with 304 wins, and Sutton with 301. It was the first time that 300-game winners met each other since Tim Keefe of the New York Giants and Pud Galvin with the Pittsburgh Pirates faced off in 1889. Neither Niekro nor Sutton were involved in the decision as the Angels scored six runs in the eighth inning to win 9–3.

July 7 — The Angels outlast the Brewers to win 3–1 in 16 innings in Milwaukee. The score was 0–0 after 15 innings with Mike Witt (nine innings), Donnie Moore (three innings) and Terry Forster (three innings) combining on the shutout. Dick Schofield led off the 16th with a triple, and after two unintentional walks, Wally Joyner cleared the bases with a another triple. Doug Corbett allowed a run in the bottom of the 16th, but nailed down the save.

The win put the Angels into first place with a record of 44–37. The club remained in first for the rest of the season.

July 8   The Angels clobber the Brewers 14–3 in Milwaukee.

July 10   After scoring three runs in the top of the 12th inning, the Angels lead 7–4 with two out in the bottom half, but wind up losing 8–7 to the Red Sox in Boston. Todd Fischer relieved Mike Cook with the score 7–7 and runners on first and third. Before delivering a pitch, Fischer committed a balk by taking his hand out of his glove while standing on the mound to allow Dwight Evans to score from third.

Fischer never pitched in another big-league game. His career in the majors consisted of nine contests, all in relief, 17 innings, an 0–0 record and a 4.24 ERA. The July 10 debacle was just the fourth appearance of Cook's career. He pitched only once more in 1986 before returning to the minors.

July 13   The Angels trounce the Red Sox 12–3 in Boston.

Wally Joyner drove in runs in ten straight games from July 4 through July 13. He had 14 RBIs during the streak. In nine games from July 8 through July 19, Joyner collected 21 hits in 39 at-bats.

July 23   Brian Downing hits a walk-off homer in the tenth inning to defeat the Brewers 3–2 at Anaheim Stadium. Kirk McCaskill pitched all ten innings and struck out 12.

July 31   Brian Downing and Bob Boone both hits grand slams to account for all of the runs of an 8–5 win over the Athletics in Oakland. Downing's homer was struck off Eric Plunk in the third inning. Boone cleared the bases with a slam against Plunk in the fourth.

August 7   Jack Howell hits a walk-off homer in the 12th inning to defeat the Mariners 4–3 at Anaheim Stadium. The Angels tied the score 3–3 with one out in the ninth on an RBI-single from George Hendrick.

August 12   The Angels retire Rod Carew's number 29 during ceremonies prior to a 12-inning, 5–4 win over the Twins at Anaheim Stadium.

Carew was the first player with a number retired by the Angels. Number 26 was retired by the club in 1982 in honor of owner Gene Autry, who was considered to be the "26th man" on the roster. The Twins also retired Carew's number 29 in 1987. He played for Minnesota from 1967 through 1978 and the Angels from 1979 through 1985. The Angels have also retired numbers 11 (Jim Fregosi), 30 (Nolan Ryan) and 50 (Jimmie Reese). Number 42 is retired throughout baseball for Jackie Robinson. In 2009, the Angels had several numbers in "limbo" and weren't assigned to anyone. Among those were 15 (Tim Salmon), 16 (Garret Anderson), 17 (Darin Erstad) and 31 (Chuck Finley).

August 16   Mike Witt pitches a two-hitter to defeat the Athletics 5–2 at Anaheim Stadium. The only Oakland hits were a home run from Dwayne Murphy with one out in the first inning and a double from Mike Davis in the eighth.

Witt finished the season with an 18–10 record, 208 strikeouts and a 2.84 ERA in 269 innings.

AUGUST 20   The only Angels' hit off Walt Terrell of the Tigers during a 3–0 loss at Anaheim Stadium is a double by Wally Joyner with two out in the ninth inning. It was the second time in 1986 that Joyner broke up a no-hitter in the ninth (see June 16, 1986).

The Angels had a record of 67–56 on August 23 and a three-game lead in the AL West. California put the pennant away with 21 wins in 26 games from August 24 through September 22.

AUGUST 26   A bowie hunting knife with a five-inch blade is thrown at Wally Joyner as he walks toward the dugout after the Angels 2–0 win over the Yankees in New York. Joyner was grazed on the left arm by the butt end of the weapon, avoiding injury.

AUGUST 29   In one of the most amazing rallies in club history, the Angels score eight runs in the ninth inning to defeat the Tigers 13–12 at Anaheim Stadium. With Randy O'Neal pitching for Detroit, Dick Schofield led off the ninth with an infield single. After Rick Burleson lined out, Wally Joyner walked. Brian Downing singled to load the bases, and Jack Howell drove in two runs with a double. Willie Hernandez relieved O'Neal and surrendered back-to-back, run-scoring singles to George Hendrick and Bobby Grich to make the score 12–9. Gray Pettis grounded into a force play at second base for the second out, and pinch hitter Ruppert Jones walked to load the bases. Dick Schofield, who started the rally with a single, ended the game with a walk-off grand slam. The drive was fair by only a few feet above the short wall in left field and the leaping attempt of Dave Collins.

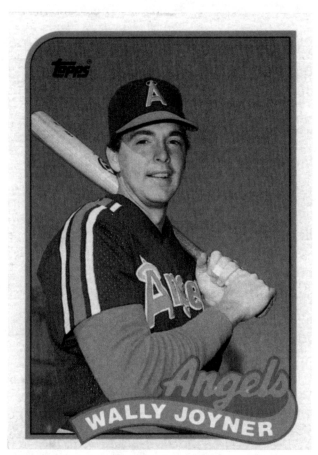

Wally Joyner captured the hearts of Angels fans in his rookie year in 1986 and remained a popular player throughout his six years with the team.

AUGUST 30   The Angels strike with a come-from-behind, ninth-inning rally for the second day in a row when Doug DeCinces hits a two-run, one-out, walk-off homer to defeat the Tigers 5–4 at Anaheim Stadium.

SEPTEMBER 6	Reggie Jackson collects his 2,500th career base hit with a double off Brad Arnsberg in the eighth inning of a 9–2 victory over the Yankees at Anaheim Stadium.
SEPTEMBER 10	The Angels a take seesaw, 14-inning, 7–6 decision from the Indians at Municipal Stadium. The Angels scored twice in the ninth to tie the contest 4–4 when Wally Joyner doubled in a run and crossed the plate on a single from Jack Howell. Doug DeCinces hit a two-run homer in the top of the 12th, but Cleveland rallied to two in their half to make the score 6–6. Mike Ryal drove in the winning run with a single in the 14th. Ryal entered the game as a pinch-hitter for George Hendrick in the ninth inning remained in the batting order as a right fielder.
SEPTEMBER 13	The Angels edge the White Sox 3–2 in 15 innings in Chicago. The winning run scored on a double from Dick Schofield and a single by Gary Pettis. Mike Witt (nine innings), Donnie Moore (three innings), Gary Lucas (two innings) and Terry Forster (one inning) pitched for California.
SEPTEMBER 17	Brian Downing hits a two-run, walk-off homer in the tenth inning to defeat the Royals 3–1 at Anaheim Stadium.
SEPTEMBER 18	Reggie Jackson hits three homers, drives in seven runs and scores four during an 18–3 thrashing of the Royals at Anaheim Stadium. Jackson hit a two-run homer off Dave Leonard in the first inning and a three-run shot against David Cone in the fourth. After drawing walks in the sixth and seventh, Reggie stroked a two-run homer facing Dan Quisenberry in the eighth. The Angels collected 20 hits in all from 12 different players.
SEPTEMBER 19	A day after the Angels score 18 runs and collect 20 hits, Joe Cowley of the White Sox pitches a no-hitter to defeat the Angels 7–1 at Anaheim Stadium. It wasn't pretty, as Cowley walked seven in addition to his eight strikeouts. The Angels scored in the sixth on three straight walks and a sacrifice fly from Reggie Jackson. Doug DeCinces made the final out by grounding into a double play from shortstop Ozzie Guillen to second baseman Jack Perconte to first baseman Russ Morman. The game was also the 2,000th of Bobby Grich's career.

Grich retired at the end of the 1986 season with 2,008 career games.

SEPTEMBER 20	Wally Joyner scores from third base on a passed ball with one out in the ninth inning to defeat the White Sox 8–7 at Anaheim Stadium.
SEPTEMBER 21	John Candelaria (seven innings) and Donnie Moore (two innings) combine on a two-hitter to defeat the White Sox 3–0 at Anaheim Stadium. The only Chicago hits were singles by Ivan Calderon in the second inning and Dave Cochrane in the eighth.
SEPTEMBER 26	The Angels clinch the AL West title with an 8–3 win over the Rangers at Anaheim Stadium. Brian Downing hit two homers and drove in five runs.
OCTOBER 1	Dick Schofield singles to lead off the ninth inning with a single to break up the no-hit bid of Royals pitcher Danny Jackson. Jackson also gave up a one-out single to Doug DeCinces before closing out a 2–0 win over the Angels in Kansas City.

October 4 — John Candelaria (six innings) and Vern Ruhle (three innings) combine on a two-hitter in Arlington to defeat the Rangers 2–0 in Arlington. The only Texas hits were singles by Orlando Mercado in the third inning and Pete Incaviglia in the fourth. The Angels also collected only two hits off Ed Correa. Brian Downing drove in both runs with a double in the second.

> *The Angels faced the Red Sox in the American League Championship Series. Managed by John McNamara, the Sox had a 95–66 record to win the AL East for the first time since 1975. McNamara managed the Angels in 1983 and 1984. The ALCS went from a best-of-five series to a best-of-seven format in 1985.*

October 7 — In the first game of the ALCS, the Angels cruise to an 8–1 win over the Red Sox at Fenway Park. Roger Clemens, who had a 24–4 record in 1986, was the Boston starter but was hammered by California batters for eight runs in 7 2/3 innings. The Angels broke the game open with four runs in the second. Brian Downing drove in four runs. Mike Witt pitched a complete game five-hitter.

October 8 — The Red Sox even the series by routing the Angels 9–2 in Boston. The game was close until Boston scored three in the seventh for a 6–2 lead.

October 10 — The Angels take a two-games-to-one lead with a 5–3 victory before 64,206 at Anaheim Stadium. The Angels snapped a 1–1 tie with three runs in the seventh after two were out. Dick Schofield hit a solo homer off Oil Can Boyd, Bob Boone singled and Gary Pettis added another home run.

October 11 — The Angels move within one victory of the World Series with an incredible 4–3 triumph over the Red Sox in 11 innings before 64,223 at Anaheim Stadium. Roger Clemens carried a 3–0 lead into the bottom of the ninth. Doug DeCinces opened the frame with a towering homer to center. Dick Schofield and Bob Boone then hit consecutive one-out singles to left. John McNamara pulled Clemens for reliever Calvin Schiraldi and Gene Mauch pinch-ran Devon White for Boone. Pettis greeted Schiraldi with a double off the left field wall that Jim Rice lost in the lights, scoring Schofield and sending White to third. After Ruppert Jones was walked intentionally to load the bases, Bobby Grich fanned for the second out. With the count 1–2, Brian Downing was hit by a pitch to score the tying run. Jerry Narron, who replaced Boone as the California catcher, opened the 11th with a single, went to second on a sacrifice by Pettis and scored on a walk-off single from Bobby Grich.

October 12 — The Angels suffer the worst loss in team history with an 11-inning, 7–6 defeat at the hands of the Red Sox before 64,233 at Anaheim Stadium. Boston scored first on a two-run homer by Rich Gedman off Mike Witt in the second. The Angels responded with a solo home run by Bob Boone in the third and a two-run shot from Bobby Grich in the sixth for a 3–2 lead. Grich's homer glanced off center fielder Dave Henderson's glove after he lost sight of the ball in the sun. Henderson had just come into the game as a replacement for Tony Armas, who sprained an ankle. Two California insurance runs were added in the seventh. The Angels headed into the ninth with a 5–2 lead and Witt still on the mound. The club was just three outs from the first World Series berth in franchise history. Bill Buckner led off the ninth with a single. One out later, ex-Angel Don Baylor hit a two-run homer to cut the lead to 5–4. Dwight Evans popped up for the second out. Police encircled the field to protect it from the impending celebration. Gene Mauch brought in Gary Lucas to relieve Witt and face Gedman, who called time to ask the umpires to have a sign removed from his line of vision in center field. The sign read: "Another Boston Choke." Lucas hit Gedman with the first pitch. It was the first time that Lucas hit a batter in four years. Lucas was replaced by Donnie Moore to face Dave Henderson, who appeared to be the goat of the game for knocking Grich's drive over the fence. Moore had a 1–2 count on Henderson, putting the Angels one strike away from the American League pennant. After a ball on a low pitch, Henderson fouled off two Moore deliveries. On Moore's third 2–2 pitch, Henderson lined a homer into the left field seats for a 6–5 Boston lead. The Angels tied the game in the ninth, however, on a single by Bob Boone, a sacrifice and another single by Ron Wilfong to tie the score 6–6. Following a single by Dick Schofield and a walk, the bases were loaded with one out, but the Angels failed to score again. Moore was still pitching in the 11th when the Sox scored the winning run. Boston loaded the bases on a hit batsman and two singles. Henderson stepped to the plate again and hit a sacrifice fly into center field. Calvin Schiraldi pitched a perfect 11th to seal the Boston victory (see July 18, 1989).

OCTOBER 14   The Red Sox force a seventh game by defeating the Angels 10–4 at Fenway Park. Still reeling from their game five loss, the Angels scored twice in the top of the first, but the Sox countered with two in their half, then broke the 2–2 deadlock with five runs in the third off Kirk McCaskill.

OCTOBER 15   The Red Sox move on to the World Series by defeating the Angels 8–1 at Fenway Park. It was over early, as the Sox scored three times in the second inning and four in the fourth for a seven-run lead. All seven runs off John Candelaria were unearned.

The Red Sox would experience their own meltdown of historic proportions in the World Series against the Mets. Leading 5–3 with two out in the tenth inning in game six against the Mets at Shea Stadium, the Sox were one out from their first world championship since 1918. The Mets rallied for three runs to win 6–5. In game seven, Boston led 3–0 in the sixth inning but wound up losing 5–3.

DECEMBER 19   The Angels trade Alan Mills and Rick Romanick to the Yankees for Butch Wynegar.

DECEMBER 24   Reggie Jackson signs a contract as a free agent with the Athletics.

Jackson went back to Oakland where he starred from 1967 through 1975. He played only one more big-league season and hit .220 with 15 homers.

1987

Season in a Sentence
A year after the collapse in the 1986 postseason, the Angels are one-half game out of first place on August 5 in 1987, then tumble into last place by the end of the season.

Finish • Won • Lost • Pct • GB
Sixth (tie)   75   87   .463   10.0

Manager
Gene Mauch

Stats   Angels • AL • Rank
Batting Avg: .252   .265   14
On-Base Pct: .324   .333   11
Slugging Pct: .401   .425   14
Home Runs: 172   11
Stolen Bases: 125   7
ERA: 4.38   4.46   7
Errors: 117   7
Runs Scored: 770   9
Runs Allowed: 803   8

Starting Lineup
Bob Boone, c
Wally Joyner, 1b
Mark McLemore, 2b
Doug DeCinces, 3b
Dick Schofield, ss
Jack Howell, lf-3b
Gary Pettis, cf
Devon White, rf-cf
Brian Downing, dh

Pitchers
Mike Witt, sp
Don Sutton, sp
Willie Fraser, sp-rp
John Candelaria, rp
Jerry Reuss, rp
De Wayne Buice, rp
Gary Lucas, rp
Greg Minton, rp
Chuck Finley, rp
Jack Lazorko, rp-sp

Attendance
2,696,299 (second in AL)

Club Leaders
Batting Avg: Wally Joyner   .285
On-Base Pct: Brian Downing   .400
Slugging Pct: Wally Joyner   .528
Home Runs: Wally Joyner   34
RBI: Wally Joyner   117
Runs: Brian Downing   110
Stolen Bases: Devon White   32
Wins: Mike Witt   16
Strikeouts: Mike Witt   192
ERA: Willie Fraser   3.92
Saves: De Wayne Buice 17

JANUARY 7   Rick Burleson signs a contract with the Orioles as a free agent.

APRIL 7   The Angels open the season with a 7–1 victory over the Mariners before 37,097 at Anaheim Stadium. Brian Downing collected two doubles and drove in three runs. Gary Pettis added three hits, including a double, and scored three runs. Mike Witt pitched a complete game and allowed five hits.

Ken Brett replaced Ron Fairly in the Angels broadcast booth in 1987. Brett announced Angels games until 1995.

APRIL 13   Devon White hits a two-run homer in the tenth inning to defeat the Mariners 5–3 in Seattle.

As a 24-year-old rookie in 1987, White hit 24 homers, stole 32 bases and scored 103 runs, but had an on-base percentage of only .306 and struck out 135 times.

APRIL 14   Brian Downing leads off the game with a home run, but the Angels lose 6–4 to the Mariners in Seattle.

APRIL 15	Brian Downing leads off the game with a home run for the second day in a row, and the Angels defeat the Mariners 4–0 in Seattle.
APRIL 18	The Angels edge the Twins 1–0 at Anaheim Stadium. Butch Wynegar drove in the lone run with a single in the seventh inning. John Candelaria (7 1/3 innings) and Donnie Moore (1 2/3 innings) combined on the shutout.
MAY 3	Doug DeCinces belts a grand slam off Wes Gardner in the sixth inning of an 11–4 triumph over the Red Sox at Anaheim Stadium.
MAY 5	The Angels use solo homers by Brian Downing in the fourth inning and Jack Howell in the sixth to defeat the Brewers 2–0 at Anaheim Stadium. Don Sutton (seven innings) and Donnie Moore (two innings) combined on the shutout.

> *After blowing the lead in game five of the 1986 ALCS (see October 12, 1986), Moore was limited to 14 games in 1987 because of a nerve irritation in his rig cage. De Wayne Buice succeeded Moore as the Angels closer. Buice had one of the most unusual careers in baseball history. He was a 29-year-old rookie in 1987 after bouncing around the minors for a decade, including stops in Canada and Mexico. In November 1987, Buice was looking for a restaurant in Yorba Linda, California, and went into a baseball card shop called The Upper Deck for directions. The owner recognized Buice and offered him a 12 percent stake in a baseball card company he was starting if Buice would get him in touch with the Players' Association to obtain a license. Buice agreed, became an executive with Upper Deck and earned more than $15 million with the company. After his big-league career ended in 1989, Buice was involved in the ownership of several minor leagues teams as well.*

MAY 9	Wally Joyner collects a three-run homer, a double and a single during an 8–1 win over the Red Sox in Boston unaware of his brother's death. After the game, Joyner was informed that his 31-year-old sibling died of a heart attack.
MAY 13	Mike Ryal hits a pinch-hit homer in the eighth inning, then adds another home run in the ninth as a first baseman, but the Angels lose 10–7 to the Tigers in Detroit.
MAY 15	John Candelaria is arrested for the second time in less than a month for driving while intoxicated. The Angels placed Candelaria on the disabled list for "personal reasons."
MAY 20	Wally Joyner smacks a walk-off homer in the tenth inning to defeat the Blue Jays 5–4 at Anaheim Stadium. Toronto scored three runs in the ninth inning to tie the score 4–4.
MAY 27	Jack Howell hits a pinch-hit homer in the sixth inning, then adds another home run in the eighth as a left fielder, but the Angels lose 8–6 to the Orioles in Baltimore.
JUNE 1	The Angels sign Greg Minton, most recently with the Giants, as a free agent.

> *Minton was released by the Giants, but gave the Angels four excellent seasons out of the bullpen.*

JUNE 2	In their first pick in the amateur draft, the Angels select catcher Greg Orton from Cal Poly.

Orton played five seasons in the majors, all with the Angels, and hit just .200 with four homers in 401 at-bats. Other future major leaguers drafted and signed in 1987 were David Holdredge (supplemental first round choice), Kevin Flora (second round), Mark Holzemer (fourth round) and Ruben Amaro (11th round).

June 5 The White Sox score four runs in the first inning and the Angels respond with six tallies in the fifth to win 6–4 at Anaheim Stadium. Jack Howell put California into the lead with a three-run homer.

June 6 Ruppert Jones hits a walk-off homer in the tenth inning to down the White Sox 2–1 at Anaheim Stadium.

June 8 In the a match-up of two starting pitchers with 300 or more career wins, Phil Niekro of the Indians (314 wins) bests Don Sutton (312) in a 2–0 decision over the Angels at Anaheim Stadium.

June 14 Dick Schofield caps a 12–0 win over the Royals in Kansas City with a grand slam off Bob Shirley in the ninth inning. It was Shirley's first appearance with the Royals after being released by the Yankees.

June 19 The Angels sign Jerry Reuss, most recently with the Reds, as a free agent.

June 21 The Angels score seven unearned runs in the third inning and defeat the Royals 8–0 at Anaheim Stadium. Jerry Reuss pitched the shutout in his first game with the Angels. He entered the game with an 0–5 record and a 7.79 ERA in 1987 with the Dodgers and Reds.

Reuss was 4–5 with a 5.25 ERA with the Angels before the club released him at the end of the 1987 season.

June 23 Devon White homers from both sides of the plate during an 8–6 win over the Rangers in Arlington. White homered from the left side of the plate against Charlie Hough in the sixth inning and from the right side facing Mitch Williams in the ninth.

June 28 The Angels hit six home runs and rout the White Sox 13–3 in Chicago. Wally Joyner homered twice with Brian Downing, Devon White, George Hendrick and Ruppert Jones adding the others. Hendrick homered as a pinch hitter for Mike Ryal in the third inning, and Jones homered batting for Hendrick in the fifth. Both Hendrick and Jones also played in left field after pinch-hitting.

June 29 The Angels extend their winning streak to eight games with an 11–4 decision over the Indians in Cleveland.

The Angels were 30–38 on June 20, they won 26 of their next 40 games to pull within one-half game of first place on August 5. On August 6 and 7, the Angels lost back-to-back games to the Mariners by scores of 15–4 and 14–0 in Seattle, which sent the club into a downward spiral. California was 19–35 over the last 54 games as hopes for a second straight pennant evaporated quickly.

July 1 Devon White collects four hits, including a homer and a double, and scores four runs in six at-bats during a 10–3 thrashing of the Indians in Cleveland.

	On the same day, the Angels signed Tony Armas, most recently with the Red Sox, as a free agent.
JULY 2	Mark McLemore hits a two-out, two-run walk-off homer in the 13th inning to defeat the Brewers 9–7 at Anaheim Stadium. Milwaukee scored twice with two out in the ninth to tie the game 7–7.
	The home run was McLemore's first in the majors, and it came in his 261st at-bat.
JULY 5	Brian Downing's walk-off single in the 12th inning defeats the Brewers 5–4 at Anaheim Stadium.
JULY 6	The Angels win with a walk-off hit in the 12th inning for the second game in a row for a 10–7 decision over the Red Sox at Anaheim Stadium. Boston led 7–0 before the Angels scored four runs in the seventh inning and three in the eighth. In the seventh, Wally Joyner tripled in two runs with two out, then scored on a home run by Doug DeCinces. In the eighth, Mike Ryal hit a two-run homer, and Joyner doubled in the tying run. In the 12th, Jack Howell belted a three-run homer with two out.
JULY 17	Brewers second baseman Dale Sveum hits three homers against the Angels to lead his team to a 12–2 victory in Milwaukee.
JULY 28	The Angels sign Bill Buckner, most recently with the Red Sox, as a free agent. Later that day, Buckner made his debut with the Angels and collected three hits, including a double, in five at-bats during a 9–2 victory over the Athletics in Oakland.
	Buckner came to the Angels nine months after gaining notoriety for costing the Red Sox a shot at winning the 1986 World Series by allowing a ground ball to roll through his legs in game six against the Mets. He played in 76 games for the Angels over two seasons and batted .288.
AUGUST 3	During an 11–3 Angels loss to the Twins at the Metrodome, Minnesota pitcher Joe Niekro is ejected in the fourth inning after umpires discover an emery board in his pocket.
AUGUST 4	In a match-up of starting pitchers with at least 300 wins, Don Sutton (317 wins) beats Steve Carlton (328 wins) and the Twins 12–3 at Anaheim Stadium. The 645 combined wins is the most ever accumulated by two pitchers starting the same major league game.
AUGUST 17	With the Angels trailing 4–2, Devon White hits a grand slam off Dave Leiper in the seventh inning, which leads to a 6–4 victory over the Athletics at Anaheim Stadium.
AUGUST 29	The Angels trade Bill Merrifield and Miguel Garcia to the Pirates for Johnny Ray.
AUGUST 31	The Angels blow a 6–0 lead, but survive to beat the Blue Jays 8–7 at Exhibition Stadium. Toronto scored seven runs in the seventh inning to take the lead, but California came back with a run in the ninth inning and another in the 11th for the victory. The winning run scored on a passed ball.
SEPTEMBER 10	The Angels take a thrilling ten-inning, 8–7 decision over the Rangers at Anaheim Stadium. The Angels led 3–2 heading into the ninth, but Texas scored five runs

to take a 7–3 advantage. All five runs crossed the plate after two were out. In the bottom half, Devon White beat out a chopper in front of the plate for a single and Tack Wilson walked. Both advanced on a ground out. Pinch hitter Jeff Eppard beat out a grounder fielded by pitcher Dale Mohorcic, but White was unable to score. Mike Ryal, pinch-hitting for Gary Pettis, belted a grand slam to tie the score. In the tenth, Devon White hit a walk-off homer for the victory.

The game was the second of only seven that Wilson played for the Angels and the second of Eppard's big-league career.

SEPTEMBER 15 The Angels trade John Candelaria to the Mets for Jeff Richardson and Shane Young.

SEPTEMBER 16 Bob Boone catches his 1,919th big-league game to pass Al Lopez for the all-time record. The Angels won 6–4 over the Royals in Kansas City.

Lopez caught 1,918 games between 1928 and 1947. Boone finished his career in 1990 with 2,225 games as a catcher. He held the record until 1993. Carlton Fisk played long enough to catch 2,226 games and beat Boone by one appearance behind the plate. Ivan Rodriguez broke Fisk's record in 2009.

SEPTEMBER 23 The Angels release Doug DeCinces.

SEPTEMBER 26 Brian Downing hits two homers, a double and a single in five at-bats, but the Angels lose 11–10 to the Indians in ten innings in Cleveland.

OCTOBER 3 Wally Joyner hits three homers during a 12–5 win over the Indians at Anaheim Stadium. All three were solo shots off Ken Schrom in the first and third innings and Sammy Stewart in the sixth. Brian Downing and Jack Howell also homered for the Angels, both off Schrom in the first.

Downing batted .272 with 29 homers in 1987.

DECEMBER 1 Chili Davis, most recently with the Giants, signs a contract with the Angels as a free agent.

Davis played with the Angels, mostly as a designated hitter, from 1988 through 1990, and after two seasons with the Twins, again from 1993 through 1996. He hit 136 home runs in an Angels uniform. Chili's given name was Charles Theodore Davis. He acquired the nickname after a bad haircut. A friend commented that it looked as though the barber used a chili bowl. Davis was also the first player born in Jamaica to appear in a major league game. The Angels had two Jamaican-born players from 1988 through 1990. The other one was Devon White, who became the second player from Jamaica to reach the big leagues with the Angels in 1985. Both Davis and White hailed from Kingston and emigrated to the United States as youngsters. Davis grew up in Los Angeles and White in New York City. Through 2009, the only other two individuals born in Jamaica to play in the majors were Rolando Roomes and Justin Masterson. Like Davis and White, Roomes and Masterson grew up in the United States.

DECEMBER 5 The Angels trade Gary Pettis to the Tigers for Dan Petry.

1988

Season in a Sentence

After Gene Mauch resigns as manager during spring training and is replaced by Cookie Rojas, the Angels put together a mid-season streak of 31 victories in 42 games, yet finish 12 games under .500.

Finish • Won • Lost • Pct • GB

Fourth   75   87   .463   29.0

Managers

Cookie Rojas (75–79) and Moose Stubing (0–8)

Stats

Stats	Angels	AL	Rank
Batting Avg:	.261	.259	6
On-Base Pct:	.318	.324	9
Slugging Pct:	.385	.391	9
Home Runs:	124		10
Stolen Bases:	86		12
ERA:	4.32	3.97	13
Errors:	135		13
Runs Scored:	714		6
Runs Allowed:	771		13

Starting Lineup

Bob Boone, c
Wally Joyner, 1b
Johnny Ray, 2b-lf
Jack Howell, 3b
Dick Schofield, ss
Tony Armas, lf-cf
Devon White, cf
Chili Davis, rf
Brian Downing, dh
Mark McLemore, 2b

Pitchers

Mike Witt, sp
Willie Fraser, sp
Chuck Finley, sp
Kirk McCaskill, sp
Dan Petry, sp
Terry Clark, sp
Brian Harvey, rp
Greg Minton, rp
Stew Cliburn, rp

Attendance

2,340,925 (sixth in AL)

Club Leaders

Batting Avg:	Johnny Ray	.306
On-Base Pct:	Brian Downing	.362
Slugging Pct:	Brian Downing	.442
Home Runs:	Brian Downing	25
RBI:	Brian Downing	93
Runs:	Johnny Ray	81
	Chili Davis	81
Stolen Bases:	Dick Schofield	20
Wins:	Mike Witt	13
Strikeouts:	Mike Witt	133
ERA:	Mike Witt	4.15
Saves:	Brian Harvey	17

JANUARY 5   Don Sutton signs a contract with the Dodgers as a free agent.

MARCH 11   Gene Mauch leaves the Angels during spring training in Palm Springs because of a case of bronchitis. Advance scout Cookie Rojas was named interim manager.

MARCH 26   Just nine days prior to the season opener, Gene Mauch retires. Cookie Rojas was named manager to replace Mauch.

> Rojas was 49 years old and a native of Havana, Cuba. He played in the majors from 1962 through 1977, mostly with the Phillies and Royals. Rojas displayed his versatility by playing all nine positions, plus designated hitter, during his career and was named to five All-Star teams as a second baseman. He had never managed before in either the minors or majors when appointed by the Angels. Mauch's retirement ended his career as manager at the age of 62 after 26 seasons with the Phillies (1960–68), Expos (1969–75), Twins (1976–80) and Angels (1981–83 and 1985–87). No one managed longer without placing a team in the World Series, which will be his unfortunate legacy. Three of his clubs were

on the brink of reaching the Fall Classic, only to lose. Mauch's 1964 Phillies blew a 6½-game lead in the final two weeks of the season, and his 1982 and 1986 Angels squandered two-game leads in the American League Championship Series. Usually saddled with clubs that possessed little talent, he won 1,902 games and lost 2,037 as a big-league skipper. Second to Mauch in most seasons managed without reaching the World Series is Jimmie Dykes, who guided six clubs over 21 seasons from 1934 through 1961 to a record of 1,406–1,541. Dykes, however, played in three Fall Classics with the Athletics in 1929, 1930 and 1931. Mauch never played in the postseason in nine seasons as a player.

In his nine seasons with the Angels, long and lanky Mike Witt gave the Angels many excellent innings and American League batters many nightmares.

MARCH 29   Jerry Reuss signs a contract with the White Sox as a free agent.

APRIL 4   The Angels open the season with an 8–5 loss to the White Sox in Chicago. The Angels led 4–3 until the Sox scored five times in the seventh. Mike Witt was the starting and losing pitcher. Johnny Ray homered in the losing cause.

APRIL 6   In his debut with the Angels, Dan Petry pitches six shutout innings, but gets a no decision because his relievers allow two runs in the ninth to tie the game 2–2. The Angels went on to win 4–2 in ten innings on a two-run single by Bill Buckner.

April 8	In the home opener, the Angels lose 8–2 to the Athletics before 45,586 at Anaheim Stadium.
	A Sony Jumbotron color video board was installed above the upper deck at Anaheim Stadium in 1988. Black-and-white matrix boards were placed above the right-field upper deck and the infield upper deck.
April 12	The Angels take a 12–0 lead in the fourth inning and rout the White Sox 15–6 at Anaheim Stadium. Devon White belted a grand slam off Jack McDowell in the third inning.
April 21	Johnny Ray drives in six runs on two doubles and two singles during an 11–6 triumph over the Mariners at Anaheim Stadium.
	From April 16 through April 30, Ray had an incredible streak in which he collected 29 hits in 52 at-bats, a batting average of .558. He finished the season with a .306 average, 42 doubles and six home runs. Ray played 104 games as a second baseman and 40 in left field.
May 13	Brian Downing hits a two-run homer with two out in the ninth inning to defeat the Yankees 5–4 in New York.
May 19	Trailing 6–1, the Angels explode for seven runs in the eighth inning and go on to defeat the Orioles 9–6 in Baltimore. All seven hits in the big inning were singles. Tony Armas drove in three runs with a pair of one-base hits.
June 1	With the eighth overall pick in the first round of the amateur draft, the Angels select pitcher Jim Abbott from the University of Michigan.
	Abbott was born without a right hand, but overcame the handicap to forge an outstanding career at Michigan. While preparing to pitch, Abbott would rest a right-handed throwing glove on the end of the right forearm. After releasing the ball, he would quickly slip his hand into the glove in order to field any balls hit his way and to receive the return throw from the catcher. Then he would remove the glove by securing it between his right forearm and torso, slip his hand out of the glove and remove the ball from the glove. He won the Sullivan Award as the nation's top amateur athlete and led the 1988 U.S. Olympic team to the gold medal in South Korea. During a trip to Havana with the U.S. team, even Fidel Castro wanted to meet him and obtain an autograph. Skeptics questioned whether or not Abbott could survive the rigors of the big leagues, but he proved them wrong. Abbott reached the majors in 1989 as a 21-year-old without having made a single minor league appearance despite a rocky spring training in which he allowed ten runs in 17 innings. Many dismissed his addition to the Angels roster as a publicity gimmick, but Abbott had a 12–12 record and a 3.92 earned run average. He not only had to endure the pressures of being a rookie, but was followed almost everywhere by reporters and photographers, some from as far away as Japan. By 1991, Abbott was 18–11 with a 2.89 ERA. After that season, however, he struggled, posting a 47–71 record from 1992 until his career ended in 1999. He was traded by the Angels to the Yankees following a 7–15 record in 1992, then returned to Anaheim in 1995 and 1996. Abbott suffered through a miserable year in 1996 with only two victories as opposed to 18 defeats.

The 1988 draft was arguably the best in Angels history. Other future major leaguers drafted and signed by the club were J. R. Phillips (fourth round), Gary DiSarcina (sixth round), Jim Edmonds (seventh round), Scott Lewis (11th round), Marcus Moore (17th round), Larry Gonzales (22nd round) and Damion Easley (30th round).

June 5   Johnny Ray's suicide squeeze in the 11th inning scores Darrell Miller from third base with the winning of a 6–5 decision over the Brewers in Milwaukee.

June 7   Brian Downing's home run off Charlie Hough in the sixth inning accounts for the lone run of a 1–0 win over the Rangers in Arlington. Chuck Finley ($8^{2}/_{3}$ innings) and Bryan Harvey (one-third of an inning) combined on the shutout.

Harvey was signed by the Angels as an undrafted free agent after being bypassed by all 26 major league clubs in 985 following a four-year career at North Carolina-Charlotte. When he was signed by the Angels, Harvey was playing with his father on a nationally known slo-pitch softball team called Howard's Furniture. Bryan became the Angels closer by 1988, a job he held for five seasons. Harvey ranks third in saves in franchise history with 126.

June 10   The Angels edge the Royals 1–0 at Anaheim Stadium. Dan Petry pitched the shutout. Brian Downing drove in the lone run with a single in the eighth inning. It was the second time in a span of three games in which Downing accounted for the only RBI in a 1–0 contest.

The Angels bottomed out with a record of 24–40 on June 15, and Cookie Rojas had a punching bag installed in the runway from the dugout to the clubhouse to allow the players to relieve their frustration. The club then put together an extraordinary streak of 31 wins in 42 games from June 16 through August 2 to pull four games above .500 at 55–51. The Angels were 20–36 from August 3 through the end of the season, however, and finished the year with 18 defeats in their last 20 games, including a season-ending 12-game losing streak.

June 17   Bob Boone collects five hits in five at-bats during a 9–7 victory over the Royals in Kansas City.

June 21   Chili Davis homers in the tenth inning to defeat the Twins 5–4 in Minneapolis.

June 25   The first pitch of the game between the Angels and Brewers at Anaheim Stadium is delivered with starting center fielder Devon White in the clubhouse talking on the telephone. Milwaukee lead-off batter Jim Gantner took a called strike from Mike Witt before the umpires realized the Angels had only eight men on the field. The pitch was nullified, and Gantner singled. The Angels went on to win 7–3, and White reached base in all three plate appearances on two singles and a walk.

June 27   Trailing 3–0, the Angels score five runs in the third inning and six in the fourth and rout the Twins 16–7 at Anaheim Stadium.

July 6   Chili Davis homers in the tenth inning to defeat the Blue Jays 5–4 in Toronto. It was his second tenth-inning home run in a span of 16 days.

1980s

JULY 8 — The Angels erupt for eight runs in the fourth inning for a 10–0 lead and defeat the Indians 10–6 at Municipal Stadium. Tony Armas started the rally with a double, then added another two-bagger to drive in two runs with two out. Cleveland pitcher Bud Black loaded the bases by hitting Jack Howell, Devon White and Johnny Ray with pitches in a span of four batters. Howell was struck above the right ear. He walked off the field under his own power and was taken to the hospital for precautionary X-rays. When White was plunked, he started toward Black but was tackled by home plate umpire Larry Young as both benches emptied and some players wrestled near the mound. After Ray was hit by a pitch, Jon Perlman relieved Black, and Wally Joyner brought all three runners across the plate with a double.

JULY 14 — Devon White accounts for both runs of a 2–0 triumph over the Tigers in Detroit with RBI-singles off Jack Morris in the third and fifth innings. Kirk McCaskill pitched the shutout.

JULY 15 — Bob Boone appears in his 2,000th career game as a catcher, and the Angels defeat the Tigers 6–4 in Detroit.

JULY 27 — Wally Joyner drives in six runs and scores the winning run of a 12-inning, 9–8 win over the Athletics at Anaheim Stadium. After Oakland scored four runs in the top of the first inning, Joyner hit a two-run homer in the bottom of the first and a three-run shot in the third, both off Britt Burns, for the 6–4 California lead. The A's surged back ahead 8–6, but the Angels scored two in the seventh, the second on Joyner's RBI-single, to tie the score 8–8. In the 12th, Joyner led off with a walk and crossed the plate on Brian Downing's triple.

JULY 28 — Brian Downing drives in the winning run in extra innings for the second day in a row with a home run in the 11th inning to down the White Sox 9–8 in Chicago.

JULY 30 — Chili Davis homers twice and drives in five runs during a 15–14 slugfest against the White Sox at the original Comiskey Park. Chicago took a 9–5 lead in the third inning, but the Angels came back with three tallies in the fifth inning and three in the sixth to pull ahead 11–9. The score was 15–11 when the White Sox scored three times in the ninth on two home runs off Donnie Moore. Dick Schofield, Darrell Miller and Jack Howell also homered for the Angels. Miller entered the game in the sixth inning as a pinch runner for Bob Boone and remained in the contest as a catcher. Howell pinch-hit for Gus Polidor in the sixth, stayed in the lineup at third base and hit his home run in the seventh.

Moore had a rocky year in 1988 with a 4.91 ERA in 27 games and 33 innings. He was released by the Angels on August 26. Moore tried to catch on with the Royals during spring training in 1989, but was released again (see July 18, 1989).

AUGUST 10 — Willie Fraser pitches a one-hitter to defeat the Mariners 2–1 at Anaheim Stadium. The lone Seattle hit was a long home run by Alvin Davis leading off the seventh inning.

Fraser was otherwise ineffective in 1988, with a 12–13 record and a 5.41 ERA in 197$^{1}/_{3}$ innings.

AUGUST 16 — The Angels score seven runs in the third inning for an 11–0 lead and defeat the Yankees 15–6 in New York. Chili Davis collected two of the Angels' eight hits in the big inning with a pair of singles. On the negative side, Willie Fraser allowed a club-record five home runs. Don Mattingly hit two of them, with Claudell Washington, Dave Winfield and Randy Velarde adding the rest.

August 26 — The Angels down the Yankees 7–6 in 12 innings at Anaheim Stadium. Tony Armas tied the score 6–6 on a home run with two out in the ninth. Johnny Ray drove in the winning run with a single.

August 27 — The Angels collect nine runs and nine hits in the second inning and thrash the Yankees 12–0 at Anaheim Stadium. Seven California batters in a row garnered hits off Charles Hudson on singles by Bob Boone and Dick Schofield, a double from Devon White, Johnny Ray's single, Wally Joyner's double, a single by Brian Downing and a home run off the bat of Jack Howell. Rookie Terry Clark pitched a complete game in what would prove to be his only career shutout.

The August 27 win also proved to be Clark's last as a member of the Angels. Clark pitched his first big-league game in 1988 at the age of 27 and started his career with a 5–0 record, before finishing his rookie campaign at 6–6. He was released by the Angels following the 1989 season. By the time his career ended in 1997, Clark had a 10–23 record with seven clubs after losing 23 of his last 28 decisions.

August 28 — The Angels rout the Yankees for the second day in a row with a 13–2 decision at Yankee Stadium.

September 10 — Two pitchers making their debuts with the Angels figure in a 17th-inning run and a 3–2 loss to the Rangers in Arlington. Vance Lovelace made his big-league debut in the 17th with two out and a runner on second. Lovelace walked Pete O'Brien and was relieved by Rich Monteleone, who hadn't pitched in the majors since April 29, 1987 when he was a member of the Mariners. Monteleone gave up a walk-off double to Ruben Sierra.

September 18 — The Angels take a thrilling 6–5 decision over the Rangers at Anaheim Stadium. Texas scored four runs in the top of the ninth for a 5–4 advantage, but the Angels responded with two in their half. The game-winning rally consisted of three consecutive singles by Darrell Miller, Johnny Ray and Bob Boone to load the bases, and a two-run, walk-off single by Wally Joyner.

The Angels didn't win again in 1988. The club closed out the year with a 12-game losing streak.

September 23 — Before Cookie Rojas completes his first season as manager, the Angels fire him. The club was 75–79 and had lost ten of the previous 12 games. Coach Moose Stubing was named interim manager. The Angels lost all eight games played under Stubing's leadership. He was a coach with the Angels from 1985 through 1990, then scouted for the organization from 1991 until 2007. With the exception of one game as interim manager of the Marlins in 1996, Rojas never managed again in the majors.

October 3 — The Angels trade David Holdredge to the Phillies for Lance Parrish.

Parrish was the Angels starting catcher for three seasons and made the All-Star team in 1990.

NOVEMBER 3   The Angels trade Paul Sorrento, Mike Cook and Ron Wassenaar to the Indians for Bert Blyleven and Kevin Trudeau.

Blyleven was 37 years old with a 254–226 lifetime record, 3,500 strikeouts and 55 career shutouts in 18 big-league seasons when acquired by the Angels. He was coming off a 1987 campaign in which he was 10–17 with an ERA of 5.43 and appeared to be finished. Blyleven was born in Holland but grew up in the Orange County town of Garden Grove, located adjacent to Anaheim. Coming home seemed to do him a world of good, as Blyleven made a remarkable comeback in 1989 by going 17–5 with five shutouts and an earned run average of 2.73. It proved to be his one good season, however. He had a records of 8–7 in 1990, and after sitting out all of 1991 with a shoulder injury, went 8–12 in 1992. Blyleven ended his career with 287 wins, 250 losses, 3,701 strikeouts and 60 shutouts. The Angels traded three prospects to obtain Blyleven, and only Sorrento became a big-league regular. A first baseman, Sorrento was blocked by Wally Joyner on the California depth chart.

NOVEMBER 14   A week after George Bush defeats Michael Dukakis in the Presidential election, the Angels named 44-year-old Doug Rader as manager.

Nicknamed the "Red Rooster" for his red hair, Rader was a fiery but fun-loving third baseman in the majors from 1967 through 1977, mostly with the Astros. He previously managed the Rangers from 1983 through 1985 to a record of 155–200. Prior to his appointment as skipper of the Angels, Rader was employed by the franchise as a scout and minor league instructor. He was an odd combination of disciplinarian and practical joker. Rader once greeted his dinner guests in the nude. In 1989, his Angels were 91–71, but fell to 80–82 in 1990. The club was 61–63 in 1991 when Rader was dismissed.

NOVEMBER 30   Bob Boone signs a contract as a free agent with the Royals.

1989

Season in a Sentence
With a vastly improved pitching staff, the Angels lead the Western Division for 49 days and win 91 games, 16 more than the previous season, under new manager Doug Rader.

Finish • Won • Lost • Pct • GB
Third   91   71   .562   8.0

Manager
Doug Rader

Stats   Angels • AL • Rank
Stats	Angels	AL	Rank
Batting Avg:	.256	.261	11
On-Base Pct:	.310	.326	13
Slugging Pct:	.386	.384	6
Home Runs:	145		1
Stolen Bases:	89		11
ERA:	3.28	3.88	2
Errors:	96		2
Runs Scored:	669		12
Runs Allowed:	578		2

Starting Lineup
Lance Parrish, c
Wally Joyner, 1b
Johnny Ray, 2b
Jack Howell, 3b
Dick Schofield, ss
Chili Davis, lf
Devon White, cf
Claudell Washington, rf
Brian Downing, dh
Kent Anderson, ss

Pitchers
Bert Blyleven, sp
Chuck Finley, sp
Mike Witt, sp
Kirk McCaskill, sp
Jim Abbott, sp
Bryan Harvey, rp
Greg Minton, rp
Bob McClure, rp
Willie Fraser, rp

Attendance
2,647,291 (third in AL)

Club Leaders
Batting Avg:	Johnny Ray	.289
On-Base Pct:	Brian Downing	.354
Slugging Pct:	Chili Davis	.436
Home Runs:	Chili Davis	22
RBI:	Chili Davis	90
Runs:	Devon White	86
Stolen Bases:	Devon White	44
Wins:	Bert Blyleven	17
Strikeouts:	Chuck Finley	156
ERA:	Chuck Finley	2.57
Saves:	Bryan Harvey	25

JANUARY 17   The Angels sign Claudell Washington, most recently with the Yankees, as a free agent.

APRIL 4   Eleven days after the Exxon Valdez spills oil into Alaska's Prince William Sound, the Angels open the season with a 9–2 loss to the White Sox before 33,265 at Anaheim Stadium. It was the Angels 13th loss in a row dating back to the end of the 1988 season. The two California runs came on homers by Claudell Washington and Devon White. Washington's homer was struck in a pinch-hit role in his first plate appearance with the Angels. Mike Witt was the starting and losing pitcher.

APRIL 5   The Angels break their 13-game losing streak with a 6–4 victory over the White Sox at Anaheim Stadium. The club lost its last 12 contests in 1988 and on Opening Day in 1989. Batting lead-off, Brian Downing hit the first pitch of the first inning for a home run off Eric King. Lance Parrish collected four hits, including a double, in four at-bats in his second game with the Angels.

APRIL 9   The Angels score seven runs in the third inning for a 13–3 lead and defeat the Mariners 13–5 at Anaheim Stadium. All seven hits in the big inning were singles by seven different players.

APRIL 15	The Angels rout the Mariners 10–0 in Seattle. Bert Blyleven pitched the shutout. Brian Brady doubled as a pinch hitter in his major league debut. He had only one more big-league at-bat, and struck out, to finish his brief career with a batting average of .500.
APRIL 25	President George Bush throws out the ceremonial first pitch before an 8–1 loss to the Orioles at Anaheim Stadium.
APRIL 26	Brian Downing's home run off Jack Morris in the second inning accounts for the lone run of a 1–0 victory over the Tigers at Anaheim Stadium. Chuck Finley (six innings), Greg Minton (1 2/3 innings) and Bryan Harvey (1 1/3 innings) combined on the shutout.

> *Harvey struck out 78 batters and allowed only 36 hits in 55 innings in 1989, but walked 41 and had an ERA of 3.44.*

APRIL 28	Kirk McCaskill pitches a one-hitter and beats the Blue Jays 9–0 at Anaheim Stadium. McCaskill went to the mound in the ninth inning with a no-hitter still in progress but allowed a lead-off double to pinch hitter Nelson Liriano.
APRIL 29	Johnny Ray drives in the tying run with a single in the eighth inning and the winning run with a walk-off sacrifice fly in the tenth to defeat the Blue Jays 4–3 at Anaheim Stadium.
APRIL 30	The Angels edge the Blue Jays 1–0 in 11 innings at Anaheim Stadium. The winning run scored on doubles by Johnny Ray and Lance Parrish. It was the second day in a row that the Angels defeated Toronto in extra innings. Mike Witt (ten innings) and Bob McClure (one inning) combined on the shutout.
MAY 6	The Angels play at Exhibition Stadium in Toronto for the last time and defeat the Blue Jays 5–4 with two runs in the ninth inning.
MAY 8	The Angels score all nine runs of a 9–2 victory over the Tigers in Detroit in the fourth inning. Wally Joyner started the rally with a double. Later in the inning, Brian Downing and Joyner hit back-to-back triples. Downing's three-bagger was struck with the bases loaded.
MAY 17	The Angels score five runs in the first inning off Roger Clemens to account for all of the runs in a 5–0 triumph over the Red Sox at Anaheim Stadium. Chili Davis hit a three-run double with two out and scored on Lance Parrish's home run. Jack Howell tied a major league record for third basemen by starting four double plays.
MAY 21	Catcher Bob Schroeder hits a grand slam off Bill Wegman in the third inning of a 12–9 win over the Brewers at Anaheim Stadium.

> *The Angels led the AL in home runs in 1989 with 145, but scored 24 fewer runs than the White Sox, who were last in homers with 94. Angels batters led the league in strikeouts (1,011), were last in walks (429), 12th in runs scored (669), and 13th in on-base percentage (.310).*

May 26	Chuck Finley pitches a one-hitter to defeat the Red Sox 5–0 in Boston. Finley had a no-hitter in progress until Jody Reed hit a looping single that fell in front of center fielder Devon White with two out in the eighth inning.
	The Angels pitching staff improved dramatically from the previous season. In 1988, the club ranked 13th in ERA with a figure of 4.32. In 1989, the club ranked second in the AL with an earned run average of 3.28.
May 29	Lance Parrish collects four hits, including a homer, and scores four runs in four plate appearances to lead the Angels to a 12–3 trouncing of the Brewers in Milwaukee.
	The Angels had a 33–16 record on May 30 and led the AL West by six percentage points over the Athletics.
June 5	In the first round of the amateur draft, the Angels select pitcher Kyle Abbott from Long Beach State University.
	The 1989 draft was the second in a row in which the Angels picked a pitcher named Abbott. In 1988, it was Jim Abbott. Kyle was 4–17 with a 5.20 ERA during a four-year career. He pitched for the Angels in 1992 and was 1–14 with the Phillies in 1994. Other future major leaguers drafted and signed by the Angels in 1989 were Joe Grahe (second round), Tim Salmon (third round), Erik Bennett (fourth round), Paul Swingle (29th round), Hilly Hathaway (35th round) and Chad Curtis (45th round). Salmon, who played at Grand Canyon University, proved to be one of the best players ever drafted by the Angels.
June 24	Chuck Finley strikes out 15 batters, and the Angels defeat the Orioles 8–3 at Anaheim Stadium.
June 27	Jack Howell homers in the tenth inning to defeat the Indians 2–1 in Cleveland.
July 1	The Angels score a single run in the first, second, fourth, fifth, sixth and seventh innings and defeat the Twins 6–1 in Minneapolis.
July 4	Tony Armas hits a three-run, walk-off homer with two out in the ninth inning to defeat the Rangers 5–2 at Anaheim Stadium.
July 11	The American League wins the All-Star Game before 64,036 at Anaheim Stadium. The NL scored twice in the first inning. Leading off the bottom half, Bo Jackson of the Royals hit a 448-foot home run on the second pitch from Giants pitcher Rick Reuschel. It was the first time in his career that Jackson batted lead-off. Red Sox third baseman Wade Boggs followed Jackson to the plate and hit another homer on a 3–2 pitch to tie the score 2–2. The AL added a run in the second inning and two more in the third. Nolan Ryan, at the age of 42, pitched two scoreless innings (the second and third) for the American League. Devon White was the only Angel to play in the contest and was retired in his only plate appearance. Chuck Finley was on the AL roster, but didn't pitch. Angels coach Jimmie Reese threw out the ceremonial first pitch, and former President Ronald Reagan attended the game and made an appearance in the broadcast booth in the first inning.

> *Future Hall of Famers on the rosters of the two clubs included Wade Boggs, Tony Gwynn, Kirby Puckett, Cal Ripken, Nolan Ryan, Ryne Sandberg, Mike Schmidt and Ozzie Smith. Other stars included Harold Baines, Jose Canseco, Will Clark, Andre Dawson, Julio Franco, Pedro Guerrero, Barry Larkin, Don Mattingly, Mark McGwire, John Smoltz, Darryl Strawberry and Tim Wallach.*

JULY 13 — After trailing 4–0 at the end of the second inning, the Angels rout the Orioles 13–5 in Baltimore.

JULY 17 — The Angels play at SkyDome in Toronto (now known as Rogers Centre) for the first time and lose a double-header to the Blue Jays by scores of 6–4 and 5–4.

JULY 18 — Wally Joyner's homer off Jimmy Key in the sixth inning on an 0–2 pitch accounts for the only run of a 1–0 win over the Blue Jays in Toronto. Bert Blyleven pitched the shutout.

> *On the same day, former Angels pitcher Donnie Moore shot his wife and committed suicide. Moore shot his wife, Tonya, three times with a pistol, the incident occurring in front of their three children at their Anaheim Hills home. Tonya was wounded in the neck, lungs and liver. Daughter Demetria, who was 17 years old, fled the house and drove her mother to the hospital. Back inside the house, still in the presence of his ten-year-old son, Donnie, Jr., Moore shot himself in the head. Tonya survived the shooting. Moore never got over yielding the runs in game five of the 1986 ALCS against the Red Sox, which cost the Angels a chance to reach the World Series (see October 12, 1986). He struggled through the 1987 and 1988 seasons with a sore shoulder and was booed by fans nearly every time he took the mound. Moore was released by the Angels on August 26, 1988. He had been released from the Royals' Class AAA farm team in Omaha five weeks before his suicide.*

JULY 20 — Wally Joyner's walk-off single in the ninth inning beats the Tigers 4–3 at Anaheim Stadium. Chuck Finley pitched a complete game, made 138 pitches and struck out 12.

JULY 21 — Wally Joyner hits a two-run, walk-off homer in the ninth inning to defeat the Tigers 8–7 at Anaheim Stadium. It was the second game in a row won by Joyner on a walk-off hit.

JULY 22 — The Angels outlast the Tigers 5–4 in 16 innings at Anaheim Stadium. Chili Davis drove in the winning run with a single. It was the third win in a row on a walk-off hit. Willie Fraser (four innings), Bryan Harvey (two innings), Greg Minton (three innings) and Dan Petry (two innings) combined for 11 innings of shutout relief, allowing just three hits.

JULY 23 — The Angels beat the Tigers in their final at-bat for the fourth game in a row. The Angels trailed 4–3 heading into the ninth. With one out, Dick Schofield, Claudell Washington and Johnny Ray hit consecutive singles to score the tying run. Devon White walked to load the bases, and Wally Joyner was hit by a pitch to bring across the winning tally. It was the third time in a span of four days in which Joyner contributed a walk-off run batted in.

> *The Angels had a 63–39 record and a 2½-game lead in the AL West on July 29.*

Jimmie Reese

Jimmie Reese's number 50 was retired by the Angels in 1995, a year after his death at the age of 92. He is the only individual to have his number retired by a major league club for which he didn't play, manage or own.

Reese was born Hyam Soloman in New York City in 1901. He changed his name to avoid the brunt of the prejudice that Jewish players endured in that era. Reese became a batboy with the Los Angeles Angels of the Pacific Coast League in 1919, a job he held for five years. He began his professional playing career as a second baseman with the Oakland Oaks of the PCL in 1924.

Reese made it to the majors leagues in 1930 with the Yankees and was a roommate of Babe Ruth. Playing mainly as a backup to second baseman Tony Lazzeri, Reese hit .346 in 188 at-bats. After playing for the Yanks again in 1931 and the Cardinals in 1932, his big-league career ended with a .278 average and eight home runs in 232 games.

Returning to the PCL, Reese played for the Angels again from 1933 through 1936 and San Diego in 1937 and 1938. Following a stint in the service and as a scout for the Boston Braves, Reese was a coach in the Pacific Coast League for more than two decades beginning in 1948 with San Diego, Hawaii, Seattle and Portland.

Reese asked the Angels for a job in 1972 when he was 71 and was appointed conditioning coach. He held the position until his death even though he was more than 70 years older than many of the players he was training. He became a beloved figure with the Angels, and Nolan Ryan even named one of his sons Reese in Jimmie's honor.

AUGUST 4   The Angels trade Roberto Hernandez and Mark Doran to the White Sox for Mark Davis.

> *Hernandez made his major league debut in 1991 and developed into one of the best relievers in the game. During his 17-year career, Hernandez saved 326 games for ten clubs. An outfielder, Davis played in only three big-league games.*

AUGUST 6   Bryan Harvey strikes out all three batters he faces in the ninth inning to close out a 6–0 victory over the Brewers in Milwaukee.

AUGUST 9   Bryan Harvey strikes out all three batters he faces in the ninth inning to close out a 4–1 win over the Mariners in Seattle. The performance gave Harvey six consecutive strikeouts over two games.

AUGUST 10   Chuck Finley strikes out 12 batters in nine innings, but the Angels lose 3–2 to the Mariners in ten innings in Seattle.

AUGUST 15   Third baseman Bobby Rose collects his first three major league hits, one of them a triple, during a 3–2 win over the Twins at Anaheim Stadium.

AUGUST 20   Kirk McCaskill pitches the Angels to a 1–0 victory over the Indians at Anaheim Stadium. Wally Joyner drove in the lone run of the game with a sacrifice fly in the seventh inning.

> *At the end of the day, the Angels had a 74–48 record and led the AL West by two percentage points over the Athletics. The Angels dropped out of first the following day and never again regained the top spot in the division in 1989.*

SEPTEMBER 6	Two weeks after Pete Rose is suspended from baseball for life because of his connections to gambling, the Angels trade Mark McLemore to the Indians for Ron Tingley.
SEPTEMBER 9	Devon White steals four bases, three of them in succession in one inning, during an 8–5 win over the Red Sox at Anaheim Stadium. In the sixth inning, White singled and stole second, third and home on pitcher Oil Can Boyd and catcher Rich Gedman. White also singled and swiped second in the eighth. Later in the inning, Mark McLemore broke the 5–5 tie with a three-run single.
SEPTEMBER 10	The Angels edge the Red Sox 2–1 in 14 innings at Anaheim Stadium. The winning run scored on an error by shortstop Luis Rivera.
SEPTEMBER 12	Wally Joyner's walk-off single in the ninth inning beats the Yankees 7–6 at Anaheim Stadium.
SEPTEMBER 13	The Angels win in their final at-bat for the third game in a row when Wally Joyner strokes a walk-off single in the tenth inning to defeat the Yankees 4–3 at Anaheim Stadium. It was the second game in a row in which Joyner had a walk-off RBI. Brian Downing tied the score 3–3 with a homer leading off the ninth inning.
SEPTEMBER 21	The Angels score three runs with two out in the ninth to tie the Indians 4–4 in Cleveland, but wind up losing 5–4 in 17 innings.

Heading into the game, the Angels were 2½ games behind the Athletics with 10 contests left on the schedule. Beginning with the tough 17-inning defeat, the Angels lost six games in a row to end any hopes for the postseason.

SEPTEMBER 28	Bert Blyleven throws his 60th career shutout in defeating the Royals 2–0 at Anaheim Stadium.

Blyleven ranks ninth all-time in shutouts. There are 20 pitchers in baseball history with 50 or more shutouts, and Blyleven is the only one who is not in the Hall of Fame. Among pitchers since 1970, Blyleven has the second most shutouts. Nolan Ryan beat him by one with 61. In addition, Blyleven was fifth in career strikeouts at the end of the 2009 season with 3,701. There are 11 pitchers with at least 2,850 strikeouts who are eligible for the Hall of Fame, and Blyleven is the only one of the 11 who has failed to make it. In career strikeouts, Blyleven ranks only behind Nolan Ryan, Randy Johnson, Roger Clemens and Steve Carlton.

DECEMBER 1	Six weeks after the World Series between the Giants and Athletics is interrupted by an earthquake, the Angels sign Mark Langston, most recently with the Expos, as a free agent.

At the time of the signing, Langston was 86–76 in six big-league seasons, most of them on Mariners teams with losing records. He led the AL in strikeouts as a rookie in 1984 and again in 1986 and 1987. He went to the Expos in a trade on May 25, 1989, which sent a struggling young left-hander named Randy Johnson from Montreal to Seattle. As an Angel, Langston was involved in a no-hitter in his debut with the club (see April 11, 1990) and had a 19–8 record with a 3.00 ERA in 1991. He was an All-Star that season and again in 1992 and 1993. Langston played eight seasons with the Angels with an overall record of 88–74.

THE STATE OF THE ANGELS

The Angels wallowed in mediocrity throughout most of the 1990s. There were three winning clubs (1995, 1997 and 1998), six with losing records (1990, 1992, 1993, 1994, 1996 and 1999) and one that finished at .500 (1991). No team won more than 85 games or had a winning percentage above .538. The franchise also had a name change, switching from the California Angels to the Anaheim Angels between the 1996 and 1997 seasons. Overall, the Angels were 738–817, a winning percentage of .475, which ranked 10th among the 13 teams that played in the American League during the entire decade. American League champions were the Athletics (1990), Twins (1991), Blue Jays (1992 and 1993), Indians (1995 and 1997) and Yankees (1996, 1998 and 1999). AL West champs were the Athletics (1990 and 1992), Twins (1991), White Sox (1993), Mariners (1995 and 1997) and Rangers (1996, 1998 and 1999). There were no pennant winners in 1994 due to the players' strike.

THE BEST TEAM

The best team was also the most heartbreaking. The 1995 Angels were 78–67 in the strike-shortened season, but had an 11-game lead in August, only to finish second to the Mariners.

THE WORST TEAM

The worst team was the 1994 edition, which had a record of 47–68 and a winning percentage of .409 when the players' strike ended the season.

THE BEST MOMENT

A reconfigured Anaheim Stadium returned to its original purpose as a baseball-only facility in 1998.

THE WORST MOMENT

At 1:47 a.m. on May 21, 1992, a bus carrying the Angels crashed, causing several injuries, the most serious to manager Buck Rodgers, who was sidelined for three months.

THE ALL-DECADE TEAM • YEARS W/ANGELS

Player	Years
Lance Parrish, c	1989–92
Darin Erstad, 1b	1996–2006
Randy Velarde, 2b	1996–99
Dave Hollins, 3b	1997–98
Gary DiSarcina, ss	1989–2000
Garret Anderson, lf	1994–2009
Jim Edmonds, cf	1993–99
Tim Salmon, rf	1992–2006
Chili Davis, dh	1988–90, 1993–96
Chuck Finley, p	1986–99
Mark Langston, p	1990–97
Jim Abbott, p	1989–92, 1995–96
Troy Percival, p	1995–2004

With the exception of shortstop, the Angels' infield was in an almost-constant state of flux throughout the decade. Other outstanding Angels players during the 1990s were left fielder Luis Polonia (1990–93) and pitcher Bryan Harvey (1986–92).

THE DECADE LEADERS

Batting Avg:	Garret Anderson	.300
On-Base Pct:	Tim Salmon	.393
Slugging Pct:	Tim Salmon	.524
Home Runs:	Tim Salmon	196
RBI:	Tim Salmon	660
Runs:	Tim Salmon	608
Stolen Bases:	Luis Polonia	174
Wins:	Chuck Finley	135
Strikeouts:	Chuck Finley	1,784
ERA:	Chuck Finley	3.76
Saves:	Troy Percival	139

THE HOME FIELD

Anaheim Stadium was enclosed in 1979 and 1980 when the Rams moved from Los Angeles to Anaheim. The football team moved to St. Louis in 1995, and the Angels entered negotiations with the city of Anaheim to change the ballpark back to a baseball-only facility. This was accomplished by 1998. Capacity was downsized from 64,593 to 45,000, and the name on the stadium was changed to Edison International Field of Anaheim, although it was most commonly known simply as Edison Field. Drawing fans was a problem throughout much of the 1990s. The club finished eighth in attendance in 1992, the first time the club was in the bottom half of the AL since 1976. The Angels didn't finish higher than fifth in the league in attendance from 1991 through 2002.

THE GAME YOU WISHED YOU HAD SEEN

Mark Langston (seven innings) and Mike Witt (two innings) combined on a no-hitter on April 11, 1990 to beat the Mariners 1–0 at Anaheim Stadium. It was also Langston's first game as an Angel.

THE WAY THE GAME WAS PLAYED

Baseball experienced one of its pivotal transitions during the 1990s, as offensive numbers soared to new heights. Fueled by expansion to 30 teams, newer ballparks with fences closer to home plate and the use of performance-enhancing substances, the average number of home runs in the AL increased from 123 per team in 1989 to 188 per team in 1999, with a peak of 196 in 1999. The average number of runs per game leaped from 8.6 in 1989 to 10.4 in 1999 with a high of 10.8 in 1996. The trend of the 1970s and 1980s toward artificial turf ended as every new ballpark on the drawing board featured a grass field. Most of the new ballparks, beginning with Camden Yards in Baltimore in 1992, had "retro" features that tried to emulate the older, classic venues. Four new teams were added in Miami, Denver, St. Petersburg and Phoenix. Beginning in 1994, there were three divisions in each league, adding a new tier of playoffs. Inter-league play started in 1997, giving the Angels a chance to settle their rivalry with the Dodgers on the field during the regular season.

THE MANAGEMENT

Gene Autry celebrated his 30th season as owner of the Angels in 1990, but was in failing health. His wife, Jackie, made many of the key decisions. In 1996, the Disney Company became a minority partner and essentially ran the day-to-day operation of the franchise with Tony Taveras as club president. Autry died in 1998 without realizing his dream of seeing the Angels play in the World Series. Following Autry's passing, Disney purchased a controlling interest in the Angels. General managers were Mike Port (1987–91), Dan O'Brien (1991), Whitey Herzog (1991–94), Bill Bavasi (1994–99) and Bill Stoneman (1999–2007). Field managers were Doug Rader (1989–91), Buck Rodgers (1991–94), Bobby Knoop (1994), Marcel Lachemann (1994–96), John McNamara (1996), Terry Collins (1997–99) and Joe Maddon (1999). Knoop and Maddon were both interim managers. In addition, John Wathan served as an interim manager for 89 games in 1992 while Rodgers was recuperating from injuries suffered in a crash of the Angels team bus (see May 21, 1992). Maddon also served as an interim manager in 1996 while McNamara was recuperating from a blood clot in his leg.

THE BEST PLAYER MOVE

The best move was the selection of Garret Anderson in the fourth round of the amateur draft in 1990.

THE WORST PLAYER MOVE

The worst move was the failure to sign Wally Joyner as a free agent following the end of the 1991 season. The worst trade sent Damion Easley to the Tigers for Greg Gohr in July 1996.

1990

Season in a Sentence
Expected to challenge for the pennant after winning 91 games in 1989, the Angels lose 20 of their first 31 games and finish two games below .500.

Finish • Won • Lost • Pct • GB
Fourth   80   82   .494   23.0

Manager
Doug Rader

Stats   Angels • AL • Rank
Stat	Angels	AL	Rank
Batting Avg:	.260	.259	6
On-Base Pct:	.328	.327	6
Slugging Pct:	.391	.386	5
Home Runs:	147		4
Stolen Bases:	69		13
ERA:	3.79	3.91	5
Errors:	142		13
Runs Scored:	690		8
Runs Allowed:	706		8

Starting Lineup
Lance Parrish, c
Wally Joyner, 1b
Johnny Ray, 2b
Jack Howell, 3b
Dick Schofield, ss
Luis Polonia, lf
Devon White, cf
Dave Winfield, rf
Chili Davis, dl-lf
Donnie Hill, 2b
Dante Bichette, rf-lf
Brian Downing, dh
Lee Stevens, 1b

Pitchers
Chuck Finley, sp
Mark Langston, sp
Kirk McCaskill, sp
Jim Abbott, sp
Bert Blyleven, sp
Bryan Harvey, rp
Mark Eichhorn, rp
Willie Fraser, rp

Attendance
2,555,668 (third in AL)

Club Leaders
Batting Avg:	Lance Parrish	.268
On-Base Pct:	Lance Parrish	.338
Slugging Pct:	Lance Parrish	.451
Home Runs:	Lance Parrish	24
RBI:	Dave Winfield	72
Runs:	Dave Winfield	63
Stolen Bases:	Devon White	21
Wins:	Chuck Finley	18
Strikeouts	Mark Langston	195
ERA:	Chuck Finley	2.40
Saves:	Bryan Harvey	25

JANUARY 22   Dan Petry signs a contract with the Tigers as a free agent.

FEBRUARY 15   The owners lock the players out of spring training because of a lack of negotiations for a new basic agreement.

MARCH 18   The labor dispute between the players and owners is resolved.

> *Spring training camps opened on March 20. The season, scheduled to start on April 2, was delayed a week, with missed games made up on open dates, with double-headers, and by extending the close of the campaign by three days.*

APRIL 9   The Angels open the season with a 7–4 loss to the Mariners before 38,406 at Anaheim Stadium. Ken Griffey, Jr. then 20 years old and the youngest player in the major leagues, broke a 2–2 tie with a three-run homer in the fifth inning off Bert Blyleven. Johnny Ray homered and scored three of the four California runs.

> *Joe Garagiola and Reggie Jackson each did one-year stints in the Angels' broadcast booth in 1990. The Angels began broadcasting games on cable over Prime Sports in 1990. Prime Sports became part of the Fox network in 1996. Fox was still carrying Angels games in 2009.*

April 11   Mark Langston (seven innings) and Mike Witt (two innings) combine on a no-hitter to defeat the Mariners 1–0 at Anaheim Stadium. It was also Langston's first game as a member of the Angels. He was relieved after seven innings and 99 pitches because manager Doug Rader didn't believe Langston was ready to go nine innings following the shortened spring training (see March 18, 1990). Witt pitched a perfect game on September 30, 1984. Langston walked four and struck out three. Witt retired all six batters he faced, two on strikeouts, in his first relief appearance since 1983. In the ninth inning, Scott Bradley and Harold Reynolds both grounded out from second baseman Johnny Ray to first baseman Wally Joyner. Ken Griffey, Jr. struck out on a 2–2 pitch to end the no-hitter. The lone run scored in the seventh inning on a bases-loaded walk by Gary Eave to Dante Bichette.

April 14   The Angels take a thrilling 12-inning, 7–5 decision from the Twins at Anaheim Stadium. Minnesota took a 5–4 lead with a run in the top of the 12th. In the bottom half, Johnny Ray singled with one out and moved to second on a ground out. After Chili Davis was intentionally walked, Dante Bichette smacked a three-run, walk-off homer.

April 25   Kirk McCaskill (five innings), Mike Witt ($2^{2}/_{3}$ innings) and Mark Eichhorn ($1^{1}/_{3}$ innings) combine to allow 13 hits and four walks, but hold the Red Sox to one run for a 3–1 victory in Boston.

April 29   The Angels trade Claudell Washington and Rich Monteleone to the Yankees for Luis Polonia.

Polonia came to the Angels just a few months after serving a 60-day jail term for having sex with a 15-year-old while playing for the Yankees. Despite his past, he quickly became a fan favorite in Anaheim because of his aggressive style of baseball. Polonia hit .336 in 109 games for the Angels in 1990 and was the club's starting left fielder for four years.

May 1   Lance Parrish collects two homers, a double and a single in four at-bats during a 7–1 win over the Orioles in Baltimore. Parrish also drove in four runs and scored three.

Parrish hit .268 with 24 homers in 1990.

May 3   Ten players go to bat for the Angels and each collects exactly one hit during a 10–8 loss to the Mariners in Seattle. The ten were starters Luis Polonia, Devon White, Wally Joyner, Chili Davis, Dante Bichette, Lance Parrish, Johnny Ray, Rick Schu and Donnie Hill and pinch hitter Jack Howell.

May 6   The Angels play their first regularly scheduled Sunday night game at home and lose 4–2 to the Yankees. The contest was carried on national television by ESPN.

May 11   The Angels trade Mike Witt to the Yankees for Dave Winfield. At first, Winfield vetoed the trade, but agreed to report to the Angels on May 16 after his contract was renegotiated. The Angels accused George Steinbrenner of helping Winfield gain additional compensation in the deal. The Angels sued Steinbrenner for $2 million in damages and were awarded $250,000. Steinbrenner was banned for life from baseball in July 1990 because of his connections to Howie Spira, a known gambler with Mafia connections. Steinbrenner paid Spira $40,000 for embarrassing information on Winfield. The suspension of Steinbrenner lasted only two years.

Winfield was 38 at the time of the trade, had made 12 All-Star appearances and had collected 2,434 career hits and 359 home runs. He missed the entire 1989 season because of a herniated disk. Despite coming to the club more than a month after the season started, Winfield led the Angels in RBIs (72) and runs scored (63) along with 19 homers in 1990. He gave the Angels another solid season in 1991 before moving to the Blue Jays as a free agent.

MAY 19	The Angels outlast the Blue Jays 11–9 in Toronto. Devon White broke a 6–6 tie with a two-run homer in the seventh inning.
MAY 23	The Angels score four runs in the ninth inning to stun the Blue Jays 5–4 at Anaheim Stadium. Wally Joyner drove in the first two runs with a double and scored the tying run on a two-out double by Johnny Ray. After Donnie Hill was intentionally walked, Lance Parrish drove in the winning run with a single.
MAY 24	The Angels win on a walk-off hit for the second day in a row when Johnny Ray doubles in the 11th inning to defeat the Blue Jays 4–3 at Anaheim Stadium. Toronto scored two runs in the top of the ninth to tie the score 3–3.
MAY 25	The Angels win in their last at-bat for the third day in a row, and the second in extra innings, when Devon White scores with the winning run in the 13th inning on an error by center fielder Robin Yount for a 5–4 decision over the Brewers at Anaheim Stadium.
MAY 27	Wally Joyner hits a grand slam off Tony Fossas in the seventh inning of a 7–3 win over the Brewers at Anaheim Stadium.
MAY 28	After pitching a two-hit shutout through nine innings, Jim Abbott allows three runs and three hits in the tenth to lose 3–0 to the Indians at Anaheim Stadium.
JUNE 3	Bryan Harvey strikes out all three batters to face him in the ninth inning to close out a 7–4 victory over the Rangers in Arlington.
JUNE 4	With their first pick in the amateur draft, the Angels select pitcher Phil Leftwich from Radford University in the second round. The club didn't have a first-round pick because of free agent compensation.

Leftwich had a 9–17 record and a 4.99 ERA during a three-year career in the majors. The Angels more than made up for the mistake of choosing Leftwich by drafting Garret Anderson in the fourth round and Troy Percival in the sixth. Other future big leaguers drafted and signed by the Angels in 1990 were Doug Creek (fifth round), Mark Dalesandro (13th round), P. J. Forbes (20th round), Kent Edenfield (21st round) and Dave Berg (32nd round).

JUNE 10	Mark Langston strikes out 12 batters in eight innings, but the Angels lose 2–1 to the Rangers in Arlington.
JUNE 11	Lance Parrish hits a walk-off homer with two out in the ninth inning to defeat the Royals 3–2 at Anaheim Stadium.

June 15	Mark Langston strikes out 11 batters in eight innings, but earns a no decision in the Angels ten-inning, 2–1 loss to the Tigers in Detroit.
June 17	Lance Parrish hits a grand slam off Lance McCullers in the fifth inning of a 7–3 triumph over the Tigers in Detroit.
June 20	Mark Langston strikes out ten batters in eight innings, but loses 2–1 to the White Sox in Chicago.

Over three consecutive starts from June 10 through June 20, Langston struck out 33 batters in 24 innings while allowing five runs and 18 hits, but wound up with two losses and a no decision. The three starts came during a nine-game losing streak that sent his record to 4–13. Langston finished his first season as an Angel with 195 strikeouts in 223 innings, but was 10–17 with an ERA of 4.40.

June 22	A walk-off triple by Dave Winfield in the ninth inning scores the only run of a 1–0 victory over the Tigers at Anaheim Stadium. Chuck Finley (8 1/3 innings) and Scott Bailes (two-thirds of an inning) combined on a three-hit shutout.

Finley had a record of 18–9 with an ERA of 2.40 in 236 innings in 1990. The earned run average is the third lowest by an Angel in franchise history by a pitcher with at least 162 innings, trailing only Dean Chance (1.65 in 1964) and Nolan Ryan (2.28 in 1972).

July 6	The Angels need 16 innings to defeat the Brewers 9–8 at County Stadium. Dante Bichette drove in the winning run with a single. Willie Fraser (five innings) and Greg Minton (two innings) shut out Milwaukee on one hit over the last seven innings.
July 7	The Angels win in extra innings for the second day in a row when Jack Howell homers in the 11th inning to beat the Brewers 4–3 in Milwaukee.
July 8	The Angels blow a seven-run lead and lose 20–7 to the Brewers at County Stadium. The Angels scored two runs in the first inning, three in the second and two in the third for a 7–0 lead. Milwaukee responded with a run in the bottom of the third and six in the fourth to tie the score 7–7 before exploding for 13 runs in the fifth. The 20 runs in a span of just three innings were allowed by Bert Blyleven, Scott Bailes, Greg Minton, Mike Fetters and Mark Eichhorn. During the 13-run inning, the Brewers collected ten hits on eight singles, a double and a home run, and drew five walks. Infielder Donnie Hill pitched the eighth inning for the Angels and allowed a walk and no hits.
July 13	Lance Parrish hits a two-run homer off Todd Stottlemyre in the second inning to account for both runs of a 2–0 victory over the Blue Jays at Anaheim Stadium. Jim Abbott pitched the shutout.
July 14	Brian Downing hits a walk-off homer in the ninth inning to defeat the Blue Jays 8–7 at Anaheim Stadium. It was the sixth home run by the Angels during the game. Downing, Dave Winfield and Dante Bichette each homered twice. Each of the three hit home runs in the seventh inning.

JULY 15   The Angels win with a walk-off hit for the second game in a row when Johnny Ray singles in the ninth inning to down the Blue Jays 4–3 at Anaheim Stadium.

JULY 26   Donnie Hill hits a two-run homer off Dennis Eckersley with two out in the 11th inning to defeat the Athletics 4–2 in Oakland.

JULY 31   The Angels collect 20 hits and rout the Twins 13–2 in Minneapolis.

AUGUST 1   Angels broadcaster Joe Torre becomes the manager of the St. Louis Cardinals. Torre had been a member of the Angels' broadcast team since 1985.

Though rarely dominant, Chuck Finley was a consistently effective pitcher for the Angels during his 14 years with the team, winning 15 or more games in six seasons.

Torre managed the Cardinals until May 1995. He led the Yankees to five World Series and four world championships as manager from 1996 through 2007, then took over as skipper of the Dodgers in 2008.

AUGUST 7   Dave Winfield collects his 2,500th career hit with a single off Tom Bolton in the first inning of a 6–3 loss to the Red Sox at Anaheim Stadium.

AUGUST 8   With two out in the bottom of the 11th inning, Brian Downing singles and Lance Parrish homers for an 8–6 win over the Red Sox at Anaheim Stadium.

AUGUST 11 The Angels score seven runs in the fourth inning, the last three on a three-run homer by Chili Davis, and defeat the Orioles 12–4 at Anaheim Stadium.

AUGUST 14 Luis Polonia hits an inside-the-park grand slam off Tom Leary in the second inning of a 9–5 win over the Yankees at Anaheim Stadium. On a sinking liner to right field, Jesse Barfield missed a shoestring catch, then casually chased the ball to the fence while Polonia raced around the bases. Polonia had been traded by the Yankees to the Angels on April 29.

August 17	Chuck Finley pitches the Angels to a 1–0 win over the Red Sox in Boston. The lone run scored on a single by Johnny Ray in the ninth inning.
	On the same day, the Angels traded Mark McLemore to the Indians for Ron Tingley.
August 18	Playing third base, Pete Coachman delivers two singles in five at-bats in his major league debut as the Angels defeat the Red Sox 4–3 in Boston.
	Coachman was 28 years old when he made his debut. He had two hits in each of his first big major league games. Coachman played only 16 games in the majors, however, and had 14 hits and a .311 batting average.
August 25	With two out in the ninth inning and the Angels trailing 2–0, Lee Stevens hits a two-strike pitch off Bobby Thigpen for a three-run homer to defeat the White Sox 3–2 in Chicago.
August 26	The Angels play at old Comiskey Park in Chicago for the last time and defeat the White Sox 4–3.
August 29	The Angels break a 2–2 tie with seven runs in the seventh inning to beat the Rangers 9–2 at Anaheim Stadium. Lance Parrish capped the rally with a three-run homer.
September 2	Jack Howell homers in the fifth inning off Alex Fernandez to account for the lone run of a 1–0 win over the White Sox at Anaheim Stadium. Chuck Finley (7 1/3 innings) and Bryan Harvey (1 2/3 innings) combined on the shutout.
September 3	The Angels score six runs in the sixth inning on only two hits, both singles, and beat the Yankees 7–0 in New York. The Angels were helped during the six-run rally by four walks and an error.
September 6	The Angels erupt for six runs in the 11th inning and defeat the Yankees 12–6 in New York.
September 13	The Angels score all seven of their runs in the seventh inning and beat the Mariners 7–1 at Anaheim Stadium.
September 14	Kirk McCaskill gives up back-to-back home runs to Ken Griffey, Sr. and Ken Griffey, Jr. during a 7–5 Angels win over the Mariners at Anaheim Stadium. Batting second, Griffey, Sr. homered in the first inning. Four pitches later, Griffey, Jr. went deep. Griffey, Sr. was 40 years old and Junior was 20. They were the first father-and-son team to be active at the same time and the first to play together on the same team. They are the only father-and-son combo to homer in the same game. Griffey, Sr. was signed by the Mariners on August 29, 1990, following his release by the Reds.
September 21	The Angels score seven runs in the seventh inning and down the Royals 12–5 in Kansas City.
September 27	The Angels take an exciting 7–6 decision from the Royals at Anaheim Stadium. Johnny Ray hit a three-run homer with two out in the eighth inning for a 5–4 California lead, but Kansas City scored twice in the ninth for a 6–5 advantage.

The Angels bounced back with two tallies in the bottom of the ninth for the victory. Devon White drove in the winning run with a single.

October 3 On the final day of the season, the Angels score seven runs in the fourth inning and beat the Athletics 11–6 in Oakland.

After making 96 errors in 1989, the Angels committed 142 in 1990. The bulk of the increase was on the left side of the infield, anchored by Jack Howell and Dick Schofield. In 1989, Angels third basemen committed 16 errors and shortstops 17. In 1990, there were 34 errors by third basemen and another 34 by shortstops.

December 2 The Angels trade Devon White, Willie Fraser and Marcus Moore to the Blue Jays for Junior Felix, Luis Sojo and Ken Rivers.

When his batting average dipped to .213 in July during the 1990 season, White was sent to the minors for three weeks to correct his swing. It didn't work. He finished the year with a .217 average and an on-base percentage of only .290. After leaving Anaheim, White played 11 more seasons in the majors and appeared in two All-Star Games. The Angels received little in compensation for trading White.

December 12 The Angels sign Floyd Bannister, most recently with the Royals, as a free agent.

1991

Season in a Sentence
The Angels move into first place on July 3, but quickly skid out of the race leading to the firing of Doug Rader in August.

Finish • Won • Lost • Pct • GB
Seventh   81   81   .500   14.0

Managers
Doug Rader (61–63) and Buck Rodgers (20–28)

Stats	Angels	AL	Rank
Batting Avg:	.255	.260	9
On-Base Pct:	.312	.329	13
Slugging Pct:	.374	.395	13
Home Runs:	115		13
Stolen Bases:	94		11
ERA:	3.69	4.09	2
Errors:	102		3
Runs Scored:	653		13
Runs Allowed:	649		2

Starting Lineup
Lance Parrish, c
Wally Joyner, 1b
Luis Sojo, 2b
Gary Gaetti, 3b
Dick Schofield, ss
Luis Polonia, lf
Junior Felix, cf
Dave Winfield, rf
Dave Parker, dh
Dave Gallagher, cf
Donnie Hill, 2b-ss

Pitchers
Mark Langston, sp
Jim Abbott, sp
Chuck Finley, sp
Kirk McCaskill, sp
Bryan Harvey, rp
Mark Eichhorn, rp
Scott Bailes, rp

Attendance
2,416,236 (sixth in AL)

Club Leaders
Batting Avg:	Wally Joyner	.301
On-Base Pct:	Wally Joyner	.360
Slugging Pct:	Wally Joyner	.488
Home Runs:	Dave Winfield	28
RBI:	Wally Joyner	96
Runs:	Luis Polonia	92
Stolen Bases:	Luis Polonia	48
Wins:	Mark Langston	19
Strikeouts:	Mark Langston	183
ERA:	Jim Abbott	2.89
Saves:	Bryan Harvey	46

JANUARY 23   Six days after the United States and its allies launch an air attack on Iraq to start the Persian Gulf War, the Angels sign Gary Gaetti, most recently with the Twins, as a free agent.

> Gaetti was a two-time All-Star and four-time Gold Glove winner in Minnesota. He proved to be a poor investment, as he hit just .234 with 30 homers in 1,092 at-bats before being released in June 1993. After leaving Anaheim, Gaetti revived his career, clubbed 35 homers for the Royals in 1995 and was active in the majors until 2000.

JANUARY 29   Chili Davis signs a contract as a free agent with the Twins.

> Davis would return to the Angels in 1993 after two seasons in Minnesota.

MARCH 14   Two weeks after President George Bush orders a cease fire to end the Persian Gulf War, the Angels trade Dante Bichette to the Brewers for Dave Parker.

> Bichette was 27 at the time of the trade. He went to the Rockies in 1993, and helped by the thin, mile-high atmosphere in Denver, put up some tremendous batting numbers. Bichette was the runner-up in the MVP voting in 1995 and

made four All-Star teams with Colorado. Parker was 39 and hit only .232 with 11 homers for the Angels in 1991, the last season of his career.

MARCH 18　　Batting with one hand, Jim Abbott belts a 400-foot triple off Rick Reuschel of the Giants during an exhibition game in Mesa, Arizona.

APRIL 9　　The Angels open the season with a 3–2 victory over the Mariners in Seattle. Playing in his first game with the Angels, Dave Parker homered in his first plate appearance and tripled in his second. Chuck Finley pitched seven shutout innings before allowing two runs in the eighth.

Ken Wilson joined the Angels broadcasting team in 1991. He previously announced games for the Mariners (1977–82), Reds (1983–85) and Cardinals (1986–90) in addition to serving as the lead play-by-play man in the NHL for the Chicago Blackhawks and St. Louis Blues. Wilson remained with the Angels until 1995.

APRIL 13　　Dave Winfield collects three homers, a double and a single, drives in six runs, and scores four in six at-bats during a 15–9 thrashing of the Twins in Minneapolis. Winfield's 15 total bases is a club record. He hit two-run homers off Mark Guthrie in the first and third innings, then hit a solo shot off Larry Casian in the fifth. Winfield had three plate appearances to hit his fourth home run and tie a major league record. Although he failed, Winfield collected two more hits. He added a double against Terry Leach in the sixth, and after grounding out facing Steve Bedrosian in the eighth, singled off Gary Wayne in the ninth. The Angels garnered 21 hits in all.

On the same day, Brian Downing signed a contract as a free agent with the Rangers.

APRIL 15　　In the home opener, the Angels lose 5–2 to the Athletics before 44,339 at Anaheim Stadium.

APRIL 19　　Chuck Finley pitches a two-hitter to defeat the Twins 2–0 at Anaheim Stadium. The only Minnesota hits were a single by Kirby Puckett in the first inning and a double from Greg Gagne in the sixth.

The Angels received excellent seasons from their top three starters. Finley was 18–9 with a 3.80 ERA. Mark Langston had a 19–8 record, a 3.00 earned run average and 183 strikeouts in 246 1/3 innings. Jim Abbott put together the best season of his career. After losing his first four decisions and in danger of being sent to the minor leagues, he finished 18–11 accompanied by an ERA of 2.89. It's the only time in major league history that three left-handers on one club won at least 18 games. The club struggled mightily to find a fourth and fifth starter, however. The starters outside of Finley, Langston and Abbott were 15–38 with an ERA of 5.12. Take number four starter Kirk McCaskill out of the equation, and the various number five starters were 5–19 and an earned run average of 6.03. Bryan Harvey bailed out many a starting pitcher with 46 saves and a 1.60 ERA in 63 games and 78 2/3 innings. He allowed 51 hits and 17 walks while striking out 101 batters. Overall, the Angels allowed the second fewest runs in the AL (649), but also scored the second fewest (653).

APRIL 30　　After the Indians score a run in the top of the 11th inning, the Angels respond with two in their half to win 6–5 at Anaheim. Junior Felix tied the score 5–5 with a one-out homer, his first as a member of the Angels. The winning run scored on consecutive singles by Luis Polonia, Dick Schofield and Jack Howell.

On the same day, the Angels fired Mike Port as general manager and replaced him with Dan O'Brien, Sr. Port was let go because of "philosophical differences" in the front office. O'Brien had been Port's assistant. Prior to coming to Anaheim, O'Brien had been the general manager of the Mariners from 1981 through 1983 and had also worked in the front offices of the Rangers and Indians. O'Brien was demoted to a role of assistant general manager again in September when the Angels hired Whitey Herzog.

MAY 5 — Trailing 3–0, the Angels score six runs in the fourth inning and win 6–4 over the Orioles at Anaheim Stadium.

MAY 7 — Bryan Harvey strikes out all three batters he faces in the ninth inning to close out a 7–4 triumph over the Yankees at Anaheim Stadium.

MAY 10 — Wally Joyner hits a grand slam off Eric King in the seventh inning of a 12–2 victory over the Indians in Cleveland.

MAY 13 — Luis Polonia collects five hits, including a triple, in six at-bats during a 9–5 win over the Indians in Cleveland. Polonia also stole two bases.

MAY 19 — Dave Gallagher collects five hits in five at-bats during a 10–2 win over the Orioles in Baltimore.

MAY 20 — The Angels sign Fernando Valenzuela, most recently with the Dodgers, as a free agent.

Valenzuela became a national phenomenon as a rookie with the Dodgers in 1981 when he started the season with an 8–0 record. Five of the eight victories were shutouts. Fernando was released by the Dodgers during spring training in 1991. After three minor league appearances in which he pitched 17 innings without allowing an earned run, he made two starts for the Angels on June 7 and June 12, but was rocked for nine runs in 6²/₃ innings and was released. After pitching a season in his native Mexico, Valenzuela played for the Orioles, Phillies, Padres and Cardinals from 1993 through 1997.

MAY 28 — The Angels play at new Comiskey Park (now known as US Cellular Field) for the first time and lose 6–5 to the White Sox.

JUNE 1 — Luis Polonia collects five hits, including a double, in six at-bats during an 11–8 win over the Blue Jays in Toronto. He also stole two bases. It was Polonia's second five-hit, two-stolen base game in less than three weeks. Dave Winfield walloped a grand slam off Willie Fraser in the third inning.

JUNE 3 — With their first pick in the amateur draft, the Angels select first baseman Eduardo Perez from Florida State University.

Eduardo was the son of Tony Perez, who fashioned a Hall of Fame career from 1964 through 1986 and appeared in four World Series with the Reds. Eduardo played the first three seasons (1993–95) of his 13-year big-league career with the Angels. Never a starter, Eduardo played for six clubs and hit .247 with 79 homers in 1,800 at-bats. Other future major leaguers drafted and signed by the Angels in 1991 were Jorge Fabregas (supplemental first round pick), Chris Prichett (second round), Chris Turner (seventh round), Mark Sweeney (ninth round), Shad Williams (17th round) and Orlando Palmeiro (33rd round).

June 4   Chuck Finley pitches a two-hitter to defeat the Red Sox 2–0 at Anaheim Stadium. The only Boston hits were singles by Ellis Burks in the second inning and Mike Greenwell in the sixth.

June 24   Dave Winfield hits for the cycle, including two singles, during a 9–4 victory over the Royals in Kansas City. Facing starter Hector Wagner, Winfield singled in the first inning, doubled in the third and homered in the fifth. Winfield added another single in the sixth off Tom Gordon. Infielder Bill Pecota took the mound in the eighth and allowed a triple to Winfield to complete the cycle.

Wagner never appeared in another big-league game. His career lasted only seven games. The contest was the first of two in which Pecota appeared as a pitcher during his nine years in the majors.

June 28   Wally Joyner collects four hits, including a homer and two doubles, and drives in five runs during a 10–8 win over the Rangers at Anaheim Stadium.

July 2   Max Venable hits a grand slam off Mark Gubicza in the second inning of a 10–5 win over the Royals at Anaheim Stadium.

July 3   The Angels take over first place with a 4–3 victory over the Royals in Kansas City. California had a record of 44–33.

The stay in first lasted only one day. The Angels lost 30 of their next 44 games to drop quickly out of the race.

July 18   The Angels take a thrilling 5–4 decision from the Indians at Anaheim Stadium. The score was 1–1 before Cleveland scored three runs in the top of the ninth before the Angels responded with four tallies in the bottom half. The four runs scored on only two hits, both singles. The winning run scored on a bases-loaded walk to Dick Schofield with two out.

July 25   The Angels play at Memorial Stadium in Baltimore for the last time, and lose 8–4 to the Orioles.

July 30   Bryan Harvey strikes out all four batters he faces in the eighth and ninth innings to close out a 4–2 win over the Indians in Cleveland.

August 7   Wally Joyner hits two homers and drives in five runs to lead the Angels to an 8–1 win over the Twins at Anaheim Stadium.

August 14   Dave Winfield hits his 400th career homer during a 7–4 win over the Twins in Minneapolis. The milestone was struck in the fourth inning off David West.

AUGUST 15	Lance Parrish hits his 300th career homer in the third inning of a 9–1 win over the Twins in Minneapolis. The milestone was struck off Scott Erickson.
AUGUST 24	A home run by Dave Winfield off Kevin Morton in the seventh inning accounts for the only run of a 1–0 victory over the Red Sox at Anaheim Stadium. Kirk McCaskill (eight innings) and Bryan Harvey (one inning) combined on the shutout.
AUGUST 26	The Angels fire Doug Rader as manager and replace him with 53-year-old Buck Rodgers. The club had a 61–63 record at the time of the switch.

> *Rodgers played his entire nine-year major league career as a catcher with the Angels from 1961 through 1969. He had previously managed the Brewers (1980–82) and Expos (1985–91) to a record of 644-619. Rodgers lasted until May 1994 as skipper of the Angels, but failed to achieve a winning record with the club. Rader never managed another major league team.*

AUGUST 28	The Angels edge the Tigers 1–0 at Anaheim Stadium. The lone run scored on a double by Luis Polonia in the sixth inning. Jim Abbott (7 1/3 innings), Mark Eichhorn (two-thirds of an inning) and Bryan Harvey (one inning) combined on the shutout.
SEPTEMBER 2	Junior Felix collects four hits, including two doubles, and drives in five runs during a 7–6 win over the Brewers in Milwaukee.
SEPTEMBER 6	The Angels score two runs in the ninth inning to beat the Brewers 2–1 at Anaheim Stadium. With one out, Luis Polonia walked, and Junior Felix, Wally Joyner and Dave Winfield delivered consecutive singles.

> *On the same day, the Angels hired Whitey Herzog as general manager, succeeding Dan O'Brien, who had replaced Mike Port on April 30. O'Brien remained with the organization as an assistant to Herzog. In 1974 Herzog had worked for the Angels as a coach and served a four-game stint as interim manager. He had an impressive resume when hired a second time by the Angels. After a playing career as a mediocre outfielder with four clubs from 1956 through 1963, Herzog had a run of success as manager of the Rangers (1973), Royals (1975–79) and Cardinals (1980–90). His Kansas City clubs won the AL West in 1976, 1977 and 1978. In St. Louis, Herzog won the World Series in 1982 and reached the Fall Classic again in 1985 and 1987. He also ran the front office during most of his term with the Cards. Herzog's official title with the Angels was senior vice president/director of player personnel. He failed to revive the franchise, however, in part because he refused to move to California and ran the club from his suburban Kansas City home with a telephone, a satellite dish, a fax machine, and file cabinets. Herzog was replaced by Bill Bavasi in 1994.*

SEPTEMBER 7	The Angels defeat the Brewers 1–0 at Anaheim Stadium. Dave Winfield drove in the lone run with a single in the first inning. Chuck Finley (7 2/3 innings), Mark Eichhorn (one-third of an inning) and Bryan Harvey (one inning) combined on the shutout.
SEPTEMBER 8	The Angels beat the Brewers 1–0 for the second day in a row. The victory completed a three-game sweep of Milwaukee in which the Angels scored only four runs. The lone run scored in the sixth inning on a double by Gary Gaetti. Jim Abbott (six innings), Mark Eichhorn (two innings) and Bryan Harvey (one inning) combined on the shutout.

SEPTEMBER 10	In his major league debut, starting pitcher Kyle Abbott strikes out the side in the first inning and allows two runs in six innings of work, but the Angels lose 6–2 to the Rangers at Anaheim Stadium.
SEPTEMBER 14	At Anaheim Stadium, the Angels beat the White Sox 3–2 with three straight singles in the tenth inning, the last two on bunts. Gary Gaetti led off the tenth with a pop fly single which fell safely in center field. Shawn Abner followed by beating out a bunt. Luis Sojo beat out another bunt, and Gaetti scored on a bad throw to first base by pitcher Bobby Thigpen.
SEPTEMBER 23	The Angels score seven runs in the first inning for a 7–0 lead, then hang on to defeat the Blue Jays 10–9 at Anaheim Stadium.

> *Luis Sojo's season ended two weeks early because of a bizarre injury. Marines at Camp Pendleton had given Wally Joyner a knife as a gift. As a gag, Lance Parrish took the knife and jabbed Sojo in the rear end. Startled, Sojo jumped away and suffered a gash on his thumb and another on his pinkie, which required a total of ten stitches.*

SEPTEMBER 24	Jim Abbott strikes out 13 batters in ten innings, but loses 3–0 to the Blue Jays at Anaheim Stadium. Abbott shut out Toronto on two hits through nine innings, but gave up a three-run homer to Pat Borders in the tenth.
OCTOBER 6	On the last day of the season, Bryan Harvey strikes out four of the five batters to face him in the eighth inning to close out a 3–1 win over the Royals at Anaheim Stadium. Gary Gaetti drove in all three California runs with a homer in the fifth inning.

> *The win gave the Angels an 81–81 record on the season. Despite finishing at .500, the Angels finished in seventh place in a seven-team division. Ten of the 14 AL teams had winning records in 1991.*

DECEMBER 8	The Angels trade Kyle Abbott and Ruben Amaro to the Phillies for Von Hayes.
DECEMBER 9	Wally Joyner signs a contract as a free agent with the Royals.

> *The Angels believed that Lee Stevens was ready to take over at first base and failed to sign Joyner despite a season in 1991 in which he hit .301 with 21 homers and 96 RBIs. One of the most popular players ever to don an Angels uniform, Joyner was only 29 when he signed with the Royals and had eight seasons ahead of him as an above-average starting first baseman. Meanwhile, Stevens failed to live up to his potential.*

DECEMBER 10	The Angels trade Dave Gallagher to the Mets for Hubie Brooks.
DECEMBER 19	Dave Winfield signs a contract as a free agent with the Blue Jays.

> *At 40, Winfield had one great season left in him. He was fifth in the MVP voting in 1992 and helped Toronto win the World Series.*

DECEMBER 28	Kirk McCaskill signs a contract as a free agent with the White Sox.

1992

Season in a Sentence
Buck Rodgers misses three months because of injuries suffered in a bus crash in May; the club loses 11 games in a row in June and July and scores fewer runs than any team in the AL.

Finish • Won • Lost • Pct • GB
Fifth (tie)   72   90   .444   24.0

Managers
Buck Rodgers (19–20), John Wathan (39–50) and Rodgers again (14–20)

Stats

Stats	Angels	AL	Rank
Batting Avg:	.243	.259	14
On-Base Pct:	.298	.328	14
Slugging Pct:	.338	.385	14
Home Runs:	88		11
Stolen Bases:	160		2
ERA:	3.84	3.94	8
Errors:	134		11
Runs Scored:	579		14
Runs Allowed:	671		6

Starting Lineup
Mike Fitzgerald, c
Lee Stevens, 1b
Luis Sojo, 2b
Gary Gaetti, 3b-1b
Gary DiSarcina, ss
Luis Polonia, lf-dh
Junior Felix, cf
Chad Curtis, rf-lf-cf
Hubie Brooks, dh
Rene Gonzalez, 3b-2b
Von Hayes, rf

Pitchers
Mark Langston, sp
Jim Abbott, sp
Chuck Finley, sp
Julio Valera, sp
Bert Blyleven, sp
Joe Grahe, rp
Chuck Crim, rp
Steve Frey, rp
Mark Eichhorn, rp

Attendance
2,065,444 (eighth in AL)

Club Leaders

Batting Avg:	Luis Polonia	.286
On-Base Pct:	Chad Curtis	.341
Slugging Pct:	Chad Curtis	.372
Home Runs:	Gary Gaetti	12
RBI:	Junior Felix	72
Runs:	Luis Polonia	83
Stolen Bases:	Luis Polonia	51
Wins:	Mark Langston	13
Strikeouts:	Mark Langston	174
ERA:	Jim Abbott	2.74
Saves:	Joe Grahe	21

January 3 The Angels sign Don Robinson, most recently with the Giants, as a free agent.

February 2 The Angels sign Ken Oberkfell, most recently with the Astros, as a free agent.

February 14 The Angels sign Alvin Davis, most recently with the Mariners, as a free agent.

March 16 Angels pitcher Matt Keough is rushed to the hospital after being struck in the right temple by a foul ball off the bat of John Patterson of the Giants while sitting in the dugout during an exhibition game in Scottsdale, Arizona. Keough hadn't pitched in the majors since 1986. He played four seasons in Japan from 1987 through 1990. Following the accident, he never played in the big leagues again.

April 7 The Angels lose 10–4 to the White Sox before an Opening Day crowd of 32,160 at Anaheim Stadium. In his first plate appearance with the Angels, Von Hayes hit a two-run homer. Starting at second base, Bobby Rose also homered. Mark Langston was the starting pitcher and allowed seven runs in three innings.

The Angels lost their first four games in 1992, then nosed four games above .500 on May 9 at 17–13. A severe slide ruined the season, however, and by July 9, the club had a record of 32–52.

APRIL 12 — The Angels outslug the Brewers 13–9 at Anaheim Stadium. Playing third base, Rene Gonzalez hit a three-run homer and a double in his first game in an Angels uniform.

On the same day, the Angels traded Dick Schofield and Julian Vasquez to the Mets for Julio Valera.

APRIL 13 — In relief of Jim Abbott, Bryan Harvey strikes out four of the five batters to face him in the eighth and ninth innings to close out a 3–0 win over the Rangers in Arlington.

APRIL 16 — The Angels score three runs in the ninth inning to defeat the Rangers 3–2 in Arlington. Chad Curtis started the rally with a double. Gary Gaetti drove in the winning run with a sacrifice fly.

Only five-foot-nine, Curtis was 45th-round draft choice in 1989 out of Grand Canyon University, where he was a teammate of Tim Salmon. A rookie outfielder in 1992, Curtis won his way into the hearts of Angels fans with his unbridled hustle and was a three-year starter for the club before a trade to the Tigers. Later, he starred in the 1999 World Series for the Yankees against the Braves with two homers in game three, including a walk-off blast in the tenth inning.

APRIL 21 — Bryan Harvey strikes out all three batters he faces in the ninth inning to close out a 3–2 win over the Athletics in Oakland.

APRIL 23 — Angels batting coach Deron Johnson dies of lung cancer at the age of 53. Johnson had been a coach with the club since 1989.

APRIL 26 — Trailing 5–1, the Angels erupt for six runs in the eighth inning to defeat the Mariners 7–5 at Anaheim Stadium. During the rally, seven Angels batters reached base on singles by Von Hayes, Hubie Brooks and Alvin Davis, a triple from Gary Gaetti, Lance Parrish's single, a walk to Rene Gonzalez, and a single by pinch hitter John Morris. The hit by Morris drove in the go-ahead run and sparked a bench-clearing brawl. Chad Curtis, running for Parrish, twisted around catcher Dave Valle to avoid the tag and landed on the plate. Though umpire Rocky Roe signaled Curtis safe, Valle tagged him hard triggering the brawl. Valle and Curtis were ejected.

APRIL 29 — Jim Abbott issues a bases-loaded walk to Pat Tabler with two out in the ninth inning to lose 1–0 to the Blue Jays in Toronto.

APRIL 30 — Junior Felix collects four hits in four at-bats and drives in six runs to lead the Angels to an 8–5 win over the Indians in Cleveland. Felix hit a three-run homer in the third inning and added singles in the fifth, seventh and ninth.

The game was played while riots swept through South Central Los Angeles after a jury acquitted four white police officers on all but one count, following a 1991 videotaped beating of African-American motorist Rodney King. The death toll in the violence was put at 52.

May 9	Chad Curtis hits his first major league homer in the first inning and adds an RBI-double in the sixth for the only two Angels runs in a 2–1 win over the Blue Jays at Anaheim Stadium.
May 19	In the game as a pinch hitter, Bobby Rose homers in what proves to be his last big-league at-bat during a ten-inning, 5–4 loss to the Yankees in New York. Two days later, Rose was placed on the disabled list after spraining his ankle in a bus crash (see May 21, 1992), and when he came off of it, he was sent to the minors. Rose finished his four-year career with five home runs in 200 at-bats over 73 games.
May 21	The Angels are involved in an horrific bus crash in New Jersey following a 12-inning, 3–2 loss to the Yankees at Yankee Stadium.

> *At 1:47 a.m., en route from New York to Baltimore, the Angels' team bus went out of control, crashed through a guardrail, skidded about 400 feet into a grove of trees and overturned on its side. The accident happened on the New Jersey Turnpike near Deptford Township, about 20 miles from Philadelphia. Manager Buck Rodgers, sitting in the front seat, suffered elbow, knee and rib injuries and was sidelined for three months. First baseman Alvin Davis had a bruised kidney. Ten others, including coach Rod Carew, were injured. The team traveled in two buses, and most of the players were in the other bus. Those in the second bus helped rescue the injured. Police speculated that the driver fell asleep at the wheel. Coach John Wathan served as interim manager in Rodgers' absence. The Angels were 39–50 under Wathan.*

May 22	The Angels play at Camden Yards in Baltimore for the first time and lose 5–3 to the Orioles.
May 30	Bert Blyleven wins his first game since July 20, 1990 with seven shutout innings in a 3–1 decision over the Indians at Anaheim Stadium. Blyleven missed 21 months because of rotator cuff surgery.
June 1	With their first pick in the amateur draft, the Angels select pitcher Pete Janicki from UCLA.

> *Janicki never reached the majors. It set the stage for a very weak draft. Future big leaguers chosen and signed by the Angels in 1992 were Jeff Schmidt (supplemental first round), Bill Simas (sixth round), Travis Driskill (11th round), John Snyder (13th round), Aaron Guiel (21st round) and Anthony Chavez (50th round).*

June 10	Luis Polonia steals four bases in extra innings, but the Angels lose 3–2 in 12 innings to the White Sox in Chicago. Polonia stole second and third in the tenth and repeated the feat in the 12th. An unusual situation occurred late in the game when Mark Langston ended up as the Angels' designated hitter. With the club trailing 1–0, Langston pinch-ran for DH Hubie Brooks and scored on a two-run single by Rene Gonzalez, which put the Angels into a 2–1 lead. After the Sox tied the contest 2–2 with a tally in the bottom half, John Wathan had no positions players to replace Brooks and had little choice but to leave Langston in the game. He batted in the tenth and 12th innings and struck out twice.

June 16	The Angels retire Nolan Ryan's number, 30, in ceremonies prior to a 4–1 win over the Rangers at Anaheim Stadium. The game drew a crowd of 51,401 on a Tuesday night.
June 17	Mark Langston pitches a two-hitter to beat the Rangers 3–0 at Anaheim Stadium. The only Texas hits were singles by Al Newman in the third inning and John Cangelosi in the sixth. One night after being honored by the Angels, Nolan Ryan pitched a complete game for the Rangers.
June 20	The Angels bury the Athletics 10–0 at Anaheim Stadium.
June 26	Chad Curtis hits two homers and drives in five runs during a 10–1 victory over the Mariners in Seattle.
June 27	Chad Curtis drives in the only two Angels runs of a 2–1 victory over the Mariners with a double in the second inning.
July 8	The Angels lose their 11th game in a row by dropping a 5–4 decision to the Tigers in Detroit.
July 9	The Angels break their 11-game losing streak by defeating the Tigers 6–1 in Detroit.

During the 11-game losing streak, the Angels scored only 22 runs.

July 10	The Angels beat the Tigers 2–1 in Detroit on back-to-back homers by John Morris and Ron Tingley off Bill Gullickson in the fifth inning.

The home run by Morris was his only one in 57 at-bats as a member of the Angels and the last of eight he struck in seven big-league seasons.

July 25	In only his second major league game, Tim Fortugno pitches a three-hit shutout and strikes out 12 batters to defeat the Tigers 3–0 at Anaheim Stadium.

Fortugno was 30 years old when he reached the majors after bouncing around the minors with four different organizations. After the July 25 shutout, he never won another game for the Angels. Fortugno's next big-league win was in 1994 as a member of the Reds. He finished his three-year career with a 3–4 record and a 5.06 ERA.

July 30	Trailing 5–1, the Angels explode for five runs in the eighth inning to defeat the Mariners 6–5 at Anaheim Stadium. Junior Felix drove in the first two runs with a bases-loaded single, and Gary Gaetti put California into the lead with a three-run homer.
August 11	Making a rare start in left field, Rob Ducey draws a bases-loaded walk from Mike Fetters in the tenth inning to give the Angels a 1–0 win over the Brewers at Anaheim Stadium. Chuck Finley (nine innings) and Joe Grahe (one inning) combined on the shutout.

Grahe started the season in the Angels starting rotation and was sent to the minors in May with a 2–3 record and a 5.90 ERA. He was recalled in June after

Bryan Harvey hurt his elbow and became the Angels' closer. As a reliever in 1992, Grahe had 21 saves and a 1.80 earned run average in 55 innings.

AUGUST 12   Mark Langston (eight innings) and Joe Grahe (one inning) combine on a two-hitter to defeat the Brewers 2–1 at Anaheim Stadium. The only Milwaukee hits were a double by Pat Listach and a single from Dante Bichette, both in the fourth inning.

AUGUST 19   A two-run single by Gary DiSarcina on a two-strike pitch with two out in the ninth inning downs the Red Sox 3–2 in Boston.

A native of the Boston suburb of Malden, Massachusetts, DiSarcina changed his uniform number from 11 to 33 during the 1992 season to honor Celtics star Larry Bird.

AUGUST 20   In the second inning, Lee Stevens doubles in a run and scores on a single by Gary DiSarcina for the only two runs of a 2–0 triumph over the Red Sox in Boston. Bert Blyleven (6 1/3 innings), Scott Bailes (one-third of an inning), Chuck Crim (1 1/3 innings) and Joe Grahe (one inning) combined on the shutout.

AUGUST 23   Luis Sojo breaks a 3–3 tie with a two-run homer in the tenth inning, and the Angels defeat the Yankees 7–3 in New York.

AUGUST 28   After missing more than three months recuperating from injuries suffered in the May 21 bus crash, Buck Rodgers returns to the team, but the Angels lose 7–1 to the Red Sox at Anaheim Stadium.

SEPTEMBER 1   Gary Gaetti collects four hits, two of them home runs, in five at-bats to lead the Angels to a 7–6 victory over the Indians at Anaheim Stadium.

SEPTEMBER 2   Tim Salmon hits a walk-off homer in the 15th inning to defeat the Indians 3–2 at Anaheim Stadium. Chuck Finley (ten innings) and Scott Lewis (five innings) pitched for the Angels.

A native of Long Beach, Salmon made his major league debut on August 21, 1992 and remained with the Angels until his career ended at the close of the 2007 season. Due to his late call-up in 1992, Salmon was eligible for the Rookie of the Year Award in 1993 and captured the honor by batting .283 with 31 homers and 95 RBIs. On the all-time career leader lists in franchise history, Salmon ranks first in home runs (299), first in walks (970), second in games played (1,672), second in at-bats (5,934), second in runs (986), second in hits (1,674), second in total bases (2,958), second in doubles (339), second in RBIs (1,016), second in on-base percentage (.385) and third in slugging percentage (.498). Despite his impressive accomplishments, Salmon was never named to an All-Star team.

SEPTEMBER 4   Lee Stevens hits a grand slam off Rick Sutcliffe in the fourth inning, but the Angels lose 8–7 to the Orioles at Anaheim Stadium.

SEPTEMBER 16   A single by Luis Sojo in the 13th inning provides the winning run in a 2–1 decision over the Mariners at the Kingdome. The story in the early part of the game was the tremendous duel between Randy Johnson and Mark Langston. Johnson pitched the first nine innings for Seattle and allowed only one hit while striking out 15. The first California run scored in the fourth inning on a single by Hubie Brooks and an error by second baseman Bret Boone. Langston fanned 12 batters in ten innings.

SEPTEMBER 26 — The Angels edge the White Sox 1–0 in Chicago. The lone run scored on a single by Chad Curtis in the third inning. Chuck Finley (seven innings), Scott Lewis (1 1/3 innings) and Steve Frey (two-thirds of an inning) combined on the shutout.

SEPTEMBER 30 — George Brett collects his 3,000th career hit with a single off Tim Fortugno in the seventh inning of a 4–0 Angels loss to the Royals at Anaheim Stadium. It was Brett's fourth single of the game.

OCTOBER 2 — Mark Langston strikes out 13 batters during a 6–3 win over the Rangers at Anaheim Stadium.

The Angels' offense in 1992 finished last in the AL in batting average (.243), on-base percentage (.298), slugging percentage (.338) and runs (579). The clean-up hitters, primarily Hubie Brooks (68 games), Gary Gaetti (39 games) and Von Hayes (23 games) were particularly abysmal, combining for a .200 batting average, .237 on-base percentage and .308 slugging percentage. In all, the Angels used 138 different batting orders in 162 games.

NOVEMBER 17 — Two weeks after Bill Clinton defeats George Bush in the Presidential election, the Angels lose Bryan Harvey and Junior Felix to the Marlins and Brett Merriman to the Rockies in the expansion draft.

The Angels exposed Harvey after he missed most of the 1992 season with elbow trouble. He had one good season left in the tank and was the Marlins' first All-Star when he saved 45 games with a 1.70 ERA in 59 games and 69 innings in 1993. After that season, Harvey's elbow miseries returned, and he was out of baseball by 1995.

DECEMBER 6 — The Angels trade Jim Abbott to the Yankees for J. T. Snow, Jerry Nielsen and Russ Springer.

The charismatic Abbott was a fan favorite and the trade angered the Angels followers, especially since it was put together to acquire a first baseman, a position held by Wally Joyner, another enormously popular player, from 1986 through 1991. Joyner left Anaheim for Kansas City as a free agent at the end of the 1991 season. Abbott struggled over most of the remainder of his career, which ended in 1999. He played for the Angels again in 1995 and 1996. The son of former Los Angels Rams receiver Jack Snow, J. T. played four seasons with the Angels as a first baseman. He started fast in 1993 with six homers and a .407 batting average through his first 15 games, but suffered through a horrendous skid in which he collected 13 hits in 135 at-bats and was sent to the minors in late July when his average dipped to .223. Snow won the first two of his six Gold Gloves as an Angel, but never fully developed as a hitter.

DECEMBER 8 — The Angels trade Luis Sojo to the Blue Jays for Kelly Gruber.

DECEMBER 11   The Angels sign Chili Davis, most recently with the Twins, as a free agent.

> *Davis previously played for the Angels from 1988 through 1990. His second term lasted from 1993 through 1996, during which he was the club's number one designated hitter.*

 ## Spring Training in Sunny California

The Angels spent at least part of spring training in Palm Springs, California, from 1961 through 1992. The club was the last in the major leagues to train in California. With the move by the Angels to Tempe, Arizona, in 1993, every big-league club held spring training in either Arizona or Florida. The first team to train in California was the Chicago Cubs in Los Angeles in 1903. During much of the 1930s, 1940s and early 1950s, spring training in California was commonplace, with up to four teams in the state, mostly in Los Angeles and Orange and San Bernadino Counties. Teams moved out of California when Pacific Coast League franchises entered into an agreement in which they would not rent out their ballparks to major league clubs. No team used the state for spring training purposes from 1954 through 1960. The following is a list of teams that trained in California. In some cases, teams trained in two different cities in the same year.

Location	Team	Year(s)
Anaheim	Philadelphia Athletics	1940–42
Anaheim	St. Louis Browns	1946
Burbank	St. Louis Browns	1949–52
Catalina Island	Chicago Cubs	1921–42; 1946–51
El Centro	Chicago White Sox	1952–53
Hollywood	Pittsburgh Pirates	1948
Holtville	Angels	1966–79
Los Angeles	Chicago Cubs	1903–04
Los Angeles	New York Giants	1907; 1932–33
Los Angeles	Chicago White Sox	1908
Palm Springs	Chicago White Sox	1951
Palm Springs	Angels	1961–92
Palo Alto	Detroit Tigers	1932
Pasadena	Chicago Cubs	1917–20
Pasadena	Chicago White Sox	1933–42; 1946–52
Paso Robles	Chicago White Sox	1913–15
Paso Robles	Pittsburgh Pirates	1924–34
Redondo Beach	Boston Red Sox	1911
Sacramento	Detroit Tigers	1931
San Bernadino	Pittsburgh	1935; 1937–42; 1946; 1949–52
San Bernadino	St. Louis Browns	1948; 1953
San Francisco	Chicago White Sox	1909–10
Santa Monica	Chicago Cubs	1905
Stockton	St. Louis Cardinals	1925

1993

Season in a Sentence
Embarking on a youth movement, the Angels win 13 of their first 18 games, but wind up with 91 defeats, one more than the previous season.

Finish • Won • Lost • Pct • GB
Fifth (tie)   71   91   .438   23.0

Manager
Buck Rodgers

Stats

Stats	Angels	AL	Rank
Batting Avg:	.260	.267	11
On-Base Pct:	.330	.337	8
Slugging Pct:	.380	.408	13
Home Runs:	114		13
Stolen Bases:	169		2
ERA:	4.34	4.32	8
Errors:	120		9
Runs Scored:	684		13
Runs Allowed:	770		9

Starting Lineup
Greg Myers, c
J. T. Snow, 1b
Torey Lovullo, 2b
Rene Gonzalez, 3b
Gary DiSarcina, ss
Luis Polonia, lf
Chad Curtis, cf
Tim Salmon, rf
Chili Davis, dh
Stan Javier, cf-lf
Damion Easley, 2b

Pitchers
Mark Langston, sp
Chuck Finley, sp
Scott Sanderson, sp
John Farrell, sp
Phil Leftwich, sp
Steve Frey, rp
Gene Nelson, rp
Ken Patterson, rp
Joe Grahe, rp

Attendance
2,057,460 (eighth in AL)

Club Leaders

Batting Avg:	Chad Curtis	.285
On-Base Pct:	Tim Salmon	.382
Slugging Pct:	Tim Salmon	.536
Home Runs:	Tim Salmon	31
RBI:	Chili Davis	112
Runs:	Chad Curtis	94
Stolen Bases:	Luis Polinia	55
Wins:	Chuck Finley	16
	Mark Langston	16
Strikeouts:	Mark Langston	196
ERA:	Chuck Finley	3.15
Saves:	Steve Frey	13

JANUARY 15   The Angels trade Lee Stevens to the Expos for Keith Morrison. On the same day, the Angels signed Stan Javier, most recently with the Phillies, as a free agent.

JANUARY 27   Hubie Brooks signs a contract as a free agent with the Royals.

FEBRUARY 11   The Angels sign Scott Sanderson, most recently with the Yankees, as a free agent.

Sanderson was 7–2 on May 27, then lost nine in a row before being sold to the Giants on August 3.

FEBRUARY 23   The Angels open their new spring training headquarters in Tempe, Arizona. The club had trained in Palm Springs, California, since 1961, and at both Palm Springs and Mesa, Arizona, from 1984 through 1992.

APRIL 6   Six weeks after a terrorist bomb explodes in the parking garage of the World Trade Center, killing six people, Mark Langston pitches a three-hitter to defeat the Brewers 3–1 before an Opening Day crowd of 33,635 at Anaheim Stadium. Langston also picked three runners off base. J. T. Snow hit a solo homer in the fourth inning, and Gary DiSarcina added a two-run shot in the fifth. It was Snow's first game with the Angels and his first big-league home run.

> Langston was 16–11 with a 3.20 ERA and 196 strikeouts in 256 1/3 innings in 1993. Chuck Finley had a 16–14 mark and 187 strikeouts in 251 2/3 innings along with an earned run average of 3.15. The remaining starters were wretched, combining for 25 wins, 46 defeats and an ERA of 5.42. In all, the club used 24 pitchers during the season, 12 of them in starting roles.

APRIL 12

The Angels score six runs in the ninth inning to cap a 12–5 rout of the Brewers in Milwaukee.

APRIL 14

The Angels score five runs in the eighth inning and six in the ninth to cap a 12–2 rout of the Brewers in Milwaukee.

> *The Angels featured new uniforms in 1993, replacing those which had gone virtually unchanged since 1971 (see April 6, 1971). The 1993 jerseys harkened back to the original 1961 design (see April 15, 1961), with "Angels" written in red and outlined in blue on both the home and road shirts. On the left shoulder was a "C" and "A" intertwined. The navy blue caps also had an interlocking "C" and "A" in red and outlined in white with a red bill. In addition, the pullover shirts were replaced with the more traditional button-down look.*

APRIL 17

Chad Curtis steals four bases during a 7–5 win over the Orioles in Baltimore. Curtis swiped second and third in the third inning following a single and repeated the feat in the ninth after a walk.

> *The Orioles ended up with three men on third base in the eighth inning. With the bases loaded and one out, Mike Devereaux hit a fly ball to Chad Curtis in center field. Curtis threw to the plate. Jeff Tackett, the runner on third returned to the base after running halfway home. Brady Anderson, who was on second, advanced to third. Chito Martinez, the base runner on first, rounded second and headed for third. Angel catcher John Orton walked to third where he tagged all three runners. Tackett was called out on a force, and Martinez was called out completing the inning-ending double play.*

APRIL 22

Three days after the raid on the Branch Davidian complex in Waco, Texas, Chuck Finley pitches a two-hitter to defeat the Indians 8–0 at Anaheim Stadium. The only Cleveland hits were singles by Alvaro Espinosa and Kenny Lofton in the third inning.

> *Former major league outfielder Billy Sample was a member of the Angels broadcasting team in 1993 and 1994.*

APRIL 25

Solo homers by Torey Lovullo in the fifth inning and Tim Salmon in the seventh, both off Roger Clemens, beats the Red Sox 2–1 at Anaheim Stadium. The home run by Lovullo was his first as a member of the Angels.

APRIL 28

A walk-off homer by Tim Salmon leading off the ninth inning beats the Yankees 3–2 at Anaheim Stadium.

> *The victory gave the Angels a 13–5 record and a 2 1/2-game lead in the AL West. The club was 43–43 and two games out of first on July 11 before sliding quickly out of the pennant race.*

MAY 19	Chad Curtis hits a two-run single in the eighth inning to account for the only runs of a 2–0 win over the White Sox in Chicago. Mark Langston (7 1/3 innings) and Joe Grahe (1 2/3 innings) combined on the shutout.
MAY 24	Luis Polonia ties a major league record when he is caught stealing three times in three attempts during a 14-inning, 4–3 loss to the Mariners in Seattle. Polonia was out trying to swipe second in the first, third and 12th innings. He was thrown out twice on pitchouts. The Mariners won despite leaving 19 men on base, 13 of them between the eighth and 12th innings. During the eighth and ninth, the two clubs combined to make 22 lineup changes.
	Polonia finished the season with 55 stolen bases in 79 attempts.
MAY 30	The Angels score seven runs in the second inning for a 7–0 lead and hang on for a 7–5 triumph over the Orioles at Anaheim Stadium. Tim Salmon capped the rally with a three-run homer.
JUNE 3	With the third overall pick in the amateur draft, the Angels select pitcher Brian Anderson from Wright State University.
	Anderson signed a contract with the Angels on July 30, and after four appearances in the minors, made his major league debut on September 10. In three seasons with the club, he was 13–13 with a 5.45 ERA in 212 2/3 innings before being traded to the Indians. Anderson had a 13-year career in the majors with four clubs and finished with a record of 82–83. He pitched in the World Series with the Indians in 1997 and the Diamondbacks in 2001. Other future major leaguers drafted and signed by the Angels in 1993 were Ryan Hancock (second round), Matt Perisho (third round), Andrew Lorraine (fourth round), George Arias (seventh round), Jamie Burke (ninth round), Todd Greene (12th round), Keith Luuloa (33rd round).
JUNE 17	The Angels lose 18–2 to the Rangers at Anaheim Stadium. Juan Gonzalez drove in eight runs. Chili Davis pitched the eighth and ninth innings and faced seven batters. He retired six of them and hit another with a pitch. Larry Gonzalez (no relation to Juan) entered the game as a catcher for the Angels in the fifth inning and singled in his first big-league plate appearance. He finished the day one-for-two, and never played in another major league game, to complete his "career" with a .500 batting average.
JUNE 18	Chili Davis hits a two-run, walk-off homer in the ninth inning to defeat the White Sox 9–8 at Anaheim Stadium.
	Davis batted only .243 in 1993, but managed to hit 27 homers and drive in 112 runs.
JUNE 26	Chili Davis hits a grand slam off Willie Banks in the sixth inning to account for all of the runs in a 4–0 victory over the Twins in Minneapolis. Chuck Finley pitched a three-hit shutout.
JULY 7	The Angels score three runs in the ninth inning to defeat the Red Sox 7–6 at Anaheim Stadium. Gary DiSarcina and Greg Myers started the rally with back-to-back doubles. Tim Salmon drove in the winning run with a single.

July 8	For the second day in a row, the Angels score three runs in the ninth inning, this time to down the Yankees 4–3 at Anaheim Stadium. Damion Easley drove in the winning run with a single.
July 11	The Angels outlast the Yankees 4–3 in 14 innings at Anaheim Stadium. Torey Lovullo drove in the winning run with a single. Chuck Finley (nine innings), Gene Nelson (three innings), Steve Frey (one innings) and Doug Linton (one inning) pitched for California.
July 13	At Camden Yards in Baltimore, Mark Langston is the American League starter in the All-Star Game and gives up two runs in the first inning before shutting out the Nationals in the second. The AL won 9–3.
July 15	Back-to-back homers by Chad Curtis and Tim Salmon off Mark Clark in the sixth inning provide the only two Angels runs in a 2–1 victory over the Indians in Cleveland.
July 18	The Angels play at Municipal Stadium in Cleveland for the last time and lose 2–1 to the Indians.
July 25	The Angels score eight runs in the second inning for an 8–0 lead, but wind up losing 9–8 to the Yankees in New York. The Yanks scored twice in the ninth for the win. It was the Angels' ninth loss in a row.
July 26	The Angels extend their losing streak to ten games with an 11–4 defeat at the hands of the Athletics at Anaheim Stadium.
July 27	The Angels end their ten-game losing streak with a 15–8 win over the Athletics at Anaheim Stadium. Playing in his first big-league game, Eduardo Perez hit a homer and a double, drove in three runs and scored three.
July 31	In just his fifth major league game, Eduardo Perez hits a two-run, walk-off homer in the ninth inning to defeat the Twins 4–3 at Anaheim Stadium.
August 3	The Angels sell Scott Sanderson to the Giants.
August 12	The Angels play at Arlington Stadium for the last time and lose 4–2 to the Rangers.
August 15	The Angels collect 22 hits and wallop the Mariners 14–2 in Seattle. Heading into the contest, the Angels had scored a total of 14 in their previous six games.
August 18	Leading 6–2, the Angels allow six runs in the ninth inning and lose 8–6 to the Tigers at Anaheim Stadium.

> *Tim Salmon homered in four straight games from August 16 through August 19. During the three-game series against the Tigers in Detroit, all Angels losses, Salmon hit one homer on the 16th, one on the 17th and two on the 18th. He added another on the 19th in a 12-inning, 5–4 victory over the Brewers at Anaheim Stadium.*

August 21	Chili Davis hits a walk-off homer in the tenth inning to defeat the Brewers 7–6 at Anaheim Stadium.

AUGUST 24	Chuck Finley pitches a two-hitter, but loses 1–0 to the Orioles in Baltimore. In the first inning, Finley walked two and allowed a two-out single to Cal Ripken to account for the lone run.
AUGUST 25	Mark Langston (eight innings) and Mike Butcher (one inning) combine on a two-hitter for a 2–1 win over the Orioles in Baltimore. Langston had a no-hitter in progress until Cal Ripken singled in the seventh. Chris Hoiles added a single with two out in the ninth.
SEPTEMBER 14	Major League Baseball announces its three-division alignment and extra round of playoffs to be put into effect for the 1994 season. The Angels were placed in the Western Division with the Athletics, Rangers and Mariners.
SEPTEMBER 15	The Angels trounce the Mariners 15–1 at Anaheim Stadium. Chili Davis drove in six runs with a pair of three-run homers in the first and eighth innings. Tim Salmon hit a grand slam in the fourth off Tim Leary.
DECEMBER 7	Stan Javier signs a contract as a free agent with the Athletics.
DECEMBER 20	Luis Polonia signs a contract with the Angels as a free agent.

1994

Season in a Sentence
The Angels are 21 games below .500 and suffering through their third straight losing season, but only 5½ games out of first in a weak division, when the players go on strike in August.

Finish • Won • Lost • Pct • GB
Fourth   47   68   .409   5.5

Managers
Buck Rodgers (16–23),
Bobby Knoop (1–1) and
Marcel Lachemann (30–44)

Stats

Stats	Angels	AL	Rank
Batting Avg:	.264	.273	11
On-Base Pct:	.332	.345	12
Slugging Pct:	.409	.434	12
Home Runs:	120		8
Stolen Bases:	65		10
ERA:	5.42	4.80	12
Errors:	76		3
Runs Scored:	543		14
Runs Allowed:	660		11

Starting Lineup
Chris Turner, c
J. T. Snow, 1b
Harold Reynolds, 2b
Damion Easley, 3b-2b
Gary DiSarcina, ss
Jim Edmonds, lf
Chad Curtis, cf
Tim Salmon, rf
Chili Davis, dh
Spike Owen, 3b
Bo Jackson, lf

Pitchers
Chuck Finley, sp
Mark Langston, sp
Phil Leftwich, sp
Brian Anderson, sp
Joe Magrane, sp-rp
Joe Grahe, rp
Bob Patterson, rp
Mike Butcher, rp
Mark Leiter, rp
Craig Lefferts, rp
John Dopson, rp

Attendance
1,512,662 (ninth in AL)

Club Leaders

Batting Avg:	Chili Davis	.311
On-Base Pct:	Chili Davis	.410
Slugging Pct:	Chili Davis	.561
Home Runs:	Chili Davis	26
RBI:	Chili Davis	84
Runs:	Chili Davis	72
Stolen Bases:	Chad Curtis	25
Wins:	Chuck Finley	10
Strikeouts:	Chuck Finley	148
ERA:	Chuck Finley	4.32

JANUARY 12   Whitey Herzog resigns as general manager of the Angels and is replaced by 36-year-old Bill Bavasi.

> *Bavasi was the son of Buzzie Bavasi, who was general manager of the Angels from 1977 through 1984. The younger Bavasi was hired as assistant general manager in September 1993. Before that, he was the team's director of minor league operations. Bavasi remained as general manager of the Angels through the end of the 1999 season.*

JANUARY 13   The Angels sign Craig Lefferts, most recently with the Rangers, as a free agent.

JANUARY 17   An earthquake centered in the San Fernando Valley suburb of Northridge, 20 miles northwest of downtown Los Angeles rocks Southern California at 4:30 a.m.. The quake resulted in the deaths of 72 people and injured more than 9,000.

> *Anaheim Stadium was about 50 miles from Northridge, but suffered significant damage. The scoreboard, located on the roof above left field, collapsed into*

hundreds of seats. Fortunately, the stadium was empty due to the time the earthquake occurred. Repairs were completed in time for the start of the 1994 baseball season, and the monitor was reinstalled on the back of the upper deck stands.

January 31 — The Angels sign Bo Jackson, most recently with the White Sox, as a free agent.

Jackson was one of the most celebrated athletes in America as a two-sport star during the 1980s. His name became known even among those who didn't follow sports with his "Bo Knows" television commercials for Nike. A star running back at the University of Auburn, he won the Heisman Trophy in 1985. He excelled as an outfielder with the Kansas City Royals from 1986 through 1990, and as a running back with the Los Angeles Raiders from 1987 through 1990. But an injury in a January 1991 playoff game against the Bengals led to hip replacement surgery and ended his football career. Jackson played 23 games for the White Sox in 1991, and after sitting out the 1992 season, appeared in 85 contests in 1993 while playing with an artificial hip and hit .232 with 16 homers. With the Angels in 1994, his last big-league season, Jackson played in 75 games, batted .279 and homered 13 times.

March 21 — The Angels sign Mark Leiter, most recently with the Tigers, as a free agent.

March 29 — The Angels trade Hilly Hathaway to the Padres for Harold Reynolds.

April 5 — The Angels open the season with an 8–2 win over the Twins in Minneapolis. Mark Langston was the starting and winning pitcher. Damion Easley collected three hits, including a double, and scored three runs. Chili Davis drove in three.

April 9 — Pitching five days after the death of his nine-month-old son, Ryan, from spinal muscular dystrophy, Mark Leiter allows two runs in six innings of a 6–4 win over the Brewers in Milwaukee.

April 11 — In the home opener, the Angels score five runs in the ninth inning but lose 9–6 to the Indians before 37,285 at Anaheim Stadium. Chili Davis homered.

April 13 — Bo Jackson hits a three-run homer with one out in the ninth to tie the score 5–5, but the Angels end up losing 6–5 in ten innings to the Indians at Anaheim Stadium.

April 15 — The Angels score seven runs in the ninth inning and one in the tenth to stun the Blue Jays 14–13 at Anaheim Stadium and give the club one of the most improbable victories in franchise history. The Angels led 6–3 before Toronto plated five runs in the eighth inning and five in the ninth for a 13–6 advantage. Jim Edmonds drove in the first run in the ninth with a one-out, bases-loaded single. Tim Salmon followed with a walk to force in the second tally. Singles by Chili Davis and Damion Easley and a sacrifice fly from Eduardo Perez brought home three more, but the Angels still trailed 13–11 with two out. Bo Jackson then walked to reload the bases, and Harold Reynolds hit a ground rule double to tie the score 13–13. In the tenth, the first two batters were retired before Salmon singled, Davis walked and Easley delivered a walk-off single for the 14–13 triumph.

Edmonds was a rookie in 1994, the first of six seasons in which he was a starting outfielder. Edmonds was an All-Star in 1995 and followed with three more excellent seasons, but played only 55 games in 1999 due to injuries. In one of the worst trades in club history, he was dealt to the Cardinals in March 2000.

April 20 — The Angels break a 2–2 tie with six runs in the ninth inning and beat the Orioles 8–2 in Baltimore.

April 21 — The Angels survive a five-run Orioles rally in the ninth inning to win 11–8 in Baltimore. All five runs scored after the first two batters were retired.

April 26 — Jim Edmonds suffers through a wild ride in an ambulance after being injured in the second inning of a 6–3 win over the Yankees in New York.

Edmonds was struck below the left ear by a throw from Yankee shortstop Mike Gallego. The ambulance was headed for Columbia Presbyterian Hospital in Manhattan, but the driver took a wrong turn and ended up on the George Washington Bridge and wound up in New Jersey. Returning on the bridge, the ambulance was stopped at the toll booth for a $4 toll. Fortunately, Edmonds wasn't seriously injured and was playing again within a few days.

May 3 — Chili Davis hits a grand slam off Terry Mulholland in the eighth inning, but the Angels lose 6–5 to the Yankees at Anaheim Stadium.

May 9 — The Angels play at the Ballpark in Arlington for the first time and lose 11–3 to the Rangers.

May 10 — Tim Salmon collects four hits, including a double and a triple, in five at-bats during an 8–6 win over the Rangers in Arlington.

May 11 — Chili Davis homers from both sides of the plate during an 13–1 trouncing of the Rangers in Arlington. Batting left-handed, Davis homered off Rich Heiling in the third inning. Hitting from the right side, Chili homered facing Darren Oliver in the seventh. Davis also tripled against Heiling in the first. In addition, Tim Salmon, Dwight Smith and Jim Edmonds hit homers for the Angels. Salmon also hit three singles for his second straight four-for-five game.

The homer by Edmonds was the first of his career.

May 13 — The Angels collect 22 hits and rout the Mariners 13–1 in Seattle. Tim Salmon continued his incredible streak of hitting by garnering five hits, in five at-bats with two homers, a double and two singles. He also scored four runs and drove in five.

In three consecutive games on May 10, 11 and 13, Salmon had 13 hits in 15 at-bats. The 13 hits included three homers, a triple and two doubles and tied an American League record for most hits in three straight games. Salmon also homered in four straight games on May 10, 11, 13 and 15. From May 6 through May 15, he hit seven homers and 17 RBIs in nine games in addition to 23 hits in 40 at-bats. Salmon followed his Rookie of the Year campaign of 1993 with a .287 batting average, 23 homers and 70 RBIs in 1994.

May 17	With the club holding a record of 16–23, the Angels fire Buck Rodgers as manager and hire 42-year-old Marcel Lachemann. Coach Bobby Knoop was interim manager for two games until Lachemann could arrive in Anaheim.
	Lachemann had a three-year big-league playing career as a pitcher with the Athletics from 1969 through 1971. He was the pitching coach for the Angels from 1984 through 1993 before moving to the Marlins in 1994, where his brother Rene was manager. They were the first pair of brothers to manage in the majors at the same time since George and Harry Wright in 1879. Marcel managed the Angels' ill-fated 1995 team, which blew an 11-game lead in August and finished second to the Mariners. He resigned as manager of the club in August 1996. Rodgers never managed another major league team.
May 18	Chuck Finley strikes out 12 batters in eight innings and beats the White Sox 3–2 at Anaheim Stadium.
May 30	The Angels play at Jacobs Field in Cleveland for the first time and lose 10–2 to the Indians.
June 2	With their first pick in the amateur draft, the Angels select outfielder McKay Christensen from Clovis West High School in Fresno, California.
	Christensen was traded to the White Sox before making his major league debut in 1999. His career in the majors lasted only 99 games. The 1994 draft was largely a fruitless exercise as none of those chosen ever had to worry about being besieged by autograph seekers. The only others selected and signed by the Angels that year who later reached the big leagues were Jason Dickson (sixth round), Bret Hemphill (14th round) and Mike Holtz (17th round).
June 14	Chuck Finley pitches the Angels to a 1–0 victory over the Royals in Kansas City.
June 16	Chili Davis homers off Kirk McCaskill in the tenth inning to defeat the White Sox 6–5 in Chicago.
	Davis hit .311 with 26 homers and 84 RBIs in 1994.
June 17	On the day that 95 million Americans tune in to watch the eight-hour police chase of O. J. Simpson through the streets and freeways of Greater Los Angeles, the Angels erupt for five runs in the ninth inning to defeat the White Sox 5–3 in Chicago. Chad Curtis started the rally with a double. Three straight walks forced in a run, and an infield single by J. T. Snow scored another. A base on balls to Tim Salmon brought home the tying run, and Chili Davis broke the deadlock with a two-run single.
June 25	Trailing 7–5, the Angels explode for seven runs in the eighth inning to defeat the Rangers 12–7 at Anaheim Stadium. Chili Davis put the Angels into the lead with a two-run single and Tim Salmon capped the rally with a three-run homer.
June 29	Scott Brosius of the Athletics hits a walk-off homer off Chuck Finley with one out in the ninth inning to beat the Angels 1–0 in Oakland. The blast was the first hit off Finley since the second inning.

1990s

July 1 — The Angels and Orioles combine for 11 home runs in a 14–7 Baltimore win at Camden Yards. The Angels hit five homers, all off Mike Mussina in the first five innings of the game. Tim Salmon connected for two with Chili Davis, Jim Edmonds and Chad Curtis adding the rest. Jeffrey Hammonds homered twice for the Orioles. Chris Hoiles, Cal Ripken, Leo Gomez and Rafael Palmeiro each struck one home run.

At the time, the 11 home runs tied a major league record. Since then, the White Sox and Tigers combined for 12 homers on May 28, 1995 in Detroit, and the same two clubs hit 12 again in Chicago on July 2, 2002.

July 2 — One day after the 11-home run outburst, the Angels and Orioles combine for only seven hits in a 1–0 California win in Baltimore. Mark Langston pitched a three-hit shutout. The lone run scored on a single by Tim Salmon in the eighth inning.

July 5 — Catcher Chris Turner collects five hits, two of them doubles, in five at-bats during a 10–3 win over the Red Sox in Boston.

The five-hit game was an anomaly for Turner. He had only 36 hits and a .242 batting average in 1994. Turner garnered 90 hits and a .237 average during his eight-year career.

July 13 — Jimmy Reese, a coach with the Angels since 1972 and a beloved figure throughout the organization, dies at the age of 92.

July 16 — The Angels score two runs in the ninth inning to beat the Orioles 4–3 at Anaheim Stadium. Bo Jackson homered with one out to tie the score. The winning run scored on a single by Gary DiSarcina and a triple from Spike Owen.

July 18 — The Angels score nine runs in the first inning and beat the Red Sox 13–4 at Anaheim Stadium. Eight of the runs crossed the plate after two were out, four of them on a grand slam by J. T. Snow off Tim Van Egmond. Jim Edmonds hit a double in his first at-bat and a triple in his second trip to the plate. There were three other extra base hits for a total of six in the inning. Damion Easley also tripled, and Chad Curtis and Spike Owen each doubled.

July 21 — The Angels score a single run in seven different innings, but lose 11–7 to the Yankees at Anaheim Stadium. The Angels scored in every inning except the first and sixth.

July 28 — Kenny Rogers of the Rangers pitches a perfect game against the Angels and wins 4–0 at the Ballpark in Arlington. Rogers threw 98 pitches and struck out eight. In the ninth inning, Rex Hudler flied out to center fielder Rusty Greer; Chris Turner grounded out from shortstop Esteban Beltre to first baseman Will Clark; and Gary DiSarcina flied out to Greer.

Rogers' gem is the only perfect game ever thrown against the Angels. Mike Witt pitched a perfect game for the Angels against the Rangers at old Arlington Stadium on September 30, 1984.

July 30 — Chili Davis drives in seven runs and homers from both sides of the plate during a 14–4 rout of the Rangers in Arlington. Batting right-handed, Davis hit a grand slam off Brian Bohannon in the third inning. Hitting from the left side while facing Cris Carpenter, Davis collected a sacrifice fly in the fourth and a two-run homer in the sixth.

August 6   The Angels hit five homers, but lose 16–10 when the White Sox score six runs in the tenth inning at Anaheim Stadium. Tim Salmon and J. T. Snow each homered twice, and Chili Davis once.

August 7   For the second day in a row, the White Sox erupt in extra innings by scoring five times in the 12th against the Angels for a 10–5 win at Anaheim Stadium.

August 10   In the last game before the strike, the Angels defeat the Royals 2–1 at Anaheim Stadium.

August 12   With about 70 percent of the season completed, the major league players go on strike.

> *The strike, baseball's eighth interruption since 1972, had been anticipated all season. The owners wanted to put a lid on escalating payrolls by capping salaries and revising, if not eliminating, salary arbitration procedures. The players, who were obviously not interested in these reforms, had only one weapon once these talks broke down: a strike.*

September 14   The owners of the 28 major league clubs vote 26–2 to cancel the remainder of the season, including the playoffs and the World Series.

November 30   The Angels sign Mitch Williams, most recently with the Astros, as a free agent.

December 14   The Angels sign Lee Smith, most recently with the Orioles, as a free agent.

> *Smith was near the end of a career in which he accumulated 478 saves. In 1995 with the Angels, he saved 37 games and posted a 3.47 ERA in 52 games and $49^{2}/_{3}$ innings. In November 1995, Smith tore a tendon in his knee when he stepped in a hole while hunting near his home in Castor, Louisiana. The injury required surgery, and he lost his job as a closer in 1996 to Troy Percival. Smith was traded to the Reds in May of that season.*

December 15   Joe Grahe signs a contract as a free agent with the Rockies.

1995

Season in a Sentence
After finishing the 1994 season with the worst record in the American League, the Angels hold a 11-game lead on August 9 but wind up finishing second to the Mariners in the AL West and second in the wild-card race.

Finish • Won • Lost • Pct • GB
Second 78 67 .538 1.0

In the wild-card race, the Angels finished in second place, 1½ games behind.

Manager
Marcel Lachemann

Stats   Angels • AL • Rank
Stats	Angels	AL	Rank
Batting Avg:	.277	.270	5
On-Base Pct:	.350	.344	5
Slugging Pct:	.448	.427	3
Home Runs:	186		2
Stolen Bases:	58		13
ERA:	4.52	4.71	6
Errors:	95		4
Runs Scored:	801		2
Runs Allowed:	697		5

Starting Lineup
Jorge Fabregas, c
J. T. Snow, 1b
Damion Easley, 2b
Tony Phillips, 3b-lf
Gary DiSarcina, ss
Garret Anderson, lf
Jim Edmonds, cf
Tim Salmon, rf
Chili Davis, dh
Greg Myers, c
Rex Hudler, 2b
Spike Owen, 3b-ss-2b

Pitchers
Chuck Finley, sp
Mark Langston, sp
Shawn Boskie, sp
Brian Anderson, sp
Jim Abbott, sp
Lee Smith, rp
Bob Patterson, rp
Troy Percival, rp
Mike James, rp
Mike Butcher, rp
Mike Bielecki, rp-sp

Attendance
1,748,680 (sixth in AL)

Club Leaders
Batting Avg:	Tim Salmon	.330
On-Base Pct:	Tim Salmon	.429
	Chili Davis	.429
Slugging Pct:	Tim Salmon	.594
Home Runs:	Tim Salmon	34
RBI:	Jim Edmonds	107
Runs:	Jim Edmonds	120
Stolen Bases:	Rex Hudler	13
	Tony Phillips	13
Wins:	Chuck Finley	15
	Mark Langston	15
Strikeouts:	Chuck Finley	195
ERA:	Chuck Finley	4.21
Saves:	Lee Smith	37

MARCH 1   With the players' strike not yet settled, the Angels use replacement players for an exhibition game in Tempe against Arizona State University. The Angels won 13–5 before a crowd of only 350.

APRIL 2   The 234-day strike of Major League Baseball players comes to an end.

The season was scheduled to begin on April 26, with each team playing 144 games. The replacement players were either released or sent to minor league teams.

APRIL 12   The Los Angeles Rams formally announce their move to St. Louis.

The Rams played at the Memorial Coliseum in Los Angeles from 1946 through 1979 and Anaheim Stadium from 1980 through 1994. The transfer of the franchise left the Angels as the only tenants of the stadium. On July 22, the

Los Angeles Raiders moved back to Oakland, which left the Los Angeles without an NFL team for the first time since 1945. The Raiders resided in Oakland from 1960 through 1981 and L.A. from 1982 through 1994 before heading back to the Bay Area.

APRIL 13 The Angels trade Chad Curtis to the Tigers for Tony Phillips.

Phillips had an 18-year major league career, which lasted from 1982 through 1999, primarily with the Athletics and Tigers. He played in at least 97 games at seven different positions, including all three in the outfield, third, second and short in the infield, and as a designated hitter. With the Angels in 1995, Phillips played mostly at third base and in left field, and he batted .261 with 113 walks, 119 runs and 27 homers. He went to the White Sox as a free agent in 1996, then played in 105 games with the Angels in 1997 after returning to the club in a trade. During his second turn in Anaheim, Phillips was arrested for possession of cocaine (see August 10, 1997).

APRIL 18 The Angels sign Scott Sanderson, most recently with the White Sox, as a free agent.

APRIL 26 Seven days after the bombing of a federal office building in Oklahoma City, which resulted in the deaths of 168 people, the Angels lose the strike-delayed opener 5–4 to the Tigers before 51,145 at Anaheim Stadium. Season tickets holders were admitted for free, and all other tickets cost only $1.00. Tim Salmon and Alan Allanson both homered. It was Allanson's first game with the Angels and his first major league homer since 1991. Chuck Finley was the starting and losing pitcher.

Mario Impemba joined the Angels broadcast team in 1995. He announced Angels games until 2001.

APRIL 28 Tim Salmon homers in the tenth inning to defeat the Blue Jays 7–6 in Toronto.

Salmon had the best season of his career in 1995 with a .330 batting average, 111 runs scored, 34 doubles, 34 homers and 105 RBIs.

MAY 5 In an odd game at Anaheim Stadium, both the Angels and Mariners collect eight hits, but the Angels win 10–0. Five California pitchers combined on the shutout and were backed by four double plays.

MAY 10 Chili Davis collects five hits, including a home run and a double, and drives in five runs in five at-bats during an 11–2 thrashing of the Rangers at Anaheim Stadium.

MAY 11 Chili Davis collects three singles in three at-bats during a 6–2 loss to the Rangers at Anaheim Stadium. The three-for-three afternoon gave Davis hits in eight consecutive at-bats over two games.

Davis batted .318 with 20 home runs in 1995.

MAY 16 Down 6–0, the Angels score four runs in the fourth inning, one in the fifth, three in the sixth and one in the ninth to defeat the Twins 9–6 in Minneapolis. Tony Phillips put the Angels into the lead with a two-run homer in the sixth.

MAY 18   The Angels score seven runs in the third inning to outlast the Twins 15–9 in Minneapolis. The Twins also scored seven times in the sixth. Andy Allanson drove in six runs with two homers and two singles. Entering the contest, he had only one run batted in on the season, that with a solo homer on April 26, and was hitless in his previous 19 at-bats. After the outburst, Allanson played in 25 more major league games and collected only three RBIs without a single home run.

> *On the same day, the Walt Disney Company agreed to buy 25 percent of the Angels from the family of Gene Autry. Under the terms of the agreement, the Disney Company would have the option of buying the rest of the stock at a later date. Autry was 86 years old and had owned the team since its inception in December 1960. The Disney Company effectively took control of the franchise in 1996 when it was able to gain enough support on the board of directors to name Tony Tavares as team president. Autry remained as chairman of the board until his death in 1998. The Angels were the second of two sports franchises owned by Disney. The corporation founded the Anaheim Mighty Ducks of the National Hockey League in 1993. Disney sold the Angels to a group headed by Arte Moreno in 2003, and the Mighty Ducks (now known as the Ducks) to Henry and Susan Samueli in 2005.*

MAY 23   Chuck Finley strikes out 15 batters, pitches a two-hitter and beats the Yankees 10–0 at Anaheim Stadium. The only New York hits were a triple by Russ Davis in the sixth inning and a single from Randy Velarde with two out in the ninth.

> *Finley was 15–12 with a 4.21 ERA and 195 strikeouts in 203 innings in 1995.*

MAY 25   The Angels erupt for nine runs in the second inning and pummel the Yankees 15–2 at Anaheim Stadium. J. T. Snow capped the rally with a grand slam off Melido Perez.

> *Snow batted .289 with 24 homers and 102 RBIs in 1995.*

MAY 29   With the Angels trailing 4–0, Tim Salmon ties the score 4–4 with a grand slam off Mike Mussina in the third inning, sparking a 6–5 win over the Orioles at Anaheim Stadium.

JUNE 1   With the first overall pick in the amateur draft, the Angels select outfielder Darin Erstad from the University of Nebraska in the first round of the amateur draft.

> *A native of Jamestown, North Dakota, Erstad was not only an outfielder with Nebraska, but was the punter on the 1994 national champion football team. He reached the majors in 1996 and played 11 seasons with the Angels. Erstad was an All-Star in 1998 and 2000 and is the only player in baseball history to win Gold Gloves in both the infield and the outfield. He won the award as an outfielder in 2000 and 2002 and at first base in 2004. Darin ranks fifth all-time among Angels in games played (1,320), fourth in at-bats (5,258), fourth in runs (818), fourth in hits (1,505), fourth in total bases (2,186), fourth in doubles (279) and fourth in RBIs (625). He also holds single-season records for highest batting average (.355 in 2000), most hits (240 in 2000) and most total bases (366 in 2000). Other future major leaguers drafted and signed by the Angels in 1995 were Jarrod Washburn (second round), Brian Cooper (fourth round) and Justin Baughman (fifth round).*

June 4 — Before a pitch is thrown in a game against the Yankees in New York, the bat of Tony Phillips is confiscated by the umpires, who respond to a request by Yankee manger, Buck Showalter, who suspected Phillips of using cork in his bat. The Yankees won 11–3. The following day, the bat was X-rayed by the American League, and no cork was found.

June 6 — A day after being exonerated by the American League of bat-tampering charges, Tony Phillips hits two homers and two singles in six at-bats to lead the Angels to a 12–3 win over the Red Sox in Boston.

June 14 — Tony Phillips collects five hits, including two doubles, in five at-bats, but the Angels lose 8–5 to the Twins at Anaheim Stadium.

June 17 — The Angels score two runs in the ninth inning and one in the 13th to defeat the White Sox 4–3 at Anaheim Stadium. The two tallies in the ninth crossed the plate with two outs. Garret Anderson was hit by a pitch with the bases loaded to narrow the gap to 3–2, and Gary DiSarcina followed with a walk to force across the tying run. DiSarcina ended the game with a walk-off single.

> *Anderson played 15 seasons with the Angels from 1994 through 2008 and was an AL All-Star in 2002, 2003 and 2005. He is the all-time career franchise record holder in games (2,013), at-bats (7,989), runs (1,024), hits (2,386), total bases (3,743), doubles (489), RBIs (1,292) and extra base hits (796) and is second in home runs (272), third in triple (35) and fifth in slugging percentage (.469).*

June 23 — The Angels wallop the Mariners 14–4 in Seattle.

> *The Angels offense scored 543 runs in 115 games in 1994, an average of 4.7 per contest, which ranked last in the American League. The club improved dramatically in 1995, with 801 runs in 145 games, an average 5.5 a game, which ranked second in the AL.*

June 27 — Tim Salmon collects two singles and two homers in four at-bats, but the Angels lose 8–5 to the Rangers in Arlington.

June 29 — The Angels score 11 runs in the first inning and trounce the Rangers 20–4 in Arlington. After the opening salvo, the Angels added three runs in the fifth inning, three in the sixth, one in the seventh and two in the ninth. All 11 runs in the first scored after two were out. The rally consisted of a three-run triple by J. T. Snow, six singles, three walks, a hit batsman, two errors and a passed ball. The Angels garnered 21 hits in all with 16 singles, three doubles, two triples and no home runs. Jim Edmonds had four of the hits to run his hitting streak to 23 games.

> *Edmonds hit .290 with 120 runs scored, 33 homers and 107 RBIs in 1995. During the 23-game hitting streak, he had 41 hits in 100 at-bats.*

July 4 — The Angels celebrate the holiday by feasting the Blue Jays 14–0 at Anaheim Stadium.

July 6 — The Angels score seven runs in the third inning and rout the Blue Jays 10–1 at Anaheim Stadium. Damion Easley capped the rally with a three-run homer.

July 8	Mark Langston pitches a three-hit shutout to defeat the Brewers 1–0 at Anaheim Stadium. Garret Anderson drove in the lone run of the game with a sacrifice fly in the second inning.
July 13	Tim Salmon hits a three-run homer in the tenth inning to defeat the Tigers 8–5 in Detroit.
July 16	The Angels sweep the Tigers 6–4 and 13–6 in a double-header in Detroit. In the second tilt, called after eight innings by rain, Jim Edmonds collected two homers, a double and a single in five at-bats, and drove in five runs.
July 18	Albert Belle of the Indians hits a walk-off grand slam off Lee Smith with one out in the ninth inning to defeat the Angels 7–5 in Cleveland.
July 22	Jim Edmonds hits two homers and scores four runs during a 13–3 rout of the Tigers at Anaheim Stadium.
July 23	The Angels score 13 runs and win with a double-digit margin for the second day in a row by a clobbering of the Tigers 13–2 at Anaheim Stadium.

Over 30 games from July 14 through August 13, Garret Anderson collected 55 hits in 127 at-bats, an average of .433. He also hit 10 homers and drove in 38 runs during that span.

July 26	Chili Davis hits a grand slam off Dennis Martinez in the third inning of a 6–3 win over the Indians at Anaheim Stadium.

The Angels were 22–6 from July 2 through August 2 and scored 212 runs in the 28 games, an average of 7.6 runs per outing.

July 28	The Angels rout the Brewers 13–6 at Anaheim Stadium.

On the same day, the Angels traded McKay Christensen, John Snyder, Andrew Lorraine and Bill Simas to the White Sox for Jim Abbott and Tim Fortugno. The return of Abbott, who became a folk hero when he played previously for the Angels from 1989 through 1992, pleased the fan base, but his return to Anaheim was unsuccessful. After a 5–4 record in 1995, Abbott was a horrendous 2–18 in 1996 with an ERA of 7.48 and was sent to the minors for two weeks in August, where he was 0–2 in four starts. It was the first time that Abbott played in the minor leagues.

August 4	Tim Salmon collects two homers and four RBIs during a 6–4 loss to the Rangers at Anaheim Stadium. It capped a streak in which Salmon had eight consecutive multi-hit games. During those eight contests, from July 27 through August 4, Salmon collected 19 hits, including five homers and four doubles, in 31 at-bats and drove in 17 runs.

On the same day, the Angels signed Dick Schofield, most recently with the Dodgers, as a free agent. He previously played for the Angels from 1983 through 1992.

A consummate team player, Garrett Anderson played 14 full seasons with the Angels at all three outfield positions, providing steady production at the plate.

August 9   The Angels down the Royals 9–1 in Kansas City.

> The victory gave the Angels a record of 60–36 and an 11-game lead in the AL West. The 11-game margin was the largest of the season. The Mariners and Rangers were tied for second with won-lost ledgers of 49–47.

August 14   The Angels win an 11–10 thriller from the White Sox in ten innings in Chicago. The Angels led 7–0 after three innings, fell behind 10–8, then won with single runs in the eighth, ninth and tenth. Greg Myers won the contest with a homer in the tenth. He entered the fray as a substitute catcher in the eighth inning after Jorge Fabregas was lifted for a pinch runner.

> The following day, the Angels beat the White Sox again 7–3 in Chicago. The win gave California a 64–38 record and a 10½-game lead. In an incredible reversal, the club then lost 28 of its next 37 games. The Mariners won 34 of 51 between August 5 and September 29.

AUGUST 31	Paul O'Neill hits three homers for the Yankees during an 11–6 win over the Angels in New York.
SEPTEMBER 3	The Angels lose their ninth game in a row by dropping an 8–1 decision to the Red Sox in Boston. The streak reduced the Angels' lead over the Mariners in the AL West to 5½ games.
SEPTEMBER 5	Brian Anderson allows four homers in the second inning of an 8–0 loss to the Orioles in Baltimore. Chris Hoiles led off the inning with a home run, and after Harold Baines was retired, Jeff Manto, Mark Smith and Brady Anderson hit consecutive homers. Cal Ripken, Jr. homered off Mark Holzemer in the sixth. It was Ripken's 2,130th consecutive game, tying Lou Gehrig's record.
SEPTEMBER 6	At Camden Yards in Baltimore, the Angels are part of baseball history when Cal Ripken, Jr. takes the field for his 2,131st consecutive game, breaking the record set by Lou Gehrig between 1925 and 1939. The crowd included President Bill Clinton and Vice President Al Gore. The record wasn't actually broken until the middle of the fifth inning when the game became official. At that point, there was a 22-minute delay while Ripken was honored. In the sixth, he homered off Shawn Boskie. The Orioles won 4–2.

Ripken's streak ended in 1998 at 2,632 games.

SEPTEMBER 8	Both lead-off batters homer in the first inning of a 9–3 win over the Twins at Anaheim Stadium. Chuck Knoblauch homered off Mark Langston in the top half, and Tony Phillips went deep on Jose Parra in the bottom half.
SEPTEMBER 10	The Angels use nine pitchers during a ten-inning, 9–8 loss to the Twins at Anaheim Stadium. The nine were Jim Abbott, Mike Bielecki, Rich Monteleone, Mike James, Bob Patterson, Troy Percival, Lee Smith, Mark Holzemer and John Habyan.

The Angels led the AL West by six games with a record of 72–56 on September 12. A nine-game losing streak, started the following day, knocked the club out of the first perch.

SEPTEMBER 20	The Angels drop into a tie for first place with the Mariners after losing 9–6 to the Athletics in Oakland. All six California runs scored in the ninth inning.
SEPTEMBER 21	The Angels fall into second place one game behind the Mariners after losing 8–3 to the Rangers in Arlington. The Angels led the Yankees in the wild-card race by one-half game.
SEPTEMBER 23	The Angels fall into second place in the wild-card race, 1½ games behind the Yankees, with a 5–1 loss to the Rangers in Arlington.
SEPTEMBER 24	The Angels break a nine-game losing streak by beating the Rangers 5–0 in Arlington. Jim Abbott pitched the shutout.
SEPTEMBER 26	The Angels fall three games out of first place by losing 10–2 to the Mariners in Seattle. The Angels were 1½ games back of the Yankees in the wild-card race. There were six games left on the schedule.

SEPTEMBER 27   The Angels pull back to within two games of first by defeating the Mariners 2–0 in Seattle. Chuck Finley (6⅓ innings), Troy Percival (1⅔ innings) and Lee Smith (one inning) combined on a three-hit shutout. The Angels trailed the Yankees by 1½ games in the wild card race.

> *After the September 27 win, there were four regular-season games remaining for the Angels, each against the Athletics at Anaheim Stadium from September 28 through October 1. The Mariners were scheduled to play the Rangers in Arlington on the same four days. The Yankees closed out the regular season with three contests against the Blue Jays in Toronto.*

SEPTEMBER 28   The Angels defeat the Athletics 4–1 at Anaheim Stadium, but remain two games behind in the AL West when the Mariners win 6–2 over the Rangers in Arlington. The Angels pulled within one game of the idle Yankees in the wild-card race.

SEPTEMBER 29   The Angels defeat the Athletics 9–6 at Anaheim Stadium, but remain two games behind in the AL West when the Mariners also win 4–3 over the Rangers in Arlington. The Yankees maintained their one-game lead in the wild-card chase by defeating the Blue Jays 4–3 in Toronto.

SEPTEMBER 30   On the second-to-last day of the regular season, the Angels pull to within one game of the Mariners in the AL West race by defeating the Athletics 9–3 at Anaheim Stadium while Seattle loses 9–2 to the Rangers in Arlington. The Yankees remained one game ahead of the Angels in the wild-card standings by downing the Blue Jays 6–1 in Toronto.

OCTOBER 1   On the last day of the regular season, the Angels force a one-game playoff to determine the AL West champion by winning 8–2 over the Athletics at Anaheim Stadium while the Mariners lose 9–3 to the Rangers in Arlington. The Yankees clinched the wild-card berth by winning 6–1 over the Blue Jays in Toronto. The Yanks won 11 of their last 12 regular season games.

> *At the end of play on October 1, the Angels and Mariners had records of 78–66 in the strike-shortened 144-game season, while the Yankees were 79–65.*

OCTOBER 2   In the playoff game to determine the AL West champion, Randy Johnson strikes out 12 and allows only three hits to lead the Mariners to a 9–1 win over the Angels at the Kingdome in Seattle. Mark Langston was the Angel starter and loser.

> *According to a system developed by statistician Clay Davenport at Baseball Prospectus, the failure of the 1995 Angels to reach the postseason was by far the worst collapse in baseball history. Davenport's analysis has revealed that the Angels' chances of making the playoffs on August 20 was 8,332–1, or a 99.998 percent chance of making the playoffs. The Angels not only blew a huge lead in the AL West race (11 games on August 9, and 9½ games on August 20), but a nearly equal advantage in the wild-card race. The next-worst collapses were 500–1 by the 2007 New York Mets and 384–1 by the 1951 Brooklyn Dodgers. Ironically, the Angels' fold in 1995 may have saved baseball in Seattle. A referendum was on the ballot in a special election in September to build new stadiums for baseball and football in the city to replace the Kingdome. Up to that point, the Mariners had two winning seasons in 18 years, the best of which was*

an 83–79 mark in 1991. Voters defeated the issue, and the Mariners threatened to move out of the city. But the club's division title in 1995 revived interest in the franchise, and a stadium bill was approved by the Washington State legislature in October. As a result, Safeco Field was built and opened in 1999.

November 21 Seven weeks after O. J. Simpson is acquitted in the murders of his ex-wife, Nicole, and her companion, Ron Goldman, the Angels sign Randy Velarde, most recently with the Angels, as a free agent.

December 5 The Angels sign Jack Howell and Tim Wallach as free agents.

The Angels signed two third basemen in one day. Howell was previously a member of the Angels from 1985 through 1991. From 1992 through 1995, he played in Japan. Wallach played 16 seasons with the Expos and Dodgers before arriving in Anaheim. After 57 games with the Angels, he went back to the Dodgers in July 1996.

1996

Season in a Sentence
The hangover from the 1995 collapse permeates the franchise, as the Angels lose 91 games, and change managers three times.

Finish • Won • Lost • Pct • GB
Fourth   70   91   .435   19.5

In the wild-card race, the Angels finished in tenth place, 17½ games behind.

Managers
Marcel Lachemann (52–59) and John McNamara (18–32)

Stats

Stats	Angels	AL	Rank
Batting Avg:	.276	.277	9
On-Base Pct:	.338	.350	11
Slugging Pct:	.431	.445	10
Home Runs:	192		9
Stolen Bases:	53		14
ERA:	5.31	4.99	13
Errors:	95		4
Runs Scored:	762		13
Runs Allowed:	943		13

Starting Lineup
Jorge Fabregas, c
J. T. Snow, 1b
Randy Velarde, 2b
George Arias, 3b
Gary DiSarcina, ss
Garret Anderson, lf
Jim Edmonds, cf
Tim Salmon, rf
Chili Davis, dh
Rex Hudler, 2b
Don Slaught, c

Pitchers
Chuck Finley, sp
Shawn Boskie, sp
Mark Langston, sp
Jason Grimsley, sp
Dennis Springer, sp
Jim Abbott, sp
Troy Percival, rp
Mike James, rp

Attendance
1,820,521 (eighth in AL)

Club Leaders
Batting Avg:	Jim Edmonds	.304
On-Base Pct:	Jim Edmonds	.375
Slugging Pct:	Jim Edmonds	.571
Home Runs:	Tim Salmon	30
RBI:	Tim Salmon	98
Runs:	Tim Salmon	90
Stolen Bases:	Rex Hudler	14
Wins:	Chuck Finley	15
Strikeouts:	Chuck Finley	215
ERA:	Chuck Finley	4.16
Saves:	Troy Percival	36

JANUARY 20   Tony Phillips signs with the White Sox as a free agent.

FEBRUARY 29   The Angels purchase Don Slaught from the Reds.

APRIL 2   The Angels open the season with a 15–9 loss to the Brewers before 27,836 at Anaheim Stadium. The Brewers broke a 1–1 tie with eight runs in the third inning, seven of them off Chuck Finley. There were 22 Milwaukee hits during the contest. Jim Edmonds homered and drove in four runs. Chili Davis also hit a home run and added two singles.

> *Steve Physioc and Jerry Reuss joined the Angels broadcasting team in 1996. The pair replaced Ken Wilson and Ken Brett. Reuss pitched 22 seasons in the majors from 1969 through 1990 including a stint with the Angels in 1987. He announced Angels games for three years. Physioc has had a longer impact, as he was still on the job in 2009. Previously, he was a baseball announcer for the Reds (1983–86), Giants (1987–90), ESPN (1989–95) and Padres (1995). Physioc has also been an announcer for the Cincinnati Bengals of the NFL and Golden State Warriors and Vancouver Grizzlies of the NBA as well extensive work in both college football and basketball. The 1996 season also saw a change in the Angels' television outlet from KTLA to KCAL. KTLA had been telecasting Angels games since 1964.*

APRIL 3   On the day that "unibomber" Theodore Kaczynski is arrested in Montana, Gary DiSarcina hits a walk-off single in the 11th inning to defeat the Brewers 3–2 at Anaheim Stadium. Milwaukee tied the game by scoring two runs in the ninth after the first two batters were retired.

> *On the same day, the Angels and the city of Anaheim agree to renovate Anaheim Stadium. Under the terms of the contract, the stadium would be upgraded and modernized and returned to its original purpose and the baseball-only facility with the removal of the outfield seats. The renovations were completed in time for the start of the 1998 season.*

APRIL 5   For the second game in a row, the Angels win with a walk-off single in the 11th inning, this time from Jack Howell to down the White Sox 7–6 at Anaheim Stadium.

APRIL 7   In his first start with the Angels, Don Slaught homers in the fourth inning of a 6–5 win over the White Sox at Anaheim Stadium.

APRIL 15   The Angels score six runs in the fourth inning to take a 9–1 lead, but wind up losing 11–10 to the Mariners at the Kingdome. Seattle tied the game 10–10 with four tallies in the seventh, then broke the deadlock in the eighth. Mike Aldrete hit a grand slam for the Angels off Edwin Hurtado.

APRIL 17   Michelle Carew, the daughter of Angels coach Rod Carew, dies at the age of 18. Her Panamanian-Jewish heritage dramatically lowered the possibility of finding a matching donor for a bone marrow transplant. In spite of Rod's heartfelt pleas for those of a similar ethnic background to come forward, no donor could be found. A statue of her has been installed at Angel Stadium of Anaheim.

APRIL 19	Actor Charlie Sheen purchases 2,615 seats in the left-field stands at Anaheim stadium in the hopes of catching a home run ball. None came his way during a 4–3 win over the Tigers.
APRIL 22	Troy Percival strikes out all three batters he faces in the ninth inning to close out a 6–5 triumph over the Tigers at Anaheim Stadium.

> *Percival was drafted as a catcher out of the University of California at Riverside in 1990. He was converted into a pitcher in the Angels minor league system in 1991. Percival made his major league debut in 1995 and was the Angels closer from 1996 through 2004. He recorded a club-record 324 saves during that period, with a high of 42 in 1998, and was named to the All-Star team in 1996, 1998, 1999 and 2001. During the 1996 season, Percival had 36 saves, a 2.31 ERA and 100 strikeouts in 62 games and 74 innings.*

MAY 10	The Angels outslug the Indians 13–8 at Anaheim Stadium. All 21 runs scored in the first five innings.
MAY 21	Rex Hudler and Don Slaught lead off the first inning with back-to-back homers to spark the Angels to a 5–2 victory over the Orioles in Baltimore.
MAY 26	Rex Hudler collects five hits, including a home run, in five at-bats to lead the Angels to a 12–2 trouncing of the Red Sox at Anaheim Stadium.
MAY 27	The Angels trade Lee Smith to the Reds for Chuck McElroy.
MAY 28	The Angels collect only two hits off Kenny Rogers, but win 1–0 over the Yankees at Anaheim Stadium. Rogers, who pitched a perfect game against the Angels in 1994 while playing for the Rangers, had a no-hitter in progress until Garret Anderson led off the eighth inning with a single. In the ninth, Rex Hudler reached first base on an error, advanced to third on a double by Randy Velarde. After Tim Salmon was intentionally walked, Rogers issued a base on balls to Chili Davis to force in the lone run of the game. Jason Grimsley pitched the shutout.

> *The shutout was the only one of Grimsley's career, which lasted from 1989 through 2006 and included 72 starts and 480 relief appearances.*

JUNE 1	The Angels score all eight of their runs in an 8–3 win over the Orioles at Anaheim Stadium in the third inning. Gary DiSarcina led off the big inning with a single and capped the rally with a three-run homer. Tim Salmon contributed a three-run double.
JUNE 5	The Angels draft future major leaguers Scott Schoeneweis (third round), Jerrod Riggan (eighth round) and Greg Jones (42nd round). The club didn't possess a first-round choice because of free agent compensation for signing Randy Velarde. Schoeneweis survived testicular cancer as a 19-year-old student-athlete at Duke University before reaching the big leagues.
JUNE 9	Switch-hitting J. T. Snow has a big day during a 13-inning, 8–6 victory over the Indians at Jacobs Field. Batting right-handed, Snow singled off ex-Angel Brian Anderson in the second and homered in the fourth. Hitting from the left side, Snow doubled in the 11th facing Jose Mesa and walloped a game-winning, two-run homer

against Julian Tavarez in the 13th. Ryan Hancock became the first Angels pitcher to collect a hit since the designated hitter rule was created in 1972 with a single in the 13th. He scored on Snow's second homer. The Angels were forced to use their pitchers as hitters when Rex Hudler was moved from designated hitter to second base in the ninth inning. Cleveland scored in the inning to tie the contest 6–6.

The hit came in Hancock's only career plate appearance in a career which lasted only 11 games. He made his major league debut the previous day. Hancock was also the starting quarterback for Brigham Young University in 1992.

JUNE 10   In the tenth inning at Kansas City, Chili Davis and J. T. Snow both homer for a 7–5 victory over the Royals. It was Snow's second extra-inning homer in two days. The long drive cleared the waterfall display in right field. Chuck McElroy was the winning pitcher with two-thirds of an inning of relief.

JUNE 11   The Angels break a 7–7 tie with three runs in the seventh inning and outlast the Royals 11–9 in Kansas City. For the second day in a row, Chuck McElroy was the winning pitcher with 1²⁄₃ innings of relief.

JUNE 12   Chuck McElroy is the winning pitcher for the third game in a row, all against the Royals in Kansas City, this time by pitching two-thirds of an inning during a ten-inning, 4–3 victory. Tim Wallach delivered the winning blow with a homer in the tenth inning.

JUNE 15   The Angels trade Ben Van Ryn to the Cardinals for Pat Borders.

JUNE 19   The Angels break a 2–2 tie with seven runs in the seventh inning, then add five more in the eighth to win 14–2 over the White Sox at Anaheim Stadium.

JUNE 27   The Athletics smack eight homers by seven different players to defeat the Angels 18–2 at Anaheim Stadium. Eric Young hit two of the eight home runs. The others were garnered by Jose Herrera, Jason Giambi, Mark McGwire, Geronimo Berroa, Terry Steinbach and Mike Bordick. Shad Williams and Rich Monteleone each surrendered three homers, and Shawn Boskie two.

JUNE 30   After the Athletics score 35 runs in the first three games of a four-game series at Anaheim Stadium, the Angels avoid a sweep by winning 1–0. The lone run scored in the first inning when Randy Velarde beat out an infield single, moved to second on a groundout and advanced two bases on a wild pitch. Ryan Hancock (seven innings), Mike James (one inning) and Troy Percival (one inning) combined on the shutout.

JULY 4   Randy Velarde runs his hitting streak to 21 games during an 11-inning, 8–7 loss to the Athletics in Oakland.

During the 21-game hitting streak, Velarde collected 35 hits in 86 at-bats for a batting average of .407.

JULY 5   After the Angels score three times in the top of the first, the Athletics explode for 13 runs in the bottom half and go on to win 16–8 in Oakland. The 16 combined runs were the most in the first inning of a major league game since 1894. In his first start since pitching seven shutout innings against the A's five days earlier,

	Ryan Hancock surrendered eight runs in two-thirds of an inning. The other five first-inning tallies were given up by Brad Pennington (three) and Jim Abbott (two). Hancock, Pennington and Abbott combined to give up nine hits (six singles, two doubles and a home run), five walks and a hit batsman. Matt Stairs drove in six runs in the big inning on a grand slam and a two-run double.
JULY 15	Trailing 7–0, the Angels score a run in the fourth inning, three in the fifth and six in the seventh to defeat the Rangers 10–7 in Arlington. Garret Anderson put the Angels into the lead with a two-out, two-run single.
JULY 22	Jim Edmonds hits a homer off Omar Olivares in the third inning for the lone run of a 1–0 triumph over the Tigers at Anaheim Stadium. Chuck Finley (7 2/3 innings) and Troy Percival (1 1/3 innings) combined on the shutout.
	Edmonds hit .304 with 27 homers in 1996.
JULY 25	The Angels score four runs in the ninth inning to shock the Brewers 5–4 at Anaheim Stadium. J. T. Snow led off the inning with a home run. After singles by Rex Hudler and Garret Anderson and two outs, Gary DiSarcina ended the game with a three-run homer.
JULY 27	On the day a bomb explodes in an Atlanta park filled with people attending the Olympics, J. T. Snow hits a grand slam off Ben McDonald in the second inning of a 7–0 victory over the Brewers at Anaheim Stadium.
	On the same day, the Angels traded Pat Borders to the White Sox for Robert Ellis.
JULY 31	The Angels trade Damion Easley to the Tigers for Greg Gohr.
	Easley was 27 when traded and frustrated the Angels by failing to come close to fulfilling his potential. Often injured, he hit .239 in 350 games over five seasons with the club. The trade proved to be one of the worst in Angels history, as Easley blossomed in Detroit as a power-hitting second baseman, and was still active in the majors in 2009. The overall number one choice in the amateur draft in 1989, Gohr pitched only 15 games for the Angels.
AUGUST 6	Marcel Lachemann resigns as manager of the Angels with the club holding a record of 52–59. He admitted that he lost the ability to motivate the team. The resignation came a month after his brother Rene was fired as manager of the Marlins. John McNamara, who managed the Angels in 1983 and 1984, was appointed to guide the club for the remainder of the season. In a highly unorthodox move, Lachemann returned to the Angels in 1997 and 1998 as a pitching coach under Terry Collins. Lachemann never managed another big-league team.
	McNamara was hospitalized on August 21 with a potentially life-threatening blood clot in his leg. Coach Joe Maddon took over as manager for 22 games while McNamara recuperated. Terry Collins was hired to manage the club after the end of the season (see November 4, 1996).
AUGUST 10	The Royals hammer the Angels 18–3 at Anaheim Stadium.

AUGUST 14	Trailing 6–0, the Angels score four runs in the second inning and four more in the third and win 8–7 over the Indians at Anaheim Stadium. Randy Velarde broke the 6–6 tie with a two-run double.
AUGUST 21	Chili Davis homers from both sides of the plate during a 7–1 win over the Yankees in New York. Batting right-handed, Davis homered off Jimmy Key in the first inning and then went deep again from the left side facing Gene Nelson in the ninth.
AUGUST 23	Chili Davis homers in the second inning and Jim Edmonds wallops a home run in the ninth, both off David Wells, to account for the only runs of a 2–0 win over the Yankees in New York. Shawn Boskie (6 1/3 innings), Mike Holtz (1 1/3 innings) and Troy Percival (1 1/3 innings) combined on the shutout.
AUGUST 25	The Angels score seven runs in the fourth inning on the way to a 13–0 rout of the Orioles in Baltimore. Randy Velarde hit a grand slam off Scott Erickson.
AUGUST 29	Garret Anderson drives in seven runs during a 14–3 trouncing of the Yankees at Anaheim Stadium. Anderson hit a grand slam off Wally Whitehurst in the first inning, then added a two-run double in the sixth and a run-scoring two-bagger in the eighth.
SEPTEMBER 8	The Angels turn a triple play in the sixth inning of a 4–2 win over the Twins in Minneapolis. With runners on first and second, Ron Coomer grounded to third baseman Jack Howell, who stepped on third and went around the horn to second baseman Rex Hudler and first baseman J. T. Snow.
SEPTEMBER 20	After the Rangers score in the top of the tenth inning, the Angels respond with two runs in the bottom half to win 6–5 at Anaheim Stadium. The first two batters were retired before George Arias and Rex Hudler singled and Garret Anderson delivered a two-run, walk-off double.
SEPTEMBER 23	Troy Percival strikes out all three batters he faces in the ninth inning to close out a 4–3 victory over the Mariners at Anaheim Stadium.
SEPTEMBER 25	Both lead-off batters homer in the first inning of an 11–2 loss to the Mariners at Anaheim Stadium. Seattle's Joey Cora homered off Shawn Boskie, and Randy Velarde cleared the wall with a drive against Salomon Torres.
SEPTEMBER 27	Garret Anderson collects a team-record six hits in seven at-bats during a 4–3 win in 15 innings over the Rangers in Arlington. All six hits were singles and were delivered in the second, fifth, seventh, ninth, 11th and 15th innings. The hit in the 15th drove in the winning run. Anderson had three hits off Ken Hill and one each against Danny Patterson, Mike Hennaman and Matt Whiteside.
OCTOBER 28	The Angels trade Chili Davis to the Royals for Mark Gubicza and Mike Bovee.

> *Davis had one good season left in his arsenal and hit 30 homers for Kansas City in 1997. Gubicza pitched two games for the Angels, both starts, and had an 0–1 record and a 20.25 ERA in 4 2/3 innings. Bovee's big-league career lasted three games.*

NOVEMBER 4	The day before Bill Clinton wins re-election by defeating Bob Dole in the Presidential election, the Angels announce that 47-year-old Terry Collins will be the team's new manager.

> *An infielder in the Pirates and Dodgers organizations, Collins never played in the majors. He managed the Astros from 1994 through 1996. Collins was fired after the Astros finished second to the Cardinals in the NL Central race by compiling an 8–17 record in September. He managed the Angels to winning seasons in 1997 and 1998. But Collins possessed a fiery temperament and was a strict disciplinarian whose hard-driving style alienated many veterans and ultimately divided the clubhouse. He resigned in September 1999 when the club had a dismal record of 51–82.*

NOVEMBER 19	The franchise officially changes its name from the California Angels to the Anaheim Angels.

> *The name change was in conjunction with the renovation of the stadium and the takeover of the franchise by the Disney Corporation. In order to pump money into upgrading the Angels ballpark, the city of Anaheim insisted upon Anaheim being included in the team's name, uniforms, logo and merchandise. Disney, which helped put Anaheim on the map with the opening of Disneyland, readily agreed. The corporation hoped to market Anaheim as a "destination city," much the same way it had with Orlando, Florida, where Disney World is located. The franchise was known as the Anaheim Angels until 2005 when new owner Arte Moreno decided to call the club the Los Angeles Angels of Anaheim.*

NOVEMBER 20	The Angels sign Dave Hollins, most recently with the Mariners, as a free agent.
NOVEMBER 21	Rex Hudler signs with the Phillies as a free agent.
NOVEMBER 26	The Angels trade J. T. Snow to the Giants for Allen Watson and Fausto Macey.
DECEMBER 5	The Angels trade Jeremy Blevins and Ryan Kane to the Yankees for Jim Leyritz.
DECEMBER 19	The Angels sign Eddie Murray, most recently with the Orioles, as a free agent.

> *On Opening Day in 1997, Murray was 41 years old and had 3,218 career hits and 501 home runs. In 46 games with the Angels, he batted .219 with three home runs.*

1997

Season in a Sentence
Playing as the Anaheim Angels for the first time, the club wins ten games in a row in July and takes over first place during the first half of August before finishing second.

Finish • Won • Lost • Pct • GB
Second   84   78   .519   6.0

In the wild-card race, the Angels finished in second place, 12 games behind.

Manager
Terry Collins

Stats   Angels • AL • Rank
Batting Avg: .272   .271   7
On-Base Pct: .344   .340   5
Slugging Pct: .416   .428   9
Home Runs: 161   8
Stolen Bases: 126   5
ERA: 4.52   4.56   5
Errors: 123   11
Runs Scored: 829   5
Runs Allowed: 794   6

Starting Lineup
Chad Kreuter, c
Darin Erstad, 1b
Tony Phillips, 2b-lf-dh
Dave Hollins, 3b
Gary DiSarcina, ss
Garret Anderson, lf
Jim Edmonds, cf
Tim Salmon, rf
Eddie Murray, dh
Luis Alicea, 2b
Jim Leyritz, c

Pitchers
Jason Dickson, sp
Allen Watson, sp
Chuck Finley, sp
Dennis Springer, sp
Troy Percival, rp
Mike Holtz, rp
Pep Harris, rp
Mike James, rp
Shigetoshi Hasegawa, rp

Attendance
1,767,330 (ninth in AL)

Club Leaders
Batting Avg: Garret Anderson   .303
On-Base Pct: Tim Salmon   .394
Slugging Pct: Tim Salmon   .517
Home Runs: Tim Salmon   33
RBI: Tim Salmon   129
Runs: Dave Hollins   101
Stolen Bases: Darin Erstad   23
Wins: Jason Dickson   13
                Chuck Finley   13
Strikeouts: Chuck Finley   155
ERA: Chuck Finley   4.23
Saves: Troy Percival   27

JANUARY 19 The Angels sign Luis Alicea, most recently with the Cardinals, as a free agent.

JANUARY 24 The Angels purchase Shigetoshi Hasegawa from Orix in Japan's Pacific League.

Hasegawa was the seventh Japanese-born player in major league history and the first with the Angels. He pitched five seasons with the club.

MARCH 9 Randy Velarde tears a ligament in his right elbow while throwing from the outfield during pre-game drills. His only appearance all year was as a pinch runner in a game on September 1.

MARCH 16 Chuck Finley breaks a bone below his right eye when hit by a bat which slips out of the hands of Mike James during batting practice. Finley also suffered a cut that required 19 stitches. He missed four weeks of action.

APRIL 2 On Opening Day, the Red Sox score four runs in the ninth inning to stun the Angels 6–5 before 30,874 at Anaheim Stadium. Troy Percival took the mound in the ninth with a 5–2 lead and retired the first two batters to face him. In an unexpected reversal of form, the next seven Boston batters reached base on a double, a walk, a single, two more walks, a hit batsman and another single. The second and third walks and the hit batsman occurred with the bases loaded. Jim Edmonds homered in the losing cause.

Anaheim Stadium underwent extensive renovation in 1997 as most of the double-decked outfield seats were removed in order to return the ballpark to its original purpose as a baseball-only facility. For the first time since 1979, the San Gabriel Mountains, Santa Ana Mountains and the Brea Hills were visible from the seats. There were only 33,851 seats available for sale in 1997, however, because much of the stadium was under construction. Despite contending for the pennant, attendance was a problem all year, as the club drew 1,767,330, the lowest figure of any 162-game season between 1978 and the present.

Tim Salmon played his entire 14-year career with the Angels. Though he was never selected for the All-Star Game, he was a consistent hitter and solid fielder and a fan favorite.

APRIL 4   Tim Salmon hits a walk-off grand slam off Paul Shuey in the 11th inning to defeat the Indians 8–6 at Anaheim Stadium. Cleveland scored twice in the top of the inning. The Angels loaded the bases on singles by Darin Erstad and Luis Alicea and a walk to Jim Edmonds before Salmon's slam.

The Angels had dramatically altered uniforms in 1997. Created by Disney studios, the jerseys were sleeveless and pinstriped with a stylized form of the team name with an enlarged angel wing to the right of the "A." The design was widely ridiculed and lasted only five seasons.

APRIL 15 — Jim Leyritz hits a two-run double with two out in the ninth inning to defeat his ex-Yankee teammates 6–5 at Yankee Stadium. Leyritz played for the Yankees in the 1996 World Series victory over the Braves and hit a key home run in game four.

APRIL 18 — During an off-day, Darin Erstad flies to his hometown of Jamestown, North Dakota, to help neighbors stack sand bags as they fought flooding.

APRIL 20 — Tim Salmon collects four hits, two of them double, and drives in five runs in five at-bats during an 11–1 thrashing of the Royals in Kansas City.

Sparky Anderson served as an analyst on Angels telecasts in 1997 and 1998.

APRIL 29 — Three Angels outfielders record assists during a 5–4 triumph over the Red Sox in Boston. In the third inning, Rudy Pemberton was thrown out at home by center fielder Orlando Palmeiro. Later in the inning, Wil Cordero was caught in a rundown between second and third after hitting a double fielded by left fielder Garret Anderson. In the fourth, Tim Naehring was gunned down out third base by right fielder Tim Salmon.

The Angels radio broadcasts moved from KMPC to KLAC in 1997. KMPC had been the radio outlet since 1961. The club returned to KMPC (now KSPN) from 2003 through 2007.

MAY 9 — Batting lead-off, Darin Erstad hits the first pitch of the first inning from Cal Eldred for a home run, but the Angels lose 5–4 to the Brewers in Milwaukee.

MAY 12 — Trailing 6–2, the Angels explode for 13 runs in the seventh inning and defeat the White Sox 16–8 at Anaheim Stadium. The 13 runs scored on 11 hits, an error, two walks, a hit batsman and a wild pitch. Those collecting hits were Gary DiSarcina (two singles), Darin Erstad (double and single), Jim Edmonds (home run), Dave Hollins (two singles), Jim Leyritz (two singles), Garret Anderson (single) and Tim Salmon (single). Salmon and Luis Alicea drew the walks and Edmonds was hit by a pitch. Erstad drove in three runs, and DiSarcina, Erstad, Edmonds, Hollins and Leyritz each crossed the plate twice.

MAY 13 — Trailing 3–0, the Angels erupt for seven runs in the third inning and hold on to down the White Sox 8–7 at Anaheim Stadium. Playing in his 3,000th major league game, Eddie Murray collected two singles in three at-bats.

MAY 14 — Down 5–0, the Angels score two runs in the third inning, two in the fourth and two in the fifth to defeat the Orioles 6–5 at Anaheim Stadium. It was the third day in a row in which the Angels won after trailing by at least three runs. Jim Edmonds put the Angels into the lead with a two-run homer.

MAY 17 — After falling behind 5–0, the Angels score four runs in the sixth inning and two in the eighth to defeat the Brewers 6–5 at Anaheim Stadium. During the eighth-inning rally, Jack Howell doubled in a run and scored the go-ahead tally on Darin Erstad's single.

The 1997 season was the last for the Brewers in the American League. The club moved to the NL in 1998.

MAY 18	The Angels trade Chuck McElroy and Jorge Fabregas to the White Sox for Tony Phillips and Chad Kreuter. Phillips played previously for the Angels in 1995.
MAY 20	The Angels outlast the Mariners 11–9 at Anaheim Stadium. The Angels scored seven runs in the fourth inning to take a 7–2 lead, fell behind 9–7, then added a run in the seventh and three in the eighth for the victory. Tim Salmon drove in the three eight-inning runs with a bases-loaded double.
MAY 21	The Angels collect 21 hits and clobber the Mariners 18–3 at Anaheim Stadium.
MAY 23	The Angels reach double figures in runs for the third game in a row by defeating the Blue Jays 12–2 in Toronto.
MAY 28	The Angels score five runs in the ninth inning to defeat the Athletics 14–10 in Oakland.
JUNE 3	With the third overall pick in the amateur draft, the Angels select third baseman Troy Glaus from UCLA.

Glaus made his major league debut on July 31, 1998 and played seven seasons with the Angels. He was an All-Star in 2000, 2001 and 2003 and set a single-season franchise record with 47 homers in 2000. Other future major leaguers drafted and signed by the Angels in 1997 include Matt Wise (sixth round), Steve Green (tenth round), Doug Nickle (13th round), Mike Colangelo (21st round) and Scot Shields (38th round).

JUNE 5	The Angels sign Kevin Gross, most recently with the Rangers, as a free agent.
JUNE 10	Center fielder Jim Edmonds makes a highlight reel catch for the ages during a 6–2 win over the Royals in Kansas City. With the score 1–1 with two out in the fifth inning and two runners on base, Edmonds raced toward the wall for a long drive hit by David Howard and dived head first on the warning track with his back to the plate to snare the ball.
JUNE 12	The Angels play a National League team during the regular season for the first time and defeat the Padres 8–4 at Anaheim Stadium.
JUNE 14	The Angels play the Giants for the first time during the regular season and lose 10–3 at Anaheim Stadium.
JUNE 17	The Angels play the Dodgers for the first time during the regular season and lose 4–3 in Los Angeles. It was also the Angels' first regular season on the road against an NL team.

The Angels met the Dodgers four times in 1997, twice in Los Angeles and twice in Anaheim, and lost all four.

JUNE 18	During the sixth inning of a 7–3 loss to the Dodgers in Los Angeles, two Japanese-born pitchers face each other for first the first time in a major league game. Hideo Nomo

was the Dodgers starter and was still in the game when Shigetoshi Hasegawa went into the contest as a reliever for the Angels.

June 19 — Garret Anderson hits a two-run, walk-off single in the ninth inning to defeat the Athletics 4–3 at Anaheim Stadium.

June 23 — Jim Leyritz homers off Darren Oliver in the fifth inning to account for the lone run of a 1–0 victory over the Rangers in Arlington. Allen Watson (six innings), Shigetoshi Hasegawa (one inning), Mike Holtz (two-thirds of an inning) and Rich DeLucia (1 1/3 innings) combined on the shutout. DeLucia struck out all three batters he faced in the ninth.

June 28 — The Angels steal four bases in the seventh inning of a 6–1 triumph over the Mariners in Seattle. With two out, Derek Lowe pitching and Tony Phillips batting, Luis Alicea stole second. After Phillips was walked intentionally, Phillips and Alicea executed a double steal with Alicea taking third and Phillips second. Greg McCarthy replaced Lowe as the Seattle pitcher, and Alicea scored and Phillips advanced to third on a wild pitch. Phillips then stole home.

June 30 — The Angels play the Rockies for the first time and lose 11–7 at Coors Field in Denver.

July 2 — The Angels play the Dodgers at Anaheim Stadium for the first time during the regular season and lose 5–4.

July 5 — The Angels pull off a triple play in the fourth inning of a 5–4 victory over the Mariners at Anaheim. With Seattle runners on first and second and running with the pitch, Rich Amaral lined out to center fielder Garret Anderson. The second and third outs were recorded on forceouts by second baseman Luis Alicea and first baseman Darin Erstad.

July 6 — Chuck Finley strikes out 13 batters and pitches a complete game to defeat the Mariners 8–0 at Anaheim Stadium. Dave Hollins hit a grand slam off Josias Manzanillo in the fourth inning.

July 11 — The Angels score five runs in the first inning to spark a 14–4 win over the Athletics in Oakland.

July 17 — The Angels extend their winning streak to ten games with a 9–4 decision over the Tigers at Anaheim Stadium.

The streak gave the Angels a 52–42 record and placed the club one-half game out of first in the AL West.

July 20 — Troy Percival strikes out all three batters he faces in the ninth inning to close out a 9–5 victory over the Blue Jays at Anaheim Stadium.

July 28 — Garret Anderson hits a grand slam off Orel Hershiser in the fourth inning of a 10–7 win over the Indians in the second game of a double-header in Cleveland. The Angels also won the opener 2–0.

JULY 29	The Angels trade Jim Leyritz and Rob Sasser to the Rangers for Ken Hill.
JULY 31	Todd Greene drives in six runs with a homer, two doubles and a single in five at-bats, but the Angels lose 14–12 at Anaheim Stadium. Chicago took a 9–0 lead in the second inning, but the Angels fought back to tie the contest 11–11 by the end of the fifth. Both teams scored in the eighth, and the Sox won the game with two tallies in the ninth.
AUGUST 2	The Angels bunch all five of their runs and four of their five hits in the second inning to defeat the White Sox 5–2 at Anaheim Stadium.
AUGUST 3	Troy Percival strikes out all three batters he faces in the ninth inning to close out a 4–1 victory over the White Sox at Anaheim Stadium.

The Angels peaked on August 6 with a record of 65–49 and a one-game lead in the AL West. The club dropped out of the top spot for good on August 20. From August 10 through September 11, the Angels were 9–21.

AUGUST 10	Tony Phillips is arrested at the Ivanhoe Motel in Anaheim for possession of crack cocaine. According to police, Phillips was found "with a loaded pipe in one hand and a lighter in the other."

The Angels suspended Phillips indefinitely on August 18, but he was back in uniform two days later after an independent arbitrator overruled the suspension following a hearing. On November 3, Phillips pled guilty to one count of felony cocaine possession, but served no jail time after entering a 18-month treatment program for first-time offenders. The Angels released him on December 22. Phillips played for the Blue Jays and Mets in 1998 and the Athletics in 1999 before his career ended.

AUGUST 13	The Angels trade George Arias, Ryan Hancock and Stevenson Agosto to the Padres for Rickey Henderson.

The Angels were the fifth of nine teams for which Henderson played during his major league career. He played 32 games for the Angels and batted just .183 with two home runs.

AUGUST 15	Chuck Finley extends his winning streak to ten games with a 5–3 decision over the Brewers in Milwaukee.

The ten-game winning streak ran Finley's record to 13–6. In the third inning of his next start on August 19, a 12–4 win over the Yankees at Anaheim Stadium, Finley broke his left wrist while backing up a play at home plate and was out for the rest of the season.

AUGUST 26	In the ninth inning at Anaheim Stadium, Rickey Henderson scores from third base after Indians first baseman Jim Thome catches a pop up by Tim Salmon in foul territory to give the Angels an 8–7 victory.

Salmon batted .296 with 33 homers and 129 RBIs in 1997.

AUGUST 28	The Angels play in San Diego for the first time and lose 9–2 to the Padres at Jack Murphy Stadium.
AUGUST 29	Ken Hill hits a two-run double in the fifth inning of a 3–1 win over the Padres in San Diego. Hill was the first Angels pitcher since 1972 to record an RBI and an extra base hit.
AUGUST 30	The Angels play in San Francisco for the first time and lose 7–3 to the Giants at Candlestick Park.
SEPTEMBER 1	The day after Princess Diana dies following a car accident in Paris, the Rockies play at Anaheim Stadium for the first time and beat the Angels 4–1.
SEPTEMBER 7	The Angels outlast the Tigers to win 5–4 in 15 innings in Detroit. Robert Eenhoorn drove in the winning run with a sacrifice fly. He entered the contest as a third baseman in the 12th. Relievers Mike James, Mike Holtz, Troy Percival and Shigetoshi Hasegawa combined to strike out 16 batters over the final eight innings. Hasegawa fanned eight in four innings, hurling from the 12th through the 15th.
SEPTEMBER 8	Darin Erstad hits two homers and drives in five, but the Angels lose 12–10 to the Blue Jays in Toronto.
SEPTEMBER 15	Garret Anderson hits a three-run, walk-off homer in the ninth inning to defeat the Twins 8–5 at Anaheim Stadium.
	On the same day, Anaheim Stadium was renamed Edison International Field of Anaheim after local utility Edison International reached a deal giving it naming rights for 20 years at a price of $50 million. Edison International owned Southern California Edison, which had 4.2 million customers in 1997. After the 2003 season, Edison International exercised its option to exit the sponsorship deal. At that time, the Angels announced from then on that the stadium would be known as Angel Stadium of Anaheim.
SEPTEMBER 27	Trailing 7–2, the Angels score a run in the seventh inning, four in the eighth and one in the ninth to defeat the Rangers 8–7 at Edison International Field. Robert Eenhoorn tied the contest with a three-run double in the eighth. Eenhoorn entered the game as a third baseman in the sixth. Tim Salmon drove in the winning tally with a walk-off single.
	In the seventh inning, Eenhoorn hit his only major league home run. A native of Rotterdam in the Netherlands, he is the only Dutch-born player to homer in a big-league game. Eenhoorn played in 17 games for the Angels in 1996 and 1997. He was later the coach of the Netherlands' national baseball team from 2001 through 2008.
NOVEMBER 7	Mark Langston signs a contract with the Angels as a free agent.
NOVEMBER 18	In the expansion draft, the Angels lose Dennis Springer to the Diamondbacks and Mike Bell to the Devil Rays.
NOVEMBER 20	The Angels trade Nick Skuse to the Tigers for Phil Nevin and Matt Walbeck.

December 9 — Luis Alicea signs a contract with the Rangers as a free agent. On the same day, Jack Howell inked a free agent deal with the Astros.

December 10 — Chad Kreuter signs with the White Sox as a free agent.

December 11 — The Angels sign Omar Olivares, most recently with the Mariners, as a free agent.

December 19 — The Angels sign Cecil Fielder, most recently with the Yankees, as a free agent.

Fielder played for the Blue Jays without notable success from 1985 through 1988, then played in Japan in 1989. Returning to the U.S. with the Tigers in 1990, Fielder became the biggest story in baseball that season by smoking 51 home runs. He added 44 more in 1991 before going into a slow decline. With the Angels, he batted .241 with 17 homers in 103 games and was released in August with the club in a pennant race.

1998

Season in a Sentence
The Angels hold a 3½-game lead in September, but blow the advantage by losing 13 of their last 19 games.

Finish • Won • Lost • Pct • GB
Second 85 77 .525 3.0

In the wild-card race, the Angels finished in third place, seven games behind.

Manager
Terry Collins

Stats

Stats	Angels	AL	Rank
Batting Avg:	.272	.271	6
On-Base Pct:	.332	.340	10
Slugging Pct:	.415	.432	9
Home Runs:	147		11
Stolen Bases:	93		11
ERA:	4.49	4.65	6
Errors:	106		5
Runs Scored:	787		10
Runs Allowed:	783		6

Starting Lineup
Matt Walbeck, c
Cecil Fielder, 1b-dh
Randy Velarde, 2b
Dave Hollins, 3b
Gary DiSarcina, ss
Darin Erstad, lf-1b
Jim Edmonds, cf
Garret Anderson, rf
Tim Salmon, dh
Phil Nevin, c

Pitchers
Chuck Finley, sp
Omar Olivares, sp
Steve Sparks, sp
Jason Dickson, sp-rp
Ken Hill, sp
Troy Percival, rp
Rich DeLucia, rp
Shigetoshi Hasegawa, rp
Mike Holtz, rp
Pep Harris, rp
Allen Watson, rp-sp

Attendance
2,519,260 (sixth in AL)

Club Leaders
Batting Avg:	Jim Edmonds	.307
On-Base Pct:	Tim Salmon	.410
Slugging Pct:	Tim Salmon	.533
Home Runs:	Tim Salmon	26
RBI:	Jim Edmonds	91
Runs:	Jim Edmonds	115
Stolen Bases:	Darin Erstad	20
Wins:	Chuck Finley	11
Strikeouts:	Chuck Finley	212
ERA:	Chuck Finley	3.39
Saves:	Troy Percival	42

JANUARY 22   Rickey Henderson signs a contract with the Athletics as a free agent.

FEBRUARY 27   The Angels sign Jack McDowell, most recently with the Indians, as a free agent.

APRIL 1   The Angels open the season with a 4–1 victory over the Yankees before 43,311 at Edison International Field. All four Anaheim runs scored in the fourth inning. Gary DiSarcina led the offense with three hits, including a double. Chuck Finley pitched seven innings.

> The game was the first at remodeled Edison International Field, formerly known as Anaheim Stadium. The double-decked outfield seats, built in 1979 and 1980 when the Los Angeles Rams moved into the stadium, were replaced with outfield pavilions. A huge scoreboard was installed above the right-field seats and an out-of-town scoreboard was placed into the right-field wall. The multi-colored seats were replaced by green seats. The exterior of the stadium was also renovated as the concrete structure and ramps were painted a combination of green and sandstone. Much of the facade of the stadium was torn down to create a more open feeling for visitors. The most notable feature of the renovation was the "Outfield Extravaganza" beyond the outfield walls in which six geysers shot water 90 feet into the air, and a stream cascaded down a "mountainside" covered with real trees and artificial rocks. Fireworks shot out of the display at the start of each game and after Angels home runs and victories. The field dimensions were 333 feet down each foul line and 404 feet to center. Outside, the main entrance included two enormous Angels hats. Fans were pleased with the changes, as attendance jumped from 1,767,330 in 1997 to 2,529,210 in 1998.

APRIL 2   In his first game with the Angels, Phil Nevin drives in three runs to lead the club to a 10–2 victory over the Yankees at Edison International Field.

> Brian Barnhart spent the first of his two years as an Angels radio announcer in 1998.

APRIL 11   Making his first start with the Angels, third baseman Frank Bolick hits a home run during an 8–5 loss to the Angels in Cleveland.

> The homer by Bolick was his first in the majors since 1993 when he played for the Expos. He appeared in 21 games for the Angels and never hit another home run.

APRIL 12   Tim Salmon scores a team record five runs during a 12–1 trouncing of the Indians in Cleveland. Salmon walked and later scored in the first, second and fourth innings and homered in the seventh and ninth.

> Salmon hit .300 with 26 homers in 1998.

APRIL 15   The Angels lose 6–3 to the Yankees during an afternoon game at Shea Stadium.

> The Angels were scheduled to play a three-game series at Yankee Stadium on April 13, 14 and 15, but the first two games were postponed after a 500-pound, concrete-and-steel beam fell from beneath the upper deck into the empty seats below. The Angels dressed in the locker room used by the New York Jets when the club played there from 1964 until 1983. The Mets also played at Shea on

April 15 and beat the Cubs 2–1 in a night game. It marked the first time that American and National League games were played in the same ballpark on the same day.

APRIL 16   The Angels play the Tampa Bay Devil Rays for the first time and lose 6–5 at Edison International Field.

APRIL 24   The Angels play in St. Petersburg for the first time and defeat the Devil Rays 10–3.

APRIL 27   Chuck Finley wins his 14th consecutive game, achieved over two seasons, with a 3–1 decision over the Orioles in Baltimore. Finley won his last ten games in 1997 and his first four in 1998. While going 14–0, he had a 2.18 ERA in 124 innings over 17 starts.

MAY 1   Darin Erstad hits a grand slam off Tony Castillo in the sixth inning of a 7–1 victory over the White Sox at Edison International Field.

MAY 21   The Angels score eight runs in the seventh inning and wallop the Athletics 12–2 at Edison International Field. Jim Edmonds collected two homers and two singles in five at-bats and drove in five runs.

Edmonds batted .307, scored 115 runs and stroked 25 home runs in 1998.

MAY 25   Garret Anderson hits a grand slam off Tim Belcher in the first inning for a 4–0 lead, but the Angels wind up losing 6–4 to the Royals at Edison International Field.

MAY 31   Trailing 5–0, the Angels score three runs in the fifth inning, two in the sixth and one in the ninth to win 6–5 over the Twins in Minneapolis. The winning run scored on a triple by Jason Baughman and a sacrifice from Gary DiSarcina.

The game was played with a temporary ten-foot foul pole in left field. A violent rainstorm the previous evening snapped the cable connecting the 45-foot foul pole normally in place to the roof, causing the pole to fall over.

JUNE 2   Four bean balls lead to two brawls and 12 ejections, including both managers, during a 7–5 win over the Royals in Kansas City. The problems started in the top of the seventh when Phil Nevin was hit in the back by Royals pitcher Jim Pittsley. Nevin, who was also hit in his previous at-bat by Chris Haney, charged the mound and tried to tackle Pittsley, but the pitcher wrestled Nevin to the ground and threw several jabs. Three more batters were hit during the eighth and ninth innings by three different pitchers, two of them Angels, leading to another bench-clearing incident in which players threw punches indiscriminately. Kansas City shortstop Felix Martinez inflamed the situation by throwing a sucker punch at Frank Bolick. Managers Terry Collins of the Angels and Tony Muser of the Royals were each suspended for eight games as a result of the brawl. Nine players were suspended for from one to four days.

On the same day, the Angels selected pitcher Seth Etherton from USC with their first pick in the amateur draft. Etherton was 9–7 with a 6.30 ERA during his major league career, which lasted from 2000 through 2006. Etherton was the only player drafted and signed by the Angels in 1998 who has reached the big leagues.

JUNE 9	Darin Erstad collects five hits, including a double, in five at-bats to lead the Angels to a 10–8 win over the Diamondbacks in Phoenix. There were two grand slams in the third. Cecil Fielder hit one in the top of the inning off Willie Blair. In the bottom half, Chuck Finley issued three consecutive walks, then surrendered a homer to Yamil Benitez. The victory extended the Angels' winning streak to nine games. It was also the first time that the Angels played the Arizona franchise.
	Erstad had a five-game streak from June 6 through June 11 in which he collected 15 hits in 23 at-bats. Among the 15 hits were two doubles, a triple and two homers.
JUNE 13	The Angels score seven runs in the fifth inning and rout the Rangers 18–6 in Arlington. Gary DiSarcina collected five of Anaheim's 21 hits with two doubles, a triple and two singles in five at-bats. Jim Edmonds had four hits, three of them doubles, in six at-bats and scored four runs.
JUNE 22	After losing all four meetings in 1997, the Angels finally beat the Dodgers in a regular-season game by overcoming a 4–0 deficit to win 6–5 at Edison International Field. The winning run scored in the ninth inning when Tim Salmon drew a bases-loaded walk from Jim Bruske.
	The Dodgers and Angels met on four consecutive days from June 22 through June 25, with the first two games in Anaheim and the last two in Los Angeles.
JUNE 30	The Angels defeat the Giants 4–3 at Edison International Field to close the month of June with a 49–32 record and a 3½-game lead in the AL West.
JULY 23	The Angels score three runs in the ninth inning and one in the tenth to defeat the Twins 6–5 in Minneapolis. Cecil Fielder started the ninth-inning rally with a double and scored on a single by Tim Salmon. After the bases were loaded, Jim Edmonds brought two runs across with a two-out single. Craig Shipley drove in the winning tally with another single in the tenth.
	Shipley played the last of his 11 seasons in the majors with the Angels. When he made his major league debut with the Dodgers in 1986, Shipley was the first native of Australia to appear in a major league game since Joe Quinn in 1901.
JULY 31	Garret Anderson runs his hitting streak to a club-record 28 games during a 7–2 loss to the Red Sox at Edison International Field.
	Anderson broke the record of 25 set by Rod Carew in 1984. During the hitting streak, Anderson collected 47 hits in 116 at-bats, an average of .405.
AUGUST 10	Troy Percival strikes out all three batters he faces in the ninth inning to close out a 6–2 win over the Tigers in Detroit.
AUGUST 12	Playing in his first game with the Angels and his first in the majors since 1995, left fielder Reggie Williams collects three hits in four at-bats during a 3–2 triumph over the Tigers in Detroit.

August 19	Reggie Williams has a hand in both runs of a 2–0 win over the Tigers at Edison International Field. Williams singled and scored in the third inning and drove in a run with a single in the fifth. Jack McDowell (seven innings), Shigetoshi Hasegawa (one inning) and Troy Percival (one inning) combined on the shutout.
August 20	The Angels score six runs in the third inning and clobber the Tigers 13–2 at Edison International Field.
August 28	The Angels trade Doug Nickle to the Phillies for Gregg Jefferies.
September 2	The Angels collect 21 hits and trounce the Indians 13–2 in Cleveland. Randy Velarde had four hits, including a homer and a double, in six at-bats and scored four runs.
September 6	With the runners moving on a 3–2 pitch with two out in the first inning, Garret Anderson drives in three runs with a bases-loaded single to account for all of the runs in a 3–0 win over the Royals at Edison International Field. Chuck Finley (eight innings) and Shigetoshi Hasegawa (one inning) combined on a three-hit shutout.
	The win gave the Angels a 79–64 record and a 3½-game lead over the Rangers in the AL West.
September 9	The day after Mark McGwire hits his 62nd homer of the season, breaking Roger Maris' record, the Angels take a 10–2 lead by scoring nine runs in the third inning, and hang on to defeat the Twins 10–8 at Edison International Field.
September 12	The Orioles score three runs in the ninth inning to defeat the Angels 3–2 in Baltimore. Troy Percival took the mound with a two-run lead, then gave up a single followed by a two-run homer from Mike Bordick. A single, a stolen base and another single from Eric Davis drove in the winning run.
	The Angels had a record of 57–97 during the month of September from 1992 through 1998.
September 17	The Angels drop out of first place with a 7–6 loss to the Rangers in Arlington.
	The Angels moved back into a tie for first with the Rangers on September 20 with a record of 83–72. Next up was a three-game series against Texas at Anaheim Stadium beginning on September 21. The Angels lost all three and were outscored 25–3 by dropping a pair of 9–1 decisions and another of 7–1.
September 24	Gary DiSarcina collects five hits, including two doubles, in five at-bats during a 10–6 triumph over the Athletics in Oakland.
	Steve Sparks was an unexpected find for the Angels in 1998. A knuckleball pitcher, he made his major league debut at the age of 29 with the Brewers in 1995, after missing much of the 1994 season after he tore up his shoulder while demonstrating to teammates how he could tear a phone book in half. Sparks was acquired by the Angels at the end of the 1996 campaign, then missed all of 1997 after undergoing Tommy John Surgery. He was called up from the minors by the Angels in June 1998 despite going a combined 0–8 at Class AA Midland and

Class AAA Vancouver. Sparks won his first three decisions as an Angel and finished the campaign 9–4. He slipped to 5–11 in 1999, however, his last season with the club.

OCTOBER 2   Gene Autry, owner of the Angels since their inception in December 1960, dies at the age of 91. With Autry's passing, the Disney Corporation took control of 100 percent of the stock in the franchise.

DECEMBER 11   The Angels sign Mo Vaughn, most recently with the Red Sox, as a free agent.

Vaughn was the biggest prize on the free agent market during the 1998–99 offseason. Over the previous six seasons, he averaged 36 homers, 111 RBIs and a .315 batting average. Vaughn was 31 when signed by the Angels and was not only expected to lead the batting attack, but the clubhouse as well. He gave the club two decent seasons in 1999 and 2000 with a combined 69 homers and 225 runs batted in, but his batting average (.276), on-base percentage (.362) and slugging percentage (.503) were well short of the numbers he posted in Boston. Part of the problem was an injured ankle that never healed properly. In the first inning of his very first regular season with the Angels, on April 6, 1999, Vaughn tumbled down the dugout steps chasing a foul fly and suffered a severe sprain. Vaughn missed the entire 2001 season because of a ruptured left bicep and was traded to the Mets in December 2001.

DECEMBER 23   The Angels sign Tim Belcher, most recently with the Royals, as a free agent.

DECEMBER 28   Gregg Jefferies signs with the Tigers as a free agent.

1999

Season in a Sentence
Expected to contend for a pennant, Terry Collins resigns as manager with the club holding a 51–82 record, leading to the offseason hiring of Mike Scioscia.

Finish • Won • Lost • Pct • GB
Fourth   70   92   .432   25.0

In the wild-card race, the Angels finished in seventh place, 24 games behind.

Managers
Terry Collins (51–82) and Joe Maddon (19–10)

Stats	Angels	AL	Rank
Batting Avg:	.256	.275	14
On-Base Pct:	.319	.347	13
Slugging Pct:	.395	.439	13
Home Runs:	158		11
Stolen Bases:	71		12
ERA:	4.79	4.86	5
Errors:	106		3 (tie)
Runs Scored:	711		13
Runs Allowed:	826		4

Starting Lineup
Matt Walbeck, c
Darin Erstad, 1b-lf
Randy Velarde, 2b
Troy Glaus, 3b
Gary DiSarcina, ss
Orlando Palmeiro, lf-rf
Garret Anderson, cf
Tim Salmon, rf
Mo Vaughn, dh-1b
Todd Greene, dh
Andy Sheets, ss
Jeff Huson, 2b
Jim Edmonds, cf

Pitchers
Chuck Finley, sp
Omar Olivares, sp
Tim Belcher, sp
Steve Sparks, sp
Ken Hill, sp
Troy Percival, rp
Mark Petkovsek, rp
Shigetoshi Hasegawa, rp
Mark Magnante, rp
Alan Levine, rp

Attendance
2,253,123 (seventh in AL)

Club Leaders
Batting Avg:	Garret Anderson	.303
On-Base Pct:	Mo Vaughn	.358
Slugging Pct:	Mo Vaughn	.508
Home Runs:	Mo Vaughn	33
RBI:	Mo Vaughn	108
Runs:	Garret Anderson	88
Stolen Bases:	Darin Erstad	13
	Randy Velarde	13
Wins:	Chuck Finley	12
Strikeouts:	Chuck Finley	200
ERA:	Chuck Finley	4.43
Saves:	Troy Percival	31

FEBRUARY 21   Nine days after President Bill Clinton is acquitted following an impeachment trial, Gary DiSarcina walks into the backswing of coach George Hendrick, who was hitting fungoes, and breaks his left forearm. The mishap occurred on the first day of spring training. DiSarcina was out of action until June.

MARCH 29   The Angels trade Phil Nevin and Keith Volkman to the Padres for Andy Sheets and Gus Kennedy.

MARCH 30   The Angels trade Dave Hollins to the Blue Jays for Tomas Perez.

APRIL 6   The Angels open the season with a 6–5 win over the Indians before 39,936 at Edison International Field. The Angels took a 3–2 lead in the fourth inning when Tim Salmon and Garret Anderson hit home runs on consecutive pitches from Jaret Wright. Cleveland surged back ahead, but Anaheim won the contest with two runs in the seventh and one in the eighth. Troy Glaus drove in the winning run with a double.

Rex Hudler began the broadcasting phase of his career in 1999 as a TV analyst alongside Steve Physioc. Hudler was already a fan favorite in Anaheim because of his role as the club's ever-hustling utility player from 1994 through 1996. His 13-year big-league career ended with the Phillies in 1998.

APRIL 9 — Orlando Palmeiro leads off the first inning of an 8–4 win over the Rangers in Arlington with a home run. The homer was the only one Palmeiro hit during his first six years in the majors, which spanned 966 at-bats from 1995 through 2000.

APRIL 10 — The Angels score in seven of their nine turns at-bat and defeat the Rangers 10–0 in Arlington.

APRIL 12 — The Angels collect 20 hits, including a club-record ten doubles, during a 13–5 win over the Rangers in Arlington. Troy Glaus contributed three doubles, Tim Salmon two, and Randy Velarde, Darin Erstad, Garret Anderson, Todd Greene and Andy Sheets contributed one each. Salmon had four hits in all and drove in five runs.

APRIL 15 — Tim Salmon drives in six runs with two homers and a double during a 12–1 win over the Athletics in Oakland. One of the home runs was a grand slam off Kevin Jarvis in the sixth inning.

APRIL 16 — Todd Greene hits a grand slam off Jamie Moyer in the sixth inning of a 9–5 victory over the Mariners at Edison International Field.

APRIL 26 — Darin Erstad hits a walk-off homer in the 11th inning to defeat the Blue Jays 4–3 at Edison International Field.

APRIL 28 — The Angels escape with a 12–10 win over the Blue Jays at Edison International Field. The Angels took a 10–0 lead in the fourth inning only to watch Toronto score ten answered runs to tie the contest 10–10. Anaheim won with two tallies in the eighth on a home run by Mo Vaughn.

APRIL 29 — Andy Sheets hits a grand slam off Roy Halladay in the first inning of a 17–1 drubbing of the Blue Jays at Edison International Field. The Angels scored seven runs in the first and five in the third to take a 12–0 lead.

MAY 12 — Chuck Finley (eight innings) and Troy Percival (one inning) combine on a three-hitter to beat the Yankees 1–0 in New York. Finley recorded four strikeouts in the third inning. The feat was made possible when Derek Jeter swung and missed on a two-strike pitch that sailed past catcher Charlie O'Brien. Finley also fanned Scott Brosius, Chuck Knoblauch and Paul O'Neill in the third. Andy Sheets drove in the lone run with a double off David Cone in the seventh inning.

Finley was the first Angels pitcher to strike out four batters in an inning since Ryne Duren in 1961. Finley struck out four in an inning again three months later on August 15.

MAY 14 — Mo Vaughn drives in six runs with a grand slam and a two-run single during an 8–3 win over the Devil Rays at Edison International Field. The slam was struck off Bobby Witt in the sixth inning.

May 19	Andy Sheets hits a two-run double with two out in the ninth inning to down the Orioles 5–4 in Baltimore.
May 22	Unable to control his knuckleball, Steve Sparks walks six batters and hits four, including three in a row, but the Angels emerge with an 8–6 victory over the Devil Rays in St. Petersburg. He hit Jose Canseco with a pitch in the first inning. In the fourth, Sparks put two runners on base, then plunked Paul Sorrento, Miguel Cairo and Kevin Stocker to force in two runs. Sparks hit the three batters in a span of just four pitches.
May 23	After being held to just one hit through the first nine innings by Ryan Rupe, the Angels erupt for four runs in the tenth off reliever Roberto Hernandez to defeat the Devil Rays 4–0 in St. Petersburg. Rupe had a no-hitter in progress until Darin Erstad singled leading off the seventh. Chuck Finley (nine innings) and Troy Percival (one inning) combined on a three-hit shutout.
June 2	With their first pick in the amateur draft, the Angels select pitcher John Lackey from Grayson County Junior College in Texas. The club lost its first round choice to the Red Sox as compensation for signing Mo Vaughn.
	Lackey moved into the Angels' starting rotation in 2002 and has become one of the best pitchers ever drafted by the franchise. Other future major leaguers drafted and signed by the Angels in 1999 have been Dusty Bergman (sixth round), Robb Quinlan (tenth round), Alfredo Amazaga (13th round), Gary Johnson (19th round) and Tom Gregorio (27th round).
June 5	Matt Walbeck hits a grand slam off Chan Ho Park in the fourth inning for a 4–0 lead, but the Angels lose 7–4 to the Dodgers in Los Angeles. Devon White put the Dodgers into the lead with a grand slam off Tim Belcher in the sixth.
	A fight broke out in the bottom of the fifth shortly after Walbeck's slam. Dodgers pitcher Chan Ho Park bunted up the first base line and was tagged hard in the chest by Belcher. Park took a few steps back and karate-kicked Belcher in the midsection. Belcher proceeded to throw Park to the ground and pummel him.
June 11	The Angels play the Diamondbacks for the first time at Edison International Field and lose 12–2.
June 13	Playing in his first major league game, Angels left fielder Mike Colangelo collides with center fielder Reggie Williams while chasing a fly ball in the seventh inning of a 13-inning, 3–1 loss to the Diamondbacks at Edison International Field. Omar Olivares had an odd stat line. He hit four batters with pitches and threw four wild pitches, but walked only one in $8^{1}/_{3}$ innings.
	Colangelo suffered a torn ligament in his thumb and never played in another game for the Angels. He didn't play in another contest in the majors until 2001 when he was a member of the Padres.
June 24	Two players whose last name begin with the letter "V" have big days during a 12–7 triumph over the Mariners in Seattle. Mo Vaughn collected five hits on two homers,

a double and two singles in six at-bats and drove in six runs. Randy Velarde also had five hits, including a homer, in six at-bats. Velarde batted second in the lineup and Vaughn third. The Angels trailed 7–3 before scoring six runs in the eighth inning and three in the ninth. It was also the last time that the Angels played at the Kingdome.

JUNE 26   Tim Belcher breaks the little finger of his left hand while making a tag at home plate in the fourth inning of a 5–4 win over the Athletics at Edison International Field. Belcher tagged Ryan Christenson, who was caught in a rundown. Belcher was out of commission for six weeks.

JULY 15   A double by Randy Velarde and a single from Mo Vaughn in the tenth inning beat the Dodgers 7–6 at Edison International Field.

The victory gave the Angels a 41–45 record. The following day, the club started an 11-game losing streak. From July 16 through September 2, the Angels lost 37 of 47 games, leading to the resignation of Terry Collins.

JULY 20   Batting leadoff, Darin Erstad hits the first pitch of the first inning from Andy Ashby for a home run, but the Angels don't score again and lose 2–1 to the Padres at Edison International Field.

JULY 25   Albert Belle hits three homers to lead the Orioles to an 11-inning, 8–7 win over the Angels in Baltimore. Belle's third homer was struck off Troy Percival with two out in the ninth inning and tied the score 7–7.

JULY 27   The Angels end an 11-game losing streak with a 10–5 victory over the Devil Rays in St. Petersburg.

JULY 29   The Angels trade Omar Olivares and Randy Velarde to the Athletics for Jeff DaVanon, Nathan Haynes and Elvin Nina.

AUGUST 1   Steve Sparks (eight innings) and Troy Percival (one inning) combine on a two-hitter to defeat the Twins 2–1 at Edison International Field. Sparks had a no-hitter in progress until Terry Steinbach led off the seventh with a single. Chad Allen also singled in the eighth.

AUGUST 15   Chuck Finley strikes out 12 batters in $6^{2/3}$ innings, and the Angels defeat the Tigers 10–2 in Detroit. Finley recorded four strike outs in the first inning, setting down Deivi Cruz, Juan Encarnacion, Dean Palmer and Tony Clark in order. Palmer reached base by swinging and missing on a two-strike pitch, which sailed past catcher Bengie Molina. It was also the Angels last game at Tiger Stadium.

Molina played in his first season with the Angels in 1998 and was the starting catcher from 2000 through 2005. Jose Molina, Bengie's younger brother by $10^{1/2}$ months, was the Angels backup catcher from 2001 through 2004. A third Molina, Yadier, was nine years younger than Bengie and broke in as a catcher with the Cardinals in 2004. All three were still active in the majors in 2009.

AUGUST 31   Leading 12–4, the Angels allow ten runs in the eighth inning, which results in an astonishing 14–12 loss to the Indians in Cleveland. The ten runs were allowed by Mark Petkovsek (five), Shigetoshi Hasegawa (one) and Troy Percival (four) on nine hits (seven singles, a double and a home run), a walk and a hit batsman. The Indians took the lead on a three-run homer by Richie Sexson. After Sexson's home run, Percival hit David Justice with a pitch. Justice charged the mound and hurled his helmet at Percival, sparking a brawl in which the Angels pitcher suffered a cut and a bruise under his right eye.

SEPTEMBER 3   With tears in his eyes, Terry Collins announces his resignation as manager of the Angels at a press conference with the club holding a record of 51–82. Three months earlier the front office gave Collins a two-year contract extension. Coach Joe Maddon served as interim manager for the remainder of the season and guided the club to a 19–10 mark.

SEPTEMBER 7   The Angels score six runs in both the fourth and eighth innings and trounce the White Sox 14–1 at Edison International Field.

SEPTEMBER 11   Eric Milton of the Twins pitches a no-hitter to defeat the Angels 7–0 in Minneapolis. Milton struck out 13 and walked two. The last out was recorded on a swinging strikeout by Jeff DaVanon.

> *There were many unusual aspects to the no-hitter. First of all, the game started at 11:05 a.m. to allow sufficient time for a college football game that evening hosted by the University of Minnesota against Louisiana-Monroe. The Twins allowed anyone wearing pajamas to be admitted free of charge. The official attendance was 11,222. Interim manager Joe Maddon also rested many of his regulars, including Mo Vaughn, Gary DiSarcina, Garret Anderson, Jim Edmonds, Tim Salmon and Darin Erstad, because the Angels played the previous evening.*

SEPTEMBER 14   Trailing 6–1 at the end of the sixth inning, the Angels score two runs in the seventh, two in the eighth and three in the ninth to win 8–6 in the first game of a double-header in Kansas City. Tim Salmon supplied a three-run homer in the ninth to put the Angels into the lead. The Angels came from behind again in the second tilt with two runs in the ninth to win 6–5. Darin Erstad drove in the go-ahead run with a single.

SEPTEMBER 15   A home run by Darin Erstad off Lance Carter with two out in the ninth inning beats the Royals 1–0 in Kansas City. It was the third game in two days in which the Angels won in the ninth, and the second contest in succession in which Erstad delivered the game-winning RBI. Chuck Finley (eight innings) and Troy Percival (one inning) combined on the shutout.

SEPTEMBER 21   In the ninth inning at Edison International Field, Troy Percival strikes out Jose Canseco, Fred McGriff and Herbert Perry, all on called third strikes, to close out a 7–5 win over the Devil Rays.

SEPTEMBER 24   The Angels play at Safeco Field in Seattle for the first time and lose 4–3 in ten innings to the Mariners.

OCTOBER 1   Jeff DaVanon hits a walk-off homer in the ninth inning to beat the Rangers 7–6 at Edison International Field. The homer was also DaVanon's first in the majors.

> *On the same day, Bill Bavasi resigned as general manager of the Angels. He had been the general manager since 1994.*

October 2   The Angels score seven runs in the seventh inning and rout the Rangers 15–3 at Edison International Field. Tim Salmon had a big day with two homers, a double and a single in five at-bats along with five RBIs and four runs scored.

October 3   In the last game of the season, the Angels edge the Rangers 1–0 at Edison International Field. The lone run scored on a home run by Tim Salmon off Mike Morgan in the seventh inning. Jarrod Washburn (8 2/3 innings) and Lou Pote (one-third of an inning) combined on the shutout.

November 1   The Angels announce the hiring of 55-year-old Bill Stoneman as general manager.

Stoneman was a pitcher in the majors from 1967 through 1974 and posted a record of 54–85 with the Cubs, Expos and Angels. He was 1–8 as an Angel in 1974. Stoneman had been the Expos vice president for baseball operations since 1983 when hired by the Angels. He helped transform the Angels into perennial contenders during his eight years as general manager of the franchise. Stoneman hired Mike Scioscia as manager and put together the club that won the World Series in 2002. Many argued that Stoneman was too cautious, and there were few bold moves during his tenure, but he was the most successful general manager in franchise history before exiting the job in 2007.

November 17   The Angels hire 40-year-old Mike Scioscia as manager.

Scioscia was well known in Southern California because of his role as a catcher with the Dodgers from 1980 through 1992. His only previous managing experience was one season at Class AAA Albuquerque in 1999, guiding the club to a record of 65–74. Scioscia was the Dodgers bench coach in 1997 and 1998. He became the most successful manager in Angels history with a world championship in 2002 and six consecutive winning seasons beginning in 2004.

December 16   Chuck Finley signs a contract as a free agent with the Indians.

Finley spent 14 seasons with the Angels. After leaving Anaheim, he spent three more years in the majors with the Indians and Cardinals and posted records of 16–11, 8–7 and 11–15.

THE STATE OF THE ANGELS

The Angels posted losing records during the decades of the 1960s, 1970s and 1990s and were exactly at .500 (783–783) during the 1980s. The club not only had a winning record during the 2000s for the first time but achieved several other franchise firsts including the American League pennant (2002), world championship (also in 2002) and 100-win season (2008). Prior to the 2005 season, the Angels had back-to-back winning seasons only three times (1978–79, 1985–86 and 1997–98) and never three in a row. The 2009 season was the sixth winning season in succession. The Angels made the postseason as a wild card in 2002 and won the AL West in 2004, 2005, 2007, 2008 and 2009. Overall, the Angels were 900–720, a winning percentage .556, which was the third best in the AL, trailing only the Yankees and Red Sox. AL champs were the Yankees (2000, 2001, 2003 and 2009), Angels (2002), Red Sox (2004 and 2007), White Sox (2005), Tigers (2006) and Rays (2008). AL West champs outside of Anaheim were the Athletics (2000, 2002, 2003 and 2007) and Mariners (2001).

THE BEST TEAM

The 2002 world champions have to be ranked number one. The club was 99–63 and won the wild card during the regular season, then dispatched the Yankees, Twins and Giants in the postseason. The 2008 team posted a franchise-best 100–62 record and had the best record in the American League, but lost the Division Series to the Red Sox.

THE WORST TEAM

The only teams with losing records during the decade were in 2001 and 2003. The 2001 squad was worse than the 2003 squad with a record of 75–87.

THE BEST MOMENT

In the 42nd season of the franchise's history, the Angels reached the World Series in 2002 for the first time and beat the Giants in seven games.

THE WORST MOMENT

The Angels suffered through the death of another young player on April 9, 2009 when Nick Adenhart was killed in an auto accident.

THE ALL-DECADE TEAM • YEARS W/ANGELS

Player	Years
Bengie Molina, c	1998–2004
Darin Erstad, 1b	1996–2006
Adam Kennedy, 2b	2000–06
Chone Figgins, 3b	2002–09
Orlando Cabrera, ss	2005–07
Garret Anderson, lf	1994–2008
Torii Hunter, cf	2008–09
Tim Salmon, rf	1992–2006
Vladimir Guerrero, dh	2004–09
John Lackey, p	2002–09
Jerrod Washburn, p	1998–2004
Jered Weaver, p	2006–09
Francisco Rodriguez, p	2002–09

Guerrero was a regular as a designated hitter only in 2009 after playing mostly in right field from 2004 through 2008. He is listed here as the DH because of a lack of viable alternatives. No one has played 100 or more games at designated hitter in consecutive season for the Angels since Chili Davis did it four years in a row from 1993 through 1996. First base was likewise a problem in Anaheim for most of the 2000s. Erstad, Salmon and Anderson were also on the 1990s All-Decade Team. Other prominent Angels during the decade included third baseman Troy Glaus (1998–2004), shortstop David Eckstein (2001–04) and pitchers Joe Saunders (2005–09) and Erwin Santana (2005–09). Glaus was the MVP in the 2002 World Series.

THE DECADE LEADERS

Batting Avg:	Vladimir Guerrero	.319
On-Base Pct:	Vladimir Guerrero	.381
Slugging Pct:	Vladimir Guerrero	.546
Home Runs:	Vladimir Guerrero	173
RBI:	Vladimir Guerrero	616
Runs:	Chone Figgins	596
Stolen Bases:	Chone Figgins	280
Wins:	John Lackey	102
Strikeouts:	John Lackey	1,201
ERA:	Kelvim Escobar	3.60
Saves:	Francisco Rodriguez	208

THE HOME FIELD

There were few major modifications to the Angels home field during the decade other than a name change from Edison International Field to Angel Stadium of Anaheim on December 29, 2003. The Angels passed the three million mark in attendance for the first time in 2003. The 2009 season was the seventh in a row in which the club drew three million or more.

THE GAME YOU WISHED YOU HAD SEEN

The Angels seemed to be on the brink of elimination in game six of the 2002 World Series, played in Anaheim on October 26. Trailing the Giants 5–0, the Angels rallied with three runs in the seventh inning and three in the eighth to win 6–5.

THE WAY THE GAME WAS PLAYED

The offensive explosion of the 1990s continued into the 2000s, as did the trend toward baseball-only ballparks with grass fields. About mid-decade, allegations of the use of performance-enhancing drugs became a hot topic, and Major League Baseball instituted much harsher penalties for players caught using the substances. The disparity in payroll and success on the field between the large- and small-market clubs continued to increase.

THE MANAGEMENT

Arte Moreno purchased the Angels from the Disney Corporation in 2003. General managers were Bill Stoneman (1999–2007) and Tony Reagins (2007–present). Mike Scioscia managed the club on the field during the entire decade.

THE BEST PLAYER MOVE

The best player move was the acquisition of Chone Figgins from the Rockies for Kimera Bartee in July 2001.

THE WORST PLAYER MOVE

The worst move was trading Jim Edmonds to the Cardinals for Kent Bottenfield and Adam Kennedy in March 2000.

2000

Season in a Sentence

In his first season as manager, Mike Scioscia brings the Angels back above .500 with a vastly improved offense.

Finish • Won • Lost • Pct • GB

Third 82 80 .506 9.5

In the wild-card race, the Angels finished in sixth place, nine games behind.

Manager

Mike Scioscia

Stats

Stats	Angels	AL	Rank
Batting Avg:	.280	.276	5
On-Base Pct:	.352	.349	6
Slugging Pct:	.472	.443	1
Home Runs:	236		3
Stolen Bases:	93		7
ERA:	5.00	4.91	9
Errors:	134		12 (tie)
Runs Scored:	864		6
Runs Allowed:	869		9

Starting Lineup

Bengie Molina, c
Mo Vaughn, 1b
Adam Kennedy, 2b
Troy Glaus, 3b
Benji Gil, ss
Darin Erstad, lf
Garret Anderson, cf
Tim Salmon, rf
Scott Spezio, dh-1b
Orlando Palmeiro, lf-rf
Kevin Stocker, ss

Pitchers

Scott Schoeneweis, sp
Ramon Ortiz, sp
Kent Bottenfield, sp
Jarrod Washburn, sp
Troy Percival, rp
Shigetoshi Hasegawa, rp
Mark Petkovsek, rp
Mike Holtz, rp
Alan Levine, rp

Attendance

2,066,977 (eighth in AL)

Club Leaders

Batting Avg:	Darin Erstad	.355
On-Base Pct:	Darin Erstad	.409
Slugging Pct:	Troy Glaus	.604
Home Runs:	Troy Glaus	47
RBI:	Garret Anderson	117
	Mo Vaughn	117
Runs:	Darin Erstad	121
Stolen Bases:	Darin Erstad	28
Wins:	Shigetoshi Hasegawa	10
Strikeouts:	Scott Schoeneweis	78
ERA:	Scott Schoeneweis	5.45
Saves:	Troy Percival	32

JANUARY 11 — Ten days after the dawn of the new millennium and the end of worries about the Y2K problem, the Angels sign Scott Spezio, most recently with the Athletics, as a free agent.

JANUARY 26 — The Angels sign Kent Mercker, most recently with the Red Sox, as a free agent.

MARCH 23 — The Angels trade Jim Edmonds to the Cardinals for Adam Kennedy and Kent Bottenfield.

> Edmonds had been the Angels starting center fielder since 1995 and played well when in the lineup, but was often injured. In 1999, he was limited to 55 games after he tore up his shoulder while weight lifting. Edmonds also drew criticism for appearing unmotivated, and his poor body language and occasional lackadaisical effort irritated management. Teammates questioned his desire and willingness to play hard. Edmonds turned 30 during the 2000 season and gave the Cardinals 42 homers, 108 RBIs and a .295 batting average. He continued his high level of play, both offensively and defensively for six years and averaged 35 homers, 98 runs batted in and a .292 average from 2000 through 2005.

Edmonds played in the All-Star Game in 2000, 2003 and 2005, and in the World Series in 2004 and 2006. Kennedy was the Angels starting second baseman for seven years, but couldn't compensate for the loss of Edmonds, in what has become one of the worst trades in franchise history.

APRIL 3   The Angels open the season with a 3–2 loss to the Yankees before 42,704 at Edison International Field. Tim Salmon homered in the second inning. Ken Hill was the starting and losing pitcher.

APRIL 5   Darin Erstad collects four hits, including two doubles and a homer, and drives in five runs in five at-bats to lead the Angels to a 12–6 victory over the Yankees at Edison International Field.

Erstad had one of the greatest offensive seasons in Angels history in 2000. He had slumped badly throughout the 1999 season, with a .253 batting average and 13 home runs in 142 games. A year later, Erstad led the American League in hits with 240 and batted .355 along with 121 runs, 39 doubles, 25 homers, 100 RBIs and .541 slugging percentage. Each of the 100 runs were driven in while batting in the leadoff spot in the batting order. The only other players with 240 or more hits in a season since 1930 are Wade Boggs (240 in 1985) and Ichiro Suzuki (242 in 2001 and 262 in 2004). Erstad turned 26 in 2000 and looked like a coming superstar, but his batting average fell to .258 and his slugging percentage plummeted to .360 in 2001 as his magical season proved to be a fluke. His batting averages from 1999 through 2001 were .253, .355 and .258, and his slugging percentages were .374, .541, .360. Erstad never again came close to his 2000 numbers. In no other season has he batted higher than .295, scored over 100 runs or collected more than 177 hits in becoming one of the game's great one-year wonders.

Darin Erstad produced a career year in 2000, batting .355 with a league-leading 240 hits while also winning a Gold Glove for his defense.

APRIL 11	Troy Percival strikes out all three batters he faces in the ninth inning to close out a 5–4 victory over the Blue Jays at Edison International Field.
APRIL 18	Adam Kennedy drives in eight runs during a 16–10 win over the Blue Jays at SkyDome. Kennedy hit a grand slam off Frank Castillo in the fourth inning, then added a bases-loaded triple in the fifth and a run-scoring single in the ninth. The Angels scored five runs in the top of the ninth to take a 16–4 lead, then survived a six-run Blue Jays rally in the bottom half. Both benches emptied in the ninth when Toronto reliever John Frascatore hit Scott Spezio with a pitch.
	Daron Sutton, the son of former Hall of Fame pitcher Don Sutton, worked in the Angels radio booth in 2000 and 2001.
APRIL 20	Trailing 11–1, the Angels score eight runs in the sixth inning, but are unable to sustain the momentum and lose 12–11 to the Blue Jays in Toronto.
APRIL 21	The Angels use six homers to defeat the Devil Rays 9–6 in St. Petersburg. Mo Vaughn, Tim Salmon and Troy Glaus each hit two homers, and the feat was accomplished in two innings. All three homered in the fourth off Dwight Gooden. Vaughn and Salmon homered on consecutive pitches, and Glaus' blast followed a walk to Garret Anderson. The drive lodged in a catwalk that helps support the roof of Tropicana Field. The score was 6–6 in the ninth with Robert Hernandez on the mound for Tampa Bay when Vaughn and Salmon again hit back-to-back homers. After Anderson struck out, Glaus hit his second home run.
	The Angels hit a club record 236 home runs in 2000, breaking the previous standard of 192 in 1996. Troy Glaus led the way with an individual club record of 47. Prior to 2000, the club standard was 39 homers by Reggie Jackson in 1982. Glaus also batted .284, scored 120 runs and drove in 100. Mo Vaughn hit 36 home runs, Garret Anderson 35, Tim Salmon 34, Darin Erstad 25, Scott Spezio 17 and Bengie Molina 14. In addition, the Angels scored 864 runs in 2000, which is also a franchise record.
APRIL 29	Tim Salmon hits a walk-off homer in the 13th inning to defeat the Devil Rays 7–6 at Edison International Field.
MAY 8	Mo Vaughn hits two homers and drives in five runs as the Angels overcome an 8–4, fourth-inning deficit to win 9–8 over the Athletics at Edison International Field. Vaughn's three-run homer in the sixth put the Angels into the lead.
MAY 12	Bengie Molina collects two homers, a double and a single and scores four runs in five at-bats, but the Angels lose 12–11 to the Rangers at Edison International Field. Over 14 games from May 12 through June 2, Molina collected 30 hits in 58 at-bats for a batting average of .517.
	On the same day, Angels pitcher Kent Mercker was hospitalized for bleeding in his brain. He had left the game the night earlier complaining of headaches and dizziness. Mercker was released from the hospital two days later and was playing again in August.
MAY 14	With one out in the ninth inning, Troy Glaus and Scott Spezio hit back-to-back homers in the ninth inning to down the Rangers 7–6 at Edison International Field.

May 21	Garret Anderson hits a grand slam off Chris Fussell in the third inning, but the Angels lose 10–6 to the Royals at Edison International Field.
May 24	Troy Glaus homers in the tenth inning to defeat the Twins 7–6 in Minneapolis. Mo Vaughn collected five hits, including two doubles, in five at-bats.
May 28	The Angels club four home runs, including three in a row, in the fifth inning of an 8–4 win over the Royals in Kansas City. Darin Erstad hit the first of the quartet of homers with a three-run blast. After Adam Kennedy flied out, Mo Vaughn, Tim Salmon and Garret Anderson hit back-to-back-to-back home runs.
May 29	Troy Glaus hits a home run in the tenth inning to defeat the Indians 3–2 in Cleveland. It was his second game-winning, tenth-inning homer in six days.
June 5	With two picks in the first round of the amateur draft, the Angels select pitcher Joe Torres from Gateway High School in Kissimmee, Florida, and pitcher Chris Bootcheck from Auburn University.
	Torres never reached the majors and Bootcheck has yet to come close to reaching his potential. Other future major leaguers drafted and signed by the Angels in 2000 have been Tommy Murphy (third round), Bobby Jenks (fifth round), Mike Hensley (tenth round) and Mike Napoli (17th round).
June 6	The Angels score two runs in the ninth inning to defeat the Giants 6–5 at Edison International Field. The pair of ninth-inning runs were driven in on singles by Darin Erstad and Mo Vaughn. Barry Bonds hit a 493-foot homer to right field in the third.
	In the seventh inning with the Angels trailing 4–1, the Rally Monkey made its first appearance. Video board operators Dean Fraulino and Jaysen Humes took a clip of a monkey jumping around from the 1994 Jim Carrey movie Ace Ventura: Pet Detective, *and superimposed the words "Rally Monkey" above it. The video clip became so popular that the club hired Katie, a white-haired capuchin monkey, to star in original clips for later games.*
June 7	Darin Erstad hits two homers and drives in five runs to lead the Angels to a 10–9 triumph over the Giants at Edison International Field.
June 20	Tim Salmon hits a grand slam off Jeff Suppan in the third inning, but the Angels lose 8–6 to the Royals at Edison International Field.
June 24	Garret Anderson, Troy Glaus and Scott Spezio hit three consecutive home runs off Eric Milton in the second inning against the Twins at Edison International Field, but the Angels lose 11–5.
June 25	Darin Erstad hits a home run at both ends of an 11-inning, 7–6 win over the Twins at Edison International Field. Erstad hit a homer leading off the first inning, then added a wall-off blast in the 11th.
July 7	Bengie Molina hits a grand slam off Scott Karl in the fifth inning of a 12–4 win over the Rockies at Anaheim Stadium.

July 18	Troy Glaus triples in the 11th inning and scores on a wild pitch by Trevor Hoffman to defeat the Padres 3–2 in San Diego. The Padres tied the score 2–2 in the ninth when Ruben Rivera hit an inside-the-park homer off Troy Percival on a two-out, two-strike pitch.
July 21	Orlando Palmeiro reaches base five times in five plate appearances on four singles and a walk and scores four runs during a 12–3 victory over the Athletics in Oakland.
July 24	The Angels score three runs in the ninth inning and one in the 12th to down the Rangers 6–5 in Arlington. With two out in the ninth, a runner on first base and the Angels trailing 5–2, Bengie Molina doubled in a run and scored on a homer by Scott Spezio. In the 12th, Tim Salmon singled in the winning run. Darin Erstad tied a major league record for most putouts by a left fielder in a game with 12.
July 28	Trailing 7–3, the Angels erupt for seven runs in the sixth inning to defeat the White Sox 10–7 at Edison International Field. Mo Vaughn broke the 7–7 deadlock with a three-run homer.
July 29	The Angels trade Kent Bottenfield to the Phillies for Ron Gant.
July 31	Trailing 4–1, the Angels explode for four runs in the ninth inning to stun the Tigers 5–4 at Edison International Field. Tim Salmon led off the ninth with a home run. After two walks and two outs, Scott Spezio delivered a three-run, walk-off homer.
August 12	Troy Glaus collects two homers and a double and drives in five runs to lead the Angels to a 9–6 triumph over the Yankees at Edison International Field. Troy's first homer was a grand slam off Denny Neagle in the second inning.
August 16	The Angels purchase David Eckstein from the Red Sox organization.

Eckstein was a second baseman as a minor leaguer in the Red Sox system and was purchased by the Angels with the idea that he might be a useful utility infielder. A 26-year-old rookie in 2001, he won the Angels starting shortstop job and exceeded all expectations. Generously listed at five-foot-eight and with few appreciable baseball skills, Eckstein became a fan favorite with his heart and determination and was a key contributor to the 2002 world championship team.

August 18	The Angels shock the Yankees by scoring five runs in the ninth inning and one in the 11th to win 9–8 in New York. The first run of the stirring ninth-inning rally crossed the plate on a ground out by Darin Erstad. At that point, the Angels trailed 8–4 with two out and a runner on second base. Orlando Palmeiro doubled in a run to narrow the gap to 8–5, and two pitches later, Mo Vaughn walloped a three-run homer off Mariano Rivera. In the tenth, the Yankees put runners on first and second with two out, but Erstad ended the inning by making a diving catch in center field. Erstad then broke the 8–8 tie with a home run in the 11th.

During July and August, Shigetoshi Hasegawa pitched 34 1/3 innings and allowed only one run, and that one was unearned. He made 66 appearances, all in relief, during the 2000 season, pitched 95 2/3 innings and had an ERA 3.48. With a 10–5 record, Hasegawa led the Angels in victories. No starter won more than eight games, and Scott Schoeneweis led the club in innings with 170. He was also the only individual with more than 127⅔ innings pitched. In all, the Angels used 16 different pitchers in a starting role.

SEPTEMBER 1   Mo Vaughn hits a grand slam off Lorenzo Barcelo in the fifth inning for an 8–2 lead, but the Angels lose 9–8 in Chicago when the White Sox score a run in the seventh inning and six in the eighth.

SEPTEMBER 3   The Angels lose a 13–12 battle to the White Sox at Comiskey Park. The Angels scored four runs in the first inning, but the Sox bounced back with nine tallies in their half. Starting Ramon Ortiz gave up all nine runs, yielding eight hits and two walks in two-thirds of an inning. The Angels recovered from the opening salvo and took a 12–10 lead, but the White Sox responded once again and won the game with a run in the seventh inning and two in the eighth. The Angels hit five home runs during the contest. Darin Erstad connected for a pair of homers, with Tim Salmon, Troy Glaus and Scott Spezio adding the rest.

The September 1 and September 3 setbacks were part of a six-game losing streak that sent the Angels out of the pennant race. During the six-game streak, the pitching staff surrendered 58 runs. On August 29, the club was 68–64 and four games out of first.

SEPTEMBER 4   The Angels play at Comerica Park in Detroit for the first time, and lose 5–0 to the Tigers.

SEPTEMBER 6   Scott Schoeneweis (eight innings) and Troy Percival (one inning) combine on a two-hitter to edge the Tigers 1–0 at Comerica Park. The only Detroit hits were singles by Brad Ausmus in the third inning and Bobby Higginson in the seventh.

SEPTEMBER 15   The Angels score seven runs in the sixth inning to take a 15–2 lead and wallop the Twins 16–5 in Minneapolis. The Angels collected 21 hits during the game.

SEPTEMBER 23   The Angels trounce the Rangers 15–4 in Arlington. Mike Scioscia tied a major league record by using four pinch runners (Jason Baughman, Scott Spezio, Shawn Wooten and Bengi Gil) in the seventh inning.

SEPTEMBER 24   Mo Vaughn hits a grand slam off Mike Venafro in the eighth inning of a 9–2 victory over the Rangers in Arlington.

SEPTEMBER 28   Troy Glaus leads off the 14th inning with a home run before the Angels add two insurance runs to win 6–3 in Oakland.

SEPTEMBER 30   The Mariners score in eight of nine innings and clobber the Angels 21–9 at Edison International Field.

DECEMBER 7   Jason Dickson signs with the Blue Jays as a free agent.

DECEMBER 10   Ron Gant signs with the Rockies as a free agent.

DECEMBER 11   The day before the Supreme Court declares George Bush the winner in the disputed Presidential election against Al Gore, the Angels sign Pat Rapp, most recently with the Orioles, as a free agent.

2001

Season in a Sentence
The Angels' home run production plummets from 236 in 2000 to 158 in 2001, and the club finishes 41 games out of first.

Finish • Won • Lost • Pct • GB
Third   75   87   .463   41.0

In the wild-card race, the Angels finished in sixth place, 25 games behind.

Manager
Mike Scioscia

Stats
Stats	Angels	AL	Rank
Batting Avg:	.261	.267	11
On-Base Pct:	.327	.334	9
Slugging Pct:	.405	.428	12
Home Runs:	158		10
Stolen Bases:	116		8
ERA:	4.20	4.47	5
Errors:	103		3
Runs Scored:	691		12
Runs Allowed:	730		4

Starting Lineup
Bengie Molina, c
Scott Spezio, 1b
Adam Kennedy, 2b
Troy Glaus, 3b
David Eckstein, ss
Garret Anderson, lf
Darin Erstad, cf
Tim Salmon, rf
Orlando Palmeiro, dh-rf-lf
Benji Gil, ss
Shawn Wooten, c-dh-1b

Pitchers
Ramon Ortiz, sp
Jarrod Washburn, sp
Scott Schoeneweis, sp
Rat Rapp, sp
Ismael Valdez, sp
Troy Percival, rp
Mike Holtz, rp
Alan Levine, rp
Ben Weber, sp
Shigetoshi Hasegawa, rp
Lou Pote, rp

Attendance
2,000,919 (eighth in AL)

Club Leaders
Batting Avg:	Garret Anderson	.289
On-Base Pct:	Troy Glaus	.367
Slugging Pct:	Troy Glaus	.531
Home Runs:	Troy Glaus	41
RBI:	Troy Glaus	108
Runs:	Troy Glaus	100
Stolen Bases:	David Eckstein	29
Wins:	Ramon Ortiz	13
Strikeouts:	Ramon Ortiz	135
ERA:	Jarrod Washburn	3.77
Saves:	Troy Percival	39

JANUARY 4   The Angels sign Ismael Valdez, most recently with the Dodgers, as a free agent.

JANUARY 5   Kent Mercker signs with the Red Sox as a free agent.

JANUARY 16   The Angels sign Jose Canseco, most recently with the Yankees, as a free agent.

The Angels released the controversial Canseco on March 28. He later signed with the White Sox and closed out his career in Chicago by playing 76 games in 2001 with 16 homers and a .258 batting average.

JANUARY 21   In an effort to conserve electricity during California's energy crisis, the Angels turn off Edison Field's "Big A" and "Little A" signs. The landmark beacons had been illuminated 24 hours a day. Under the new guidelines, they were turned on only for stadium events.

JANUARY 25   The Angels sign Wally Joyner, most recently with the Braves, as a free agent.

Joyner was a hero in Anaheim when he played for the Angels from 1986 through 1991, but his return wasn't successful. After batting .243 with three homers in 148 at-bats and 53 games, he retired on June 14, his 39th birthday.

MARCH 28   The Angels trade Darren Blakely to the Yankees for Glenallen Hill.

APRIL 3   The Angels open the season with a 3–2 loss to the Rangers in Arlington. Darin Erstad collected three hits, including two doubles, in four at-bats and drove in both Anaheim runs. Scott Schoeneweis was the starting and losing pitcher. Jarrod Washburn was the scheduled starter, but he was scratched because of strep throat.

APRIL 10   The Angels lose the home opener 7–5 to the Rangers before 42,784 at Edison International Field. Glenallen Hill hit a home run.

APRIL 12   Clutch hitting leads to a 13–3 rout of the Rangers at Edison International Field. The Angels collected six hits in nine at-bats with runners in scoring position and left only three men on base.

APRIL 13   Garret Anderson hits a two-run, walk-off homer in the ninth inning, which defeats the Mariners 4–3 at Edison International Field.

In 2000, Anderson batted .289 with 28 home runs and 123 runs batted in.

MAY 13   The Angels score seven runs in the ninth inning to cap a 14–2 win over the Tigers in Detroit.

Bengie Molina went on the disabled list on May 5 with an injured hamstring. His brother Jose was called up from the minors to replace him. Jose joined his older sibling on the DL on May 21 with a broken thumb.

MAY 23   Scott Schoeneweis allows 12 hits and a club-record 11 runs in four innings of pitching, and the Angels lose 12–5 to the Orioles in Baltimore.

JUNE 5   In the first round of the amateur draft, the Angels select first baseman Casey Kotchman from Seminole Junior College in Florida. Other future major leaguers drafted and signed by the Angels in 2001 have been Jeff Mathis (supplemental first round choice), Dallas McPherson (second round), Jake Woods (third round), Steven Shell (also in the third round), Matthew Brown (tenth round), Ryan Budde (12th round), Mike Gorneault (19th round) and Steve Andrade (32nd round).

JUNE 8   Garret Anderson's homer off Giovanni Carrara in the second inning accounts for the lone run in a 1–0 win over the Dodgers in Los Angeles. Ismael Valdez (6 2/3 innings), Alan Levine (one inning), Mike Holtz (one-third of an inning) and Troy Percival (one inning) combined on the shutout.

JUNE 10   Garret Anderson's homer in the tenth inning beats the Dodgers 6–5 in Los Angeles.

JUNE 12   The Angels play at Pac Bell Park in San Francisco for the first time and lose 3–2 to the Giants.

June 16	Garret Anderson's walk-off single defeats the Dodgers 6–5 at Edison International Field.
June 17	The Angels score four times in the ninth inning to stun the Dodgers 6–4 at Edison International Field. With one out, Darin Erstad hit a two-run double to tie the score. Two pitches later, Troy Glaus clobbered a two-run, walk-off homer. It was the second game in a row won with a walk-off base hit.

Glaus batted only .250 in 2001, but had 40 homers and 108 RBIs and scored an even 100 runs.

June 23	The Angels collect only two hits off Jamie Moyer and Brian Fuentes, but beat the Mariners 2–1 in Seattle. Shawn Wooten singled in a run in the fifth inning, and David Eckstein homered in the sixth.

The Angels used 15 different players as starters at the designated hitter position in 2001. Shawn Wooten and Orlando Palmeiro tied for the team lead in starts at DH with just 25.

June 26	The Rangers erupt for seven runs in the 11th inning off reliever Mark Lukasiewicz to defeat the Angels 8–1 at Edison International Field.
July 7	The Angels hit four homers during a 10–3 win over the Rockies in Denver. Benji Gil walloped two home runs with Jerry DaVanon and Garret Anderson each adding one.
July 8	The Angels homer five times during an 11–3 victory over the Rockies in Denver. Darin Erstad and Scott Spezio each hit two home runs and Garret Anderson one.
July 13	The Angels trade Kimera Bartee to the Rockies for Chone Figgins.

The deal received almost no attention at the time, but it has become one of the best in Angels history. Listed at five-foot-nine and 155 pounds, Figgins didn't make his major league debut until 2002, and he was 27 when he won a job as a regular in the Angels lineup. He's been a fixture ever since, and in 2007 established himself as the club's all-time stolen bases leader, passing previous record-holder Gary Pettis. Following the trade, Bartee played in only 12 big-league games and was hitless in 15 at-bats.

July 17	Trailing 7–2, the Angels score two runs in the seventh inning, three in the eighth, and one in the ninth to defeat the Padres 8–7 at Edison International Field. Benji Gil tied the game 7–7 with a two-run, three-run homer in the eighth. Shawn Wooten forced across the winning run by drawing a walk from Trevor Hoffman with the bases loaded in the ninth.
July 20	The Orioles-Angels game in Baltimore is postponed because of a persistent fire aboard a train that derailed near Camden Yards. The derailment of the 60-car freight train carrying hydrochloric acid and other hazardous chemicals took place on July 18 and also postponed games against the Rangers on that date and on July 19.
July 21	The Angels overcome a disastrous ninth inning to win 6–5 over the Orioles at Camden Yards. The Angels had a 5–2 lead with two out in the ninth and a Baltimore

runner on first base before Troy Percival gave up three runs to tie the score. In the top of the tenth, Scott Spezio tripled with two out and crossed the plate on a Bengie Molina single. In the bottom half, Shigetoshi Hasegawa retired the Orioles in order.

Percival appeared to be the pitcher of record, but wasn't given credit for the victory. The official scorer invoked a little-used rule that says that a victory in such a situation can be withheld from a pitcher if he has been "ineffective" and can be awarded to a succeeding reliever who helps preserve the win. The scorer gave the win to Hasegawa.

JULY 26 Playing the Devil Rays at Edison International Field, the Angels score four runs in the first inning before a batter is retired when David Eckstein walks and Troy Glaus, Darin Erstad and Garret Anderson hit three consecutive homers. The three home runs were struck in a span of five pitches off Ryan Rupe. The Angels went on to win 5–3.

AUGUST 2 The Angels break a 4–4 tie with six runs in the sixth inning and defeat the Red Sox 13–4 in Boston.

The Angels peaked on August 19 with a record of 66–58 and were six games behind in the wild-card race. The Angels went 9–29 the rest of the way, however, and lost 19 of their last 21 games.

AUGUST 22 Benjie Molina collects four hits, including a homer and a double, in four at-bats during a 4–2 win over the Red Sox at Edison International Field.

AUGUST 23 With three singles and a double, Bengie Molina goes four-for-four for the second game in a row. The Angels lost 7–6 to the Red Sox at Edison International Field.

Including a hit in his final at-bat on August 20, a 6–1 loss to the Red Sox in Anaheim, Molina had hits in nine consecutive plate appearances. From August 20 through August 28, he had 14 hits in a span of 18 at-bats—a homer, two doubles and 11 singles.

SEPTEMBER 1 The Angels win an 11–9 battle with the Twins in Minneapolis. The Angels took a 6–2 lead in the third, fell behind 9–8, then won with a run in the eighth and two in the ninth. Troy Glaus broke the 9–9 tie with a double.

SEPTEMBER 11 Two hijacked commercial airliners strike and destroy the twin towers of the World Trade Center in New York in the worst terrorist attack ever perpetrated on American soil. A third hijacked plane destroyed a portion of the Pentagon in Northern Virginia just outside Washington D.C, and a fourth crashed in rural Pennsylvania. Some 3,000 were killed, including about 2,800 at the World Trade Center.

Almost immediately, Commissioner Bud Selig canceled the slate of games scheduled for that day, including the Angels-Mariners match-up at Edison International Field. Later in the week, Selig announced that all games through Sunday, September 16 would be postponed. The contests were made up by extending the regular season by a week. When play resumed, heightened security and an air of patriotism accompanied every game. Fans endured close scrutiny by stadium personnel. "God Bless America" replaced "Take Me Out To The Ball Game" as the song of choice during the seventh-inning stretch.

SEPTEMBER 18	In the first game since the September 11 terrorist attacks, the Angels lose 4–0 to the Mariners in Seattle.
SEPTEMBER 29	Troy Glaus drives in six runs with two homers, a double and a single in five at-bats to lead the Angels to a 13–2 thrashing of the Rangers at Edison International Field.

The victory was the only one achieved by the Angels over the last 14 games of the season.

DECEMBER 26	The Angels sign Aaron Sele, most recently with the Mariners, as a free agent.
DECEMBER 27	The Angels trade Mo Vaughn to the Mets for Kevin Appier.

Vaughn missed the entire 2001 season after surgery to repair a torn biceps tendon in his left arm. He never recovered from his injuries and played only 166 more games after the trade. Appier gave the Angels one solid season and helped the club reach the World Series in 2002.

2002

Season in a Sentence
After a 6–14 start, the Angels win 99 games, reach the postseason as a wild card, dispatch the Yankees and Twins in the playoffs to win the first AL pennant in franchise history, then defeat the Giants in a thrilling seven-game World Series.

Finish • Won • Lost • Pct • GB
Second   99   63   .611   4.0

In the wild-card race, the Angels finished in first place, six games ahead.

AL Division Series
The Angels defeated the New York Yankees three games to one.

AL Championship Series
The Angels defeated the Minnesota Twins four games to one.

World Series
The Angels defeated the San Francisco Giants four games to three.

Manager
Mike Scioscia

Stats

Stats	Angels	AL	Rank
Batting Avg:	.282	.264	1
On-Base Pct:	.341	.331	4
Slugging Pct:	.433	.424	6
Home Runs:	152		10
Stolen Bases:	117		3
ERA:	3.69	4.46	2
Errors:	87		2
Runs Scored:	851		4
Runs Allowed:	644		1

Starting Lineup
Bengie Molina, c
Scott Spezio, 1b
Adam Kennedy, 2b
Troy Glaus, 3b
David Eckstein, ss
Garret Anderson, lf
Darin Erstad, cf
Tim Salmon, rf
Brad Fullmer, dh
Orlando Palmeiro, rf-lf

Pitchers
Jarrod Washburn, sp
Ramon Ortiz, sp
Kevin Appier, sp
Aaron Sele, sp
John Lackey, sp
Troy Percival, rp
Ben Weber, rp
Alan Levine, rp
Brendan Donnelly, rp
Scott Schoeneweis, rp

Attendance
2,305,547 (seventh in AL)

Club Leaders

Batting Avg:	Adam Kennedy	.312
On-Base Pct:	Tim Salmon	.380
Slugging Pct:	Garret Anderson	.539
Home Runs:	Troy Glaus	30
RBI:	Garret Anderson	123
Runs:	David Eckstein	107
Stolen Bases:	Darin Erstad	23
Wins:	Jarrod Washburn	18
Strikeouts:	Ramon Ortiz	162
ERA:	Jarrod Washburn	3.15
Saves:	Troy Percival	40

JANUARY 4   Tony Tavares resigns as president of the Angels. He had held the position since 1995. Bill Stoneman, who was vice president and general manager, took over from Tavares in running the day-to-day operations of the franchise.

JANUARY 14   Shigetoshi Hasegawa signs with the Mariners as a free agent.

JANUARY 17   The Angels trade Brian Cooper to the Blue Jays for Brad Fullmer.

JANUARY 28   Ismael Valdez signs with the Rangers as a free agent.

MARCH 9	Two brawls mar a spring training game against the Padres in Tempe. The fights were triggered when Aaron Sele hit Ryan Klesko with a pitch. Scott Spezio was suspended for six games and Troy Glaus for two as a result of their participation in the melee.
MARCH 31	Playing a regular season game in March for the first time in club history, the Angels begin the 2002 season with a 6–0 loss to the Indians before 42,697 at Edison International Field. The contest was played on Easter Sunday and televised nationally by ESPN. Cleveland scored four runs in the first inning off Jarrod Washburn. Bartolo Colon pitched a complete game five-hitter.

The 2002 season was the first for Rory Markas and Terry Smith as the Angels' radio broadcasting team.

APRIL 3	Former Angels star Chuck Finley is unable to make his scheduled start for the Indians against his old club in Anaheim because of a domestic dispute with his wife. The Indians won the game 6–5.

Finley married actress Tawny Kitaen in 1997 while playing for the Angels, and the couple had two children. Tawny is best known for appearing in several videos of the band Whitesnake during the 1980s. She was then married to Whitesnake lead singer, Dave Coverdale. Finley's altercation with Kitaen occurred on April 1. While Finley was driving his vehicle along the Pacific Coast Highway in Newport Beach, she allegedly kicked him repeatedly with her high-heeled boots while his foot was on the gas pedal, and severely twisted his ear, leaving visible scrapes and abrasions. Finley was able to gain control of the car and get home safely. He filed for divorce on April 4. Tawny was ordered to undergo a substance abuse program, anger management counseling and to make a donation to a battered woman's shelter.

APRIL 16	The Angels come from behind three times to defeat the Rangers 6–5 in ten innings at Edison International Field. Texas scored three runs in the first and one in the second, but the Angels responded with a like number in their half of both innings. There was no more scoring until the Rangers plated a run in the tenth. The Angels won the contest on a two-run, walk-off double by Darin Erstad.

The team abandoned its vest-type uniforms after five years (see April 4, 1997), reverting to a more traditional design. The jerseys were now mostly red, with blue trim, and for the first time the world "Anaheim" would appear across the front on the road uniforms. The Anaheim designation lasted only two seasons, however. Beginning in 2004, "Angels" once again appeared across the front of the road shirts.

APRIL 23	The Angels lose 1–0 to the Mariners in Seattle.

The defeat dropped the Angels to 6–14 on the season. The club was already 10½ games behind first-place Seattle, which had a regular season record of 116–46 in 2001. Including the last 21 games of 2001, the Angels had a record of 8–33 over their last 41 games. Any thoughts of reaching the playoffs in 2002 seemed to be over just three weeks into the season. But in an amazing turnaround, the Angels had a record of 104–54 from April 24 through the end of the 2002 World Series.

APRIL 27	The Angels score seven runs in the fifth inning and down the Blue Jays 11–4 at Edison International Field. David Eckstein hit a grand slam off Scott Cassidy.
APRIL 28	After the Blue Jays score a run in the top of the 14th inning, David Eckstein hits a two-out, walk-off grand slam off Pedro Borbon in the bottom half for an 8–5 victory at Edison International Field. It was the second day in a row in which Eckstein hit a grand slam.
APRIL 30	The Angels rout the Indians 21–2 in Cleveland with a run in the first inning, two in the third, three in the fifth, one in the sixth, two in the seventh, ten in the eighth and two in the ninth. The ten-run eighth was achieved with eight hits (two homers, a double and five singles), two walks, a hit batsman and a wild pitch. Darin Erstad homered and walked during the long rally, Troy Glaus singled twice, and Jerry DaVanon delivered a three-run pinch homer. Overall, Glaus collected four of the Angels' 22 hits and drove in five runs.
MAY 3	The Angels extend their winning streak to eight games with a 6–4 decision over the Blue Jays in Toronto.
MAY 8	Troy Glaus hits a walk-off homer in the ninth inning to defeat the Tigers 3–2 at Edison International Field. Troy Percival struck out all three batters he faced in the top of the ninth.

Glaus hit .250 with 30 homers and 111 RBIs in 2002.

MAY 10	The Angels collect 24 hits and wallop the White Sox 19–0 at Edison International Field. The Angels broke a scoreless tie with eight runs in the third inning, then added two in the fourth, three in the fifth, three in the sixth and three in the seventh. Adam Kennedy hit two homers and two singles in five at-bats and scored four runs. Troy Glaus, Garret Anderson and Brad Fullmer also homered. Scott Schoeneweis (seven innings) and Matt Wise (two innings) combined on the shutout. The lopsided win set a franchise record for the most runs in a shutout victory. It also marked the second time in a span of eleven days in which the Angels won a game by 19 runs.

Kennedy had a breakout year in 2002 by hitting .312 with seven home runs.

MAY 11	Troy Percival strikes out all three batters he faces in the ninth inning to close out a 6–3 win over the White Sox at Edison International Field.

Percival had 40 saves, 68 strikeouts and a 1.92 ERA in 58 games and $56^{1}/_{3}$ innings in 2002.

MAY 17	The Angels extend their winning streak to eight games with an 8–4 decision over the White Sox in Chicago.
MAY 22	Trailing 5–0, the Angels score two runs in the seventh inning and five in the eighth to take a 7–5 lead, then survive a Royals rally in the ninth to win 7–6 at Edison International Field. Darin Erstad tied the score 5–5 with a two-run double, and Garret Anderson broke the deadlock with another double, which brought home of pair of runs.

The Angels won 21 of 24 games from April 24 through May 22.

MAY 25 — Tim Salmon hits a walk-off homer in the 13th inning to defeat the Twins 4–3 at Edison International Field.

Salmon batted .286 with 22 homers in 2002.

MAY 29 — The Angels break a 1–1 tie with five runs in the fifth inning and go on to trounce the Royals 12–2 in Kansas City. Playing in only his fifth major league game, Alfredo Amezaga collected four hits in five at-bats. He was in the lineup at shortstop in place of the injured David Eckstein. Amezaga was sent back to the minors the next day when Eckstein returned.

JUNE 4 — In the first round of the amateur draft, the Angels select pitcher Joe Saunders from Virginia Tech University.

After struggling for a few years, Saunders blossomed in 2008 with a 17–7 season. The only other player drafted and signed by the Angels in 2002 who has yet to reach the majors is tenth-round pick Howie Kendrick.

JUNE 5 — The Angels take a thrilling ten-inning 7–5 decision from the Rangers at Edison International Field. The Angels trailed 4–2 with one out in the ninth when Brad Fullmer and Tim Salmon hit home runs on back-to-back pitches from Hideki Irabu. After Texas scored in the top of the tenth, the Angels responded with three in their half on a double from Adam Kennedy and a single from David Eckstein to tie the score, and a two-run, walk-off home run off the bat of Troy Glaus.

JUNE 7 — The Angels play the Reds for the first time during the regular season and win 4–3 at Edison International Field.

JUNE 9 — David Eckstein hits a grand slam off Jeff Hamilton in the second inning of a 7–4 win over the Reds at Edison International Field.

The slam was the third of the season for Eckstein, who accomplished the feat on back-to-back days on April 27 and 28. He finished the season with a .293 batting average, eight homers and 107 runs scored.

JUNE 10 — The Angels play the Pirates for the first time during the regular season and win 4–3 at Edison International Field.

JUNE 18 — The Angels play the Cardinals for the first time during the regular season and lose 7–2 in St. Louis.

JUNE 26 — Trailing 6–2, the Angels score four runs in the eighth inning and one in the ninth to defeat the Rangers 7–6 in Arlington. Bengie Molina knotted the game at 6–6 with a three-run homer. Garret Anderson drove in the winning run with a double.

Anderson finished fourth in the MVP balloting in 2002 with a .306 batting average, 29 homers and 123 RBIs. He also had a league-leading, and Angels record, 56 doubles.

July 3	The Angels edge the Orioles 1–0 at Edison International Field. Darin Erstad drove in the lone run with a single in the eighth inning. Jarrod Washburn (eighth innings) and Troy Percival (one inning) combined on the shutout.
July 11	Shawn Wooten homers off Darrell May in the sixth inning to account for the lone run of a 1–0 win over the Royals in Kansas City. It was Wooten's first game of the season after missing the first half of the season following thumb surgery. Jarrod Washburn (six innings), Ben Weber (1 2/3 innings), Scott Schoeneweis (one-third of an inning) and Troy Percival (one inning) combined on the shutout.

Weber was 30 when he made his major league debut in 2000. He spent the 1997 and 1998 seasons pitching professionally in Taiwan.

July 19	Tim Salmon collects five hits, including a homer, and drives in five runs in five at-bats to lead the Angels to a 15–3 rout of the Mariners at Edison International Field. The Angels had 20 hits in all and scored eight runs in the sixth inning.
July 21	Jarrod Washburn runs his winning streak to 12 games with a 7–5 decision over the Mariners at Edison International Field.

Washburn won 15 of 16 decisions from April 19 through August 11. During that stretch, he pitched 139 2/3 innings and posted an ERA of 2.64. Washburn finished the season with an 18–6 record accompanied by an earned run average of 3.15. He has been unable to build on the success of that season, however. Washburn was 29–31 with the Angels from 2003 through 2005 before going to the Mariners as a free agent. He continued to struggle after leaving Anaheim.

July 28	Shawn Wooten hits a sacrifice fly in the ninth inning to account for the lone run of a 1–0 victory over the Mariners in Seattle. Kevin Appier (eight innings) and Troy Percival (one inning) combined on the shutout.
August 6	Tim Salmon hits a grand slam off Matt Ginter in the sixth inning of an 11–2 triumph over the White Sox in Chicago.
August 10	The Angels score seven runs in the third inning and clobber the Blue Jays 11–4 in Toronto. The first five batters in the third collected hits on four straight singles and a three-run homer from Garret Anderson.
August 11	David Eckstein homers off Roy Halladay in the fourth inning to account for the lone run in a 1–0 win over the Blue Jays in Toronto. Jarrod Washburn (eight innings) and Troy Percival (one inning) combined on a three-hit shutout.
August 13	Troy Glaus is the hero of a 7–6 win over the Tigers at Edison International Field. With Detroit ahead 6–5 in the 11th inning, Glaus doubled and scored on a single by Darin Erstad. In the 12th, Glaus delivered a walk-off single for the victory.
August 16	Troy Percival strikes out all three batters he faces in the ninth inning to close out a 5–4 win over the Indians at Edison International Field.
August 18	Kevin Appier (six innings), Brendan Donnelly (one inning), Ben Weber (one inning) and Troy Percival (one inning) combine on a two-hitter to defeat the Indians 4–1

at Edison International Field. The only Cleveland hits were a single by Ellis Burks in the first inning and a double from Jim Thome in the ninth.

> *Donnelly made his major league debut in 2002 at the age of 30 after he had pitched for 14 minor league teams over ten seasons and had been released by six big-league organizations, including the Devil Rays, who let him go to clear a roster spot for Jim Morris. Morris made his major league bow at 35 and was later the subject of a Disney movie starring Dennis Quaid.*

AUGUST 21   Scott Spezio breaks a 1–1 tie with a two-run homer in the 11th inning before the Angels add two insurance runs to defeat the Yankees 5–1 in New York.

AUGUST 27   Darin Erstad collects five hits, including two doubles, in five at-bats to lead the Angels to a 7–3 triumph over the Devil Rays at Edison International Field.

AUGUST 29   Showing their dismay about tomorrow's impending strike by the players, fans at Edison International Field throw foul balls back onto the playing field during the Angels-Devil Rays game. Over 100 people were ejected for throwing trash. The Angels won 6–1. The players and owners came to agreement over a new Basic Agreement the following morning.

SEPTEMBER 5   Garret Anderson drives in seven runs and collects four hits in four at-bats during a 10–1 victory over the Devil Rays in St. Petersburg. Anderson singled in the first inning, doubled in a run in the third and then added a pair of three-run homers in the fifth and sixth.

SEPTEMBER 8   The Angels extend their winning streak to ten games with a 6–2 decision over the Orioles in Baltimore.

SEPTEMBER 12   Scott Spezio's walk-off single in the ninth inning beats the Athletics 7–6 at Edison International Field. The win put the Angels into a tie for first place with Oakland. Both clubs had records of 91–55. The A's surged past the Mariners and Angels into first with an American League record 20-game winning streak from August 13 through September 4.

SEPTEMBER 14   After the Rangers score five runs in the first inning, the Angels bounce back to win 8–6 at Edison International Field with two runs in the second inning, two in the third, three in the fifth and one in the eighth. Tim Salmon gave the Angels a 7–6 lead with a three-run homer in the fifth.

SEPTEMBER 15   The Angels take sole possession of first place with a 13–4 thrashing of the Rangers at Edison International Field. Troy Glaus led the way with three homers, six RBIs and four runs scored. The home runs came in consecutive at-bats off Kenny Rogers in the fifth inning, Jay Powell in the seventh and Juan Alvarez in the eighth.

> *The Angels were 16–1 between August 29 and September 15, and 88–41 from April 24 through September 15.*

SEPTEMBER 16   Troy Glaus hits a three-run homer in the first inning, his fourth home run in four consecutive plate appearances over two games, but the Angels don't score again and

	lose 4–3 to the Athletics in Oakland. The loss dropped the Angels into a tie for first place.
SEPTEMBER 17	Tim Salmon homers off Billy Koch in the tenth inning for the lone run of a 1–0 win over the Athletics in Oakland. Jarrod Washburn (eight innings), Ben Weber (one inning) and Troy Percival (one inning) combined on the three-hit shutout. The win put the Angels into sole possession of first place by one full game.
SEPTEMBER 18	The Angels drop back into a tie for first with a 7–4 loss to the Athletics in Oakland. Francisco Rodriguez made his major league debut at the age of 20 and pitched a scoreless eighth.

> *Rodriguez made five regular-season appearances, all in relief, and didn't allow a run while striking out 13 batters in 5 2/3 innings without a decision. He burst onto the national stage in the postseason with a 5–1 record in 11 games and 18 2/3 innings. Rodriguez struck out 28 batters, while walking five, surrendered 12 hits and had an ERA of 1.93. In his first 24 1/3 major league innings, counting the 2002 postseason, Rodriguez fanned 41 batters.*

SEPTEMBER 19	The Angels fall back out of first with a 5–3 loss to the Athletics in Oakland. There was little concern about reaching the postseason, however, as the Angels held an 8 1/2-game lead in the wild-card race.

> *The Angels lost seven of nine games from September 18 through September 27 and finished four games behind the A's.*

SEPTEMBER 26	The Angels clinch the wild-card berth in the playoffs by defeating the Rangers 10–5 in Arlington.
SEPTEMBER 28	The Angels score seven runs in the sixth inning and defeat the Mariners 8–4 at Edison Intentional Field. Brad Fullmer started the rally with a single and drove in the last two runs with a triple.
SEPTEMBER 29	On the last day of the regular season, Troy Glaus hits a grand slam off Ismael Valdez in the first inning of a 7–6 win over the Mariners at Edison International Field.

> *The Angels made the postseason for the first time since 1986. The 99–63 record was easily the best in franchise history up to that time, topping the 1982 team which was 93–69. The Angels also had the best run differential (plus 207 on 851 runs scored and 644 allowed) in the AL in 2002. The opponent in the Division Series was the Yankees. Managed by Joe Torre, the Yanks were 103–58 in 2002 and had played in the World Series five of the previous six years, winning it all in 1996, 1998, 1999 and 2000 before losing in seven games to the Diamondbacks in 2001.*

OCTOBER 1	The Angels open the Division Series with an 8–5 loss to the Yankees in New York. Troy Glaus tied the score 4–4 with a homer in the sixth inning off Roger Clemens, then broke the deadlock with another home run off Ramiro Mendoza in the eighth. But the Yanks scored four times in the eighth, the last three on a home run by Bernie Williams off Brendan Donnelly. Starter Jarrod Washburn gave up homers to Derek Jeter, Jason Giambi and Rondell White. Darin Erstad collected three hits in the losing cause.

The series was televised nationally over FOX (games one, two and four) and ABC Family (game three). The announcers were Joe Buck, Tim McCarver, Thom Brennaman, Jon Miller and Joe Morgan.

OCTOBER 2   The Angels even the series by defeating the Yankees 8–6 in New York. The Angels took a 4–0 lead in the third inning, fell behind 5–4 in the sixth, then went ahead again with three tallies in the eighth for a 7–5 advantage. Both teams scored once in the ninth. There were four Angels home runs in the game. Tim Salmon went deep in the first inning and Scott Spezio in the second. The Angels went ahead for good when Garret Anderson and Troy Glaus led off the eighth with back-to-back homers. Shawn Wooten contributed three hits. Francisco Rodriguez allowed two runs in two innings but received credit for the win.

OCTOBER 4   The Angels take a two-games-to-one lead in the best-of-five series with a 9–6 victory before 45,072 at Edison International Field. The Yankees led 6–1 before the Angels countered with two runs in the third inning, one in the fourth, one in the sixth, one in the seventh and three in the eighth. Adam Kennedy homered in the fourth inning and led off the eighth with a double. He scored on Darin Erstad's single to break the 6–6 deadlock, and Tim Salmon put the icing on the cake with a two-run homer. Francisco Rodriguez pitched two scoreless innings and was the winning pitcher for the second game in a row.

OCTOBER 5   Trailing 2–1, the Angels erupt for eight runs in the fifth inning and defeat the Yankees 9–5 before 45,067 at Edison International Field to advance to the Championship Series. It was the first time in franchise history that the Angels won a postseason series. Shawn Wooten started the rally with a home run off David Wells. With one out, the Angels received five consecutive singles from Benji Gil, David Eckstein, Darin Erstad, Tim Salmon and Garret Anderson. In all, the Angels collected ten hits in the inning off three pitchers in a span of 22 pitches.

The Angels met the Minnesota Twins in the Championship Series. Managed by Ron Gardenhire, the Twins were 94–67 during the regular season, then upset the Athletics in five games in the Division Series.

OCTOBER 8   The Angels open the Championship Series with a 2–1 loss to the Twins at the Metrodome in Minneapolis. The Twins broke the 1–1 tie with a run in the fifth inning off Kevin Appier.

The series was televisied nationally over the FOX network with Thom Brennaman and Steve Lyons serving as announcers.

OCTOBER 9   The Angels even the series with a 6–3 triumph over the Twins in Minneapolis. The Angels opened with a run in the first inning on a home run by Darin Erstad, then added three in the second. A bizarre play took place in the second when Scott Spezio stole home while Adam Kennedy tried to steal second. Spezio was caught in a rundown but scored after swiping the ball away from Minnesota catcher A. J. Pierzynski. Brad Fullmer homered in the sixth.

OCTOBER 11   The Angels take a two-games-to-one lead in the best-of-seven series with a 2–1 win over the Twins before 44,234 at Edison International Field. Garret Anderson gave the Angels a 1–0 lead with a home run in the second inning. Troy Glaus provided the Angels with a 2–1 advantage by homering in the eighth. Jarrod Washburn went seven innings and Frankie Rodriguez was the winning pitcher with a scoreless eighth.

OCTOBER 12   The Angels are one game away from playing in the World Series by defeating the Twins 7–1 before 44,830 at Edison International Field. The game was scoreless in a duel between John Lackey and Brad Radke until the Angels scored twice in the seventh. Five more runs crossed the plate in the eighth.

OCTOBER 13   The Angels win the first American League pennant in franchise history with a 13–5 trouncing of the Twins before 44,835 at Edison International Field. The Angels trailed 5–3 before erupting for ten runs in the seventh inning. Adam Kennedy hit three home runs. The first was struck off Joe Mays leading off the third. Kennedy added another solo shot in the fourth against Mays. With Johan Santana on the mound for Minnesota, Scott Spezio and Bengie Molina started the seventh with singles before Kennedy hit his third homer to put the Angels ahead 6–5. Before the inning ended, both Spezio and Kennedy added singles as the Angels never let up and scored seven more runs. The three-home-run game by Kennedy followed a regular season in which he homered just seven times in 474 at-bats. Francisco Rodriguez was the winning pitcher. It was his fourth win of the 2002 postseason.

Manager Mike Scioscia brought a new level of competitive grit to the Angels when he took the reins in 2000. Leading the team throughout the 2000s, he compiled 900 regular-season victories and a .556 win percentage.

Until the victory on October 13, 2002, the Angels were 0–6 in franchise history in games that would have put then into the World Series, losing three in a row both 1982 and 1986. The Angels played the San Francisco Giants in the fourth all-California World Series in history. Managed by Dusty Baker, the Giants won the wild card with a 95–66 record, then defeated the Braves and Cardinals in the playoffs. Both franchises were looking to erase decades of frustration. The Angels had never played in a World Series, much less won one. The Giants hadn't claimed a world championship since 1954 when the franchise played in New York. Opposing managers Mike Scioscia and Baker had been teammates on the 1981 world champion Dodgers.

OCTOBER 19   The Angels open the World Series with a 4-3 loss to the Giants before 44,603 at Edison International Field. Barry Bonds started the scoring with a home run in the second inning off Jarrod Washburn. Troy Glaus homered for the Angels in both the second and sixth innings, but the Angels were unable to erase the San Francisco lead. It was the Angels' third game-one loss in the 2002 postseason.

> *During the 2002 postseason, Glaus batted .344 with seven home runs in 61 at-bats. He was named the World Series MVP.*

OCTOBER 20   The Angels outlast the Giants 11-10 in game two before 44,584 at Edison International Field. The Angels scored five runs in the first inning to take a 5-0 lead. With one out, Scott Spezio and Brad Fullmer executed a double steal with Fullmer swiping home. It was the first steal of home in a World Series game since Tim McCarver accomplished the feat with the Cardinals in 1964. McCarver was in the broadcast booth serving as an analyst alongside Joe Buck for the FOX television network. The Giants scored four runs in the top of the second, but Tim Salmon took a two-run homer in the bottom half for a 7-4 advantage. The Giants countered with a run in the third and four in the fifth to move ahead 9-7. The Angels tied the contest with tallies in the fifth and sixth. Salmon broke the 9-9 deadlock with another two-run homer in the eighth. Barry Bonds homered in the ninth before Troy Percival closed out the victory. Francisco Rodriguez pitched three scoreless innings for his fifth win of the 2002 postseason.

> *The only other pitcher with five wins during a single postseason is Randy Johnson with the Diamondbacks in 2002.*

OCTOBER 22   The Angels take a two-games-to-one lead with a 10-4 victory over the Giants at Pac Bell Park in San Francisco. Anaheim put the game away early with four runs in the third inning and four in the fourth. Darin Erstad collected three hits, one of them a double, and Scott Spezio drove in three runs.

OCTOBER 23   The Giants even the series by defeating the Angels 4-3 in San Francisco. Troy Glaus hit a two-run homer in the third inning for a 3-0 lead, but the Giants responded with three runs in the fifth inning and another in the eighth. Francisco Rodriguez took the loss.

OCTOBER 24   The Giants move within one win of a world championship by trouncing the Angels 16-4 in San Francisco.

> *Darrin Baker, the three-year-old son of Giants manager Dusty Baker, got himself in harm's way during the game. Darrin was acting as one of the Giants batboys when he went out to retrieve Kenny Lofton's bat after Lofton's two-run triple. The problem was, J. T. Snow and David Bell were racing toward the plate as Darrin headed toward it. Snow grabbed Darrin and got the youngster out of the way to avoid a personal tragedy. Darrin's action led to a rule passed by major league owners in January 2003 that stipulated that batboys must be at least 14 years old. The next time Darrin will be able to serve as a batboy will be in 2013.*

OCTOBER 26   Trailing 5-0 in game six and on the brink of elimination, the Angels rally for three runs in the seventh inning and three in the eighth to win 6-5 before 44,506 at

Edison International Field. San Francisco starting pitcher Russ Ortiz pitched six scoreless innings and retired Garret Anderson on a grounder leading off the seventh. The Giants clubhouse was already covered in plastic sheeting to protect it from the anticipated celebratory spraying of champagne. Troy Glaus and Brad Fullmer followed with singles, and Giants manager Dusty Baker lifted Ortiz in favor of Felix Rodriguez. Baker gave Ortiz the game ball as he headed back toward the dugout. Scott Spezio was next up, and on the eighth pitch of the at-bat, belted a three-run homer which barely cleared the right-field wall. The Angels still trailed 5–3 heading into the eighth, and the Giants needed just six outs for the title. With Todd Worrell pitching for San Francisco, Darin Erstad led off the inning with a homer. After Tim Salmon and Garret Anderson singled, Robb Nen was brought in to pitch to Troy Glaus, who doubled in two runs to put the Angels ahead 6–5. Troy Percival retired the side in order in the ninth.

OCTOBER 27 The Angels win the World Series by defeating the Giants 4–1 in game seven before 44,598 at Edison International Field. Both teams scored in the second inning. In the third, David Eckstein and Darin Erstad singled, and Tim Salmon was hit by a pitch to load the bases. Garret Anderson scored all three with a double. John Lackey (five innings), Brendan Donnelly (two innings), Francisco Rodriguez (one inning) and Troy Percival (one inning) pitched for the Angels. Lackey was the first rookie to start a game seven since Babe Adams of the Pirates in 1909. Donnelly and Rodriguez were also rookies. In the ninth, Percival put runners on first and second with one out, then struck out pinch hitter Tsuyoshi Shingo and retired Kenny Lofton on a fly ball to Darin Erstad in center field.

2003

Season in a Sentence
Following the World Series win, the Angels make few changes from the 2002 cast, and attendance increases by more than 700,000 to over three million for the first time in franchise history, but the club winds up with a losing record.

Finish • Won • Lost • Pct • GB
Third   77   85   .475   19.0

In the wild-card race, the Angels finished in sixth place, 18 games behind.

Manager
Mike Scioscia

Stats
	Angels	AL	Rank
Batting Avg:	.268	.267	7
On-Base Pct:	.330	.333	8
Slugging Pct:	.413	.428	9
Home Runs:	150		12
Stolen Bases:	129		2
ERA:	4.28	4.52	6
Errors:	105		7
Runs Scored:	736		11
Runs Allowed:	743		5

Starting Lineup
Bengie Molina, c
Scott Spezio, 1b-3b
Adam Kennedy, 2b
Troy Glaus, 3b
David Eckstein, ss
Garret Anderson, lf
Darin Erstad, cf
Tim Salmon, rf-dh
Brad Fullmer, dh
Jeff DaVanon, rf
Shawn Wooten, 1b-dh-3b
Eric Owens, cf-rf
Chone Figgins, cf

Pitchers
Ramon Ortiz, sp
Jarrod Washburn, sp
John Lackey, sp
Aaron Sele, sp
Kevin Appier, sp
Troy Percival, rp
Brendan Donnelly, rp
Ben Weber, rp
Francisco Rodriguez, rp
Scot Shields, rp

Attendance
3,061,093 (third in AL)

Club Leaders
Batting Avg:	Garret Anderson	.315
On-Base Pct:	Tim Salmon	.374
Slugging Pct:	Garret Anderson	.541
Home Runs:	Garret Anderson	29
RBIs:	Garret Anderson	116
Runs:	Garret Anderson	80
Stolen Bases:	Adam Kennedy	22
Wins:	Ramon Ortiz	16
Strikeouts:	John Lackey	151
ERA:	Jarrod Washburn	4.43
Saves:	Troy Percival	33

MARCH 30   Two weeks after the start of the Iraq War, the Angels open the season in a nationally televised game on a Sunday night over ESPN and lose 6–3 to the Rangers before 43,525 at Edison International Field. John Lackey, who won game seven of the 2002 World Series, was the starting and losing pitcher.

Before the game, the American League pennant was hoisted and players received their World Series rings during a 20-minute ceremony.

APRIL 2   The Angels rout the Rangers 10–0 at Edison International Field. Mickey Callaway (six innings), Scot Shields (two innings) and Ben Weber (one inning) combined on the shutout.

APRIL 16	Trailing 6–2, the Angels score seven runs in the eighth inning, then survive a two-run Texas rally in the ninth to win 9–8 in Arlington. Bengie Molina broke the 6–6 tie with a single.
APRIL 19	The Angels score three runs in the ninth inning to defeat the Mariners 7–6 at Edison International Field. The game-winning rally consisted of four singles, two stolen bases and a Seattle error.
MAY 3	Tim Salmon runs his hitting streak to 20 games during a 7–1 loss to the Blue Jays in Toronto.
MAY 8	Garret Anderson drives in all seven Angels runs in a 7–1 win over the Indians at Edison International Field. Facing Jason Davis, Anderson singled in a run in the first inning, scored a runner from third on a ground out in the third and walloped a grand slam in the fifth. Anderson capped the day with a run-scoring double off Billy Traber in the seventh.

Anderson batted .315 with 29 homers, 116 RBIs and a league-leading 49 doubles. He also appeared in 159 games. Anderson played in at least 150 games in eight straight seasons beginning in 1996.

MAY 13	Scott Spezio homers twice during a 10–3 win over the Yankees in New York. Spezio walloped a solo shot off Mike Mussina in the fourth inning and a grand slam facing Juan Acevedo in the ninth.
MAY 15	The Disney corporation sells the Angels to 56-year-old Arte Moreno.

Moreno was the first Hispanic to own a major sports franchise in North America and the first minority to own a Major League team. Although of Mexican descent, Moreno is a fourth-generation American and was born in Tucson, Arizona. He made his money in the billboard business and sold his enterprise in 1999 for $8 billion. Moreno was previously a minority owner of the Diamondbacks from 2001 through 2003. Thus far, the Angels have been far more consistently successful under Moreno's leadership, both on the field and at the box office, than under either the Gene Autry or Disney regimes.

MAY 27	The Angels are honored for their World Series win by President George W. Bush at the White House. Later that evening, the Angels lost 12–4 to the Orioles in Baltimore.
JUNE 1	Jeff DaVanon hits two homers and two singles in five at-bats during a 9–4 win over the Devil Rays in St. Petersburg.
JUNE 3	The Angels play the Montreal Expos for the first time during the regular season and hit six homers and collect 22 hits during a 15–4 victory in San Juan, Puerto Rico. The Expos played 21 "home" games in San Juan in 2003 and 22 in 2004. Switch-hitting Jeff DaVanon homered twice for the second game in a row. In addition, he homered from both sides of the plate, connecting off right-hander Toma Ohka in the first inning and lefty Scott Stewart in the ninth. Tim Salmon, Garret Anderson, Troy Glaus and Bengie Molina also homered for the Angels.

On the same day, the Angels selected shortstop Brandon Wood from Horizon High School in Scottsdale, Arizona, in the first round of the amateur draft. Wood made his major league debut in 2007. Future major leaguers drafted and signed by the Angels in 2003 have included Sean Rodriguez (third round) and Reggie Willits (seventh round).

JUNE 4   Garret Anderson hits three homers and Jeff DaVanon has his third consecutive multi-homer game to lead the Angels to an 11–2 thrashing of the Expos in San Juan. It was also the second game in a row in which DaVanon hit homers from both sides of the plate. He went deep off right-hander Dan Smith in the sixth inning and lefty Joey Eischen in the eighth. Anderson homered off Byung-Hyun Kim in the third and fifth and Eischen in the eighth and drove in five runs. The Angels had seven home runs in all, with Troy Glaus and Brad Fullmer adding the others. There were 13 Anaheim home runs in the first two games of the series against the Expos.

DaVanon was only the third major leaguer with switch-hit homers in consecutive games, following Eddie Murray in 1987 and Ken Caminiti in 1995. He was also just the fourth player with three consecutive multi-homer games. The first three were Tony Lazzeri in 1936, Gus Zernial in 1936 and Lee May in 1969. DaVanon finished the season with 12 homers in 330 at-bats. The three games in a row in which he hit two homers were the only ones in his career in which he homered more than once. DaVanon spent eight years in the majors from 1999 through 2007 and hit 33 homers in 1,288 at-bats with four clubs.

JUNE 6   The Angels play the Marlins for the first time during the regular season and lose 4–1 in Miami.

JUNE 10 The Angels play the Phillies for the first time during the regular season and lose 3–0 at Edison International Field.

JUNE 13 The Angels play the Mets for the first time during the regular season and lose 7–3 at Edison International Field.

JUNE 14 Brad Fullmer hits a grand slam off Jason Roach during a 13–3 win over the Mets at Edison International Field. Garret Anderson collected two homers and two singles in five at-bats.

Troy Percival pitched nine consecutive hitless innings over nine appearances from June 7 through June 28.

JULY 4   Aaron Sele (five innings), Francisco Rodriguez (two innings), Brendan Donnelly (one inning) and Troy Percival (one inning) combine on a two-hitter to defeat the Athletics 1–0 in Oakland. The only A's hits were a single by Scott Hatteburg in the first inning and a double from Miguel Tejada in the sixth. The Angels collected just three hits off Mark Mulder. One of them was a double by Bengi Gil in the sixth. Gil moved to third on a sacrifice by Jose Molina and scored on a suicide squeeze by David Eckstein.

The Angels went into the All-Star break with a record of 49–43 and were 4½ games out in the wild-card race. The club went 28–42 the rest of the way, however.

JULY 13	On the night prior to the All-Star Game at U.S. Cellular Field in Chicago, Garret Anderson wins the home run hitting contest, beating out Jim Edmonds in the semi-finals and Albert Pujols 9–8 in the finals.
JULY 14	Mike Scioscia manages the American League to a 7–6 win in the All-Star Game at U.S. Cellular Field in Chicago. Garret Anderson collected three hits in four at-bats. He singled in the fourth inning, and facing Woody Williams, homered in the sixth. The AL trailed 6–4 heading into the eighth, but scored three times for the win. Anderson contributed by leading off the inning with a double. Brendan Donnelly retired the side in order in the eighth.
	Donnelly went into the All-Star break with an 0.38 ERA in 48 innings. He finished the year with a 1.58 earned run average in 63 games and 74 innings.
JULY 29	Bengie Molina ties a major league record for catchers by starting three double plays, but the Angels lose 6–2 to the Yankees at Edison International Field. The three double plays happened in the second, seventh and eighth innings when Molina caught a third strike and threw out a runner attempting to steal second base.
AUGUST 8	With the Angels trailing the Indians 1–0 with two out in the ninth in Cleveland, Garret Anderson hits a three-run homer. The Angels added two more runs and the Indians one for a 5–2 final.
AUGUST 16	Playing in his second game with the Angels, Jason Riggs takes the field wearing a uniform in which the team nickname is spelled *Angees*. Riggs played five innings before anyone noticed the mistake. The Angels won 11–7 over the Tigers at Edison International Field.
AUGUST 23	Eric Owens collects five hits in six at-bats during a ten-inning 14–8 win over the Tigers at Comerica Park. Detroit led 5–0 at the end of the sixth inning. The Angels moved ahead 7–6 in the top of the eighth, only to fall behind 8–7 in the bottom half when the Tigers crossed the plate twice. Anaheim won the game with a run in the ninth on a two-out single by Jerry DaVanon and a six-run explosion in the tenth. Garret Anderson broke the 8–8 tie with a two-run single.
SEPTEMBER 1	Scott Spezio hits a grand slam off Kenny Rogers in the third inning of a 10–2 win over the Twins in Minneapolis.
SEPTEMBER 4	Angels television broadcaster Rex Hudler is suspended indefinitely by the club following his arrest at the Kansas City International Airport for possession of marijuana and drug paraphernalia. Hudler returned to his broadcasting duties in 2004.
SEPTEMBER 16	Scott Spezio hits a three-run, walk-off homer in the ninth inning to down the Athletics 6–5 at Edison International Field.
SEPTEMBER 21	Behind 5–2, the Angels erupt for seven runs in the seventh inning and beat the Rangers 11–6 in Arlington.
SEPTEMBER 23	Tim Salmon hits a walk-off homer in the 11th inning to defeat the Mariners 2–1 at Edison International Field. Scot Shields (eight innings), Troy Percival (one inning),

Brendan Donnelly (one inning) and Francisco Rodriguez (one inning) combined on a four-hitter.

NOVEMBER 24   Seven weeks after California voters recall Governor Gary Davis and replace him with Arnold Schwarzenegger, the Angels sign Kelvim Escobar, most recently with the Blue Jays, as a free agent.

Escobar had a breakout year for the Angels with an 18–7 record in 2007, but he sat out all of 2008 with a bum shoulder and played in only one game in 2009.

DECEMBER 10   The Angels sign Bartolo Colon, most recently with the White Sox, as a free agent.

Colon gave the Angels two terrific seasons before an assortment of injuries caught up with him. Colon was 18–12 in 2004, although it came with a 5.01 ERA, and won the Cy Young Award in 2005 with a record of 21–8. He was the Angels' first Cy Young winner since Dean Chance in 1964 and the first to win at least 20 since Nolan Ryan in 1974.

DECEMBER 19   Scott Spezio signs with the Mariners as a free agent.

DECEMBER 20   The Angels sign Jose Guillen, most recently with the Athletics, as a free agent.

Guillen made his major league debut in 1997, and the Angels were already his sixth big-league club. He hit .297 with 27 home runs and 104 RBIs for Anaheim in 2004. He was suspended the last two weeks of the season and during the postseason for "inappropriate conduct" in publicly: He expressed his displeasure with Mike Scioscia after the Angels manager removed Guillen for a pinch runner during a crucial game against the Athletics.

DECEMBER 29   Edison International Field of Anaheim is renamed Angel Stadium of Anaheim after Edison International exercises an option to exit its naming rights agreement. The Angels ballpark had been known as Edison International Field since September 1997.

2004

Season in a Sentence
After bringing several high-priced free agents to Anaheim, the Angels win the AL West title in a thrilling race with the Athletics before being swept by the Red Sox in the playoffs.

Finish • Won • Lost • Pct • GB
First 92 70 .568 +1.0

AL Division Series
The Angels lost to the Boston Red Sox three games to none.

Manager
Mike Scioscia

Stats

Stats	Angels	AL	Rank
Batting Avg:	.282	.270	1
On-Base Pct:	.341	.338	6
Slugging Pct:	.419	.433	10
Home Runs:	162		10
Stolen Bases:	143		1
ERA:	4.28	4.63	4
Errors:	90		1
Runs Scored:	836		7
Runs Allowed:	734		2

Starting Lineup
Bengie Molina, c
Darin Erstad, 1b
Adam Kennedy, 2b
Chone Figgins, 3b-cf
David Eckstein, ss
Jose Guillen, lf
Garret Anderson, cf
Vladimir Guerrero, rf
Troy Glaus, dh-3b
Jeff DaVanon, cf-lf-rf

Pitchers
Bartolo Colon, sp
John Lackey, sp
Kelvim Escobar, sp
Jarrod Washburn, sp
Aaron Sele, sp
Troy Percival, rp
Francisco Rodriguez, rp
Scot Shields, rp
Kevin Gregg, rp
Ramon Ortiz, rp-sp

Attendance
3,375,677 (second in AL)

Club Leaders

Batting Avg:	Vladimir Guerrero	.337
On-Base Pct:	Vladimir Guerrero	.391
Slugging Pct:	Vladimir Guerrero	.598
Home Runs:	Vladimir Guerrero	39
RBI:	Vladimir Guerrero	126
Runs:	Vladimir Guerrero	124
Stolen Bases:	Chone Figgins	34
Wins:	Bartolo Colon	18
Strikeouts:	Kelvim Escobar	191
ERA:	Kelvim Escobar	3.93
Saves:	Troy Percival	33

JANUARY 14   The Angels sign Vladimir Guerrero, most recently with the Expos, as a free agent.

When signed, Guerrero was a month shy of his 28th birthday and had a .323 lifetime batting average. Over the previous six seasons, he had averaged 37 home runs, 110 RBIs and 100 runs scored per year. Guerrero played in only 112 games because of a bad back in 2004, however, and there were some concerns about his health. The Angels took a chance and signed Guerrero and have never regretted the decision. In his first season in Anaheim, Guerrero batted .337 with 39 home runs and 126 RBIs to win the AL MVP award. At the end of the 2009 season, Guerrero rankrd first in franchise history in batting average (.319), first in slugging percentage (.546), third in on-base percentage (.381) and fifth in home runs (173).

APRIL 6   The Angels open the season with a 10–5 win over the Mariners in Seattle. Troy Glaus homered twice and drove in four runs. Bartolo Colon made his Angels debut and allowed an unearned run in six innings.

> *Colon was 6–8 with a 6.38 ERA before the All-Star break and 12–4 with a 3.63 earned run average afterward.*

APRIL 7 — The Angels reach double digits in runs scored for the second day in a row by sinking the Mariners 10–7 in Seattle.

APRIL 8 — The Angels score five runs in the ninth inning to beat the Mariners 5–1 in Seattle. Adam Kennedy put the Angels into the lead with a two-run single.

APRIL 13 — The Angels open the home portion of the schedule with a 7–5 victory over the Mariners before 43,443 at Angel Stadium. The Angels trailed 4–0 at the end of the fourth inning. Vladimir Guerrero and Bengie Molina led the comeback with home runs. The game was Guerrero's first in Anaheim.

> *The Angels had 45 sellouts in 2004 and drew a then-record 3,375,677, some 300,000 more than the previous record of 3,061,090 set in 2003. It was also a dramatic increase over the 2,000,917 the club attracted in 2001. Arte Moreno, who purchased the franchise in May 2003, also removed "Anaheim" from the team's road uniforms and replaced it with "Angels." In addition, all references to Anaheim were removed from officially licensed merchandise, the team Web site, tickets and promotional material and replaced it with "Angels" or "Angels baseball." It was a prelude to another change in the official name of the franchise (see January 3, 2005).*

APRIL 23 — The Angels rout the Athletics 12–2 in Oakland.

APRIL 29 — The Angels score eight runs in the fourth inning and clobber the Tigers 12–3 in Detroit. Jose Guillen capped the rally with a three-run homer.

MAY 1 — The Angels edge the Twins 1–0 in Minneapolis. Chone Figgins drove in the lone run with a single in the ninth inning. Aaron Sele (five innings), Kevin Gregg (two innings), Francisco Rodriguez (one inning) and Troy Percival (one inning) combined on the shutout.

MAY 3 — After falling behind 6–2 in the sixth inning, the Angels outlast the Tigers 11–9 at Angel Stadium. Troy Glaus broke a 6–6 tie with a two-run homer in the seventh.

MAY 7 — John Lackey pitches a three-hitter to defeat the Devil Rays 1–0 at Angel Stadium. David Eckstein drove in the lone run with a single in the third inning.

MAY 8 — Shane Halter hits a pinch-hit grand slam off Trever Miller in the seventh inning of a 7–2 triumph over the Devil Rays at Anaheim Stadium. The homer was also Halter's first as a member of the Angels.

MAY 9 — The Angels run their winning streak to nine games with an 8–4 decision over the Devil Rays at Angel Stadium.

MAY 14 — Chone Figgins collects five hits and drives in six runs in five at-bats during a ten-inning, 10–9 win over the Orioles in Baltimore. The game started with David Eckstein and Figgins collecting back-to-back triples leading off the first inning. Figgins added a grand slam in the second off Kurt Ainsworth to help the Angels build a 9–0 lead. There were seven Anaheim runs scored in the second, helped by a three hit batsmen (a record), as Robb Quinlan, Eckstein and Casey Kotchman were plunked with pitches. But the Orioles scored nine unanswered runs, the last three in the ninth, to tie the score 9–9. Figgins capped his big day with a game-winning single in the tenth.

MAY 18   Adam Riggs hits a walk-off single in the 11th inning to down the Yankees 1–0 at Angel Stadium. Aaron Sele (six innings), Francisco Rodriguez (two innings), Troy Percival (one inning) and Scot Shields (two innings) combined on a brilliant three-hit shutout.

Free-swinging Vladimir Guerrero won the American League MVP Award in 2004, the first of six years with the Angels, and he remained the team's most feared hitter throughout his time in Anaheim.

The Angels had a 29–15 record and a 3 1/2-game lead on May 23. By July 21, the club was 49–45 and was six games out of first place. From there, the Angels were 43–25 to win the division.

MAY 24   Vladimir Guerrero, Jose Guillen and Jeff DaVanon hit three consecutive homers off Justin Miller in the second inning, but the Angels lose 6–5 in ten innings to the Athletics in Oakland.

MAY 30   The Angels sign Raul Mondesi, most recently with the Pirates, as a free agent.

Mondesi left the Pirates without permission to take care of a personal matter in the Dominican Republic and was released. He played eight games with the Angels and batted .118 before injuring a quad muscle. Mondesi was released by the club in July after missing a rehab appointment.

JUNE 2   Vladimir Guerrero drives in nine runs with two homers, a double, a single and a sacrifice fly in five plate appearances to lead the Angels to a 10–7 victory over the Red Sox at Angel Stadium. David Eckstein and Chone Figgins helped Guerrero achieve his big day. Eckstein collected five hits, including a double, in five at-bats. Figgins was three-for-four. Combined, the top three hitters in the Angels lineup had 12 hits in 13 at-bats. Guerrero hit a two-run homer in the first inning off Pedro Martinez to give the Angels a 2–0 lead. Vladimir added a two-run double in the third off Martinez to break a 2–2 tie. By the time Guerrero batted again in the fourth, the Angels trailed 7–4. He hit a sacrifice fly to narrow the gap to two runs. In the sixth, after Mike Timlin replaced Martinez, Guerrero put Anaheim ahead 8–7 with a three-run homer. In the seventh, Eckstein doubled in a run and crossed the plate on Guerrero's single.

JUNE 7   In the first round of the amateur draft, the Angels select pitcher Jered Weaver from California State University at Long Beach. Weaver moved into the Angels starting rotation in 2006.

JUNE 8   Angels pitchers tie a major league record by striking out 26 batters, but the club loses 1–0 in 17 innings to the Brewers at Anaheim Stadium. The pitchers were Kelvim Escobar (11 strikeouts in eight innings), Francisco Rodriguez (three strikeouts in two innings), Scot Shields (four strikeouts in two innings), Kevin Gregg (three strikeouts in two innings) and Ramon Ortiz (five strikeouts in three innings). In the process, Bengie Molina set a record for most putouts by a catcher in a game with 26. Milwaukee's Geoff Jenkins tied a big-league record by fanning six times. The lone run crossed the plate on a double in the 17th by Scott Podsednik off Oritz. The Angels collected only four hits off six Brewers hurlers. Starter Ben Sheets allowed only one hit in nine innings.

Rodriguez had a 4–1 record and 12 saves in 2004 along with a 1.82 ERA and 123 strikeouts in 69 games and 84 innings.

JUNE 11   The Angels play the Cubs for the first time during the regular season and win 3–2 at Angel Stadium.

JUNE 15   The Angels play in Pittsburgh for the first time and defeat the Pirates 4–2 at PNC Park.

June 18	The Angels play in Houston for the first time and lose 5–0 to the Astros at Minute Maid Park.
June 25	The Angels collect 22 hits and rout the Dodgers 13–0 in Los Angeles.
July 7	Jose Guillen hits two homers and a double and drives in five runs in three at-bats during a 12–0 thrashing of the White Sox in Chicago. Bengie Molina hit into a five-four-three triple play.
July 10	The Angels score seven runs in the seventh inning and trounce the Blue Jays 11–2 in Toronto. Bengie Molina hit a grand slam off Kerry Ligtenberg.
July 19	Travis Hafner hits two homers for the Indians, the second of which is a three-run shot in the tenth that beats the Angels 8–5 at Angel Stadium.
July 20	Travis Hafner hits three homers for the Indians to lead his club to a 14–5 win over the Angels at Angel Stadium. His five home runs in back-to-back games tied a major league record.
July 22	The Angels lambaste the Rangers 11–1 in Arlington.
July 25	Kevin Gregg ties a major league record by throwing four wild pitches in the eighth inning of a 6–2 loss to the Mariners in Seattle.
July 27	Bartolo Colon (seven innings), Francisco Rodriguez (one inning) and Troy Percival (one inning) combine on a one-hitter to defeat the Rangers 2–0 at Angel Stadium. The only Texas hit was a single by Matt Young in the third inning. Jose Guillen had a hand in both runs. In the fourth inning, Guillen doubled in a run and scored on Robb Quinlan's single.
	Before the game, a fight broke out between Adam Kennedy and Texas catcher Gerald Laird, a carry-over from their dispute the night before. Laird claimed that Kennedy attempted to be hit by a pitch with the bases loaded and said something to Kennedy before his next plate appearance. They clashed near the batting cage prior to the July 27 contest, and soon all players from both teams were involved before tempers cooled.
July 28	John Lackey (8 1/3 innings) and Troy Percival (two-thirds of an inning) combine on a three-hitter to defeat the Rangers 2–0 at Angel Stadium. The save was Percival's 300th in the major leagues.
July 31	Jose Guillen collects five hits in six at-bats to lead the Angels past the Mariners 9–8 in 11 innings at Angel Stadium. The Angels trailed 5–0 at the end of the third inning, but came back to take a 7–6 advantage in the eighth. The Mariners scored a run in the ninth and another in the 11th, however, to move ahead 8–7. In the bottom of the 11th, Curtis Pride singled, and Guillen walloped a two-run walk-off homer.
	Pride played in the majors from 1993 through 2006 despite being deaf since birth. He was the first deaf player in the majors since Dick Sipek in 1945. Pride appeared in 68 games for the Angels from 2004 through 2006.

AUGUST 6	The Angels sign Andres Galarraga as a free agent.
AUGUST 8	The Angels score three runs in the ninth inning to down the Royals 6–4 in Kansas City. Jose Guillen led off the ninth with a homer. With one out and runners on second and third, David Eckstein bunted to score Darin Erstad from third. On the same play, Kennedy crossed the plate from second when pitcher Dennys Reyes threw wildly to first.
AUGUST 9	For the second night in a row, the Angels rally in the ninth inning by scoring four runs to defeat the Royals 5–3 in Kansas City. The rally consisted of three singles, two walks, two wild pitches and an error.
AUGUST 10	Robb Quinlan runs his hitting streak to 21 games during an 11–3 loss to the Orioles at Angel Stadium.

Quinlan batted .442 with 34 hits during the 21-game streak. Seven days later, his season ended when he tore an oblique muscle while taking batting practice.

AUGUST 14	Francisco Rodriguez strikes out four of the five batters to face him in the eighth and ninth innings to close out an 11–8 win over the Tigers at Angel Stadium.
AUGUST 19	Josh Paul hits a grand slam off Travis Harper in the seventh inning of a 10–7 triumph over the Devil Rays in St. Petersburg.
AUGUST 25	Jeff DaVanon hits for the cycle in a 21–6 trouncing of the Royals at Angel Stadium. DaVanon hit a double off Mike Wood in the third inning, a triple against Matt Kinney in the fourth, a single facing Shawn Camp in the fifth and a home run off Scott Sullivan in the eighth. Jose Molina hit a grand slam off Sullivan in the seventh. Molina entered the game as a substitute first baseman for Darin Erstad, who was given a rest during the rout. The Angels scored five runs in the third inning, six in the fourth, three in the fifth, two in the sixth and five in the seventh.
AUGUST 27	The Angels extend their winning streak to nine games with a 9–6 decision over the Twins in Minnesota.
AUGUST 29	Adam Kennedy hits a two-run, walk-off homer in the ninth inning to defeat the Twins 4–2 at Angel Stadium.
AUGUST 31	Alfredo Amezaga hits a grand slam off Mike Myers in the ninth inning, but the Angels lose 10–7 to the Red Sox in Boston. Amezaga entered the game as a pinch hitter for David Eckstein in the eighth.
SEPTEMBER 5	John Lackey ($7^{1}/_{3}$ innings) and Francisco Rodriguez ($1^{2}/_{3}$ innings) combine on a two-hitter to defeat the Indians 2–1 at Jacobs Field. The only Cleveland hits were doubles by Travis Hafner in the sixth inning and Ronnie Belliard in the eighth, but off Lackey.
SEPTEMBER 8	Kelvim Escobar (12 strikeouts in eight innings) and Brendan Donnelly (two strikeouts in an inning) combine to fan 14 batters, but the Angels lose 1–0 to the Blue Jays at Angel Stadium.

> *Donnelly didn't pitch until June 18 in 2004 because of an injury suffered in spring training. While shagging fly balls, Donnelly was hit in the face, breaking his nose in 20 places. It required three surgeries to set it straight.*

SEPTEMBER 12   The Angels clobber the White Sox 11–0 at Angel Stadium. Bartolo Colon (seven innings), Kevin Gregg (one inning) and Scott Dunn (one inning) combined on the shutout.

SEPTEMBER 20   In his first major league start, third baseman Dallas McPherson collects three hits, including a double, in three at-bats to help the Angels defeat the Mariners 5–2 at Angel Stadium.

> *Vladimir Guerrero left the game after being hit in the head by a pitch from Ryan Franklin. The contest was delayed for five minutes while Guerrero received medical attention and Mike Scioscia and Seattle manager Bob Melvin talked to the umpires about the beaning. The situation escalated when Scioscia yelled and gestured toward Franklin. The Mariners pitcher moved toward the Angels manager before being restrained by teammates. Scioscia was ejected.*

SEPTEMBER 24   Raul Ibanez of the Mariners collects six hits in six at-bats during a 16–6 win over the Angels at Angel Stadium. Seattle had 24 hits in all.

SEPTEMBER 24   The Angels lose 6–3 to the Athletics at Angel Stadium to fall three games behind the Oakland club in the AL West race. The Angels were tied for second with the Rangers. There were nine games left on the schedule.

SEPTEMBER 25   Jose Guillen has a confrontation with Mike Scioscia in the dugout after being lifted for a pinch runner in the eighth inning of a 5–3 loss to the Athletics at Angel Stadium.

> *After being removed from the game, Guillen threw his arms in the air, fired his helmet in Scioscia's direction and slammed his glove against the wall. Scioscia responded by suspending Guillen for "inappropriate conduct" for the remainder of the season, including the playoffs. The next day, Guillen railed against Scioscia to reporters, calling him "a piece of garbage" and saying "he can go to hell." With Adam Riggs, who hit .194 in 2004, replacing Guillen in the lineup, the Angels won seven of eight games beginning on September 25. Guillen was traded to the Nationals two months later (see November 19, 2004).*

SEPTEMBER 28   The Angels move into a tie for first place with the Athletics by defeating the Rangers 8–2 in Arlington. Vladimir Guerrero led the way with two homers, a double, a single and five runs batted in in five at-bats. There were five games left on the schedule.

> *In five games between September 27 and September 30, Guerrero collected 12 hits, five of them home runs, in 17 at-bats and drove in nine runs.*

SEPTEMBER 29   The Angels take a one-game lead in the AL West by defeating the Rangers 8–7 in 11 innings in Arlington. Trailing 6–5 with two out and no one on base, Vladimir Guerrero singled, and Curtis Pride doubled to tie the score. In the 11th, Troy Glaus hit a two-run homer for an 8–6 advantage before the Angels survived a Texas rally in the bottom half for the win.

September 30	The Angels drop back into a tie for first place with the Athletics after losing 6–3 to the Rangers in Arlington.

There were three games left on the schedule, each against the Athletics in Oakland. The formula was simple. The team that won at least two of the three games would capture the AL West crown.

October 1	The Angels take a one-game lead in the AL West by routing the Athletics 10–0 in Oakland. Alfredo Amezaga hit a grand slam off Joe Blanton in the sixth inning. Playing second base in place of the injured Adam Kennedy, Amezaga came into the game batting .155 with one home run on the season. Amezaga hit two homers in 2004, and both were grand slams. He didn't hit another home run in a major league game until 2006 when he was playing for the Marlins. Bartolo Colon (seven innings), Brendan Donnelly (one inning) and Ramon Ortiz (one inning) combined on the shutout. Andres Galarraga hit his 399th career homer. It was his only one in an Angels uniform.
October 2	The Angels clinch the AL West pennant by defeating the Athletics 5–4 in Oakland. Trailing 4–2 in the eighth, Darin Erstad doubled in two runs and crossed the plate on a single by Garret Anderson. Troy Percival pitched a one-two-three ninth.
October 3	Playing in his last major league game, Andres Galarraga is hitless in three at-bats during a 3–2 loss to the Athletics in Oakland, thereby finishing his career with 399 home runs. Others who fell just shy of 400 career home runs were Al Kaline (399), Dale Murphy (398) and Joe Carter (396).

The Angels played the Boston Red Sox in the Division Series. Managed by Terry Francona, the Red Sox were 98–64 in 2004 and won the wild-card berth.

October 5	The Angels open the Division Series by losing 9–3 to the Red Sox before 44,608 at Angel Stadium. Boston broke the game open with seven runs in the fourth inning, six of them off Jarrod Washburn, to take an 8–0 lead. Troy Glaus and Darin Erstad each collected three hits, including a home run, in the losing cause.

The series was telecast nationally over ESPN with Chris Berman, Rick Sutcliffe and Tony Gwynn serving as announcers.

October 6	The Angels lose game two 8–3 to the Red Sox before 45,188 at Angel Stadium. The Sox broke a 3–3 tie with a run in the seventh inning, then salted the game away with a four-run ninth.
October 8	The Red Sox complete the sweep of the Division Series by defeating the Angels 8–6 in ten innings at Fenway Park. Trailing 6–1, the Angels scored five runs in the seventh inning with two out on a bases-loaded walk by Mike Timlin to Darin Erstad and a grand slam by Vladimir Guerrero. David Ortiz ended the contest with a two-run, walk-off homer off Jarrod Washburn, who was making his first relief appearance since 1999. He didn't make another one until 2008 when he was a member of the Mariners.

The Red Sox moved on to the Championship Series and faced the Yankees. After falling behind three games to none, the Red Sox put together an unprecedented comeback and captured four victories in succession. In the World Series, Boston swept the Cardinals four straight to win their first world championship since 1918.

OCTOBER 15   The Angels sell Derrick Turnbow to the Brewers.

Turnbow spent most of 2003 and 2004 in the minors at Salt Lake, but when pitching for the Angels he allowed only one earned run in $21^{2}/_{3}$ innings for an ERA of 0.42. He excelled for one season in Milwaukee as a closer with 33 saves and an ERA of 1.74 in 69 games and $67^{1}/_{3}$ innings in 2005.

NOVEMBER 18   Two weeks after George W. Bush wins re-election by defeating John Kerry in the Presidential election, Troy Percival signs with the Tigers as a free agent.

Percival has struggled with arm problems since leaving the Angels. He enjoyed a comeback year in 2008 as the closer on the American League champion Tampa Bay Rays.

NOVEMBER 19   The Angels trade Jose Guillen to the Nationals for Macier Izturis and Juan Rivera.

Guillen stamped his ticket out of town when he was suspended near the end of the season (see September 25, 2004). The problems between Guillen and Scioscia were far from over, however (see June 14, 2005).

DECEMBER 6   The Angels sign Steve Finley, most recently with the Dodgers, as a free agent.

DECEMBER 11   Troy Glaus signs with the Diamondbacks as a free agent.

Glaus hit a club-record 47 homers as a 23-year-old in 2000, then added 40 more homers in 2001. He never reached those levels again as he was bogged down by an assortment of injuries. Glaus played in only 55 games in 2004. After leaving Anaheim, Glaus regained his health and was a consistently solid performer at third base with the Diamondbacks, Blue Jays and Cardinals for another four years.

DECEMBER 14   The Angels sign Paul Byrd, most recently with the Braves, as a free agent. On the same day, Ramon Ortiz was traded to the Reds for Dustin Moseley.

DECEMBER 17   The White Sox purchase Bobby Jenks from the Angels.

Jenks was a starter in the Angels farm system and struggled mightily with his control, walking 6.2 batters per nine innings over five seasons. The White Sox converted Jenks into a reliever, and he quickly developed into one of the best closers in the game.

DECEMBER 23   David Eckstein signs with the Cardinals as a free agent.

Eckstein became part of the "shortstop-go-'round" of the 2004–05 offseason. Eckstein went from the Angels to the Cardinals, Edgar Renteria moved from the Cardinals to the Red Sox, and Orlando Cabrera transferred from the roster of the Red Sox to the Angels.

2005

Season in a Sentence
Now known as the Los Angeles Angels of Anaheim, the club wins the AL West before defeating the Yankees and losing to the White Sox in the playoffs.

Finish • Won • Lost • Pct • GB
First   95   67   .586   +7.0

AL Division Series
The Angels defeated the New York Yankees three games to one.

AL Championship Series
The Angels lost to the Chicago White Sox four games to one.

Manager
Mike Scioscia

Stats

Stats	Angels	AL	Rank
Batting Avg:	.270	.268	6
On-Base Pct:	.325	.330	9
Slugging Pct:	.409	.424	9
Home Runs:	147		10
Stolen Bases:	161		1
ERA:	3.68	4.35	3
Errors:	87		2
Runs Scored:	761		7
Runs Allowed:	643		2

Starting Lineup
Bengie Molina, c
Darin Erstad, 1b
Adam Kennedy, 2b
Chone Figgins, 3b-cf-2b
Orlando Cabrera, ss
Garret Anderson, lf
Steve Finley, cf
Vladimir Guerrero, rf
Jeff DaVanon, dh-rf-lf
Juan Rivera, lf-rf-dh

Pitchers
Bartolo Colon, sp
John Lackey, sp
Paul Byrd, sp
Erwin Santana, sp
Jarrod Washburn, sp
Francisco Rodriguez, rp
Scot Shields, rp
Brendan Donnelly, rp
Esteban Yan, rp

Attendance
3,404,686 (second in AL)

Club Leaders

Batting Avg:	Vladimir Guerrero	.317
On-Base Pct:	Vladimir Guerrero	.394
Slugging Pct:	Vladimir Guerrero	.565
Home Runs:	Vladimir Guerrero	32
RBI:	Vladimir Guerrero	108
Runs:	Chone Figgins	113
Stolen Bases:	Chone Figgins	62
Wins:	Bartolo Colon	21
Strikeouts:	John Lackey	199
ERA:	Jarrod Washburn	3.20
Saves:	Francisco Rodriguez	45

JANUARY 3   Angels owner Arte Moreno announces that the name of the franchise will be changed from the Anaheim Angels to the Los Angeles Angels of Anaheim. According to the 2005 team media guide, "the inclusion of Los Angeles reflects the original expansion name and returns the Angels as Major League Baseball's American League representative in the Greater Los Angeles territory." It was the third name change in club history. The team was known as the Los Angeles Angels from its inception in December 1960 through September 1965; the California Angels from September 1965 through November 1996; and the Anaheim Angels from November 1996 through January 2005.

Moreno saw the change as part of an overall strategy to increase the team's revenue by marketing it to the entire Los Angeles area. Billboards promoting the

Angels even went up near Dodger Stadium. The suffix "of Anaheim" was tacked on to satisfy a contractual obligation with the city. The unwieldy moniker Los Angeles Angels of Anaheim became the subject of national ridicule. Moreno also encountered a substantial backlash from many Angels fans, who took pride in the city of Anaheim and the surrounding Orange County area and desired an identity distinctive from Los Angeles. Outraged Anaheim city officials responded by suing the team, claiming that the name change was in violation of the club's lease on Angel Stadium, which is owned by the city. According to the 1996 agreement, the Angels had to include Anaheim in the team name in exchange for $20 million worth of stadium improvements and other considerations. In addition to the suit, the mayors of every Orange County city as well as the mayor of Los Angeles signed a petition opposing the name change. On February 9, 2006, a jury found in favor of the team, determining that the Los Angeles Angels of Anaheim name was in compliance with the lease agreement. The city of Anaheim appealed the decision, and on December 20, 2008, the state appellate court denied the appeal. The Angels have continued to market themselves without direct reference to their location whenever possible. Neither "Los Angeles" nor "Anaheim" appears on the team's uniforms, and the Angels are not referred as "Los Angeles" by the Angel Stadium ballpark announcer nor by the Angels television or radio broadcasters, who use "Angels" or "Angels baseball" in its place. On official press releases and on the team's Web site, the entire name "Los Angeles Angels of Anaheim" is used. Major League Baseball refers to the team as "Los Angeles." In the end, the change failed to harm attendance. The Angels have drawn over three million fans every season since 2003 and have developed a rabid fan base.

JANUARY 12 The Angels sign Orlando Cabrera, most recently with the Red Sox, as a free agent.

APRIL 5 The Angels open the season with a 3–2 victory over the Rangers before 43,590 at Angel Stadium. Vladimir Guerrero drove in two runs with a homer and a double. Bartolo Colon pitched $6^{2}/_{3}$ innings for the win.

Guerrero followed his MVP season of 2004 by hitting .317 with 32 homers and 108 RBIs in 2005.

APRIL 11 Trailing 6–2, the Angels score a run in the seventh inning, two in the eighth, one in the ninth and one in the tenth to defeat the Rangers 7–6 at Arlington. Darin Erstad homered in the ninth and Orlando Cabrera in the tenth.

The Angels broke another team attendance record in 2005 by drawing 3,404,868 to Angel Stadium. The club ranked fourth in baseball in attendance, trailing only the Dodgers, Yankees and Cardinals.

APRIL 12 The Angels outslug the Rangers 13–8 in Arlington.

APRIL 15 Bartolo Colon (seven innings), Scot Shields (one inning) and Francisco Rodriguez (one inning) combine on a two-hitter to defeat the Athletics 6–1 in Oakland. The only hits by the A's were a double by Mark Kotsay and a single from Scott Hatteberg in the fourth inning.

APRIL 21 Down 5–0, the Angels score a run in the third inning, two in the fourth, one in the eighth, one in the ninth and one in the tenth to defeat the Indians 6–5 at Angel

Stadium. Garret Anderson drove in the tying run with a two-out single in the ninth. Orlando Cabrera ended the contest by belting a walk-off homer.

APRIL 24 — Steve Finley hits a home run off Joe Blanton in the seventh inning to account for the lone run of a 1–0 win over the Athletics at Angel Stadium. Kelvim Escobar (six innings), Scot Shields (1 2/3 innings) and Francisco Rodriguez (1 1/3 innings) combined on the shutout.

APRIL 26 — Alex Rodriguez hits three homers and a single and drives in ten runs to lead the Yankees to a 12–4 win over the Angels in New York. Rodriguez clubbed all three homers and accounted for nine of his ten RBIs off Bartolo Colon on a three-run homer in the first inning, a two-run shot in the third and a grand slam in the fourth.

MAY 1 — Solo homers by Jose Molina in the fourth inning and Vladimir Guerrero in the sixth, both off Johan Santana, are enough to defeat the Twins 2–1 in Minneapolis.

MAY 17 — In his major league debut, Angels starter Ervin Santana yields a cycle to the first four batters he faces in the major leagues. Facing the Indians in Cleveland, Santana surrendered a triple to Grady Sizemore, a double to Coco Crisp, a single to Travis Hafner and a homer to Ben Broussard. The Indians won the game 13–5.

MAY 20 — Juan Rivera hits a grand slam off Yhency Brazoban in the ninth inning of a 9–0 triumph over the Dodgers in Los Angeles. Rivera entered the contest in the fifth as a substitute for Vladimir Guerrero in right field.

MAY 27 — The Angels take a thrilling 9–8 decision

Speedy Chone Figgins was a feared base-stealer during his years with the Angels, leading the league in swipes in 2005.

from the Royals in ten innings at Angel Stadium. Kansas City led 4–3 at the end of the eighth, then tacked on four more runs in the ninth. The Angels tied the game 8–8 in the bottom half with an incredible five-run rally. Dallas McPherson drove in the first run with a single. With the bases loaded and none out, Adam Kennedy hit a grounder to shortstop Angel Berroa, who threw to second for an attempted force. The throw was wild, however, and all three runners scored. Kennedy wound up on second on the play and crossed the plate on a single from Chone Figgins. In the tenth, McPherson walloped a walk-off homer.

> *Figgins finished the season with a .290 batting average, 113 runs scored and 62 stolen bases. He displayed his versatility by playing in 56 games at third base, 50 in center field, 42 at second, 15 in left, eight in right, four at shortstop and seven as the designated hitter.*

May 28   The Angels score six runs in the fourth inning and clobber the Royals 14–1 at Angel Stadium.

June 4   Trailing 5–1 at the end of five innings, the Angels score a run in the sixth inning, four in the seventh, one in the eighth and six in the ninth to defeat the Red Sox 13–6 in Boston. Garret Anderson put the Angels into the lead with a three-run homer in the seventh.

> *Anderson, Tim Salmon and Darin Erstad are the only individuals to play for the Angels while they were known as the California Angels, Anaheim Angels, and Los Angeles Angels of Anaheim.*

June 6   The Angels play the Braves for the first time during the regular season and win 4–2 in Atlanta.

June 7   With their first pick in the amateur draft, the Angels select pitcher Trevor Bell from LaCrescenta High School in LaCrescenta, California.

June 10   The Angels play the Mets for the first time in New York City and win 12–2 at Shea Stadium.

June 13   The Angels play the Washington Nationals for the first time and collect 20 hits during an 11–1 win at Angel Stadium. Vladimir Guerrero collected four hits, including a homer, in four at-bats and drove in five runs. The contest also the marked the return of Jose Guillen to Anaheim. Guillen had been suspended by the Angels near the end of the previous season (see September 25, 2004).

June 14   Controversy flares during a 6–3 loss to the Nationals at Angel Stadium. With the Angels leading 3–1 in the seventh inning, Washington manager Frank Robinson called for an inspection of Brendan Donnelly's glove. Both benches cleared and Robinson and Mike Scioscia had to be physically separated. As he was being restrained by fellow Nationals players, Jose Guillen shouted angry words at the Angels, a number of whom made it clear that they believed their former teammate had been the one who told Robinson to have Donnelly's glove examined. (Several weeks later, Guillen acknowledged that he had done so.) Donnelly was ejected for having a foreign substance (pine tar) on his glove. Guillen belted a two-run homer in the eighth to tie the score 3–3, and the Nationals added three more runs for the victory.

	Donnelly was later suspended for ten days by Major League Baseball. Scioscia and Robinson were each suspended for one game.
JUNE 17	The Angels play the Marlins for the first time during the regular season and win 3–2 in 11 innings at Angel Stadium. Jeff DaVanon drove in the winning run with a walk-off single.
JUNE 18	The Angels win with a walk-off hit in extra innings for the second day in a row when Vladimir Guerrero homers in the tenth to defeat the Marlins 3–2 at Angel Stadium.
JUNE 21	Darin Erstad runs his hitting streak to 21 games during an 8–6 victory over the Rangers at Angel Stadium.
	During the streak, Erstad collected 35 hits in 91 at-bats for a batting average of .385.
JUNE 27	The Angels collect 20 hits and defeat the Rangers 13–3 in Arlington. Juan Rivera had three doubles and a single in four at-bats.
JUNE 28	Garret Anderson hits a grand slam off Brian Shouse in the 11th inning to defeat the Rangers 5–1 in Arlington. It was the Angels' eighth win in a row.
JUNE 29	Rangers pitcher Kenny Rogers shoves two cameramen before a game against the Angels in Arlington. Texas won 7–6 in 11 innings. Rogers was later suspended for 20 days and fined $50,000 by Major League Baseball.
JUNE 30	The Rangers hit eight home runs during an 18–5 win over the Angels in Arlington. Kevin Mench hit three home runs, Mark Teixeira two, and Hank Blalock, Alfonso Soriano and David Dellucci one each. Erwin Santana and Jake Woods each gave up three homers and Joel Peralta two.
JULY 1	Paul Byrd pitches a two-hitter to defeat the Royals 5–0 at Kauffman Stadium. The only Kansas City hits were a single by Matt Stairs in the fifth inning and a double from Mark Sweeney in the seventh.
	Byrd is well-known for his uncanny resemblance to actor Kelsey Grammer. He is also known for using an "old-fashioned" wind-up, in which he swings his arms back prior to going into the full wind-up. He occasionally swings his arms back twice before pitching.
JULY 6	The Angels defeat the Twins 7–6 at Angel Stadium. The win gave the Angels a 52–32 record and an 8½-game lead in the AL West.
JULY 21	With the Angels trailing 5–2, Vladimir Guerrero hits a grand slam off Tom Gordon in the seventh inning to beat the Yankees 6–5 at Angel Stadium.
JULY 28	The Angels lose 2–1 to the Blue Jays in an 18-inning marathon in Toronto. The contest was scoreless until both teams scored in the ninth. Francisco Rodriguez blew the save opportunity. Orlando Hudson drove in the winning run with a single off Scot Shields. John Lackey, Rodriguez, Brendan Donnelly, Esteban Yan, Joel Peralta and Shields combined for 17 strikeouts.

JULY 31	Bengie and Jose Molina both homer off Randy Johnson, but the Angels lose 8–7 to the Yankees in 11 innings in New York. Bengie homered in the fourth inning and Jose in the fifth. Jose drew the start at first base. Through the 2009 season, it is also the only time in his career that Jose was a starter at first.
	Bengie hit .295 with 14 homers in 2005.
AUGUST 2	Vladimir Guerrero hits two homers and drives in five runs during a 10–3 triumph over the Orioles at Angel Stadium.
AUGUST 7	Casey Kotchman reaches base four times in four plate appearances with two homers and two walks and drives in five runs during a 10–4 win over the Devil Rays at Angel Stadium. One of Kotchman's homers was a grand slam off Seth McClung in the third inning.
AUGUST 9	Vladimir Guerrero hits a grand slam off Rich Harden in the second inning of a 9–2 victory over the Athletics in Oakland.
AUGUST 11	Jason Kendall and the Athletics steal a 5–4 win from the Angels in Oakland and move into first place in the AL West. When Francisco Rodriguez muffed a routine throw from catcher Jose Molina, Kendall alertly sprinted home from third base with the winning run.
AUGUST 18	Juan Rivera collects four hits in five at-bats and drives in six runs during a 13–4 trouncing of the Red Sox at Angel Stadium. The six RBIs were attained with a pair of three-run homers in the fifth and eighth innings.
AUGUST 30	The Angels fall two games behind the Athletics with a 2–1 loss in 11 innings to the A's at Angel Stadium.
	The Angels led the AL West by 8½ games and were 10½ games ahead of third-place Oakland on July 6, then went 21–26 while the streaking A's were 34–14.
SEPTEMBER 1	The Angels move back into a tie for first place with a 3–0 win over the Athletics at Angel Stadium. Ervin Santana (8⅓ innings) and Francisco Rodriguez (two-thirds of an inning) combined on the shutout.
	Santana was born Johan Ramon Santana and used that name until 2003. He decided to change his name to avoid having the same name as pitching star Johan Santana, who debuted in the majors with the Twins in 2000.
SEPTEMBER 2	Vladimir Guerrero hits his 300th career home run in the fifth inning of a 4–1 win over the Mariners at Angel stadium. The victim of the milestone blast was Jamie Moyer.
SEPTEMBER 4	The Angels take sole possession of first place with a 5–3 win over the Mariners at Angel Stadium.
	With the exception of a tie for first with the Athletics on September 15, the Angels maintained sole possession of the top spot in the AL West for the remainder of the season. From September 16 through the end of the regular season, the Angels won 14 of 16 games.

SEPTEMBER 9   Francisco Rodriguez strikes out all three batters he faces in the 12th inning to close out a 6–5 win over the White Sox in Chicago. The winning run scored in the top half of the 12th on the heads-up base running of Vladimir Guerrero. Guerrero led off the inning with a double. Bengie Molina then bunted down the third base line, and while third baseman Geoff Blum was throwing to Ross Gload at first, Guerrero kept running when shortstop Juan Uribe was late covering third. Gload's throw home was off-line, and Guerrero scored.

SEPTEMBER 20   Bartolo Colon earns his 20th win of the season with a 2–1 decision over the Rangers at Angel Stadium.

Colon finished the season with a 21–8 record, a 3.48 earned run average and the Cy Young Award.

SEPTEMBER 24   The Angels extend their winning streak to eight games with a 7–3 decision over the Devil Rays at Angel Stadium. The victory gave the Angels a four-game lead with eight contests left on the schedule.

SEPTEMBER 27   The Angels clinch the AL West by defeating the Athletics 4–3 in Oakland.

The Angels played the Yankees in the Division Series. Managed by Joe Torre, the Yanks were 95–67 in 2005 and won the AL East. The Angels also had a 95–67 record in 2005 and won home-field advantage in the playoff series by posting a 6–4 record against the Yankees in head-to-head competition.

OCTOBER 4   The Angels open the Division Series with a 4–2 loss to the Yankees before 45,142 at Angel Stadium. New York scored three runs in the first inning off Bartolo Colon. Bengie Molina homered in the seventh inning.

The series was telecast over the FOX network (games one, four and five) and ESPN (games two and three). The announcers were Joe Buck and Tim McCarver on FOX and Jon Miller and Joe Morgan over ESPN.

OCTOBER 5   The Angels even the series with a 5–3 win over the Yankees in front of a crowd of 45,150 at Angel Stadium. The Yankees took a 2–0 lead before the Angels scored a run in the fifth inning, another in the sixth, two in the seventh and one in the eighth. Orlando Cabrera broke the 2–2 tie with a two-out, two-run single in the seventh. Bengie Molina added a home run in the eighth.

OCTOBER 7   The Angels take a two-games-to-one lead with an 11–7 victory over the Yankees in New York. The Angels took a 5–0 advantage with three runs in the first inning and two in the third off Randy Johnson, fell behind 6–5, then recaptured the lead with a two-run sixth. Garret Anderson homered in the first inning and Bengie Molina in the third. It was the third straight game in which Molina walloped a home run. In the sixth, Juan Rivera doubled and scored on a single from Darin Erstad to tie the score 6–6. Chone Figgins broke the deadlock with an RBI-single. Anderson finished the game with four hits and five RBIs.

OCTOBER 9   The Yankees force a deciding fifth game by defeating the Angels 3–2 in New York. The Angels scored twice in the sixth inning for a 2–0 lead, but the Yankees countered with a run in their half and two more in the seventh.

October 10   The Angels move on to the Championship Series with a 5–3 win over the Yankees before 45,133 at Angel Stadium. The Yankees scored two runs in the second inning, but the Angels responded with three in their half and two more in the third off Mike Mussina. Garret Anderson led off the second with a home run. Adam Kennedy gave the Angels a 3–2 lead with a two-out, two-run triple. It should have been an easy out, but center fielder Bubba Crosby and right fielder Gary Sheffield collided on the play. Bartolo Colon started for the Angels, but had to leave the contest in the second inning because of a hand injury.

October 11   The Angels open the Championship Series with a 3–2 win over the White Sox at U.S. Cellular Field in Chicago. It was the third win in three nights in three cities for the Angels, as the club traveled from New York to Anaheim to Chicago. Garret Anderson started the scoring with a homer leading off the second inning, and the Angels added two runs in the third. Paul Byrd went six innings for the win.

The series was telecast nationally over the FOX network with Joe Buck, Tim McCarver and Lou Piniella serving as announcers.

October 12   The White Sox even the series by defeating the Angels 2–1 in Chicago with a run in the controversial ninth inning. Robb Quinlan tied the score 1–1 with a homer in the fifth inning. With the score still knotted at 1–1 and two outs in the ninth, A. J. Pierzynski swung and missed at a low two-strike pitch from Kelvim Escobar. Believing the inning was over, catcher Josh Paul rolled the ball back to the mound and headed toward the dugout. After hesitating briefly, Pierzynski realized that strike three hadn't been called and ran toward first. Home plate umpire Doug Eddings ruled that the ball hit the ground, then went into Paul's glove. Pierzynski was safe at first. Three pitches later, Joe Crede hit a walk-off double that scored Pablo Ozuna, who pinch-ran for Pierzynski.

October 14   The Angels lose game three 5–2 to the White Sox before 44,725 at Angel Stadium. The Sox scored three runs in the first inning, two on a home run by Paul Konerko, off John Lackey. Orlando Cabrera hit a two-run homer for the Angels in the sixth with Chicago ahead 5–0.

October 15   The White Sox move within one game of the AL pennant by beating the Angels 8–2 before 44,857 at Angel Stadium. Paul Konerko hit a home run in the first inning for the second game in a row to give Chicago a 3–0 advantage. There was more controversy in game four. Konerko's homer came after a disputed checked swing on a 2–2 pitch. With the White Sox leading 3–1 and Angels runners on first and third in the second, Steve Finley hit into an inning-ending double play. Finley argued that catcher A. J. Pierzynski interfered with his swing by tipping his bat, but the umpires disagreed. Pierzynski homered in the fourth.

October 16   The White Sox win their first AL pennant since 1959 by defeating the Angels 6–3 before a game-five crowd of 44,712 at Angel Stadium. The Angels led 3–2 at the end of five innings before Chicago scored a run in the sixth, another in the seventh and two in the eighth.

The four White Sox victories came on complete games from Mark Buehrle, Jon Garland, Freddy Garcia and Jose Contreras. The Sox swept the Astros in the World Series to win their first world championship since 1917.

DECEMBER 7   Paul Byrd signs with the Indians as a free agent.

DECEMBER 21   The Angels trade Steve Finley to the Giants for Edgardo Alfonzo.

DECEMBER 22   Jarrod Washburn signs with the Mariners as a free agent.

2006

Season in a Sentence
The Angels fall short in their quest for a third consecutive AL West title, but achieve a milestone by posting a winning season in three consecutive seasons for the first time in franchise history.

Finish • Won • Lost • Pct • GB
Second   89   73   .549   4.0

In the wild-card race, the Angels finished in third place, six games behind.

Manager
Mike Scioscia

Stats	Angels	AL	Rank
Batting Avg:	.274	.275	8
On-Base Pct:	.334	.339	10
Slugging Pct:	.425	.437	10
Home Runs:	159		12
Stolen Bases:	148		1
ERA:	4.04	4.56	3
Errors:	124		14
Runs Scored:	766		11
Runs Allowed:	732		4

Starting Lineup
Mike Napoli, c
Howie Kendrick, 1b-2b
Adam Kennedy, 2b
Macier Izturis, 3b
Orlando Cabrera, ss
Garret Anderson, lf-dh
Chone Figgins, cf
Vladimir Guerrero, rf
Tim Salmon, dh
Juan Rivera, lf-rf
Robb Quinlan, 1b
Jose Molina, c

Pitchers
Ervin Santana, sp
John Lackey, sp
Kelvim Escobar, sp
Jered Weaver, sp
Jeff Weaver, sp
Francisco Rodriguez, rp
Scot Shields, rp
J. C. Romero, rp
Brendan Donnelly, rp
Hector Carrasco, rp

Attendance
3,406,790 (second in AL)

Club Leaders
Batting Avg:	Vladimir Guerrero	.329
On-Base Pct:	Vladimir Guerrero	.382
Slugging Pct:	Vladimir Guerrero	.582
Home Runs:	Vladimir Guerrero	33
RBI:	Vladimir Guerrero	116
Runs:	Orlando Cabrera	95
Stolen Bases:	Chone Figgins	52
Wins:	Ervin Santana	16
Strikeouts:	John Lackey	190
ERA:	John Lackey	3.56
Saves:	Francisco Rodriguez	47

FEBRUARY 6   Bengie Molina signs with the Blue Jays as a free agent.

FEBRUARY 23   The Angels sign Jeff Weaver, most recently with the Dodgers, as a free agent.

> *At the time Jeff was signed, Jered Weaver, Jeff's younger brother (by six years) was the Angels' top pitching prospect. Jered was called up from the minors on May 26 and won his first seven starts and first nine decisions. Jeff was pitching so badly, he was sent to the minors on June 30, then was traded to the Cardinals on July 5 with a record of 3–10 and a 6.29 ERA.*

APRIL 3	The Angels open the season with a 5–4 win over the Mariners at Safeco Field. Orlando Cabrera broke a 3–3 tie with a two-run single in the top of the ninth before the Mariners scored in their half. Vladimir Guerrero hit a two-run homer on a 1–0 pitch in the first. It was the second straight year that Guerrero homered on his first swing of the season.
APRIL 7	In the home opener, the Angels defeat the Yankees 4–1 before 44,221 at Angel Stadium. Orlando Cabrera homered.
APRIL 11	Adam Kennedy hits a two-run, walk-off double in the ninth inning to defeat the Rangers 5–4 at Angel Stadium.
APRIL 24	Francisco Rodriguez strikes out all three batters he faces in the ninth inning of a 3–0 win over the Tigers at Angel Stadium.
APRIL 26	John Lackey (eight innings) and Scot Shields (one inning) combine on a two-hitter to defeat the Tigers 4–0 at Angel Stadium. The only Detroit hits were singles by Craig Monroe in the fifth inning (off Lackey) and Magglio Ordonez in the ninth (against Shields).
MAY 2	Jason Kendall of the Athletics charges the mound and wrestles with John Lackey after being hit by a pitch in the sixth inning of a 10–3 Angels loss at Angel Stadium. Both dugouts and bullpens emptied, but no one was ejected.

> *Casey Kotchman began the 2006 campaign as the Angels starting first baseman, but hit just .152 in 29 games before going on the disabled list in May with mononucleosis. He missed the remainder of the season.*

MAY 4	Mike Napoli homers in his first major league plate appearance during a 7–2 win over the Tigers in Detroit. The home run came in the third inning off Justin Verlander on the fourth pitch of the at-bat. As a rookie, Napoli batted only .228, but hit 16 homers in 268 at-bats.

> *On the same day, Los Angeles psychologist Michael Cohn sued the Angels for $4,000 for sexual discrimination because he was denied a tote bag. The club gave away the tote bags to women 18 or older entering the gates at Angel Stadium as part of a promotion on Mother's Day in 2005. Cohn alleged that males and fans under 18 were "treated unequally." In February 2007, Orange County Superior Court Judge Jonathan Cannon threw the case out of court. Cohn's appeals were likewise denied.*

MAY 12	Juan Rivera hits a grand slam off Bobby Livingston in the fourth inning of a 12–7 win over the Mariners at Angel Stadium.
MAY 16	Jose Molina steals second base with his brother Bengie catching for the Blue Jays in the sixth inning of an 8–3 win at Angel Stadium. Jose came into the game with just six career stolen bases in 277 games. It was not only his lone steal of the 2006 season, but his only stolen base attempt.
MAY 17	Bengie Molina tries to seek revenge from the previous day by trying to steal second base off of his brother Jose, but is thrown out in the second inning of a 3–0 Blue Jays win over the Angels at Angel Stadium (see September 9, 2006).

May 19	The Dodgers collect 25 hits in eight turns at bat and wallop the Angels 16–3 in Los Angeles.
May 23	In the second plate appearance of his first major league game, first baseman Kendry Morales homers to help the Angels to a 7–6 victory over the Rangers in Arlington. Morales also collected two singles to complete a three-for-five day.
May 27	In his major league debut, Jered Weaver pitches seven shutout innings while allowing three hits to lead the Angels to a 10–1 triumph over the Orioles at Angel Stadium.
June 2	In his second big-league appearance, Jered Weaver pitches shutout ball over the first six innings before surrendering two runs in the seventh inning of a 10–3 triumph over the Indians in Cleveland. In his first two starts combined, Weaver began his career by pitching 13 consecutive shutout innings.
June 3	The Angels lose 14–2 to the Indians in Cleveland.
June 4	The day after losing 14–2 to the Indians in Cleveland, the Angels turn the tables and win by the same 14–2 score.
June 6	The Angels score ten runs over the last four innings and rout the Devil Rays 12–2 in St. Petersburg.

On the same day, the Angels selected catcher Hyun Choi Conger from Huntington Beach High School in Huntington Beach, California, in the first round of the amateur draft.

June 13	Jered Weaver allows one unearned run in seven innings of a 4–1 win over the Royals at Angel Stadium.

Despite a 4–0 record and a 1.37 ERA in four starts, Weaver was sent to Salt Lake City on June 16 to make room for Bartolo Colon, who was coming off the disabled list. Jered was recalled on June 30, and his brother Jeff was sent to the minors. Jeff was traded to the Cardinals on July 5.

June 24	Robb Quinlan hits a two-run homer in the 13th inning to defeat the Diamondbacks 6–4 in Phoenix.
July 1	Garret Anderson collects his 2,000th career hit during a 9–2 win over the Dodgers at Angel Stadium. The milestone hit was a single off Aaron Sele in the sixth inning.

The Angels won 13 of their first 14 games in July.

July 3	Orlando Cabrera executes a straight steal of home without drawing a throw from pitcher Chad Billingsley in the third inning of a 4–0 win over the Dodgers at Angel Stadium.
July 4	Trailing 5–2, the Angels erupt for seven runs in the sixth inning and defeat the Mariners 14–6 in Seattle. Juan Rivera hit two homers and a single in five at-bats and drove in five runs.

July 5	The Angels trade Jeff Weaver to the Cardinals for Terry Evans.

> *Weaver was traded five days after suffering the indignity of being sent to the minors to make room on the roster for his younger brother Jered. Jeff was 5–4 with a 5.18 ERA for the Cardinals, then posted a 3–2 record in five starts in the postseason, including a victory in game five of the World Series against the Tigers, which clinched the world championship.*

July 7	After giving up a double to Mark Kotsay leading off the first inning, John Lackey retires the last 27 batters to face him in a 3–0 win over the Athletics in Oakland. Lackey threw 109 pitches in the one-hit gem and struck out ten batters. The other 17 outs were recorded on four grounders and 13 fly balls.

> *Orlando Cabrera was hitless in four at-bats during the game to end his streak of reaching base in a club-record 63 consecutive games from April 25 through July 6. It was also the longest such streak in major league history since Ted Williams set the all-time record with an 84-game in 1949. Over his streak, Cabrera had a batting average of .302 with 76 hits in 251 at-bats. He also drew 27 walks and was hit by a pitch twice. Cabrera's on-base percentage over the 63 games was .372. Through 2009, the only others players with streaks of reaching base in 60 or more games were Williams (84 in 1949 and 69 in 1941), Joe DiMaggio (74 in 1941) and Bill Joyce (64 in 1891). Cabrera's on-base percentage of .372 was much lower than the other four during their streaks. Williams's was .518 in 1949 and .593 in 1941; DiMaggio's was .468; and Joyce weighed in with an on-base percentage of .463. Cabrera finished the 2006 season with a .282 batting average and a .335 on-base percentage. His on-base percentage was lower than the AL average of .339 that season. Cabrera's 45 doubles in 2006 ranks third all-time in Angels history behind Garret Anderson, who had 56 in 2002 and 49 in 2003. Vladimir Guerrero also had 45 doubles in 2007.*

July 11	Vladimir Guerrero homers off Brad Penny in the second inning of the American League's 3–2 win in the All-Star Game at PNC Park in Pittsburgh.
July 15	Vladimir Guerrero drives in five runs and passes the 1,000 mark in career runs batted in during a 9–2 triumph over the Devil Rays at Angel Stadium. Guerrero powered a grand slam off Chad Harville in the seventh inning.
July 18	The Angels extend their winning streak to eight games with a 7–5 decision over the Indians at Angel Stadium.
July 23	Jered Weaver runs his record to 7–0 after seven career starts by pitching $6^{2}/_{3}$ innings for the victory in a 3–1 decision over the Royals in Kansas City. Weaver's 7–0 mark was accompanied by a 1.15 ERA in 47 innings.
July 26	The Angels score ten runs in the second inning and collect 20 hits during a 15–6 victory over the Devil Rays in St. Petersburg. The Angels scored twice in the top of the first before Tampa Bay responded with four tallies in their half. The ten-run inning was accomplished with nine hits (five singles and four doubles), two walks, a wild pitch and an error. Both Chone Figgins and Macier Izturis hit a double and a single during the outburst. Nine different players (Robb Quinlan, Jose Molina,

Figgins, Izturis, Orlando Cabrera, Vladimir Guerrero, Juan Rivera, Tim Salmon and Howie Kendrick) scored a run. Quinlan crossed the plate twice.

JULY 28   The Angels take over first place with an 8–3 win over the Red Sox in Boston.

At the end of play on July 28, the Angels were 53–49 and led the AL West by one-half game over the Athletics. It was quite a turnaround for Mike Scioscia's club, which started 32–40. After July 28, the Angels posted a record of 36–24, but were unable to keep pace with the A's, who were 40–19 and won the division by four games.

AUGUST 5   Vladimir Guerrero draws four walks, three of them intentional, during a 10–3 win over the Rangers at Angel Stadium.

AUGUST 16   A brawl erupts in the ninth inning of a 9–3 win over the Rangers in Arlington. The ruckus was started when Adam Kennedy charged the mound after being hit by a pitch from Scott Feldman. It took about four minutes to restore order. Kennedy, Brendan Donnelly and Kevin Gregg drew four-game suspensions for their roles in the brawl. Mike Scioscia was given a three-game ban.

AUGUST 18   Jeff Weaver pitches seven shutout innings in a 3–0 win over the Mariners in Seattle. The victory gave Weaver a career record of 9–0.

Weaver's 9–0 record tied the American League record for most consecutive wins at the start of a career. Whitey Ford was 9–0 for the Yankees in 1950. The major league record is held by Hooks Wiltse, who was 12–0 with the 1904 New York Giants.

AUGUST 24   Jeff Weaver allows only one run in six innings, but winds up as the losing pitcher in a 2–1 contest against the Red Sox at Angel Stadium. It was the first loss of his major league career after starting 9–0.

Weaver finished his rookie campaign with an 11–2 record and a 2.56 ERA.

SEPTEMBER 2   The Angels explode for five runs in the tenth inning to win 7–2 over the Tigers in Detroit. Chone Figgins cleared the bases with a three-run triple, and Orlando Cabrera added a two-run homer. The Angels tied the game 2–2 in the ninth with a two-out, RBI-single from Vladimir Guerrero.

Guerrero batted .329 with 33 homers and 116 RBIs in 2006.

SEPTEMBER 4   The Angels edge the Orioles 1–0 at Angel Stadium. Adam Kennedy drove in the lone run with a single in the fourth inning. Jeff Weaver (seven innings), Scot Shields (one inning) and Francisco Rodriguez (one inning) combined on the shutout.

Rodriguez had 47 saves and a 1.73 ERA in 69 games and 73 innings in 2006. He struck out 98 batters.

SEPTEMBER 5   Adam Kennedy hits a three-run, walk-off homer in the tenth inning to defeat the Orioles 5–2 at Angel Stadium.

SEPTEMBER 9	Bengie Molina steals second base with his brother Jose catching for the Angels in the fourth inning of a 2–1 loss to the Blue Jays at Angel Stadium.
	Bengie came into the contest with only two stolen bases in nine attempts in 818 career games. He attempted to steal a base only twice all season, and both were with his brother Jose catching (see May 16, 2006 and May 17, 2006). Through the 2009 season, Bengie hadn't attempted to steal another base.
SEPTEMBER 13	Freddy Garcia retires the first 23 Angels to face him before Adam Kennedy singles with two out in the eighth inning of a 9–0 White Sox win at Angel Stadium. After Kennedy hit, Garcia retired the next four hits to close out the near-perfect game.
SEPTEMBER 15	Vladimir Guerrero homers in the 11th inning to down the Rangers 2–1 in Arlington.
SEPTEMBER 16	Batting out of the ninth spot in the batting order, Chone Figgins hits for the cycle in just four plate appearances, but the Angels lose 12–6 to the Rangers in Arlington. Figgins singled in the second inning, homered in the fifth and doubled in the seventh off Adam Eaton, and tripled in the ninth against Nick Masset.
SEPTEMBER 24	Ervin Santana (eight innings) and J. C. Romero (one inning) combine on a two-hitter to defeat the Athletics 7–1 in Oakland. The only hits by the A's were a single by Eric Chavez in the second inning and a triple from Marco Scutaro in the sixth.
SEPTEMBER 27	Tim Salmon collects his 299th career homer in the first inning of a 6–5 win over the Rangers at Angel Stadium.
	Salmon missed all of 2005 with injuries and returned for one final campaign in 2006. He batted .265 with nine homers in 211 at-bats and 76 games. When Salmon struck home run number 299, he had already decided to retire at the end of the season. His quest for his 300th homer fell short. Salmon is the only player in major league history to end his career with exactly 299 home runs. Others who fell just shy of 300 were Rickey Henderson (297), Robin Ventura (294) and Kent Hrbek (293).
SEPTEMBER 30	Francisco Rodriguez strikes out all three batters he faces in the ninth inning to close out a 7–6 triumph over the Athletics at Angel Stadium.
OCTOBER 1	The Angels honor Tim Salmon on the occasion of his last major league game by cutting his name and jersey number into the infield and outfield grass at Angel Stadium.
NOVEMBER 22	The Angels sign Gary Matthews, most recently with the Rangers, as a free agent.
NOVEMBER 28	Adam Kennedy signs with the Cardinals as a free agent.
DECEMBER 11	The Angels sign Darren Oliver, most recently with the Mets as a free agent.
DECEMBER 15	The Angels trade Brendan Donnelly to the Red Sox for Phil Seibel.
DECEMBER 26	The Angels sign Shea Hillenbrand, most recently with the Giants, as a free agent.

2007

Season in a Sentence
The Angels win 94 games and the AL West, but the playoff run ends quickly when the club suffers a sweep at the hands of the Red Sox.

Finish • Won • Lost • Pct • GB
First   94   68   .580   6.0

AL Division Series
The Angels lost to the Boston Red Sox three games to one.

Manager
Mike Scioscia

Stats	Angels	AL	Rank
Batting Avg:	.284	.271	4
On-Base Pct:	.345	.338	3
Slugging Pct:	.417	.423	9
Home Runs:	123		12
Stolen Bases:	139		2
ERA:	4.23	4.50	5
Errors:	101		9
Runs Scored:	822		4
Runs Allowed:	731		5

Starting Lineup
Mike Napoli, c
Casey Kotchman, 1b
Howie Kendrick, 2b
Chone Figgins, 3b
Orlando Cabrera, ss
Garret Anderson, lf
Gary Matthews, cf
Vladimir Guerrero, rf
Shea Hillenbrand, dh
Reggie Willits, lf
Macier Izturis, 3b-2b

Pitchers
John Lackey, sp
Kelvim Escobar, sp
Jered Weaver, sp
Ervin Santana, sp
Joe Saunders, sp
Bartolo Colon, sp
Francisco Rodriguez, rp
Scot Shields, rp
Darren Oliver, rp
Chris Bootcheck, rp
Justin Speier, rp
Dustin Moseley, rp

Attendance
3,365,632 (second in AL)

Club Leaders
Batting Avg:	Chone Figgins	.330
On-Base Pct:	Vladimir Guerrero	.403
Slugging Pct:	Vladimir Guerrero	.547
Home Runs:	Vladimir Guerrero	27
RBI:	Vladimir Guerrero	125
Runs:	Orlando Cabrera	101
Stolen Bases:	Chone Figgins	41
Wins:	John Lackey	19
Strikeouts:	John Lackey	179
ERA:	John Lackey	3.01
Saves:	Francisco Rodriguez	40

JANUARY 24   Darin Erstad signs with the White Sox as a free agent.

APRIL 2   The Angels open the season with a 4–1 win over the Rangers before 43,906 at Angel Stadium. John Lackey was the starting pitcher and went five innings. Justin Speier (two innings), Scot Shields (one inning) and Francisco Rodriguez (one inning) combined for four innings of hitless relief. Casey Kotchman homered. Vladimir Guerrero hit a double on the first pitch of his first at-bat. It was the third consecutive season in which he collected an extra base hit on his first swing of the season. Guerrero homered in 2005 and 2006.

Guerrero batted .324 with 27 homers and 125 RBIs in 2007.

APRIL 10   The Angels lose to the Indians 7–6 before 19,031 at Miller Park in Milwaukee.

The game was played in Milwaukee because of a freak spring snowstorm in Cleveland. In the home opener on April 6 against the Mariners at Jacobs Field, the Indians were one strike away from a 4–0 win over the Mariners when the contest was stopped by snow with two out in the top of the fifth. After a wait of an hour and 17 minutes, the game was called because of the snowy conditions. The scheduled contests for April 7, April 8 and April 9 against Seattle were also postponed. The Angels were slated to come to Cleveland for three games from April 10 through April 12 with the prospect of more cold weather. In addition, the turf at Jacobs Field was in an unplayable condition because of the snow. It was then decided to move the Angels-Indians series to Milwaukee under the roof at Miller Park. The Angels won 4–1 on April 11 and lost 4–2 on April 12.

APRIL 16   In the worst school shooting in U. S. History, 33 people, including the shooter, are killed on the campus of Virginia Tech University.

APRIL 20   As the only active player from Virginia Tech, Angels pitcher Joe Saunders is given special dispensation to wear a Virginia Tech cap during the game against the Mariners at Angel Stadium to honor the victims of the massacre on campus four days earlier. Saunders also wore the initials "VT" on his cleats and drew the Virginia Tech logo on the back of the pitcher's mound before the game. Saunders pitched six shutout innings, and the Angels won 8–4.

APRIL 24   The Angels blow a seven-run lead, but manage to pull out a 9–8 win in ten innings over the Tigers at Angel Stadium. The Angels led 7–0 at the end of the third inning, but Detroit battled back and took an 8–7 advantage in the ninth on a two-run homer by Magglio Ordonez off Francisco Rodriguez. The Angels tied the score with a run in the bottom of the ninth and won the contest in the tenth without a ball leaving the infield. Kendry Morales started the tenth with an infield single and moved to second on error, then was lifted for pinch runner Reggie Willits. Willits advanced to third on a bunt and scored on a groundout.

Born in 1981 in Chickasaw, Oklahoma, Willits was named after Reggie Jackson. Willits and his wife began building a home in Fort Cobb, Oklahoma in 2003 with the first completed structure being a standalone 90 foot by 35 foot batting cage. He decided to save money and work on his game by moving the family into the batting cage, outfitted with an open floor plan. He made his major league debut in 2006 with the unusual uniform number of 77. Through 2009, Willits had 804 major league at-bats, all with the Angels, without hitting a home run.

MAY 1   Vladimir Guerrero hits a grand slam off Zack Greinke in the first inning to spark a 7–5 win over the Royals in Kansas City.

Mark Gubicza joined to Angels television team during games in 2007. He previously hosted the pregame and postgame shows. Gubicza moved to radio alongside Rudy Markas in 2008.

MAY 9   The Angels take sole possession of first place with a 3–2 victory over the Indians at Angel Stadium.

The Angels had a record of 18–16 on May 9, and were never out of first place for the rest of the season. By May 22, the club was 5½ games ahead of the second place Athletics and eight games up on June 24. The margin dropped to one game on July 20 and was still at one game on August 25. From that point, the Angels quickly pulled away and were 9½ games ahead by September 11.

MAY 14   Casey Kotchman hits a grand slam off Kevin Millwood in the first inning of a 7–2 triumph over the Rangers in Arlington.

JUNE 3   A two-run walk-off homer by Vladimir Guerrero in the ninth inning downs the Orioles 3–2 at Angel Stadium.

JUNE 4   The Angels collect 23 hits, score eight runs in the eighth inning, and wallop the Twins 16–3 at Angel Stadium. Gary Matthews hit a grand slam in the eighth off Jason Miller. It was one of his four hits during the evening. Orlando Cabrera picked up four hits, including a double, in five at-bats and scored four runs.

JUNE 12   Kelvim Escobar strikes out 14 batters in six innings, but the Angels lose 5–3 to the Reds at Great American Ballpark. It was the first time that the Angels played a game in Cincinnati.

Escobar had an 18–7 record and a 3.40 ERA in 2007. John Lackey was the ace of the staff with a 19–9 mark and an earned run average of 3.01.

JUNE 16   Francisco Rodriguez strikes out all three batters he faces in the ninth inning to close out a 3–0 win over the Dodgers in Los Angeles. Jeff Weaver (5⅓ innings), Darren Oliver (two-thirds of an inning) and Scot Shields (two innings) preceded Rodriguez to the mound.

JUNE 16   Chone Figgins collects six hits in six at-bats to lead the Angels to a 10–9 win over the Astros at Angel Stadium. It was also the first time that the Astros

John Lackey won 102 regular-season games during his eight years with the Angels but is best remembered by the team's fans for winning Game Seven of the 2002 World Series as a rookie.

played a game in Anaheim. Figgins picked up his first four hits off Chris Sampson with singles in the first, second and fourth innings and a double in the sixth. Figgins singled off Chad Qualls in the seventh for hit number five. The Angels scored five runs in the inning to wipe out a 9–4 deficit. Figgins stepped to the plate again with two out in the ninth, a runner on first base, and Trevor Miller on the mound, and delivered a game-winning single. To date, Figgins is the only player in major league history with six hits, including a walk-off hit, in a nine-inning game. The only other Angel with six hits in a game is Garret Anderson on September 27, 1996.

Figgins was limited to 115 games in 2007 because of injuries, but batted .330 with 41 stolen bases. From May 31 through the end of the season, Figgins batted .381 in 352 at-bats.

June 20 — Right fielder Terry Evans hits a home run in the second inning of an 8–4 win over the Astros at Angel Stadium. It was Evans's first major league hit and it came in his left field second plate appearance.

Evans was hitless in his next 11 big-league at-bats. He didn't collect his second hit until September 30, 2009. Through the end of the 2009 season, he had yet to hit another home run in the majors.

June 22 — Orlando Cabrera hits a ground rule walk-off single to score Chone Figgins from third base with the winning run in the 11th inning of a 5–4 decision over the Pirates at Angel Stadium. Cabrera's drive bounced over the left-field wall, but he was awarded only a single since it ended the game.

June 24 — For the second time in three days, the Angels win with a walk-off ground rule single, this time by Erick Aybar in the tenth inning to down the Pirates 54 at Angel Stadium. Aybar's drive bounced over the right-field fence to score Howie Kendrick from second base.

June 29 — Aubrey Huff hits for the cycle for the Orioles, but the Angels win 97 in Baltimore. Howie Kendrick broke the 7–7 tie with a two-run homer in the ninth.

July 3 — Brad Wilkerson of the Rangers hits three homers and drives in six runs during an 8–3 win over the Angels in Arlington.

July 9 — On the night before the All-Star Game, Vladimir Guerrero wins the Home Run Derby at A T & T Park in San Francisco.

July 27 — The Angels score six runs in the first inning and defeat the Tigers 11–6 at Angels Stadium.

July 28 — The Angels break a 3–3 tie with seven runs in the eighth inning and defeat the Tigers 10–3 at Angel Stadium.

July 29 — The Angels score 12 runs in the first three innings and defeat the Tigers 13–4 at Angel Stadium to complete a three-game series sweep of Detroit. The Angels scored at least ten runs in all three games.

July 31 — Gary Matthews collects four extra base hits during an 8–0 win over the Mariners in Seattle. Facing Jeff Weaver, Matthews homered in the second inning and doubled in the third. He followed with a double off Ryan Rowland-Smith in the fifth and a homer against Mark Lowe in the seventh.

The Angels had three sons of former major leaguers on the club in 2007. Gary Matthews is the son of Gary Matthews, Sr. Justin Speier is the son of Chris Speier. The elder Matthews and Speier were teammates with the Giants from 1972 through 1976. Darren Oliver is the son of Bob Oliver, who played for the Angels from 1972 through 1974.

AUGUST 2 — Vladimir Guerrero homers twice during a 6–4 win over the Athletics in Oakland.

AUGUST 3 — Vladimir Guerrero hit two home runs for the second game in a row, but the Angels lose 8–4 to the Athletics in Oakland.

AUGUST 10 — Macier Izturis hits a grand slam off Scott Baker in the sixth inning of a 10–1 triumph over the Twins at Angel Stadium.

AUGUST 20 — Howie Kendrick and Ryan Budde hit back-to-back doubles in the tenth inning to defeat the Yankees 7–6 at Angel Stadium. Budde entered the game as a substitute catcher in the ninth. The walk-off double was his first career RBI.

Through the end of the 2009 season, Budde had yet to drive in another run as a major leaguer.

AUGUST 21 — Garret Anderson sets a club record with ten runs batted in during an 18–9 victory over the Yankees at Angel Stadium. In the first inning, Anderson doubled in two runs off Mike Mussina. In the second, Anderson batted against Mussina again and hit another two-bagger to drive in another run. In the third, Anderson walloped a three-run facing Edwar Ramirez. After just three innings, the Angel outfielder had already driven in six runs. Anderson grounded out leading off the fifth, but stepped to the plate in the sixth with the bases loaded and hit a grand slam off Sean Henn. The major league record for RBIs in a game is 12, and Anderson had a shot at the mark in the eighth. He batted against Marcus Gwyn with two out and runners on first and second, but grounded out.

Anderson failed to drive in a run in his two previous games and in any of the four contests following his ten-RBI outburst. But from August 26 through September 7, however, he set another club record by driving in runs in 12 consecutive games, falling just one game shy of the American League record of 13. During the 12 games, Anderson hit seven homers and drove in 22 runs. He also collected 20 hits in 42 at-bats for a batting average of .476. Over 21 games from August 21 through September 12, Anderson drove in 37 runs. He finished the season with 80 runs batted in 108 games.

SEPTEMBER 12 — The Angels rout the Orioles 18–6 at Camden Yards. The Angels scored the 18 runs on 14 hits, benefiting from 13 walks issued by Baltimore pitchers. The only Angel to play all nine innings was Howie Kendrick, as Mike Scioscia emptied his bench in the late innings to rest his regulars.

SEPTEMBER 16 — Jim Thome hits his 500th career homer to help the White Sox defeat the Angels 9–7 in Chicago. The milestone was struck off Dustin Moseley in the sixth inning.

SEPTEMBER 23	The Angels clinch the AL West title with a 7–4 win over the Mariners at Angel Stadium.
SEPTEMBER 28	Vladimir Guerrero drives in both runs of a 2–0 win over the Athletics in Oakland with a sacrifice fly in the first inning and a homer in the fourth. John Lackey (seven innings), Justin Speier (one inning) and Francisco Rodriguez (one inning) combined on the shutout.

The Angels played the Boston Red Sox in the Division Series. Managed by Terry Francona, the Red Sox won the AL East with a record of 96–66.

OCTOBER 3	The Angels open the Division Series with a 4–0 loss to the Red Sox at Fenway Park. Josh Beckett pitched the complete game shutout. He retired 19 batters in a row from the first inning through the seventh.

The series was televised nationally over TBS. The announcers were Ted Robinson and Steve Stone.

OCTOBER 5	Manny Ramirez hits a three-run, walk-off homer off Francisco Rodriguez with two out in the ninth inning to beat the Angels 6–3 in game two of the Division Series in Boston. The Angels issued four intentional walks to David Oritz.
OCTOBER 7	The Red Sox complete the three-game sweep of the Angels with a 9–1 win before 45,262 at Angel Stadium. The Sox extended a 2–0 lead to 9–0 by scoring seven runs in the eighth inning.

The Angels were outscored 19–4 during the series.

OCTOBER 16	Bill Stoneman retires as general manager of the Angels at the age of 63. He had been the general manager since 1999 and guided the club through it's most successful period, which included the world championship in 2002. Stoneman was succeeded by 40-year-old Tony Reagins, who became the fourth African-American general manager in major league history. He previously held the position of director of player development since 2002.
NOVEMBER 19	The Angels trade Orlando Cabrera to the White Sox for Jon Garland.
NOVEMBER 21	The Angels sign Torii Hunter, most recently with the Twins, as a free agent.

2008

Season in a Sentence
The Angels win 100 games and post the best record in the American League, both franchise firsts, but lose to the Red Sox in the first round of the playoffs for the second year in a row and the third time in five seasons.

Finish • Won • Lost • Pct • GB
First   100   62   .617   +21.0

AL Division Series
The Angels lost to the Boston Red Sox three games to one.

Manager
Mike Scioscia

Stats	Angels	AL	Rank
Batting Avg:	.268	.268	7
On-Base Pct:	.330	.336	11
Slugging Pct:	.413	.420	9
Home Runs:	159		9
Stolen Bases:	129		2
ERA:	4.00	4.36	3
Errors:	91		5
Runs Scored:	765		10
Runs Allowed:	697		5

Starting Lineup
Jeff Mathis, c
Casey Kotchman, 1b
Howie Kendrick, 2b
Chone Figgins, 3b
Erick Aybar, ss
Gary Matthews, lf-rf-cf
Torii Hunter, cf
Vladimir Guerrero, rf
Garret Anderson, dh-lf
Juan Rivera, lf-dh
Macier Izturis, ss
Mike Napoli, c
Mark Teixeira, 1b

Pitchers
Ervin Santana, sp
Joe Saunders, sp
Jon Garland, sp
John Lackey, sp
Jered Weaver, sp
Francisco Rodriguez, rp
Scot Shields, rp
Justin Speier, rp
Darren Oliver, rp
Jose Arredondo, rp

Attendance
3,336,747 (second in AL)

Club Leaders
Batting Avg:	Vladimir Guerrero	.303
On-Base Pct:	Chone Figgins	.367
Slugging Pct:	Vladimir Guerrero	.521
Home Runs:	Vladimir Guerrero	27
RBI:	Vladimir Guerrero	91
Runs:	Vladimir Guerrero	85
	Torii Hunter	85
Stolen Bases:	Chone Figgins	34
Wins:	Joe Saunders	17
Strikeouts:	Ervin Santana	214
ERA:	Joe Saunders	3.41
Saves:	Francisco Rodriguez	62

FEBRUARY 25   Bartolo Colon signs with the Red Sox as a free agent.

MARCH 31   The Angels open the season with a 3–2 loss to the Twins in Minneapolis. Jered Weaver was the starting and losing pitcher. Casey Kotchman collected three hits.

APRIL 2   The Angels edge the Twins 1–0 in Minneapolis. The lone run scored in the seventh when Howie Kendrick singled, advanced to second on a sacrifice, third on a ground out and home on a wild pitch. Joe Saunders (eight innings) and Francisco Rodriguez (one inning) combined on the shutout.

Saunders was 17–7 with a 3.41 ERA in 2007.

APRIL 4   In the home opener, the Angels lose 11–6 to the Rangers before 43,383 at Angel Stadium. All six Angels runs scored in the ninth inning in a futile rally.

APRIL 7	After the Indians score three runs in the top of the ninth inning to take a 4–2 lead, Torii Hunter hits a walk-off grand slam in the bottom half for a 6–4 victory. The bases were loaded with one out on a walk to Gary Matthews, a single by Vladimir Guerrero and another walk to Garret Anderson. Hunter also hit a solo homer in his previous plate appearance in the eighth.
APRIL 9	Mike Napoli hits a grand slam off Paul Byrd in the second inning of a 9–5 triumph over the Indians at Angel Stadium.
APRIL 26	Vladimir Guerrero collects his 2,000th career hit during a 6–4 loss to the Tigers in Detroit. The milestone was a double off Denny Batista in the eighth inning.
MAY 5	The Angels score four runs in the ninth inning to defeat the Royals 4–0 in Kansas City. The four-run rally consisted of a triple from Erick Aybar, Casey Kotchman's single, and back-to-back, two-out homers from Garret Anderson and Brandon Wood.
MAY 6	Garret Anderson drives in all five runs of a 5–3 victory over the Royals in Kansas City. Anderson hit a three-run homer in the fourth inning and run-scoring singles in the fifth and seventh, all off Brian Bannister.
MAY 13	The Angels take over first place with a 2–0 win over the White Sox at Angel Stadium. The Angels remained on top of the AL West for the rest of the season.
MAY 18	Mike Napoli hits two homers and drives in five runs during a 10–2 thrashing of the Dodgers at Angel Stadium.
MAY 26	The Angels outlast the Tigers to win 1–0 in 12 innings at Angel Stadium. The lone run scored on a bases-loaded walk from Bobby Seay to Garret Anderson. Jon Garland (7 1/3 innings), Scot Shields (1 2/3 innings), Francisco Rodriguez (one innings) and Jose Arredondo (two innings) combined on a five-hit shutout.
MAY 27	The Angels win in their last at-bat for the second game in a row with two runs in the eighth inning and one in the ninth to down the Tigers 3–2 at Angel Stadium. Gary Matthews drove in the winning run with a single.
JUNE 7	Leading off the first inning, Macier Izturis hits the first pitch from Greg Smith for a home run, sparking a 5–3 win over the Athletics in Oakland.
JUNE 13	The Angels play the Braves in Anaheim for the first time and lose 5–2 at Angel Stadium.
JUNE 15	Casey Kotchman hits a two-run homer in the fifth inning to account for all of the scoring in a 2–0 win over the Braves at Angel Stadium. Joe Saunders (7 1/3 innings), Scot Shields (two-thirds of an inning) and Francisco Rodriguez (one inning) combined on the shutout.
JUNE 20	Ervin Santana (seven innings), Jose Arrendondo (one inning) and Justin Speier (one inning) combine on a two-hitter to defeat the Phillies 7–1 at Citizens Bank Park. It was also the first time the Angels played a game in Philadelphia. The only hits by the Phillies were a single by Shane Victorino in the first inning and a double from Chris Coste in the second.

During his six years with the Angels, closer Francisco Rodriguez led the American League in saves three times, including his record-breaking 62 saves in 2008.

June 21   Pitching one inning, Scot Shields faces five batters with one walk and four strikeouts during a 6–2 win over the Phillies in Philadelphia. Entering the fray in the eighth, Shields fanned Greg Dobbs, Jimmy Rollins and Shane Victorino, but Victorino reached first base when he swung and missed on a two-strike pitch that sailed past catcher Jeff Mathis for a wild pitch. After walking Pat Burrell, Shields struck out Ryan Howard.

June 23   The Angels play the Nationals in Washington for the first time and win 3–2 at Nationals Park.

June 28   Jeff Weaver (six innings) and Jose Arrendondo (two innings) hold the Dodgers without a hit, but the Angels lose 1–0 in Los Angeles. The Dodgers scored the lone run in the fifth inning. Matt Kemp reached base when Weaver couldn't handle a twisting roller between the mound and the first base line. At first, it was ruled a hit, then changed to an error. On a stolen-base attempt, Kemp went from first to third when the throw from catcher Jeff Mathis sailed into center field. Kemp crossed the plate on a sacrifice fly by Blake DeWitt. Weaver was lifted for a pinch hitter in the seventh.

> The Angels were the fifth team in major league history to lose a game without allowing a hit. The others were the 1964 Astros playing the Reds (with Ken Johnson pitching), the 1967 Orioles versus the Tigers (with Steve Barber and Stu Miller combining on the no-hitter), the 1990 Yankees against the White Sox (with Andy Hawkins on the mound) and the 1992 Red Sox facing the Indians

(with Matt Young as the pitcher). The Reds and the Tigers were the only teams to bat nine times. The White Sox, Indians and Dodgers batted eight times as the winning team at home.

JUNE 29   The day after a no-hitter and a 1–0 loss, John Lackey (8 2/3 innings) and Francisco Rodriguez (one-third of an inning) combine on a three-hitter to defeat the Dodgers 1–0 in Los Angeles. Mike Napoli drove in the lone run with a single in the second inning.

JULY 10   The Angels outlast the Rangers 11–10 in 11 innings in Arlington. The Angels led 10–4 in the fifth inning before allowing the Rangers to tie the game. Macier Izturis drove in the winning run with a single.

JULY 18   Garret Anderson collects four hits, including a homer, in four at-bats and drives in five runs to lead the Angels to an 11–3 trouncing of the Red Sox at Angel Stadium.

JULY 20   Francisco Rodriguez strikes out all three batters he faces in the ninth inning to close out a 5–3 triumph over the Red Sox at Angel Stadium.

JULY 23   Three Angels batters collect at least four hits during a 14–11 victory over the Indians at Angel Stadium. It was the first time in franchise history that three players had four or more hits. Casey Kotchman garnered five hits, including a double, in five at-bats. Jeff Mathis had a homer, a double, and two singles in four at-bats and drove in six runs. He powered a grand slam off Tom Mastny in the fifth inning. Howie Kendrick had three doubles to tie a club record, along with a single, in five at-bats. The Angels had 19 hits in all.

JULY 26   Torii Hunter reaches base five times in five plate appearances with two homers, a single and two walks, scores four runs and drives in five to lead the Angels to an 11–6 win over the Orioles in Baltimore.

JULY 29   John Lackey narrowly misses a no-hitter before settling for a two-hitter and a 6–2 defeat of the Red Sox in Boston. Lackey went to the mound in the ninth with a no-hitter intact. He started the ninth by striking out Jacoby Ellsbury, then allowed a sharp single through the left side to Dustin Pedroia. Kevin Youkilis followed with a home run. Lackey walked David Ortiz with two out but finished the game.

> *On the same day, the Angels traded Casey Kotchman and Stephen Marek to the Braves for Mark Teixeira, who was in the last year of his contract and was acquired to boost the Angels batting attack. It worked, as Teixeira hit .358 with 13 homers and 43 RBIs in 54 games. In the end, the Angels couldn't keep him, however. During the following offseason, Teixeira signed a lucrative deal with the Yankees.*

JULY 31   Outfielders Juan Rivera, Torii Hunter and Vladimir Guerrero each hit three-run homers during a 12–6 triumph over the Yankees in New York. Rivera and Hunter both homered in the second inning off Andy Pettitte.

AUGUST 1   The Angels defeat the Yankees 1–0 in New York. Torii Hunter drove in the winning run with a single off Mariano Rivera in the ninth inning. Ervin Santana (eight innings) and Francisco Rodriguez (one inning) combined on the shutout.

Santana was 16–7 with a 3.49 ERA and 214 strikeouts in 219 innings in 2008.

AUGUST 3   Mark Teixeira hits a grand slam off Edwar Ramirez in the eighth inning, but the Angels lose 14–9 to the Yankees in New York. It was also the Angels' last game at old Yankee Stadium.

AUGUST 4   With two out in the ninth and Angels runners on first and second, George Sherrill of the Orioles walks Jeff Mathis and Chone Figgins to force in the winning run of a 6–5 decision at Angel Stadium. Baltimore scored four runs in the top of the ninth to knot the contest at 5–5.

AUGUST 9   The Angels break a 3–3 tie by scoring eight runs in the eighth inning and defeat the Yankees 11–4 at Angel Stadium. Vladimir Guerrero led off the big inning with a home run and later added an RBI-single.

Guerrero batted .303 with 27 home runs in 2008.

AUGUST 28   The Angels score five runs in the eighth inning to defeat the Rangers 7–5 at Angel Stadium. Juan Rivera put the Angels into the lead with a three-run double.

SEPTEMBER 3   Jered Weaver cuts a finger on his pitching hand when it is snagged by a staple in the upholstery of the dugout bench during a 9–6 loss to the Tigers in Detroit. Weaver missed a scheduled start because of the cut.

SEPTEMBER 8   A sixth-inning brawl highlights a 12–1 win over the Yankees at Angel Stadium.

Torii Hunter was the instigator of the fracas by charging hard into catcher Ivan Rodriguez on a play at the plate. Hunter failed to slide and was out easily. After the play, Hunter tripped on a bat and stumbled into Rodriguez. The two began shoving each other. and both benches and bullpens emptied, but no punches were thrown. Hunter and Rodriguez were ejected. "The ghetto came out in me, and I hate that," explained Hunter afterward. "I want to apologize to the fans."

SEPTEMBER 10   The Angels clinch the AL West pennant with a 4–2 victory over the Yankees at Angel Stadium.

SEPTEMBER 11   With a scoreless ninth inning in a 7–4 win over the Mariners at Angel Stadium, Francisco Rodriguez records his 57th save of 2008 to tie the single-season major league record set by Bobby Thigpen of the White Sox in 1990 (see September 13, 2008).

SEPTEMBER 12   Mike Napoli hits a two-run, walk-off homer in the ninth inning to defeat the Mariners 5–3 at Angel Stadium.

SEPTEMBER 13   Francisco Rodriguez pitches a scoreless ninth inning to close out a 5–2 victory over the Mariners at Angel Stadium. The save was the 58th of the season for Rodriguez, breaking the record set by Bobby Thigpen.

Rodriguez finished the season with a 2–3 record, 62 saves and a 2.24 ERA in 76 games and $68^{2}/_{3}$ innings. He struck out 77 batters.

SEPTEMBER 19	The Angels collect 22 hits and win a 15–13 slugfest against the Rangers in Arlington. There were 26 runs scored by the two clubs in the first five innings. The Angels led 8–0 before Texas plated nine runs in the third. Mike Scioscia's club tied the score 9–9 with a run in the fourth, then broke the deadlock with five tallies in the fifth. The Rangers scored three runs in their half of the fifth to make the score 14–12, but couldn't retake the lead.
SEPTEMBER 21	John Lackey strikes out 12 batters and pitches six shutout innings during a 7–3 victory over the Rangers in Arlington.
SEPTEMBER 28	On the last day of the regular season, the Angels record their 100th win of the season with a 7–0 decision over the Rangers at Angel Stadium. The win broke the club record of 99 set by the 2002 world champions.

The Angels met the Boston Red Sox in the Division Series for the second year in a row. In 2007, the Red Sox swept the Angels on the way to winning the World Series. Boston also swept the Angels in the first round in 2004. Managed by Terry Francona, the Red Sox were 95–67 in 2008 and won the AL wild card. The Angels had an 8–1 record against the Sox during the regular season.

OCTOBER 1	The Angels open the Division Series with a 4–1 loss to the Red Sox before 44,996 at Angel Stadium. Boston took a 2–1 lead with two runs in the sixth inning, then added two more in the ninth.

The series was carried on national television over TBS with Chip Caray and Buck Martinez serving as announcers.

OCTOBER 3	J. D. Drew hits a two-run homer off Francisco Rodriguez in the ninth inning to lift the Red Sox to a 7–5 win over the Angels before a game-two crowd of 45,334 at Angel Stadium. Boston led 5–1 before the Angels countered with single runs in the fourth, fifth, seventh and eighth innings. Mark Teixeira tied the score 5–5 with a sacrifice fly. He also had three hits and scored three runs.
OCTOBER 5	The Angels stay alive with a 12-inning, 5–4 win over the Red Sox at Fenway Park. Erick Aybar drove in the winning run with a single. Mike Napoli led the way with two homers and a single. He also scored three runs and drove in three. Chone Figgins collected three hits, including a double. Jered Weaver pitched scoreless ball in the 11th and 12th in his first career relief appearance. The win ended the Angels 11-game losing streak to the Red Sox in the postseason dating back to the 1986 Championship Series.
OCTOBER 6	The Red Sox advance to the Championship Series by beating the Angels 3–2 in Boston. Torii Hunter tied the contest 2–2 with a two-run single in the eighth inning. Jed Lowrie won the game with a walk-off single off Scot Shields in the ninth.
DECEMBER 10	Five weeks after Barack Obama defeats John McCain in the Presidential election, Francisco Rodriguez signs a contract with the Mets as a free agent.
DECEMBER 31	The Angels sign Brian Fuentes, most recently with the Rockies, as a free agent.

2009

Season in a Sentence
Overcoming the death of Nick Adenhart in the first week of the season, the Angels reach the Championship Series before losing to the Yankees in six games.

Finish • Won • Lost • Pct • GB
First   97   65   .599 +10.0

AL Division Series
The Angels defeated the Boston Red Sox three games to none.

AL Championship Series
The Angels lost to the New York Yankees four games to two.

Manager
Mike Scioscia

Stats

Stats	Angels	AL	Rank
Batting Avg:	.285	.267	1
On-Base Pct:	.350	.336	3
Slugging Pct:	.441	.428	4
Home Runs:	173		8
Stolen Bases:	148		3
ERA:	4.45	4.46	11
Errors:	84		4
Runs Scored:	883		2
Runs Allowed:	761		8

Starting Lineup
Mike Napoli, c
Kendry Morales, 1b
Macier Izturis, 2b
Chone Figgins, 3b
Erick Aybar, ss
Juan Rivera, lf
Torii Hunter, cf
Bobby Abreu, rf
Vladimir Guerrero, dh
Howie Kendrick, 2b
Gary Matthews, cf-rf
Jeff Mathis, c

Pitchers
Jered Weaver, sp
Joe Saunders, sp
John Lackey, sp
Erwin Santana, sp
Brian Fuentes, rp
Darren Oliver, rp
Jason Bulger, rp
Kevin Jepsen, rp
Jose Arredondo, rp
Matt Palmer, rp-sp

Attendance
3,240,386 (second in AL)

Club Leaders
Batting Avg:	Erick Aybar	.312
On-Base Pct:	Chone Figgins	.395
Slugging Pct:	Kendry Morales	.569
Home Runs:	Kendry Morales	34
RBI:	Kendry Morales	108
Runs:	Chone Figgins	114
Stolen Bases:	Chone Figgins	42
Wins:	Jered Weaver	16
	Joe Saunders	16
Strikeouts:	Jered Weaver	174
ERA:	Jered Weaver	3.74
Saves:	Brian Fuentes	48

JANUARY 6 — Mark Teixeira signs a contract with the Yankees as a free agent.

JANUARY 13 — Preston Gomez, the team's assistant to the general manager, dies of injuries sustained after being struck by a car in Blythe, California. Gomez was 85. As a tribute, the Angels wore black "Preston" patches on their left sleeves during the 2009 season.

FEBRUARY 12 — Bobby Abreu, most recently with the Yankees, signs with the Angels as a free agent.

FEBRUARY 24 — Garret Anderson signs a contract with the Braves as a free agent.

APRIL 6	The Angels open the season with a 3–0 win over the Athletics before 43,220 at Angel Stadium. Joe Saunders (6 2/3 innings), Jose Arredondo (one-third of an inning), Scot Shields (one inning) and Brian Fuentes (one inning) combined on the shutout. Howie Kendrick started the scoring with a two-run homer in the third inning.
	At the end of the 2009 season, Shields ranked second in Angels history in games pitched with 448. Troy Percival is the franchise leader with 579.
APRIL 8	Appearing in his fourth major league game, Nick Adenhart pitches six shutout innings, but the Angels lose 6–4 to the Athletics at Angel Stadium.
APRIL 9	Just hours after pitching six shutout innings, Nick Adenhart is pronounced dead at the University of California-Irvine Medical Center from injuries sustain in a traffic accident, which occurred just after midnight. Adenhart was 22 years of age.
	The accident took place in Fullerton about five miles from Angel Stadium. Police reported that an individual driving a red Toyota Sienna minivan traveling at 70 miles per hour ran a red light and hit a gray Mitsubishi Eclipse in which Adenhart was a passenger. Courtney Stewart, the driver of the Mitsubishi, and Henry Pearson, a passenger in the vehicle, were pronounced dead at the scene. Jon Wilhite, a third passenger, survived the crash. The driver of the minivan fled on foot, but was later apprehended and identified as 22-year-old Andrew Thomas Gallo. On May 27, 2009, Gallo was indicted by the Orange County grand jury on three counts of murder and one count each of hit-and-run and driving under the influence and causing injury. Two hours after the crash, Gallo had a blood alcohol level of .19 percent, more than twice the legal limit, and was driving with a suspended license. As this book went to press, Gallo's trial was scheduled for April 19, 2010. The Angels postponed the game of April 9. For the remainder of the season, a black patch with Adenhart's number 34 was placed just above the heart on the team's uniforms.
APRIL 10	Ceremonies are held in honor of Nick Adenhart prior to a 6–3 win over the Red Sox at Angel Stadium.
	A 75-second video of Adnehart's career was shown on the scoreboard as "Calling All Angels" by Train played on the audio system. Players and coaches from both teams then came onto the field for a 32-second moment of silence. Before the first pitch, center fielder Torii Hunter ran to the fence in center field and touched a picture of Adenhart the club had put on the wall.
APRIL 12	A high pitch from Josh Beckett of the Red Sox to Bobby Abreu in the first inning leads both benches to empty in the first inning of a 5–4 win at Angel Stadium. The teams exchanged shoves and Torii Hunter and Mike Scioscia were ejected.
APRIL 17	Team owner Arte Moreno, general manager Tony Reagins, manager Mike Scioscia, pitching coach Mike Butcher and players Jered Weaver, John Lackey and Dustin Moseley attend the funeral of Nick Adenhart in Williamsport, Maryland.
APRIL 30	The Angels play at new Yankee Stadium for the first time and lose 7–4.

The Angels Curse

For much of the first 40 years of the existence of the franchise, fans and those connected with the club often talked about "The Angels Curse" as a series of untimely deaths, accidents and unfathomable losses plagued the club. The "curse" appeared to have been lifted when the Angels won the World Series in 2002, but the deaths of Preston Gomez (see January 13, 2009) and Nick Adenhart (see April 9, 2009) from injuries sustained in auto accidents ignited new discussion.

The events that led to the "curse" include:

1965
Pitcher Dick Wantz died at the age of 25 from a brain tumor just a month after pitching in only one major league game.

1968
Pitcher Minnie Rojas was paralyzed from injuries sustained in a car accident that killed his wife and two of their three children.

1972
Infielder Chico Ruiz was killed in a traffic accident.

1974
Pitcher Bruce Heinbechner died in a car accident during spring training.

1977
Infielder Mike Miley was yet another Angels player who died from injuries sustained in an automobile crash.

1978
Outfielder Lyman Bostock died from wounds suffered in a drive-by shooting.

1982
Up two games to none in the best-of-five Championship Series against Brewers, the Angels lost three in a row and failed to advance to the World series.

1986
Up three games to one in the best-of-seven Championship Series against the Red Sox, the Angeles lost three in a row. Game Five was particularly galling, as the Angeles blew a three-run lead in the ninth inning.

1989
Donnie Moore, who was the losing pitcher in game five of the 1986 ALCS, committed suicide after wounding his wife with a gun.

1992
A bus carrying manager Buck Rodgers, the coaching staff and several players, careened off the New Jersey Turnpike. Rodgers was badly injured, and it was three months before he returned to the dugout.

1995
The Angels had an 11-game lead in the AL West in August, but wound up finishing second to the Mariners.

MAY 1   The Angels blow a 9–4 lead by allowing four runs in the eighth inning and two in the ninth to lose 10–9 to the Yankees in New York. Brian Fuentes blew the save in the ninth without retiring a batter by loading the bases on a walk and two singles followed by a two-run, walkoff single from Jorge Posada.

> *The Angels were off to a slow start in 2009 with a 6–11 record on April 25. The club was still struggling with a 29–29 record on June 11 and were in second place 4½ games behind the Rangers.*

MAY 9   Joe Saunders pitches a complete game shutout to defeat the Royals 1–0 at Angel Stadium. The lone run scored in the third inning when Gary Matthews doubled, advanced to third on a bunt and crossed the plate on a sacrifice fly by Chone Figgins.

Gold Glove center fielder Torii Hunter anchors the Angels defense and provides consistent production at the plate. His leadership helped the 2009 team to win the American League Western Division championship.

May 10 — Center fielder Torii Hunter saves a 4–3 win over the Royals at Angel Stadium by leaping above the fence after a sprint of about 150 feet to rob Miguel Olivo of a home run in the ninth inning.

May 13 — Matt Palmer pitches a complete game and retires the last 19 batters to face him to defeat the Red Sox 8–4 at Angel Stadium. Palmer allowed two runs in the first inning and two in the second to put the Angels in a 4–0 hole.

May 16 — In his first start of the season after coming off of the disabled list, John Lackey lasts only two pitches, and the Angels lose 5–3 to the Rangers in Arlington. On his first pitch, Lackey threw behind the head of Ian Kinsler, who hit two homers the night before. The next pitch hit Kinsler, and Lackey was ejected by home plate umpire Bob Davidson. Lackey had been sidelined for more than a month by a forearm strain.

May 31 — Trailing 8–1, the Angels rally with four runs in the sixth inning, one in the seventh and three in the ninth to beat the Mariners 9–8 at Angel Stadium. With two out in the ninth, the Angels were still behind 8–6 with runners on first and second. Vladimir Guerrero doubled in a run and Torii Hunter was intentionally walked to load the bases. Juan Rivera drew a walk from David Aardsma to tie the score 8–8.
The winning run was driven home on a single from Kendry Morales. Morales entered the game as a pinch hitter in the sixth inning and remained in the lineup as a first baseman.

> *Morales came into the 2009 season as a 26-year-old with enormous potential, but had a .249 career batting average and 12 homers in 377 at-bats. He put together a breakout year with a .306 average, 34 homers and 108 RBIs.*

June 9	With two picks in the first round of the amateur draft in the 24th and 25th slots, the Angels select outfielder Randal Grichuk from Lamar Consolidated High School in Rosenberg, Texas, and outfielder Michael Trout from Millville High School in Millville, New Jersey. The Angeles lost their first round pick (32nd overall) to the Rockies by signing Brian Fuentes as a free agent, but gained spots from the Mets for losing Francisco Rodriguez and from the Yankees for the signing of Mark Teixeira.
June 12	Matt Palmer runs his record to 6–0 by beating the Padres 11–6 at Angel Stadium.
	Palmer entered the season as a 30-year-old with only three career games in the majors with the Giants in 2008 and had an 0–2 record and an 8.39 earned run average. He was acquired by the Angels as a free agent on January 13, 2009. During the 2009 season, Palmer had an 11–2 record and a 3.93 ERA in 40 games, 13 of them starts, and 121$^1/_3$ innings.
June 13	Torii Hunter hits three consecutive homers during a 9–1 win over the Padres at Angeles Stadium. Hunter homered off Josh Geer in the third and fifth innings and Joe Thatcher in the seventh. The Angels belted five homers in all. Kendry Morales and Jeff Mathis accounted for the other two.
June 15	The Angels take an 8–0 lead with seven runs in the fourth inning and hold on to defeat the Giants 9–7 in San Francisco.
June 20	The Weaver brothers square off as starting pitchers at Angel Stadium. Jered pitched 5$^1/_3$ innings for the Angels and allowed six runs and ten hits. Jeff went five innings for the Dodgers and gave up two runs and six hits. The Dodgers won 6–4.
June 26	The Angels score eight runs in the second inning and rout the Diamondbacks 12–3 in Phoenix. The rally included seven hits on four singles, a double, a triple and a homer.
	The Angels scored 277 runs in 38 games, an average of 7.3 runs per contest, from June 24 through August 7.
June 27	With the Angels trailing the Diamondbacks 1–0 in the sixth inning in Phoenix, Erick Aybar circles the bases on a bunt. Pitcher Doug Davis fielded Aybar's bunt and threw wildly past first base, and the ball bounced off the front of the grandstand and into right field. By the time right fielder Justin Upton tracked down the ball, Aybar was heading to third. Upton's throw sailed past third baseman Mark Reynolds, which allowed Aybar to score the tying run. Mike Napoli broke the deadlock with a homer in the ninth.
June 28	The Angels take a 9–2 lead in the fifth inning and hold on to defeat the Diamondbacks 12–8 in Phoenix. In the fourth inning, Gary Matthews hit a three-run double, advanced to third base on an error, then stole home.
July 4	The Angels fall behind 4–0 in the fifth inning then rally to rout the Orioles 11–4 at Angel Stadium.
July 5	The Angels fall behind 4–0 again, this time in the third inning, and rally to defeat the Orioles 9–6 at Angel Stadium. A 6–6 tic was broken in the seventh inning on back-to-back bases-loaded walks by Chris Ray to Juan Rivera and Mike Napoli.

JULY 8	Andruw Jones hits three homers for the Rangers during an 8–1 win over the Angels at Angel Stadium.
JULY 10	The Angels fall behind 4–0 in the second inning and rally to down the Yankees 10–6 at Angel Stadium.
JULY 11	The Angels rally from a 4–0 deficit for the fourth time in a span of seven days and beat the Yankees 14–8 at Angel Stadium. The Angels took an 8–4 lead with seven runs in the fifth inning.

The victory put the Angels into first place one-half game ahead of the Rangers with a record of 48–37. The Angels were 68–36 from June 12 through the end of the regular season.

JULY 18	Jon Wilhite, the only survivor of the crash that killed Nick Adenhart (see April 9, 2009), throws out the ceremonial first pitch prior to an 11–6 win over the Athletics in Oakland. Wilhite threw the pitch to A's catcher Kurt Suzuki. The two were teammates on the Cal State-Fullerton baseball team.
JULY 19	The Angels edge the Athletics 1–0 in ten innings in Oakland. Brian Anderson had a perfect game in progress until Bobby Abreu singled with out in the seventh. Abreu also provided the lone run of the game with a homer off Andrew Bailey with one out in the tenth. John Lackey (nine innings) and Brian Fuentes (one inning) combined on a four-hit shutout.
JULY 21	The Angels score seven runs in the seventh inning and beat the Royals 10–2 in the second game of a double-header in Kansas City. Erick Aybar hit a three-run triple during the rally. The Angels also won the opener 8–5.
JULY 23	The Angels score two runs in the ninth inning and one in the tenth to defeat the Twins 6–5 at Angel Stadium. Both runs in the ninth scored off Joe Nathan after two were out. They were driven in on singles from Gary Matthews and Howie Kendrick. Mike Napoli won the game with a walkoff double.

Napoli hit .272 with 20 home runs in 2009.

JULY 25	The Angels extend their winning streak to eight games with an 11–5 decision over the Twins at Angel Stadium. The victory included a nine-run rally in the fourth inning. Macier Izturis and Chone Figgins both collected two hits in the fourth. Izturis doubled and homered, and Figgins singled and homered.
JULY 27	Juan Rivera, Kendry Morales and Mike Napoli hit consecutive homers off Carl Pavano during a span of six pitches in the second inning, but the Angels lose 8–6 to the Indians at Angel Stadium.
JULY 31	The Angels score six runs in the 11th inning and defeat the Twins 11–5 in Minneapolis. The first eight batters in the inning reached base on six singles and two walks.
AUGUST 1	The Angels clobber the Twins 11–6 at the Metrodome.

August 2	The Angels reach double digits in runs for the third game in a row in Minneapolis by beating the Twins 13–4. Kendry Morales drove in six runs with a pair of three-run homers in the fifth and eighth innings. It was also the last time that the Angels played at the Metrodome.
August 10	Vladimir Guerrero hits the 399th and 400th homers of his career during an 8–7 win over the Rays at Angel Stadium. His second homer of the game was struck off Russ Springer in the seventh inning and broke a 7–7 tie.
August 16	The Angels explode for nine runs in the 13th inning and defeat the Orioles 17–8 in Baltimore. The first five batters of the 13th reached on singles. Juan Rivera capped the rally with a three-run homer. The Angels garnered 23 hits during the contest. Jason Bulger struck out five batters in two innings.
August 17	Vladimir Guerrero collects two homers and drives in five runs during an 8–5 win over the Orioles in Baltimore.
August 28	Trailing 6–2, the Angels erupt for seven runs in the seventh inning and beat the Athletics 11–7 at Angel Stadium. Kendry Morales was the key to the victory with five hits and six RBIs in five at-bats. Morales homered in the second inning and doubled in the fourth off Brett Tomko; doubled in the fourth against Craig Breslo; hit a three-run homer in the seventh facing Brad Ziegler; and singled in the ninth off Santiago Casilla. The home run in the seventh gave the Angels an 8–6 lead. The four extra base hits tied a club record. In four games from August 28 through August 31, Morales collected 12 hits, including four doubles and three homers, in 17 at-bats.

On the same day, the Angels traded Sean Rodriguez to the Rays for Scott Kazmir.

August 31	The Angels trounce the Mariners 10–0 in Seattle. Joe Saunders (seven innings) and Trevor Bell (two innings) combined on the shutout.
September 2	In his debut with the Angels, Scott Kazmir loses 3–0 to the Mariners in Seattle. In the first inning, Kazmir loaded the bases with no outs, then retired 18 batters in a row. With the score 0–0, Kazmir gave up two runs in the seventh.
September 18	Scott Kazmir (six innings), Jason Bulger (one inning), Kevin Jepsen (one inning) and Brian Fuentes (one inning) combine to shut out the Rangers 2–0 in Arlington. The win gave the Angels a 7½-game lead over Texas in the AL West race.
September 28	The Angels clinch their fifth AL West title in a span of six years with an 11–0 triumph over the Rangers at Angel Stadium. Erwin Santana pitched the complete game shutout. After the game, the Angels ran to the outfield wall to touch the picture of Nick Adenhart, who died on April 9.
September 30	Matt Palmer (five innings), Darren Oliver (one inning), Jose Arredondo (one inning), Kevin Jepsen (one inning) and Rafael Rodriguez (one inning) combine on a one-hitter to defeat the Rangers 5–0 at Angel Stadium. The only Texas hit was a single by Julio Borbon leading off the first inning.

The Angels played the Red Sox in the Division Series. Managed by Terry Francona, the Sox won the wild card with a record of 95–67. It was the fourth time in six years that the two clubs met in the first round of the playoffs. The Red Sox swept the Angels in 2004, won in four games in 2007 and swept the Angels again in 2008.

OCTOBER 8   The Angels open the postseason with a 5–0 win over the Red Sox before 45,070 at Angel Stadium. John Lackey (7⅓ innings) and Darren Oliver (1⅔ innings) combined on the shutout. Torii Hunter broke a 0–0 deadlock with a three-run homer in the fifth inning.

The series was telecast nationally over ESPN. Dan Orsillo and Buck Martinez served as announcers.

OCTOBER 9   The Angels take game two with a 4–1 decision over the Red Sox before 45,223 at Angel Stadium. Jered Weaver allowed only a run and two hits in 7⅓ innings.

OCTOBER 11   The Angels complete the sweep of the Red Sox with a 7–6 win over the Red Sox at Fenway Park. The Angels trailed 5–2 before narrowing the gap with two runs in the eighth on a two-out, two-run single by Juan Rivera. Boston scored in the bottom half to take a 6–4 advantage. The first two Angels batters in the top of the ninth were retired by Jonathan Papelbon and were down to their last strike when Erick Aybar singled on an 0–2 pitch. Chone Figgins followed with a walk on a full count. Bobby Abreu fell behind 1–2, and for the third time the Angeles were one strike away from losing. After fouling off a pitch, Abreu doubled in a run. Torii Hunter was issued an intentional walk to load the bases and Vladimir Guerrero singled in two runs to provide the Angels with a 7–6 lead. Brian Fuentes retired all three batters to face him in the ninth.

The Angels met the Yankees in the Championship Series. Managed by Joe Girardi, the Yankees were 103–59 in 2009.

OCTOBER 16   The Angels open the series against the Yankees with a 4–1 loss in New York. John Lackey gave up two runs in the first inning, one on a botched play by the infield. On a pop-up by Hideki Matsui, third baseman Chone Figgins and Erick Aybar had trouble communicating, and the ball fell to the turf for a single that scored Johnny Damon from second base.

The series was televised nationally over the FOX network with Joe Buck and Tim McCarver serving as announcers.

OCTOBER 17   The Angels blow an opportunity to even the Championship Series by losing 4–3 in 13 innings to the Yankees in New York. Chone Figgins drove in a run in the top of the 11th to give the Angels a 3–2 lead, but Alex Rodriguez led off the bottom half with a homer off Brian Fuentes. The Yanks had runners on first and second with one out in the 13th when Melky Cabrera grounded to second baseman Macier Izturis, who threw wildly to second base on an attempted force play, allowing the winning run to score. The game lasted five hours and ten minutes.

OCTOBER 19   In game three, the Angels win a thrilling 5–4 decision in 11 innings over the Yankees before 44,911 at Angel Stadium. The Yankees struck in the first inning on a leadoff homer by Derek Jeter off Jered Weaver. The Angels trailed 3–0 before scoring a run in the fifth, two in the sixth and one in the seventh for a 4–3 lead. Howie Kendrick hit a solo homer in the fifth, and Vladimir Guerrero walloped a two-run shot in the sixth. A homer by Jorge Posada in the eighth tied the score 4–4. With two out in the 11th, Kendrick singled and scored on a walkoff double by Jeff Mathis. Mathis entered the game in the eighth inning after Mike Napoli was lifted for a pinch hitter.

OCTOBER 20   The Yankees take a three-games-to-one lead by trouncing the Angels 10–1 before 45,160 at Angel Stadium.

OCTOBER 22   The Angels stave off elimination by beating the Yankees 7–6 before 45,113 at Angel Stadium. The Angels scored four runs in the first inning and kept the 4–0 lead through the end of the sixth behind the pitching of John Lackey. The Yanks scored six runs in the seventh, all after two were out, off Lackey, Darren Oliver and Kevin Jepsen to move ahead 6–4. The Angels rebounded to score three times in their half. Still down 6–5 with two out in the inning, Vladimir Guerrero and Kendry Morales delivered RBI–singles. Mike Scioscia tried an unusual strategy by issuing an intentional walk to Alex Rodriguez with two out and no one on base in the ninth. It nearly backfired when the Yanks loaded the bases on a single and another walk, but Brian Fuentes retired Nick Swisher on an infield pop-up for the final out.

OCTOBER 24   Game six is postponed for a day by rain.

OCTOBER 25   The Yankees win the American League championship by defeating the Angels 5–2 in New York. Joe Saunders pitched shutout ball through the first three innings before allowing three runs in the fourth.